Carriers of Growth?

Library of Economic History

General Editor

Peer Vries (*University of Vienna*)

VOLUME 6

The titles published in this series are listed at *brill.com/lehi*

Carriers of Growth?

International Trade and Economic Development in the Austrian Netherlands

By

Ann Coenen

BRILL

LEIDEN | BOSTON

Cover illustration: Mattheas Seuter, the City of Ostend, 1740 (© Stadsarchief Oostende).
After the Closure of the River Scheldt, the Port of Ostend was the only remaining large harbour for the Austrian Netherlands, therefore it was one of the core concerns of eighteenth-century trade policy. Mattheas Seuter painted a map of the city, accompanied by deities Poseidon and Mercury as an allegory for overseas trade.

Library of Congress Cataloging-in-Publication Data
Coenen, Ann.
Carriers of growth? : international trade and economic development in the Austrian Netherlands / by Ann Coenen.
pages cm -- (Library of economic history ; volume 6)
Includes bibliographical references and index.
ISBN 978-90-04-27259-0 (hardback : alk. paper) -- ISBN 978-90-04-27260-6 (e-book : alk. paper) 1. Netherlands--Commerce--History--18th century. 2. Belgium--Commerce--History--18th century. 3. Economic development--Netherlands--History--18th century. 4. Economic development--Belgium--History--18th century. 5. Netherlands--History--1714-1795. 6. Belgium--History--1648-1794. I. Title.
HF3615.C64 2014
382.09493--dc23

2014026077

This publication has been typeset in the multilingual "Brill" typeface. With over 5,100 characters covering Latin, IPA, Greek, and Cyrillic, this typeface is especially suitable for use in the humanities. For more information, please see www.brill.com/brill-typeface.

ISSN 1877-3206
ISBN 978-90-04-27259-0 (hardback)
ISBN 978-90-04-27260-6 (e-book)

This book is printed on acid-free paper.

Aan Marah, Emma en Pieter-Jan

Contents

PART 3

International Trade in the Austrian Netherlands, a Study of Five Key Sectors

Preface

Five years ago, when I received the brilliant opportunity to start a PhD project at the University of Antwerp, my view on the subject of this volume was quite 'naïve'. Being an ambitious young scholar, I aspired to reach a solid conclusion in the unrelenting debate on trade and economic development. A region like the Austrian Netherlands, lacking colonies and major ports, and subjected by absolutist monarchs, would certainly offer proof that trade could form a severe threat and an impediment for a region's development, thus proving that international trade indeed played a huge role in history. In the end, trade indeed turned out to have had an unquestionably large impact on Early Modern economies, but in a much more layered and nuanced way than I had expected. In fact, through the study of its international trade, it was the Southern Netherlands's home market that truly entered the spotlight. Through the years, I hence experienced how history can continue to surprise and throw a different light on deeply rooted ideas – my own, for starters. Countless scholars, friends and especially those priceless combinations of both have assisted me in completing the task at hand. Without wanting to raise suspicion on complicity with the errors in the following pages, I wish to take the opportunity to thank all of them.

One of the main objectives of this volume was the critical analysis of the Habsburg customs statistics. The huge first step of this work – digitizing 33 years of trade data on thousands of commodities – would probably have taken more than four years on its own. Most fortunately, the largest part of the digitization had already been performed more than fifteen years ago. It was Koen Dries who took on this work within a project of Erik Aerts (KU Leuven) and who was willing to put his valuable database, plus his knowledge on the source, at the disposal of the Antwerp Centre for Urban History. He even converted it to up-to-date, accessible software, so that I could easily complete the few missing numbers. He can never be thanked enough.

Second, I experienced the joy of working under the wings of two highly accomplished supervisors in the period 2008–2012. Bruno Blondé and Helma De Smedt complemented each other perfectly. Not only were they able to answer nearly every question I could think of, they also took away my doubts when necessary, offered never-ending enthusiasm and were truly some of the warmest mentors a young researcher could wish for.

The list of other scholars who assisted me with valuable advice, comments or data is next to infinite: Eric Vanhaute and Glenn Rayp (Ghent University), members of the CES Leuven (Eric Buyst and Erik Aerts among others), Michaël

Serruys, Peer Vries, Greet De Bock, Willem Vereecken, Joost Jonker, Oscar Gelderblom, and of course my French colleagues Guillaume Daudin and Loïc Charles for our joint presentations all over the world. The members of the N.W. Posthumus-institute greatly aided my work by allowing me to share my research with a wider audience from its earliest stages onwards, but also by giving me a superb network of fellow historians. I explicitly want to thank Jan-Willem Veluwenkamp, Jeffrey Williamson, Jan Luiten van Zanden and Kenneth Morgan for the advice they have given me at different stages of my work.

My colleagues at the UA merit a separate section. There are few workplaces with such a huge amount of interesting, highly intelligent and warm-hearted people as the Department of History in Antwerp. I want to express my gratitude towards all of my colleagues for offering such a pleasant environment. Special thanks go to those who allowed me to use their know-how and sources (Jord Hanus, Wouter Ryckbosch, Dries Lyna, Iason Jongepier, Hilde Greefs, Bert De Munck, Maxime Van Houtven and Josefine Vanhille). Mostly, I wish to thank those colleagues who shared my little port of refuge (the *Annexe*) and made it into my second home. Maïka, Eline, Yves, Iason, Steven, Pieter, Botho, Filip, Hadewijch and Mirella: even though some of you are to blame for nurturing my coffee addiction, you have become much more than mere colleagues.

Lastly, I want to thank the large group of people who were less closely involved in the research, but who helped me in many practical ways and – more importantly – through their encouragement and trust. Thank you Pieter-Jan, Linda, Jan, Lien, Pieter, Marc, Hilde, Bart, Charel, Lucienne, Rita, Frans and Erin.

Ghent, July 2014

List of Map, Charts and Tables

Map

Charts

Tables

List of Abbreviations

NAB	National Archives Brussels
FC	Finance Council
SSW	Secretariat of State and War
AO	Auditor's Office
CAPV	Chancellerie Autrichienne Des Pays-Bas à Vienne
CGG	Conseil du Gouvernement Général
OS	Österreichisches Staatsarchiv
FHKA	Finanz- und Hofkammerarchiv
NHK	Neues Hofkammerarchiv
SITC	Standard International Trade Classification

Glossary

Baize: A thick and coarse woollen fabric

Barracan: A coarse, tightly woven and inexpensive woollen fabric. Sometimes used as a synonym for camel cloth

Bourat: A mixed fabric with a silk warp and a woollen weft

Broadcloth: A firm woollen fabric, available in many colours and finishing. It was usually quite luxurious

Caffa: A patterned or flowered type of silk velvet

Calico: A (printed) cotton fabric that originated from the city of Calicut, India

Calmande: A woollen fabric, glazed on one side

Camel cloth (*camelot*): A valuable fabric of wool or camel hair. It was originally Oriental but had a woollen version in the Netherlands

Cartload or *charretée*: Unit of measure for coal, equivalent to 5 quarters or 1500 pounds (a bit over 700 kilograms)

Combed flax: Flax from which the pieces of bark have been removed, so that it is ready to be spun

Damask: A silk fabric with a pattern woven in. Linen could also be damascened

Dimit: A twilled cotton fabric

Dimity or bombazine (*basin*): A very heavy cotton or sometimes mixed cotton fabric

Duffel: A heavy woollen fabric, fulled and raised on both sides

Flannel: A light and soft woollen fabric; it sometimes contained linen or cotton

Frisade: A type of broadcloth, but thicker and fulled hard

Fustian: A light, mixed cotton fabric. Usually, it was made from cotton and linen, but other fibres could be used as well

Kersey: Carded serge, thicker than broadcloth

Last: Unit of measure for grains. Its weight and volume varies for different types of grains. For barley, one last equals approximately 3200–3400 pounds; for wheat 4600–4800 pounds, or close to 3000 litres; and for rye 4000–4200 pounds.

Linen cloth (*toile*): Basic linen fabric, with different colours and finishings

Moquette or plush: A type of velvet with longer piles

Nanking: A yellow cotton fabric, sometimes used as a synonym for calico

Pesée: Unit of measure for coal, with a weight of 144 pounds

Quarter or *rasière*: Unit of measure. For salt, the official "*razière d'Ostende*" or "*sac de Malines*" equalled a weight of at least 270 pounds (about 126 kilograms). A quarter of coal equals 300 pounds.

Queues et pennes: Also called *bouts de laines*. These are bits and tailings of wool (wool waste), which could be used to produce broadcloth of lesser quality.

Ratteen: A woven woollen fabric, from which loose hairs have been twisted into little knots

Rollet (or batiste): Fine, satin-like type of linen cloth

Serge (*saye*): light woollen fabric

Serge (*serge*): Twilled, coarse woollen fabric

Siamoise: A light fabric with a linen warp and a cotton weft

Tick: Firm linen cloth, used for bedding. It was mainly manufactured in Turnhout.

Velvet: A delicate, shining silk fabric

Introduction

> The love for foreign goods places the biggest obstacles to the advance of our national industry, on which depends so strongly the welfare of our subjects.[1]

This assertion, from an imperial decree of Emperor Joseph II, was quoted by a Viennese weekly in 1784. The statement clearly illustrates the prevailing school of thought among early modern European monarchs as to the importance of international trade for economic development. Mercantilist views in particular were still highly *en vogue* during the second half of the eighteenth century, while Adam Smith's ideas had yet to find receptivity except among a small group of theorists. In short, trade was still generally regarded as a zero-sum game, a *guerre d'argent*.[2] Rulers hoped that by accumulating as much bullion as possible – in the first place through exports – and by instituting barriers against imports of foreign goods, they would increase the power and prestige of their realms. The preceding quote evidences that the Habsburg rulers likewise adhered to such protectionist views. No less than other European sovereigns, they were of the opinion that a favourable balance of trade was the *summum bonum* for the prosperity of their economy, and hence of their subjects. Since the treaty of Utrecht the latter had also included the inhabitants of the Southern Low Countries, a relatively small area located between the Dutch Republic and France.

Many economic historians have attached great importance to international trade of the early modern period; their work is sometimes in-line with the discourse and politics of the Habsburg princes, but more often it is based on modern trade theory. Despite the on-going research, the question as to whether and how international trade may have contributed to economic development remains highly abstruse. The debate about the possible merits and the precise impact of overseas trade for economic development is continued by contemporary historians, who variously inflate and minimize the possible influence of international trade.[3] It is clear, however, that no European country of the

1 "La passion pour les marchandises étrangères met les plus grands obstacles au progrès de l'industrie nationale, dont dépend si essentiellement le bien-être de nos sujets." NAB, SSW, 2194/2, 'Extrait de la feuille hebdomadaire intitulé: Esprit des Gazettes, Tome 10.n°1°' (Vienna, September 15th 1784).

2 "A silver war," Philippe Minard, *La Fortune du Colbertisme* (Paris: Fayard, 1998), 16.

3 For this debate, see: Ronald Findlay and Kevin H. O'Rourke, Power and Plenty. Trade, War, and the World Economy in the Second Millennium (Princeton/Oxfordshire, 2007), Patrick

 | DOI 10.1163/9789004272606_002

eighteenth century could be regarded independently from the international economy in which it was enmeshed; yet the precise nature of the influence of trade surpluses or deficits – or of any other evolution in international trade flows – remains enigmatic.[4] This is partly due to the fact that for most eighteenth-century regions it remains unclear where their trade flows originated from, what these flows were composed of, and whether the balance of trade was positive or negative.[5] However, this volume will prove that this international historiographical opposition in itself is counterproductive.

The controversy over trade and economic development began in the United Kingdom. Despite the myriad differing opinions held in the passionate debate about the role of international trade versus endogenous factors (the enclosure movement, the financial revolution, technological innovations, the battle between labour and capital, or changing behaviour) many historians have assumed that the imperial context of the Isle was immensely important for its eighteenth-century economic modernisation and even for the early onset of the industrial revolution.[6] Other economies such as those of France, the Iberian Peninsula and the Dutch Republic, have received considerable historiographical attention, albeit less so than that of England.[7] So far, no comparable efforts have been undertaken for the Habsburg Low Countries,

K. O'Brien, "European Economic Development: The Contribution of the Periphery," *Economic History Review* 35, no. 1–18 (1982), Peer Vries, *Escaping Poverty: the Origins of Modern Economic growth* (Vienna University Press, 2013), 263–271.

4 Eric J. Hobsbawm, *Industry and Empire: an Economic History of Britain since 1750* (London: 1973), 35.

5 George Maria Welling, The Prize of Neutrality. Trade Relations between Amsterdam and North America 1771–1817. A Study in Computational History, dissertation (Rijksuniversiteit Groningen 1998).

6 The literature is next to inexhaustible, but besides the authors from note 3 some interesting starting points are: Daron Acemoglu, Simon Johnson, and James Robinson, "The Rise of Europe: Atlantic Trade, Institutional Change and Economic Growth," *American Economic Review* 95, no. 3 (2005), C.A. Bayly, *The Birth of the Modern World, 1780–1914* (Oxford: Blackwell, 2004), R.A. Church and E.A. Wrigley, *The Industrial Revolutions*, 11 vols. (Oxford: Blackwell, 1994), R. Davis, *The Industrial Revolution and British Overseas Trade* (Leicester: 1979), Stanley L. Engerman, *Trade and the Industrial Revolution, 1700–1850*, 2 vols. (Cheltenham: 1996), Ronald M. Hartwell, *The Causes of the Industrial Revolution in England* (London: Methuen, 1970), Hobsbawm, *Industry*, Patrick K. O'Brien, "Mercantilism and Imperialism in the Rise and Decline of the Dutch and British Economies," *De Economist* 148 (2000).

7 F. Crouzet, *Britain, France and International Commerce* (Aldershot, 1996), Guillaume Daudin, *Commerce et Prospérité. La France au XVIIIe Siècle* (Paris: Presses de l'université Paris-Sorbonne, 2005), Jan de Vries and A. Van der Woude, *Nederland 1500–1815. De eerste Ronde van Moderne Economische Groei* (Amsterdam: 1995), J. Israel, *The Dutch Republic. Its Rise,*

though several laudable openings have been made within the study of the Habsburg economy.[8] These latter works illustrate that the Austrian Netherlands offer a new and quite different case for economic historians, and that research on the country's foreign trade during this time can provide vital new outlooks on the broader international economic history of the period.

It is nothing short of astonishing that this international debate has almost entirely overlooked both the international trade flows and the commercial policy of the Southern Low Countries. The region that after 1830 would become known as Belgium would after all not only be the first to follow in Britain's early industrial footsteps, it offers many other characteristics that grant it high comparative value. Unlike Britain, the Austrian Netherlands were a small yet very densely populated area, with a large labour surplus, hence low wages.[9] At the same time they were a rather passive player in the eighteenth-century trade scene, since after the Treaty of Utrecht (1713) the region had not been allowed to establish locally based oriental trade companies and it moreover lacked a major port after the closure of the river Scheldt. Moreover, the political economy of the region was completely different from that of its overseas neighbour. But what really sets this case study apart, is that the first findings on eighteenth-century international trade (which will be discussed extensively below) in the Austrian Netherlands have left an impression that contradicts and/or nuances many of the leading opinions about international trade.

Reminiscent of an optimistic mercantilist view held also by the Austrian overseers of the Southern Netherlands, the largely Anglo-Saxon debate on international trade predominantly tried to answer the question whether international trade can be regarded as a direct lever for early industrialisation and increased economic growth. Such a focus very easily narrows down the research either to economic modelling (calculating the balance of trade) or to the study of a limited number of successful export sectors. Moreover, it places trade diametrically opposite to all other possible factors leading up to the Industrial Revolution. However, existing research on the eighteenth-century economy of the Austrian Netherlands has brought some important

---

Greatness and Fall, 1477–1806 (Oxford: 1995), Joel Mokyr, "The Industrial Revolution and the Netherlands: Why Did It Not Happen?," *De Economist* 148 (2000).

8 Hilda Coppejans-Desmedt, "Economische Opbloei in de Zuidelijke Nederlanden," in *Algemene Geschiedenis der Nederlanden* (Utrecht: 1955), J. Lefèvre and P.F. Lefèvre, *Etude sur le Commerce de la Belgique avec l'Espagne au XVIIIe Siècle* (Brussels: 1921), Hubert Van Houtte, *Histoire Économique de la Belgique à la Fin de l'Ancien Régime* (Ghent: 1920).

9 Christiaan Vandenbroeke, "The Regional Economy of Flanders and Industrial Modernization in the Eighteenth Century," *Journal of European Economic History* 16, no. 1 (1987).

incongruities to the surface, revealing the flaws of such an approach. For example, from a comparative perspective the *industrial* towns that – from a nineteenth-century point of view – we would assume would have been boosted by international trade in fact appear to have been slow economic growers.[10] And the new industries that historiography has often put in the spotlight (cotton printing, sugar refining, etc.) did not immediately show impressive results, despite receiving significant government support, including trade barriers and lower export tariffs. On the other hand, products accounting for large export volumes (linen for instance) were supplied by sectors marked by very low wages; in other words: so-called internal or domestic factors (wages) went hand in hand with external ones (export). The relation between international trade and other economic developments is far more complex. In order to make statements on it, we need to reconcile a quantitative and a qualitative analysis. Moreover, it will be best to gradually descend from the aggregate macroeconomic level to a sectorial level.[11]

In particular, I believe that studying the differing impact of international trade on a number of representative and/or key economic sectors of the eighteenth-century economy of the region will yield the best results.[12] That does not imply that it is not useful to assess how the trade balance evolved during this era, and to estimate the value of the international trade flows, since this provides a useful contextual framework. To date, attempts to calculate trade balances in the past are very scarce and for the eighteenth-century Austrian Netherlands we lack any concrete estimate. Hence, that will be the starting point of this work. Yet to assess what the real impact of foreign trade was for the region and its inhabitants, the macro-image of international trade flows must be complemented by qualitative detail- and in-depth-analyses of the importance of trade for the development of the various sectors involved in

10 Bruno Blondé, "Transport and the Economic Development of Brabant in the 18th Century," in *Economic Growth and Structural Change. Comparative Approaches over the Long Run on the Basis of Reconstructed National Accounts. Workshop on Quantitative Economic History* (Leuven: 1993), Bruno Blondé, "Disparities in the Development of the Brabantine Urban Network: urban Centrality, Town-Countryside Relationships, and Transportation Development, 1750–1790," in *Proceedings Twelfth International Economic History Congress*, ed. C. Núnez (Madrid: 1998).

11 "Economic development" refers to both the quantitative and qualitative changes in the economy (not merely growth or increasing economic prosperity/profits/output). Such developments can differ for different stakeholders.

12 The definition of economic growth used here is: the increase of national product / national income in constant prices per capita.

trade. This will allow moving beyond matters of economic growth to economic development. To what extent did international trade contribute to the welfare or decay of certain sectors, and in which ways? It was thus necessary to select economic sectors that together spanned the entire economy: these included both traditional and new industries, everyday goods and luxury items, industrial commodities and raw produce. I did not necessarily choose the sectors with the largest productions or the highest traded values; however, the selected subsectors share a common feature, in that each commodity was part of an important international commodity chain. Of course, growth within a certain sector does not imply that there was overall growth and highlighting only a few commerce sectors overlooks the diversity of the thousands of commodities being traded at the time. However, each of the five sectors chosen here contributes vital new information to the economic history of the Austrian Netherlands.

Both the textile sector, which included brand-new products such as cotton and vested fabrics like linen and wool, and colonial products (specifically: sugar, coffee, tea, dyestuffs and cocoa) have often figured at the core of economics-related research on the eighteenth century; and they also form an interesting case for the Austrian Netherlands, since – as we will see – trade brought about a number of important changes in these sectors. Historiography has often equated cross-border commerce with colonial trade, especially in Anglo-Saxon research, but this perspective strongly limits the extent of commerce. Indeed, for other goods included in this research the focus lies on intra-European trade. Coal is a resource that (for fairly obvious reasons) has very often been linked with industrialisation, and the relation between industry and coal remains widely discussed and debated, not least because society until today craves coal and other fossil fuels. In the Belgian area, it was, perhaps surprisingly, already well-known years before the start of the Industrial Revolution. The other two commodities selected for this study – namely, salt and grain – may strike some as a curious selection. Yet there are good reasons for including chapters on these perhaps seemingly humdrum products. I will return to the specific reasons for choosing each of the five product categories; for now, however, suffice it to say that the over-arching aim was to grasp a representative 'basket' of commodities that effectively embodied the span of international trade of the day.

Not only does focusing on separate sectors greatly facilitate answering questions about the role of trade and identifying the role of international trade for each, this approach also guards us from some of the large pitfalls of research on the eighteenth-century economy. While both the quantitative data on international trade and most of the memoranda on trade in general have been provided by the central government (mainly the Austrian Netherlands' Finance

Council), a 'made-to-measure' approach for each of the selected sectors allows us to include more specific sources not only from central and local governments, but also from traders, producers, manufacturers and consumers. This way, looking into individual sectors will also reveal much about the different actors (merchants, producers and consumers, the government) and lobby groups involved in external trading relations and about the dissimilar impact of international trade on these actors and on different areas (rural versus urban for example). These are elements that are commonly obscured in more macro-economic analyses. This 'bottom-up' approach to the history of economic development in an often overlooked region will hopefully provide the necessary input to renew a line of research that, in recent years, has been dominated alternately by focuses on technology and knowledge (for example Mokyr), institutions (North, Acemoglu) and attitudes (de Vries, McCloskey, etc.).[13]

Lastly, this approach also allows us to unravel the effects of the eighteenth-century Habsburg trade policy on economic development, a subject that has seen much debate.[14] The era was characterized by a government that still very much pursued a mercantilist ideal and therefore actively sought to establish a sound trade policy. It is clear that the public administration was strongly committed to using trade in order to boost new industries, but it must be asked whether these policies indeed obtained results. Ever since classical economists

13 Acemoglu, Johnson, and Robinson, "The Rise," Acemoglu and Robinson, *Why Nations fail,* Jan de Vries, *The Industrious Revolution. Consumer Behaviour and the Household Economy, 1650 to the Present* (Cambridge: 2008), Deirdre McCloskey, *Bourgeois dignity* (Chicago: University of Chicago Press, 2010), Joel Mokyr, *The Lever of Riches: Technological Creativity and Economic Progress* (New York: Oxford University Press, 1990), Mokyr, *The Enlightened Economy. An Economic History of Britain 1700–1850* (New Haven/London, 2009), Douglass C. North and Robert Paul Thomas, *The Rise of the Western World* (Cambridge: Cambridge University Press, 1973); North, Wallis and Weingast, *Violence and Social Orders. A conceptual Framework for Interpreting Recorded Human History* (Cambridge, 2009).

14 Ann Coenen, De Oostenrijkse Nederlanden in de tweede helft van de 18de eeuw: infant industry protectionisme vóór de Industriële Revolutie?, in: *Overheid en Economie, liber amicarum voor Helma De Smedt* (forthcoming), Hilda Coppejans-Desmedt, "Aspecten van de Industriële Politiek in de Oostenrijkse Nederlanden," in *Overheid en Economie. Economische Aspecten van de Overheidspolitiek in en met Betrekking tot de Oostenrijkse Nederlanden,* ed. Helma Houtman-De Smedt (Antwerp: 1989), Cécile Douxchamps-Lefèvre, "La Politique Douanière du Gouvernement des Pays-Bas sous la Règne de Marie-Thérèse," in *Overheid en Economie. Economische Aspecten van de Overheidspolitiek in en met Betrekking tot de Oostenrijkse Nederlanden,* ed. Helma Houtman-De Smedt (Antwerp: 1989), Piet Lenders, "Ontwikkeling van Politiek en Instellingen in de Oostenrijkse Nederlanden. De Invloed van de Europese Oorlogen," *Bijdragen tot de Geschiedenis* 64, no. 1 (1981).

condemned it as a short-sighted policy sure to limit economic growth, mercantilism has had a bad press, but this research makes it possible to move beyond the impact of general measures and to look for the impact of trade policy on different sectors and stakeholders, which – as we will see – is far from unambiguous.

PART 1

Theoretical Background

CHAPTER 1

International Trade and Economic Development

In marked contrast to the state of trade-related research on the Southern Low Countries, the breadth of academic literature concerning the role of international trade in economic development is immense. Countless prominent historians have tackled the issue and contributed to the discussion. Throughout the 1990s historians generally seemed to agree with Patrick O'Brien's view that trade, though certainly important for the early modern growth of Great Britain, was far from sufficient to explain it.[1] As O'Brien's work details, the government also played an important supporting role.[2] More recently, historians have again emphasized the importance of (overseas) commerce, and this in its turn has triggered renewed disputation amongst supporters of so-called endogenous growth factors. Subsequently, literature remains flooded with very strong and distinct statements.

The reason for the high commotion is that the nature of the impact of international trade is one of the bones of contention within the multi-faceted dispute on early modern economic growth and thus inevitably the take-off of the Industrial Revolution in Western Europe. This is undoubtedly one of the most important debates in the economic history of the early modern and modern periods. No scholar claims that a thriving international trade could have had negative consequences for the economy. However, estimates of the magnitude of its impact vary from negligible to decisive. The former put more stress on the importance of endogenous factors (specific to a certain region), while the latter favour exogenous factors (supra-national), from which international trade – especially with the colonies – is by far the most important.

Thus far, most historians have attributed the advent of the industrial revolution in England primarily to endogenous causes. The agricultural conversion

1 P. Bairoch, *Economics and World History: Myths and Paradoxes* (New York: 1993), 84, C.K. Harley, "Trade: Discovery, Mercantilism and Technology," in *The Cambridge Economic History of Modern Britain*, ed. R. Floud and P. Johnson (Cambridge: Cambridge University Press, 2004), Kenneth Morgan, *Slavery, Atlantic Trade and the British Economy* (Cambridge: 2000), Kevin H. O'Rourke and Jeffrey G. Williamson, "After Columbus: Explaining Europe's Overseas Trade Boom, 1500–1800," *Journal of Economic History* 62 (2002), Kevin O'Rourke and Ronald Findlay, *Power and Plenty* (Princeton, 2007).

2 Patrick K. O'Brien, "Imperialism and the Rise and Decline of the British Economy, 1688–1989," *New Left Review* 238 (1999): 62.

 | DOI 10.1163/9789004272606_003

that took place on the British Isles from the late seventeenth century onwards has long been regarded as the necessary basis for the development of a modern industry.[3] Marxist approaches introduced class struggle – that is, the changing social and political relationships – as the primary explanation for the transition to industrial capitalism.[4] Other endogenous factors that have long been offered as explanations include the so-called financial revolution of the early eighteenth century (which led to efficient organization of banks and stock exchanges) and improvements in transport and communication infrastructures.[5] Of course, development of the necessary technology in Britain is also considered to have been a condition for the unfolding of the industrial revolution, and is occasionally even proposed as having been the main reason.[6] Often in such a materialistic approach the importance of raw materials, especially coal, returns as well. Another view, held by Douglass North and his supporters within the New Institutional Economics, prioritizes the importance of institutions (in the broad sense of the term).[7] A final possible endogenous cause consists in the assumption that British society (especially its middle class) was characterized by an openness and perceptivity to change and innovation, and that it experienced a rising demand for goods: the so-called consumer revolution.[8] Today's dominant perspectives can generally be grouped under the previous three: knowledge (or technology), institutions and attitudes.

A striking observation on the historiography stressing internal explanations is that the aforementioned authors, when discussing – or rather

3 J.A. Chartres, "Introduction," in *The Industrial Revolutions. Volume 1*, ed. R.A. Church and E.A. Wrigley (Oxford: 1994), xxviii, Patrick K. O'Brien and R. Quinault, *The Industrial Revolution and British Society* (Newcastle upon Tyne: 1993), 2. For a contemporary Malthusian, materialistic view (that also takes culture into consideration): Gregory N. Clark, *A Farewell to Alms: A Brief Economic History of the World* (Princeton: 2007).

4 S.R. Epstein, "Rodney Hilton, Marxism and the Transition from Feudalism to Capitalism," *Past and Present* 195 (2007): 252.

5 Church and Wrigley, *The Industrial Revolutions*, xix, xxvii and xxix, O'Brien and Quinault, *The Industrial Revolution and British Society*, 125–128, 130, 146, Immanuel Wallerstein, *The Modern World-System*, 4 vols, vol. 2 (New York: 1980), 105.

6 N.F.R. Crafts, "Exogenous or Endogenous Growth? The Industrial Revolution Reconsidered," *Journal of Economic History* 55 (1995), Mokyr, "The Industrial Revolution."

7 Acemoglu and Robinson, *Why Nations fail*, Acemoglu, Johnson, and Robinson, "The Rise," North, Wallis and Weingast, *Violence and Social Orders*, North and Thomas, *The Rise of the Western World.*

8 de Vries, *The Industrious Revolution*, McCloskey, *Bourgeois Virtues: Ethics for an Age of Commerce*, Deirdre Nansen McCloskey, *Bourgeois Dignity: Why Economics can't Explain the Modern World* (Chicago: University of Chicago Press, 2010).

dismissing – international trade, frequently refer to the founding father of economic theory, Adam Smith. However, these historians narrow classical Smithian theory to a single aspect: Smith's criticism against possession of colonies.[9] Already among some of his contemporaries, Smith's ideas had led to anti-commercialism (in other words a tendency to fold back on the British territory) and pro-agriculturalism (in line with the physiocrat influences on his theory). However, Smith merely scorned the monopolies of his time and did not disregard the possibility of creating mutual benefits via international trade, provided that such trade was pursued free of protectionist restrictions.[10] In fact, Smith was very much pro international trade, placing exchange at the heart of his growth model.

Directly opposed to the previously mentioned category of ideas are explanations based on external factors. Apart from various less common hypotheses – including the theory that the siren song of the reliable and highly military secured city of London could lure many Dutch, American, French and German investors – it is clearly international trade that plays the leading role here. The British colonies in particular became an extremely important outlet for the Kingdom.[11] Between 1700 and 1774, exports – mainly to the American colonial markets – rose much more sharply than European domestic demand.[12] World-systems theory has, among others, put forward the hypothesis that the expansion of the international economy to the colonies has led to higher gains which were concentrated in the hands of capitalists from the core countries, who invested those gains in Western European industrial capital. This presumably boosted the economic growth of Western Europe.[13] Recently, such a global vision has been re-introduced by the California School, with authors such as Robert Marks and Roy Bin Wong. This school has ventured upon the study of the great divergence. While not all authors discuss international trade, they found inter alia an argument for the importance of trade in the study of China, a country with a strong economy but virtually no international trade and (hence?) no industrial revolution. Closely linked to this line of thought is the study of the role of globalisation. A more recent perspective on

9 Smith called the colonies "an economic drain on the mother country." Adam Smith, *An inquiry into the nature and causes of the wealth of nation*, 1776, cited in: R.B. Sheridan, *Sugar and Slavery: an Economic History of the British West Indies 1623–1775* (Barbados: Caribbean Universities Press, 1974), 32.

10 O'Brien, "European Economic Development," 10.

11 R. Davis, *English Overseas Trade 1500–1700* (London: 1973), 39–40.

12 R. Davis, "English Foreign Trade, 1700–1774," *Economic History Review* 15 (1962).

13 O'Brien, "European Economic Development," 3.

the influence of international trade is that of changing consumption patterns.[14]

Partially influenced by Marxist theories, the adherents of external explanations are convinced that foreign trade not merely had beneficial effects, but was a primary cause of the Industrial Revolution.[15] Besides the works mentioned in this paragraph that strongly highlight overseas trade – often with a moralistic undertone, following the example of Eric Williams – international trade was generally assigned a rather indirect role. It did not give sufficient means for industrialisation, but may have exerted a significant impact on economic development through the introduction of new consumer products. Historians such as Ralph Davis and Patrick O'Brien have also – as mentioned above – acknowledged the importance of trade. However, according to O'Brien early modern overseas trade was a priori an endogenous factor, given that the impetus to the growth of trade originally came from the state.

This underlying judgment concerning the importance of the state has given rise to an opposition between classical (liberal) and mercantilist arguments. Mercantilism until today is the best-known conflict theory in the history of economic thought.[16] Yet it is far from a well-defined school of thought, with clear-cut positions, but rather the compilation of a very diverse set of policy recommendations. Sixteenth-and seventeenth-century mercantilists believed that international trade was in the first place a constant struggle, in which

14 M. Berg, "In Pursuit of Luxury: Global History and British Consumer Goods in the Eighteenth Century," *Past & Present* 182 (2004), Brewer, John and Roy Porter, eds, *Consumption and the World of Goods*, London (2007), C. Clunas, "Modernity Global and Local: Consumption and the Rise of the West," *American Historical Review* 104 (1999), Beverly Lemire, *Fashion's Favourite. The Cotton Trade and the Consumer in Britain 1660–1800* (Oxford: Oxford University Press, 1991), Trentmann, Frank, ed., *The Oxford Handbook of the History of Consumption* (2012).

15 A selection of the extensive literature on international trade and economic development: Robert Allen, "Why the Industrial Revolution was British: Commerce, Induced Invention, and the Scientific Revolution," in: *The Economic History Review* 64, 2 (2011) 357–384, Stanley L. Engerman and Patrick K. O'Brien, "The Industrial Revolution in Global Perspective," in *The Cambridge Economic History of Modern Britain*, ed. R. Floud and P. Johnson (Cambridge: 2004), Findlay and O'Rourke, *Power and plenty*, J. Inikori, *Africans and the Industrial Revolution in England: A Study in International Trade and Economic Development* (Cambridge: 2002), Morgan, *Slavery*, Kenneth Pomeranz and Steven Topik, *The World That Trade Created. Society, Culture, and the World Economy, 1400-the Present* (New York: M.E. Sharpe, 1999).

16 For an introduction to the term, see: D.C. Coleman, "ercantilism Revisited," *The Historical Journal* 23, no. 4 (1980), Eli Heckscher and L. Magnusson (ed.), *Mercantilism* (London: 1994), Minard, *La Fortune*, O'Brien, "Mercantilism."

one's own market had to be protected rigorously against foreign imports. The two most important elements in this heterogeneous line of thought were the formation of monopolies and the complementarity of economic functions. Colonies were supposed to specialize in the production of raw materials, so that the mother country could specialize in the processing thereof, in order to produce as many different products domestically – that is: on domestic territory or in the colonies – to realize a positive trade balance. The idea that even a protectionist organization of international trade can be of assistance for state development is not new – nearly every present-day industrial country protected its economy at first – but many authors, especially those inspired by Smith's laissez-faire arguments, will nonetheless, because of antipathy towards state and empire, greatly underestimate the influence of trade.[17] In O'Brien's words, these liberal historians "established an Anglo centric (and, by extension, neoliberal) case for the insignificance of trade and colonization by emphasizing 'endogenous forces'."[18] O'Brien considers such renderings severely unrealistic for studying early modern economies and seeks to accentuate the importance of the state in the industrialisation of the British economy. "Power," he notes, "as mercantilists long insisted, really mattered!"[19]

There are different problems regarding this apparent contradiction of myriad explanatory elements within historiography. First of all, most authors have not fully considered the possibility that different factors and actors might have been at work in different sectors. This problem has already been addressed by authors from the field of commodity chain analysis. In the latter field, research started from a single product category, for example sugar, tobacco or coffee, making it much easier to focus on all agents involved in a

17 B. Balassa, "The Process of Industrial Development and Alternative Development Strategies," *Essays in International Finance* 141 (1980): 5, J.E. Meade, *An Introduction to Economic Analysis and Policy* (London: 1937), 346. The "infant industry" argument for protecting developing economies is especially well known. It was first developed by A. Hamilton, *Report on Manufactures* (London: 1791) and F. List, *Das Nationale System der Politischen Oekonomie* (Jena: 1841). Mercantilism has also been opposed by the theories of mutual advantages. The latter argues that trade can be beneficial to all who participate in it through the mechanism of comparative advantages. It was a follower of Adam Smith, David Ricardo (David Ricardo, *On the Principles of Political Economy and Taxation* (1817).) who has made this mechanism widely known. For the majority of contemporary economists trade at least in theory has mutual advantages. However, the past did not meet all the conditions under which this can be the case, so among economic historians the controversy remains.

18 O'Brien, "Imperialism," 54–55.

19 Ibid.: 62.

certain trade.[20] Secondly, foreign markets are usually regarded as either suppliers or buyers, but are rarely considered as both. Hence, there is little space for changeable economic or political dynamics between regions. Lastly, the debate often assumes that sectors that would take the lead during the nineteenth-century industrial revolution already accounted for the highest growth during the century before. Consequently only the role of trade for these sectors was investigated, while it is just as well possible that not all eighteenth-century developments have a connection to the nineteenth century. This overly strong focus on the search for possible causes of the Industrial Revolution has important implications for the study of the eighteenth-century economy.[21]

Still, notwithstanding the many contradictions, this extensive literature on international trade theory provides invaluable insights into the possible gains and risks of international trade, and on the costs and benefits of protectionist measures. As we will see below, the opinions in the research on the Austrian Netherlands are much less rigidly divided, but, on the other hand, still rest on a great deal of unclarity.

20 Mintz, *Sweetness*, M. Pendergrast, *Uncommon Grounds: The History of Coffee and how it transformed our World* (1999), J.M. Price, *Tobacco in Atlantic Trade. The Chesapeake, London and Glasgow, 1675–1775* (Brookfield: 1995).

21 Maxine Berg and Pat Hudson, "Rehabilitating the Industrial Revolution," *Economic History Review* 45, no. 1 (1992).

CHAPTER 2

The Austrian Netherlands in the Second Half of the Eighteenth Century

A Cautious Recovery

In many respects the second half of the eighteenth century was a relatively prosperous era for the Southern Netherlands. The Habsburg empress Maria-Theresa came to represent an international political climate which afforded the Austrian Netherlands a period of peace and stability. Moreover, the position of the Habsburgs on the international stage was emboldened by the Treaty of Aix-la-Chapelle (1748), allowing the government to introduce a cautious but efficient customs policy. For the first time since 1648, the customs administration developed a pragmatic-mercantilist trade policy in support of the nation's domestic industries.[1] Seen in hindsight this policy may appear rather incoherent, particularly owing to its countless obscure regulations and exceptions, yet it nonetheless may have been a huge step towards achieving import-substitution in several strategic sectors and according to some even to an export-driven growth.[2] Moreover, the local administrators – though they were elected by and accountable to the Habsburg emperors – seemed to be genuinely concerned about this small corner of the empire and appeared to recognize its economic potentials. Likewise, the Austrian Netherlands were granted a larger degree of self-government than were the Habsburg hereditary lands.[3]

Although there is no small degree of dispute regarding the condition of the Austrian Netherlands' international trade flows, a somewhat broader consensus exists concerning the nation's general economic situation. For the decades before 1750 historians usually agree that economic life was, in virtually every respect, bleak and stagnant but that circumstances subsequently began to

1 It should be noted that the term "industry" needs to be taken with a pinch of salt. The manufactories of this era did not yet know the rigid division of labour that would arise during the nineteenth century.

2 Catharina Lis and Hugo Soly, "Different Paths of Development. Capitalism in the Northern and Southern Netherlands During the Late Middle Ages and the Early Modern Period," *Review. A Journal of the Fernand Braudel Center for the study of economics, historical systems, and civilizations* 20, no. 2 (1997).

3 The Prince-Bishopric of Liège was not included in the Austrian Netherlands (although it would later be part of Belgium) and this policy thus not applied to Liège.

 | DOI 10.1163/9789004272606_004

improve. Historians assume that the economy of the Southern Netherlands gradually reoriented during the second half of the eighteenth century. Although difficult years were still to follow, such as the period 1771–1775 (according to Hasquin) and the years immediately after the Brabantine Revolution, these interludes occurred amidst periods when the nation's industries were otherwise flourishing.[4] The economy in general certainly appeared to fare well during the years 1780–1785.[5] According to Chris Vandenbroeke the Habsburg economy was performing better in terms of human capital, agricultural productivity, population growth and transport infrastructure than were the respective economies of neighbouring countries.[6] Agriculture still accounted for approximately half of the gross domestic product – as was the case throughout most of Europe at the time.[7] But while agriculture certainly seemed to do well, the emerging urban industries – in the view of certain prominent economic historians (Van der Wee, Soly) – formed another backbone of the economic recovery after 1748.

Also, certain key developments in international relations were beneficial for the position of the Austrian Netherlands. Events like the four years' war between the Dutch Republic, Great Britain and France, all of whom had entered the conflict as a result of the American War for Independence, presumably created an opening for the neutral Austrian Netherlands in international trade. Previous years had seen the Southern Netherlands relegated to a generally passive role, its actions, especially those related to international trade, being dependent on the interests of more powerful nations. Every decision could lead to opposition and reprisals from other states. It was only in the second half of the eighteenth century that the Habsburg government became capable (aided by several notably bright technocrats) of developing its own trade policy. The influence of international politics upon domestic economic affairs had not played out, of course. Competition between nations remained

---

4 Hervé Hasquin, "Nijverheid in de Zuidelijke Nederlanden, 1650–1795," in *Algemene Geschiedenis der Nederlanden* (Haarlem: 1979), 158.

5 Hubert Van Houtte, "Contribution à l'Histoire Commerciale des Etats de L'empereur Joseph II (1780–1790)," *Vierteljahrschrift für Sozial- und Wirtschaftsgeschichte* 8 (1910): 355.

6 G. Dejongh and Y. Segers, "Een Kleine Natie in Mutatie. De Economische Ontwikkeling van de Zuidelijke Nederlanden/België in de Eeuw 1750–1850," *Tijdschrift voor Geschiedenis* 114 (2001): 175, Herman Van der Wee and Eddy Van Cauwenberghe, *Productivity of Land and Agricultural Innovation in the Low Countries (1250–1800)* (Leuven: Leuven University Press, 1987), Vandenbroeke, "The Regional Economy," 163.

7 Erik Aerts, "Economische Interventie van de Centrale Staat in de Spaanse en Oostenrijkse Nederlanden (1555–1795)," in *Gouvernance et Administration dans les Provinces Belgiques du XVIe au XVIIIe Siècle*, ed. S. Dubois and J. Yante (Brussels: 2009), 115.

fierce, and political measures were often implemented as a means to influence foreign trade. Great Britain, for example, barred imports of certain textile goods from the Austrian Netherlands.[8] Also, the fact that the Austrians overtly admired Colbert's economic policy likely had to do at least as much with their discontent towards the English and the Dutch than with specific esteem for the man and his ideas.[9] The British import ban on goods from the Southern Netherlands is an example of the sorts of trade measures that the Southern Netherlands, being still a generally weak region in terms of international clout and one still overshadowed in the larger European political arena, could hardly implement itself, not least as such measures could garner harsh reactions from the nation's larger economic competitors.

Nonetheless, the customs administration developed a number of ad hoc measures regarding trade relations with different countries. Differing customs tariffs had been in place since 1670, and this remained the case over a century later. These included the tariff of 1670 (specifically designed for trade with France) and the tariff of 1680, which regulated commerce with the other neighbouring countries.[10] Politics also occasionally yielded positive results. For example, the Southern Netherlands were able to benefit from being granted the status of most favoured nation. This statute was a clause in peace treaties with France and Spain dating from several decades earlier, but was only observed since 1748 and 1755 respectively.[11] Remarkably, however, the Austrian Netherlands did not form a customs union with the rest of the Habsburg Empire.[12] Various sources state that the Austrian Empire was to be treated as a singular unit – wherein the different parts were supposed to complement and benefit each other – but the Habsburg rulers, needing time to envisage a role for their newly added territory, probably never went so far as to actually do so.[13]

8 Lucienne Van Meerbeeck, *Etude des Relations Économiques des Pays-Bas avec la Grande-Bretagne au XVIIIe Siècle, et Plus Spécialement sous les Règnes de Marie-Thérèse et de Joseph II* (Brussels: 1929).

9 On the different forms of mercantilism and colbertism, see Minard, *La Fortune*, 15–16.

10 Hasquin, "Nijverheid," 125, Pierre Lebrun et al., *Essai sur la Révolution Industrielle en Belgique* (Brussels: Académie Royale de Belgique, 1979), 128–129.

11 Coppejans-Desmedt, "Aspecten," 75, H. Van Werveke, "Beschouwing over het Economisch Leven in de Zuidelijke Nederlanden tijdens de XVIIe en XVIIIe Eeuw," *Bijdragen en mededelingen van het historisch genootschap* 61 (1940): XC.

12 John Komlos, *The Habsburg Monarchy as a Customs Union* (Princeton: Princeton University Press, 1983), 4.

13 NAB, FC, 4278: Charter of the *Jointe pour le commerce avec les Pays Héréditaires*, April 10th 1753 by Karel van Lotharingen. See also: FC, 4286; 4298; 4303; 4304; SSW, 2194/2.

Besides navigating the myriad difficulties of international diplomacy, Maria Theresa also carried some of the huge debt that her father, Charles VI, had been forced to assume after the War of the Spanish Succession. During the first half of the century this debt resulted in the creation of tax revenue being a prominent motive in the government's trade policy, and, for most policy-makers, it likely remained one until the end of the century.[14] Nonetheless, the eighteenth century witnessed the birth of a much more sophisticated trade policy, in which all kinds of economic and political considerations were taken to heart. A customs bureau was established within the Finance Council, which was responsible – among other things – for the management of international trade. The bureau introduced the idea of collecting customs statistics to be used for the purpose of establishing a more efficient trade policy. These statistics, which were first devised by the general treasurer, Patrice de Nény, serve as my prime source in this study and I will revisit them throughout this work. The minister plenipotentiary, Karl von Cobenzl, strongly supported de Nény, particularly because the customs administration was regarded as the cornerstone of a mercantilist economic policy. The bureau reached its full potential during the leadership of Henri Delplancq.[15] He transformed it into a true ministry of economic affairs, with a strong focus towards achieving a positive trade balance. The complex trade policy developed within this official body was likely the only means via which to establish a modus vivendi for the various conflicting interests of producers, traders and consumers.[16]

With the economy now recovering (even if only slightly) from dire times, and entrepreneurs now being able to benefit from the less chaotic political context, just about everyone seized the opportunity to apply to the government for assistance. Everyone from regional representatives and city councils to abbeys, specific sectors or companies to even the lowliest rag-and-bone man could submit their views on international trade in one sector or even in general to the emperor (in practice to the Finance Council). Or as one merchant noted

---

14 Bruno Bernard, *Patrice-François de Neny (1716–1784). Portrait d'un Homme d'Etat*, ed. Roland Mortier and Hervé Hasquin, vol. 21, *Etudes sur le XIIIe Siècle* (Brussels: Editions de l'université de Bruxelles, 1993), 116.

15 Herman Coppens, "Bureau voor het Beheer van de Douanerechten (1737–1794)," in *De Centrale Overheidsinstellingen van de Habsburgse Nederlanden (1482–1795)*, ed. Erik Aerts (Brussels: 1995), 526.

16 Coppejans-Desmedt, "Aspecten," 79. This evolution was facilitated by the administration being able to rely on a number of highly competent councilors in different fields. Some of the most notable staff members are described by: Bernard, *Patrice-François de Neny*, 113–115.

at the time: "It is fashionable to talk a lot about commerce, especially among people who know neither its theory nor its practice."[17] Present-day scholars tend to easily dismiss these opinions as egocentric or seemingly irrational in a more nation-wide economic perspective. Such assessments are not necessarily true, for many of these various lobbies grounded their arguments in advanced theoretical, managerial, social or diplomatic frameworks. And even those whose motives were entirely self-interested cannot automatically be assumed to have been using hollow arguments. The heterogeneous and constantly evolving reality of international commerce is revealed through the lines of their requests, which, not just for historians, is a merit in itself.

---

17 "Il est fort à la mode de parler beaucoup de commerce, surtout parmis des gens qui n'en connoisent ni la theorie ni la pratique." NAB, Manuscripts, 850 A, memoirs on eighteenth-century trade, anonymous author to trade partner in Vienna, s.d., presumably 1754, p. 9.

CHAPTER 3

International Trade by a Commercially 'Passive' Participant

Although much is known about the wider political and economic developments occurring in the Austrian Netherlands during this period, and despite the broad consensus that has emerged regarding the many merits of the nation's new trade policy, we are still left with only scarce and usually indefinite statements on the nature and the impact of its international trade. The following brief overview underlines the fact that while opinions are less overtly contradictory and distinct than in the international debate on the importance of external (often colonial) commerce, they are also much more confused and hypothetical.

Our earliest notions about eighteenth-century trade derive from authors from the eighteenth and early nineteenth centuries who recorded their impressions of the state of international trade; in doing so, they illustrated views from the Habsburg period itself. The historian Briavoinne noted in the 1830s that trade had prospered, but his conclusion was drawn only from population growth and the increase in customs revenue. Briavionne attributed the alleged prosperity of trade to the downfall of the Northern Netherlands' commercial status (and that of a number of industrial competitors) and to the new and coherent customs policy. This policy of moderate Colbertism was pursued, with, however, as its main motive, the fact that customs revenue was very significant for the government.[1] Nonetheless, it contributed to the region's shift into a commercial nodal point within Western Europe. Merchant Nicolas Bacon, who resided in the Austrian Netherlands' Auditor's Office, made regular recommendations about the international trade situation. Although he believed that many measures still had to be taken – including drawing up a trade balance – he insisted that international trade constituted: "The inexhaustible source of public wealth and the strongest support of the state, [so] it

1 N. Briavoinne, *De L'industrie en Belgique. Sa Situation Actuelle. Causes de Décadence et de Prosperité.* (Brussels: Dubois, 1839), 83, N. Briavoinne, *Mémoire sur l'État de la Population, des Fabriques, de Manufactures et du Commerce dans les Provinces des Pays-Bas, depuis Albert et Isabelle jusqu'è la Fin du Siècle Dernier* (Brussels: 1841), Hervé Hasquin, *Oostenrijks België, 1713–1794. De Zuidelijke Nederlanden onder de Oostenrijkse Habsburgers* (Brussels: Gemeentekrediet, 1987), 150–152.

 | DOI 10.1163/9789004272606_005

is indispensable to protect it."[2] Of course his statement stemmed largely from his own self-interest as a trader and was at least as much wishful thinking as actual finding. Henri Delplancq, director of the *bureau de la régie*, or the customs bureau, from 1765 to 1787, was far less convinced that international trade was faring well. He sought tirelessly for ways to strengthen (export) trade, principally that with the Austrian hereditary lands.[3] The British historian James Shaw viewed the Southern Netherlands via a slightly more neutral perspective; he held that trade had experienced a revival under the Habsburgs, not least due to the country's newly active authorities. He ascribed the rise of the port of Ostend to the nearby nations being in conflict and to the port being granted free port status in 1781; moreover, the Southern Netherlands were also able to trade via Trieste and the coasts of Africa.[4] Although there was no shortage of conflicting opinions concerning the state of international trade in the eighteenth century, authors were invariably convinced that trade was a potentially tremendous source of wealth and prosperity and that its importance was undeniable. In this respect they differ from many of the previously mentioned present-day authors, who no longer necessarily regard trade as having been the principal cause for economic development.

Unsurprisingly, existing opinions about the impact of international trade on economic development in the Austrian Netherlands are thus more diverse in modern historiography as well. In the early twentieth century, Jules Mees claimed that although agriculture remained the main source of wealth in the Austrian Netherlands – as elsewhere in eighteenth-century Europe – the trade in processed products had already emerged as the second leading source and that it contained the germ of the Industrial Revolution.[5] Around the same time, Lefèvre investigated the bilateral balance of trade with Spain, which he assumed to have been highly favourable (because of the huge export of linen fabrics) and thus garnered the region significant profits.[6] Hervé Hasquin also held no doubts that international trade had played an important role in early modern development.[7] Herman Van der Wee, one of the most prominent

---

2 "La source inépuisable de l'abondance publique et par la même le plus ferme appui de l'état, il est d'une nécessité indispensable de le protéger." NAB, FC, 4279: Letter by Nicolas Bacon, August 1st, 1754.

3 J. Pricken, *La Douane Belge sous Marie-Thérèse et Joseph II* (Brussels: 1964), 23. NAB, FC, 4289, 4303, 8576, 8580.

4 James Shaw, *Essai sur les Pays-Bas Autrichiens* (London: 1788).

5 Jules Mees, "La Statistique Douanière de la Belgique dans la Seconde Moitié du XVIIIe Siècle," *Revue belge d'histoire* 1 (1914): 96–97.

6 Lefèvre and Lefèvre, *Etude*, 187.

7 Hasquin, *Oostenrijks België*.

economic historians of the Southern Netherlands, has argued that international trade was one of the motors behind European growth.[8] Sadly, none of them has ventured deeper into the subject. Hilda Coppejans-Desmedt has only added that the reason that trade – especially trade with Spain and the United Provinces – was the driving force behind the nation's economy in the eighteenth century was again the carefully developed customs policy.[9] As noted in the introduction, there is fairly broad consensus concerning the merits of the customs policy, as evidenced in works from Jan Van Houtte, Bruno Bernard as well as Lis and Soly.[10] Jonathan Israel has credited the efforts of the Habsburg rulers for strongly aiding the region in its attempts to realize import substitution for foreign goods, which enabled economic growth.[11] Lis and Soly agree that the home market could not yet be fully served (so there were virtually no exports), but that imports definitely decreased due to successful substitution of imports, sparked by government intervention.[12]

Nonetheless, many of these contemporary authors have expressed some doubts about the direct significance of trade for the region. Helma De Smedt has noted that trade with most regions (except for Spain) was purely one-directional. Even the efforts of the Austrian government to encourage trade between the nation's hereditary lands and the Southern Netherlands met with little success.[13] A major reason for this was abolishment of the Ostend Company in 1732, which rendered the Southern Netherlands a relatively passive player in

8 Herman Van Der Wee and Th. Peeters, "Een Dynamisch Model voor de Seculaire Ontwikkeling van de Wereldhandel en de Welvaart (12e–18e Eeuw)" *Tijdschrift voor Geschiedenis* (1970): 234.

9 Coppejans-Desmedt, "Economische Opbloei," 273–274.

10 Bernard, *Patrice-François de Neny*, 115, Catharina Lis and Hugo Soly, "Living Apart Together: Overheid en Ondernemers in Brabant en Vlaanderen tijdens de Tweede Helft van de 18e Eeuw," in *Arbeid in Veelvoud. Een Huldeboek voor Jan Craeybeckx en Etienne Scholliers* (Brussels: 1988), 131, Jan Van Houtte, *An Economic History of the Low Countries 800–1800* (London: Weidenfeld and Nicolson, 1977), 292.

11 Israel, *The Dutch Republic*, 1089.

12 Catharina Lis and Hugo Soly, *Een Groot Bedrijf in een Kleine Stad. De Firma De Heyder en Co. te Lier, 1757–1834* (Lier: 1987), 109–110, Lis and Soly, "Living," 131, Lis and Soly, "Different Paths."

13 Helma Houtman-De Smedt, "Charles Proli. Antwerps Zakenman en Bankier, 1723–1786. Een Biografische en Bedrijfshistorische Studie," *Verhandelingen van de Koninklijke Academie voor Wetenschappen, Letteren en Schone Kunsten van België. Klasse der letteren* 45, no. 180 (1983): 126–129, Helma Houtman-De Smedt, "De Zuidelijke Nederlanden en de Oostzee in de 18e Eeuw (Oostenrijkse Periode)," in *The Interactions of Amsterdam and Antwerp with the Baltic Region, 1400–1800* (Leiden: Martinus Nijhoff, 1983).

international trade. Jan Blomme has argued that most of the exported products were raw materials (like wool), which would have been more efficiently processed on domestic soil. Bruno Blondé has added that a number of typical new sectors (such as cotton) contributed less to economic growth than is suggested by their preponderance in historiography.[14] According to most of the aforementioned authors we first of all need to look for the causes of renewed growth in population growth, low wages, technological improvements, an increased demand for luxury, improvements in the road network and increased agricultural productivity and rental incomes.[15]

To date, almost all authors that have included the Austrian Netherlands in their inquiries are Belgians. However, their research has shown that the political economy of the Austrian Netherlands was nearly the opposite of that of Britain in the eighteenth and early nineteenth century, yet the region was second only to Britain in the development of mechanized, capital-intensive industry in the textile, metallurgical and coal sectors. This should suffice to indicate why the study of foreign trade and trade policy while the region was under the sway of Austria's 'enlightened despots', Maria Theresa and Joseph II, should be of great interest to economic historians of far more than the Low Countries alone.

Existing historiography on the Austrian Netherlands has already offered many different hypotheses regarding possible engines for development during the eighteenth century: namely agriculture, export of manufactured goods (for example linen), the production of import substitutes for foreign goods, population growth and increased demand. However, the exact role of international trade (both from the view of supply as of demand) is very rarely made explicit. Historiography still leaves us in the dark when it comes to the actual changes international trade brought about or whether its value was large enough to impact certain sectors. This is partly a consequence of the fact that comprehensive sources relating to international trade in the Austrian Netherlands

---

14 Jan Blomme and Herman Van Der Wee, "The Belgian Economy in a Long-Term Historical Perspective: Economic Development in Flanders and Brabant, 1500–1812," in *Workshop on Quantitative Economic History* (Leuven: 1993), 9, Blondé, "Transport," Blondé, "Disparities."

15 Blondé, "Disparities," 43, Jan Dhondt and M. Bruwier, "The Industrial Revolution in Belgium and Holland, 1700–1914," in *The Fontana Economic History of Europe*, ed. C. Cipolla (London: 1973), 350–351, Houtman-De Smedt, "Charles Proli," 96. For example, the suggestion that the domestic market was the largest buyer of textiles has been raised by Catharina Lis and Hugo Soly, "Restructuring the Urban Textile Industries in Brabant and Flanders During the Second Half of the Eighteenth Century," in *Textiles of the Low Countries in European Economic History*, ed. E. Aerts and J.H. Munro (Leuven: 1990).

have not been exhaustively analysed. Even Moureaux, who knew the eighteenth-century customs archive like the back of his hand, laments the need for source-based research in his study on bilateral Franco-Belgian trade.[16] Yet the highly detailed information on every imaginable cross-border trade flow not only tells us about the value of trade (which does not really matter that much) but also on the composition and evolution of trade for each product (or even the absence of trade), which enables us to also lay bare some of the assumed levers for growth mentioned above. It is in other words past time to broaden the scope of the debate and add some details about the multi-facetted influence of international trade on the variety of stakeholders and on different sectors in the eighteenth-century economy.

16 Philippe Moureaux, "Le Commerce entre la France et les Pays-Bas Autrichiens dans la Seconde Moitié du XVIIIe Siècle. Une Première Approche des Sources Quantitatives," 137.

CHAPTER 4

Sources for the History of Eighteenth-Century International Trade

As noted in the introduction, compiling sufficient empirical data on foreign trade has proven extremely difficult in much of the worldwide research on international trade. Researchers have had to suffice with conjectures based on the numbers of ships, on tax data or on merchants' accounts. Fortunately, the Austrian Netherlands are exceptionally blessed in this respect. The Habsburg rulers were extremely keen on gathering economic data; eventually preserving a huge amount of highly detailed and often standardized statistical and contextual information. Indeed, the cornerstone of the protectionist customs policy they pursued was establishing a complete record of all international trade flows.[1]

1 The Habsburg Customs Statistics: *Magnum Opus* of the Customs Administration

The so-called *Relevés Généraux Des Marchandises, Manufactures et Denrées Entrées, Sorties et Transitées*, the trade statistics collected by the customs administration, constitute the core of this volume. These statistics include import, export and transit data for over a thousand products.[2] They were compiled between 1759 and 1791 and contain traded volumes (and sometimes values) for products ranging from fruit trees, gold leaf and butter to guns, coal and luxury items. When all possible sub-categories are included, the list contains an incredible 3000 different articles, or, in short, just about every conceivable commodity that crossed the border.[3] Drawing up a *relevé général* (general

1 Cécile Douxchamps-Lefèvre, "La Statistique Douanière des Pays-Bas Autrichiens," in *Annales du Congrès de la Fédération cah de Belgique* (Brussels: 1969), 123.

2 NAB, FC, 5748–5805.

3 Two of the categories from the customs statistics merit separate mention: "cloutiers," or nailmakers, are noted among the traded goods in the years 1760–1763 and 1765–1766; "Juifs" (Jews) are noted in all years. Both categories identify persons instead of actual goods, and so we should consider why these particular people were classified as such. Most likely they were obliged to pay some kind of tax when crossing borders. In the case of nailmakers a remark noted in some of the years states that they "ont payés un sols par mois pour travailler (à fons la grand ville subalterne à Marche)." The tax was probably due when the nailmakers wished

 | DOI 10.1163/9789004272606_006

record) of all goods that went across the border was part of a broader trade policy; such efforts were intended to render a clear overview of the state of trade and customs revenues so as to develop more efficient customs regulations.[4]

The idea for the creation of the customs statistics was launched in 1754 by Patrice de Nény, general treasurer of the Austrian Netherlands and a member of the Finance Council.[5] Following his suggestion, the government named Benoît-Marie Dupuy as the first secretary of the new customs bureau, the *bureau de la régie des droits d'entrée et de sortie*, which was responsible for the customs management. Dupuy was likely a former clerk of the French *Fermes Générales*. He had arrived in Brussels with the French army during its invasion of the Austrian Netherlands in the War of Austrian Succession; he had been appointed head of the *Régie général*, established by Louis XV to collect taxes in the territories he occupied. Dupuy worked so efficiently, however, that when the peace was signed, the Habsburgs offered him a position as a special advisor to the government. Dupuy's work to modernize and reform the tax administration – modelled mainly on the French accounting procedures of the *Fermes Générales* – was strongly supported by the minister plenipotentiary Karl von Cobenzl.[6] The latter regarded the customs administration as a cornerstone of a mercantilist economic policy and thus staunchly advocated careful monitoring of import, export and transit trade.[7] Already in the 1750s Dupuy had begun to collect data for a general trade record; de Nény, however, wary of the governor's councillor keeping tabs on him, severely criticized Dupuy's work and reforms. Dupuy was finally dismissed in July 1756 and departed the Low Countries in 1757.[8] He was succeeded by Ferdinand Paradis, who produced

---

to practice their valuable skills abroad. As concerned Jews, a remark states: "Juifs qui payent le droit corporel à la sortie." It is less clear why these particular travelers were taxed, although it is likely that their respective statuses rendered them easy targets for collection of additional government revenues.

4 NAB, FC, 4279, *commerce en général 1755*.

5 Blomme and Van Der Wee, "The Belgian Economy," Douxchamps-Lefèvre, "La Statistique," 123.

6 On Dupuy and his career in the Austrian Netherlands' financial administration, see Marie-Laure Legay, "Un Français à Bruxelles: les réformes comptables de Benoît-Marie Dupuy (1746–1756)," *Comptabilités* (on line journal), 1, 2010, retrieved on 27th July 2011, http://comptabilites.revues.org/156.

7 Coppens, "Bureau," 526.

8 Legay, 'Un Français', 9. The sources also point to personal conflicts in which Dupuy was involved: NAB, FC, 4279, report on disobediences by Dupuy, July 18th 1756; 5853, complaints about Dupuy and report concerning a quarrel with a certain Poitevin, 1756.

the first complete annual record, for the year 1759, and later by Henri Delplancq (director during the period 1765–1787). It was especially under Delplancq's leadership that the bureau reached its full potential, providing not only data about external trade but also a more extensive expertise on economic and financial matters. The latter aspect likely explains why the bureau's workforce increased from a dozen clerks in the early 1750s to more than forty at the end of the 1780s.[9]

The customs statistics contain, for each of the 3000 alphabetically listed products, three columns (import, export and transit trade) and 22 rows.[10] The first 21 rows present the traded volumes per department; the final row identifies the calculated total volume for the Austrian Netherlands. The departments were: Brussels, St-Philippe (called Lillo, after 1785), Turnhout, Antwerp, Tienen, Ghent, Sint-Niklaas, Ypres, Bruges, Courtrai, Ostend, Newport, Chimay, Charleroi, Mons, Namur, Navagne (called Herve, after 1765), Luxembourg, Marche, Saint Vith and Roermond (see Map 1 for the customs offices). Unfortunately, the statistics do not account for the origins and destinations of the trade flows. The department for which they were registered offers clues about the possible final destinations; however, since goods were not necessarily registered at their points of entry or departure, such indications are far from certain.[11] Each year's information is compiled in a cardboard volume; a more luxurious copy, with a decorative leather and gold-leaf cover, was delivered annually to the monarch.[12] The goods are recorded in different units, including measures of length, weight, monetary value, and even a few units whose exact values are no longer known (namely a *lien* of glasses and a *wiege* of monkfish). Some goods were also recorded in several ways (for example partly in ells and partly in Brabantine guilders, depending on the practices of local customs

9 Coppens, "Bureau," 526, Philippe Moureaux, "Un Organe Peu Connu du Gouvernement des Pays-Bas Autrichiens: le Bureau de Régie des Droits d'Entrée et de Sortie," *Belgisch Tijdschrift voor Filologie en Geschiedenis* 44 (1966): 490–498.

10 Not every year contains exactly the same categories, therefore the total number of goods for the 33 years exceeds that of a single year. The year with the smallest amount of goods is 1779 (846); the year with the largest is 1759 (2001).

11 Merchants could apply for a permit to register goods elsewhere, for example in the city where their activities were based. To establish the importance of different trading partners, the customs statistics can be supplemented by local customs data preserved in the National Archives in Brussels for 1791–1794: NAB, FC, 5830–5846: *Relevés généraux des marchandises entrées, sorties et Transitées par les différents départements avec l'indication de la provenance ou de la destination des produits.*

12 Apparently they were never actually transported to Vienna, but remained in Brussels. Perhaps they were only symbolically directed towards the empress and emperor.

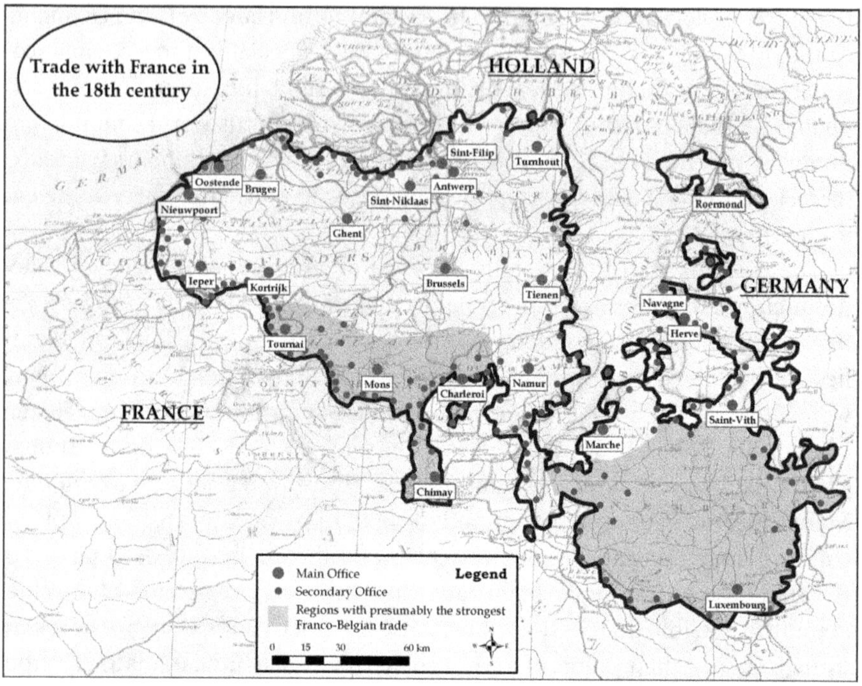

MAP 1 *Based on a Map of the customs bureaus by customs official Lorent, 1784. Digitized by Iason Jongepier.*
SOURCE: NAB, FC, 2248.

bureaus). The statistics mainly include volumes, but rarely monetary values, thereby rendering aggregation much more complicated.

The customs bureau left a large archive of information concerning the organization of its work, including regulations, personnel files, memoranda on the bureau's founding and numerous letters and decrees.[13] These show that each of the 21 *départements* had a principal bureau and a variable number of subordinate bureaus.[14] The latter were leased by the central administration to local officials. This arrangement, unfortunately, impacted the coherence of the

13 National archive Brussels, Conseil des finances, *commerce et douanes*. The Finance Council contains detailed personnel files: NAB, FC, 8563–8576, reports on customs organisation: 4294 and countless other sources on the customs administration which are described in: Coppens, "Bureau," Koen Dries, "Comité voor de Wederzijdse Handel tussen de Duitse Erflanden en de Nederlanden (1768–1777)," in *De Centrale Overheidsinstellingen van de Habsburgse Nederlanden (1482–1795)*, ed. Erik Aerts (Brussels: 1994).

14 A list of the secondary customs offices per department can be found in NAB, FC, 4294.

customs registers: as noted, products are noted alternately in monetary values and in various other units of measurement; however, it also meant that the local staff depended on thorough collecting of taxes to survive, which was an incentive for them to be meticulous. Moreover, the numerous regulations and inspections indicate the accuracy with which the sources were created.[15] The government acknowledged that fraud was a serious problem, but took several steps to address it.[16] For example, every department included an auditor and guards who were controlled by the central administration, not by the local customs officers.[17] The bureau was able to compute its statistics remarkably quickly. The local customs administration forwarded their statistics, without compiling or arranging them, to the *Bureau de la Régie*, where a large staff was assigned to compose the overall statistics. The process usually took less than six months, whereas for example its French counterpart required almost a year, and sometimes up to three years, to perform the same task. In this way the bureau was able to produce a continuous series from 1759 to 1791. In contrast, the French *Objet général* contains several blank years.[18]

The concluding of the source, in 1791, obscures some important questions about the impact of trade. To name two: How did the reopening of the river Scheldt in 1795 (it had been closed by the Dutch Republic) affect trade conditions, and how did the international blockade impact industrialization? The reopening of the Scheldt evidently benefited commerce to an immense degree; as such, it would likely be highly productive to compare commercial activity in that period with the preceding years. Likewise, the international blockade ensured that the Austrian Netherlands did not need to worry about British competition. This in itself was a windfall. Moreover, even though the roots of industrialisation had been established earlier, it was only after 1790 that industrialisation became truly visible. The available studies on trade in the nineteenth century mitigate the problem to some extent, but it remains inopportune that such an interesting source was brought to such a sudden end.[19]

Nevertheless, the fact remains that an administrative source like the *relevé* must be approached with great caution. Even though historians do not

15 NAB, FC, 6399.

16 NAB, FC, 8576.

17 G. Bigwood, *Les Impôts Généraux dans les Pays-Bas Autrichiens. Etude Historique de Législation Financière* (Leuven: 1900), 280.

18 Loïc Charles and Guillaume Daudin, "Le Bureau de la Balance du Commerce au XVIIIe Siècle," *Revue d'Histoire moderne et contemporaine* (accepted for publication).

19 For example: Karel Veraghtert, "De Havenbeweging te Antwerpen tijdens de Negentiende Eeuw" (Katholieke Universiteit Leuven, 1977).

question the source's intrinsic value, the customs statistics present various shortcomings. These weaknesses have been discussed by Cécile Douxchamps-Lefèvre, Jules Mees, Greta Devos and more recently Koen Dries (who did the largest part of the source's digitisation).[20] All the usual methodological suspects – under-registration, contraband, fraud, negligence – are present, and, as Mees and Douxchamps-Lefèvre discovered, a number of tax-exempt goods were simply not included. (It is possible to determine which goods these were, by looking them up in the tariff books.[21]) Another concern is that local employees were not always up to the task. This is evidenced by the *Bureau de la Régie* including a considerable number of misspellings and miscalculations in the tables submitted from the local customs bureaus.[22] In any case the statistics cannot be compared to contemporary administrative documents: before 1770 the staff in the regional offices was not even required to be able to read and write![23] Also, changing levels of taxation probably caused bias, since increasing taxes may have led to higher rates of tax evasion. It is even more difficult to establish whether this bias would have affected certain goods more than others (and which goods these would have been). Tax evasion was a problem the customs administration was well aware of (see for instance the chapter on the salt trade).[24] Moreover, it is nearly impossible to assess how great the impact of changing tariffs was on this source. All in all, the amounts listed clearly tended to be minima, because when traders saw the chance to avoid customs controls and the accompanying taxes, they probably rarely hesitated to do so. Even though the figures from the source suggest an illusion of exactness, we must remain cognizant that in fact they are merely indications of the magnitude of traded volumes and of the trends in trade. In particular, one should not lose sight of the reality that these customs statistics – however systematically and accurate they may appear to be – were compiled by real persons and with a specific objective, thereby rendering them unavoidably far from exact.

---

20 Greta Devos, "Oostenrijkse Douanestatistiek en de Oostendse Handel in de Tweede Helft van de XVIIIe Eeuw," in *Colloquium: Economische Geschiedenis van België* (Brussels: 1972), Douxchamps-Lefèvre, "La Statistique," Dries, "Comité," Mees, "La Statistique."

21 See below. NAB, FC, 8873–8874, Estat Ou Tarif des Droits d'entrée et sortie sur les marchandises, manufactures et denrées.

22 Mees, "La Statistique," 89–91.

23 Christine Piraux and M. Dorban, *Douane, Commerce et Fraude dans le Sud de l'Espace Belge et Grand-Ducal au XVIIIe Siècle* (Louvain-la-Neuve: Academia Bruylant, 1998), 136.

24 Smuggling received an enormous deal of attention within the sources of the *bureau de la régie*. Some more general texts can be found in NAB, FC, 4278, Consultation of August 27th 1753 by the *jointe pour le commerce avec les Pays Héréditaires*; 4284, memoir concerning smuggling (1780); 8576, notes by Delplancq (1786–1789).

In short, extreme caution is warranted when dealing with the quantitative information from the customs statistics. Nonetheless, if the source is used correctly, there are convincing arguments for not ignoring this goldmine of data. The statistics' eminent importance for uncovering trends and magnitudes in foreign trade is uncontested. That the evolutions do indeed make sense has been substantiated in the work of colleagues such as Dries Lyna, and will of course be corroborated further in my own case studies.[25] Moreover, in comparison with the statistical materials available for other countries – for example the Dutch Republic – it is no exaggeration to state that the Habsburg customs statistics are superior.[26] This fact did not escape even critics of the customs statistics.[27] These statistics, when their limitations are accounted for, provide highly valuable information not just for economic historians but also for researchers investigating material culture, social transformations and eighteenth-century society in general. For this reason the present volume includes all the yearly figures for import, export and transit of every product, not just those examined in the five case studies (see Appendix, A.1). The 21 departmental subtotals have been collected for a number of sample years (1764–1781), so as to obtain at least a snapshot of the relative weights of the different departments involved in international trade, though only for the goods included in the specific case studies.

2 The Tariff Books: A Look Behind the Curtain of the Trade Policy

By simply observing the trade figures in the customs statistics for the sectors examined in this volume, we could already attempt to draw conclusions; these would be far from certain, however, due to the source's potential pitfalls, as mentioned above. The data from the customs statistics must be tested against information from other sources. One such source that gives particularly valuable insights into the trade policy and the actors involved are the tariff books, the so-called "*Estat ou tarif des droits d'entrée et sortie sur les marchandises, manufactures et Denrées.*" It is – as are the customs statistics – part of the archives of the *bureau de la régie*.[28] However, they were not

25 Dries Lyna, "The Cultural Construction of Value: Art Auctions in Antwerp and Brussels (1700–1794)" (UA, 2010).

26 de Vries and Van der Woude, *Nederland*.

27 Mees, "La Statistique," Moureaux, "Le Commerce," 144.

28 NAB, FC, 8873–8874, Estat Ou Tarif des Droits d'entrée et sortie sur les marchandises, manufactures et denrées. Copies and appendices can be found in : NAB, FC, 8861, 5606–5608.

originally compiled by the eighteenth-century customs administration, but date to the century before. As noted in the introduction, customs duties were not identical for all of the Southern Netherlands' trading partners. A separate tariff had been established for trade with France, the original tariff dating from 1670. In 1680 duties for the other neighbouring countries were established.[29] In the second half of the eighteenth-century, the Council of Finance still verbally adhered to these original (printed) tariffs, over which neighbouring countries had exerted great influence. Yet the various copies in the archive of the customs bureau evidence countless modifications until 1792; these modifications are handwritten, in chronological order, on the flip-side of the pages.

The tariff books contain a similar alphabetized list of goods as that in the *relevé général*, but with less subcategories. The respective heights of the import and export duties of each good are printed; yet only rarely are the transit duties recorded. Unfortunately, the more recent, handwritten adjustments to the taxes are far from complete. This is because, first, the customs bureau could not keep track of all the changes – which were often only implemented locally – resulting in only the chief adjustments being included in the tariff books.[30] And, second, it was a generally deliberate policy not to make tariff changes public, owing to fear of retributions from trading partners who might oppose tax changes, and because traders could be tempted to demand certain benefits already granted to colleagues trading other commodities or in different areas.[31] Adjustments were made for different sectors at different times but were communicated only to those involved in the particular sector, and sometimes only to those who had requested the modifications. This was exacerbated by the fact that, as noted earlier, local customs bureaus were being leased out by the central administration, thereby leaving customs tariffs prone to specific cyclical and circumstantial events.[32] To find all of the missing modifications would require sifting through the countless letters and communications included in the folders on individual goods, compiled by the customs services; yet even many of these are lost to present-day researchers. In the case

29 NAB, FC, 5606, Tarif pour la levée des droits sur les marchandises, manufactures & denrées entrantes ou sortantes le Royaume de France, Pays cedé & autres. Du 18 juillet 1670. NAB, FC, 8874, Estat ou tarif des droits d'entrée et sortie sur les marchandises, manufactures et denrées. 1680, "corrigé jusqu'au mois de mars 1792," signed by Alexander Farnese.

30 Pricken, *La Douane*.

31 Lis and Soly, "Living," 133.

32 Recent work on the customs organization focuses mainly on the Walloon area. Piraux and Dorban, *Douane*.

of transit duties, compiling an overview of the tariff's evolutions is simply impossible.[33]

All in all, even though they are incomplete, the tariff books are especially useful in uncovering certain aims and aspirations regarding international trade flows. They reveal otherwise undocumented measures, such as that exports of almost every kind of weaponry were entirely prohibited during wartime. This measure was evidently adopted so to ensure that such exports did not fall into enemy hands and to assure neutrality. Another illustration of the information contained in the tariffs books is that most export tariffs were relatively high. This was logical in the case of raw materials, because governments would have wanted to encourage the processing of these materials by domestic manufactories – and thereby also support industry – but it is odd from a more mercantilist point of view, wherein rulers would have wished to support foreign trade and thereby aimed for a positive balance of trade. This raises the possibility that the government was in fact more concerned with gaining higher tax incomes than with achieving higher earnings for its inhabitants. This would be hugely important if true, as it would imply that the government was implementing not a *trade* policy but merely a tax policy. This in itself would not be highly surprising, as import and export tariffs constituted the most significant parts of the government's annual revenues.[34] This hypothesis will be tested later in this work. On the other hand, the tariffs present a clear division between manufactured and unprocessed goods, a fact that again indicates a more prudently thought-through trade policy. Indeed, the tariffs end with a note concerning goods which were not included, stating that for all "*manufactures*" the import duty amounted to three Brabantine guilders for every hundred guilders worth of goods, and that the same amount of export was taxed at only half a guilder. "*Marchandises & Denrées*" were charged two guilders for both imports and exports.[35] Finally, the tariff books also mention commodities that were exempt from duties. This allows for checking if these duty free commodities are missing from the customs statistics and to fill in the gaps mentioned by Mees and Douxchamps-Lefèvre.[36] Moreover, the tariff books can provide the modern scholar with clues about the relevance and worth of goods;

---

33 For a rare number of goods it is possible to trace the developments in transit tariffs to a larger extent, for example for coal and grains. See below.

34 Bigwood, *Les Impôts Généraux*, 219.

35 NAB, FC, 8874.

36 However, their fear that tax-exempt goods were not included does not seem especially necessary, as only in a limited number of years were certain goods (i.e. small, valuable goods such as diamonds) not included.

such information can be derived from the levels of the duties (although an expensive product, of course, may have been taxed very modestly when the government wished to boost its import or export) and from the number of times taxes were modified.

3 The Large Legacy of the *Bureau de la régie*

While we are most fortunate in having detailed registers compiled by the Habsburg administration on international trade and taxation, these registers represent but a tiny fragment of the available source materials that the administration left behind. Besides the previously mentioned quantitative sources, the customs bureau and the Finance Council of the Austrian Netherlands collected a sizable archive of myriad sources on international trade in all its aspects. These sources strengthen an actor-based approach to trade, since they also include letters from other parties than the government. International trade policy has always been the outcome of a social game of force between players maintaining differing interests. The Southern Netherlands have an especially long history of opposing economic lobby groups.[37] Although there was a clear change of climate after 1748, the 'liberal' trade lobby did not loosen its grip on political affairs.[38] Moreover, trade policy in those still turbulent times remained severely entangled with international politics. The choice between protectionism and free trade was thus much more than an individual or a technical one. Laying bare this nexus of agents will help to further our understanding of a tumultuous and dynamic era in politics and commerce. This study endeavours to determine – among other things – how government policy was shaped by customs legislation and vice versa, and how different groups in society could advance their interests. It is hoped that this actor-oriented analysis of the trade policy will give economic history a 'human face'.

Most of the sources on the international trade of the Austrian Netherlands are in the archive fund of the Finance Council, but important pieces are located

37 See for example: Maïka de Keyzer, "Opportunisme, corporatisme en progressiviteit: conflicten en vertogen van corporatieve belangengroepen in het stedelijk milieu van het achttiende-eeuwse Mechelen," *Tijdschrift voor sociale en economische geschiedenis* 7:4 (2010), 3–26.

38 H. Deceulaer, "Between Medieval Continuities and Early Modern Change: Proto-Industrialization and Consumption in the Southern Low Countries (1300–1800)," *Textile History* (2006), Ilja Van Damme, "Pendelen tussen Revoluties en Tradities: Recent Historisch Onderzoek naar de Kleinhandel in de Late Middeleeuwen en de Nieuwe Tijd (Ca. 1450-Ca. 1850)," *Stadsgeschiedenis* 2 (2007).

in the funds of the Secretariat of State and War, of the auditor's office and within the collection of manuscripts. A few interesting documents on commerce remain in the *Hofkammerarchiv* of Vienna, but most such documents are now in Brussels. The sources vary, ranging from texts about trade in general (memoranda, decrees, notes from experts, and so on) to highly specific articles (such as personal requests from merchants and entrepreneurs, patent applications and inventories). During Delplancq's administration in particular, the *bureau de la régie* truly evolved into a sort of ministry of economic affairs. The largest collections of the customs archive are grouped per the commodity they deal with. These pieces offer specific information about the trade policy, the actors and the trade flows of specific products.[39] The most extensive collections are those on textiles and grains, each of which occupies several meters of filing cabinets. For grain, unlike with other products, the customs administration also methodically gathered prices for every department.[40]

The study of this variety of documents highlights a number of contradictory trends in the commercial history of the Austrian Netherlands. Often these – as will repeatedly be the case throughout this book – sprung from the contradiction between political aspirations and economic realities, or, in other words, between discourse and facts. Both the Habsburg and local governments stressed, in all their decrees and statements, the importance of international trade and of maintaining a positive trade balance, and thus – in good mercantilist practice – appeared to be highly concerned with achieving these objectives; however, merchants and manufacturers nonetheless complained incessantly about the situation. The explanation lies partly in the precarious international situation which made it difficult to implement overt protectionist measures. Also, it should be kept in mind that the empress and emperor in Vienna may well have been more occupied with benefiting the entire empire

39 The collections on the products included in this volume can be found in the following funds: NAB, FC, 5215–5249, sel et raffineries; 4556–4560, Etoffes de laine, d'or, de soie et toiles de coton généralité, 4563–4596, étoffes de laine de toutes espèces; 4597–4598, draps faits de queues et de pennes; 4599–4609, Etoffes d'or, d'argent, de soie, velours de soie et soie crue et filée; 4610–4637, toiles de toutes genres; 4638–4644, imprimeries de toiles de coton; 4688–4689, Gazes et crêpes de soie, de fil, marli, treilli, etc; 4856–4891, laines; 4892–4899, draperies de Limbourg; 5319–5339, toiles, toilettes, Cambrai, fils, dentelles & blanchisseries; 5019–5034, charbons; 4704–4817, céréales; 4503–4537, Epiceries, thé, caffé, chocolat, drogues et teintures; 5256–5267, sucre et raffineries.

40 NAB, FC, 4818–4838 (grain prices) and 4950–4953 (flax prices). Jan Materné, *De Prijzenadministratie van de Centrale Overheid te Brussel tijdens de 18de Eeuw. Vlaamse, Brabantse, Noordnederlandse, Engelse, Duitse en Baltische Graanprijzen op de Amsterdamse Beurs (1767–1792)* (Brussels: 1994).

and its treasury, rather than just the Southern Netherlands and its traders. Also, and a point that will be examined later, industry-related concerns may have been paramount over commerce-related ones. Nonetheless, combining the data from the customs statistics with those from the contextual sources facilitates an in-depth analysis of the evolutions of imports, exports and transit, of the influence of administrative measures in the individual sectors, and, more importantly, on the differentiated impact of international trade on all parties involved. It is particularly the existence of this type of archival material that thus enables us to go beyond the macroeconomic debate and uncover the specificity of different sectors, each with their own actors and internal logic, which is otherwise hidden by the large questions on trade and development.

PART 2

International Trade in the Austrian Netherlands

An Assessment of Its Value

CHAPTER 5

The Balance of Trade

As discussed in the introduction, the question about the possible merits of overseas trade for economic development poses one of the never-ending debates in economic historiography. In order to begin solving some pieces of this puzzle, I will first of all estimate the overall worth of the international trade flows, in order to provide a contextual framework for the study of individual sectors. This has not yet been done for the Southern Low Countries in the second half of the eighteenth century, despite the necessary sources long being available and even though the region offers some very interesting characteristics compared to the research on trade for other regions on the continent. However, as noted previously, the preliminary observations about trade in the Austrian Netherlands appear to nuance the view about Britain and other bigger trading nations.[1] Research on foreign trade in the Southern Netherlands thus provides vital new outlooks onto the broader international economic history of this period.

In this chapter, I seek to make the first move towards shedding light on the complex relation between international trade and the development of the Austrian Netherlands in the second half of the eighteenth century. The first important assignment is to generate an assessment of the value of international trade for the Southern Low Countries in the second half of the eighteenth century so as to unravel the trends taking place in this field. However, an active or passive balance of trade in itself meant little for an economy. To assess the dissimilar effects of international trade I will break up the result into separate sectors and track the impact of trade on individual agents. After all, the fact that eighteenth-century governments were highly concerned with mercantilist schemes does not necessarily mean that a trade surplus had many encouraging effects on economic development. This volume therefore does not endeavour to calculate the precise value of trade and then seek mathematical correlation between international trade and growth – as other authors have done: rather, it explicitly departs from specific sectors in order to assess what international trade meant for eighteenth-century actors, and also look at

1 Ann Coenen, "Katoen en Economische Groei. De Katoenhandel in de Oostenrijkse Nederlanden tussen Politieke Ambities en Economische Realiteit 1759–1791," *Tijdschrift voor sociale en economische geschiedenis* 8, no. 2 (2011).

 | DOI 10.1163/9789004272606_007

the dissimilar roles that it might have simultaneously played.[2] The merit of estimating the worth of total trade flows is that it allows for embedding the case studies into a macroeconomic framework and estimating their relative importance within the international trade flows.

1 State of the Art

Explicit statements on the Southern Low Countries' balance of trade are in very short supply. Within the brief overview of economic historiography on the Austrian Netherlands, there were some authors who also made statements on the balance of trade. Valéry Janssens claimed – based on monetary data – that the trade balance of the Southern Low Countries was surely positive. "The expansion of the money supply during that period [1749–1780] (…) demonstrates more clearly than any argument whatsoever, and despite the spread of a completely opposite view, that the trade balance in the course of those years – with brief exceptions – showed a surplus."[3] However, Janssens actually examined the balance of payments, for which the balance of trade is only one element, besides services and other monetary flows. Anyhow, Chris Vandenbroeke agrees with Janssens' assessment.[4] Lefèvre claimed that at least in the commercial interaction with Spain the bilateral trade balance was positive for the region.[5] Lis and Soly do not mention a trade surplus, but argue that there was an increase in foreign (and domestic) demand for manufactured goods from the Austrian Netherlands, while its imports decreased.[6] Philippe Moureaux also believed that the trade deficit was reduced considerably during the second half of the eighteenth century, maybe even to the point of equilibrium.[7] This assessment is contrary to that of Hubert Van Houtte,

2 Angus Maddison, *Contours of the World Economy, 1–2030 Ad* (Oxford: Oxford University Press, 2007), Jan Luiten Van Zanden, "Early Modern Economic Growth: A Survey of the European Economy, 1500–1800," in *Early Modern Capitalism*, ed. Maarten Prak (London: Routledge, 2001).

3 Valéry Janssens, "Het Geldwezen der Oostenrijkse Nederlanden," *Verhandelingen Koninklijke Vlaamse Academie voor Wetenschappen, Letteren en Schone Kunsten van België. Klasse der letteren. Brussel* 29 (1957): 166.

4 Vandenbroeke, "The Regional Economy," 162.

5 Lefèvre and Lefèvre, *Etude*, 7, 187.

6 Lis and Soly, *Een Groot Bedrijf*, 109–110, Lis and Soly, "Living," 131, Lis and Soly, "Different Paths."

7 Philippe Moureaux, *Les Préoccupations Statistiques du Gouvernement des Pays-Bas Autrichiens et le Dénombrement des Industries dressé en 1764* (Brussels: 1971), 179–180.

who assumed that the export deficit endured after 1748.[8] Jan Blomme has added that especially industrial exports were not doing well. Exported products were mainly raw materials (like wool), which should preferably have been processed on domestic soil.[9] So far, the assessments of the balance of trade are thus not only rather broad, but also – unfortunately – contradictory.

However, even though we lack explicit estimates of the balance of trade for the Austrian Netherlands, we hold some interesting examples of trade calculations and of trade balances that were calculated for other periods or only for parts of the region. Luk Corluy mapped the main trade flows for the department of Ghent in the years 1792–1794.[10] Pierre Dardel describes the bilateral trade between the Austrian Netherlands and France in his study of Rouen. According to Dardel, exports from the region increased throughout the second half of the eighteenth century.[11] Guillaume Daudin and Loïc Charles are currently working towards determining a bilateral balance of trade based on French trade statistics.[12] Jules Mees has already used the Habsburg customs statistics to list products according to their passive or active character in the trade balance.[13] Brulez's study of the sixteenth-century balance of trade adopts a different method. For measuring imports, he uses the trade details of the allegedly most significant import goods (silk, fustian, wine, wheat, salt, wool, cloth, spices, alum and copper); and for exports he bases his calculations on the yield of the export tariff.[14] These examples are promising for the feasibility of such a project – even in instances where less detailed information is available than that for the Austrian Netherlands – and they offer the possibility to compare the results presented below.

8 Van Houtte, *Histoire*, 250.

9 Blomme and Van Der Wee, "The Belgian Economy," 9.

10 Luk Corluy, "Een Metodologische Poging tot Uitwerking van een Ekonomisch Model van de Buitenlandse Handel voor het Departement Gent in de Oostenrijkse Nederlanden tijdens de Tweede Helft van de XVIIIe Eeuw" (KUL, 1972).

11 Pierre Dardel, *Navires et Marchandises dans les Ports de Rouen et du Havre au XVIIIe Siècle* (Paris: Ecole pratique des hautes études, 1963), 78–80.

12 Loïc Charles, Ann Coenen, and Guillaume Daudin, "Comparing Early Trade Statistics: The Case of the Austrian Netherlands and France from 1759 to 1791," *EHES Conference (Dublin)* (2011), Daudin, *Commerce*, 143–147.

13 Mees, "La Statistique," 94–95.

14 Wilfrid Brulez, "De Handelsbalans der Nederlanden in het Midden van de 16de Eeuw," *Bijdragen voor de Geschiedenis der Nederlanden* XXI (1967).

2 Approach

One of the recurring themes in the discussions on trade history is how to make an acceptable and effective reconstruction of historical trade flows.[15] For the Austrian Netherlands we are blessed with the remarkably abundant data on imports, exports and transit for numerous goods, brought together in the customs statistics. However, the amount of data in the customs statistics is, as noted, immense and heterogeneous, yet the biggest fly in the ointment is the fact that the customs statistics in their original form include mostly traded volumes. For the purpose of this chapter – i.e. calculating the balance of trade – this data is only useful when converted into comparable measurements, preferably monetary values. Therefore, besides figures on trade, eighteenth-century price data is also needed for as many goods as possible.

A very small number of commodity prices can be read directly from the customs statistics, for in a few cases both the volume and the corresponding value were recorded such that the price can be calculated. This is the case for *codde* (a type of fabric) and for woollen sheets. Apart from these two textile goods, a sample yielded no other examples. Fortunately, however, for about 170 other goods – mostly ones that were traded in small quantities – we do not have to look for prices, because the size of the trade flows was only recorded in monetary value and did not require conversion. All other prices used below were found in various primary and published sources. Commodity prices can be found scattered throughout the archive fund of the Finance Council and the Secretary of State and War, though it is not always apparent how representative these figures are.[16] The customs administration itself also collected price data, in particular on grains and flax.[17] However, the largest part of the prices used here is taken from a published work: "Nederlandsche Prijsgeschiedenis" by Nicolaas Posthumus.[18] Posthumus published annual wholesale prices from the Amsterdam stock market. Since our subject is cross-border trade, we can safely assume that the prices in Posthumus's overview are largely similar to those used for wholesale commerce in the Austrian Netherlands. For grains,

---

15 Welling, "The Prize."

16 It is also not entirely clear whether these were whosale or retail prices, but since they were used by the customs administration probably the former (and Cost, Insurance and Freight included). NAB, FC, 4289, 4305, 4564, 4571, 4597, 4828 and 5320. NAB, AO, 1266. NAB, SSW, 2153.

17 NAB, FC, 4837–4838 and 4951–4953. Materné, *De Prijzenadministratie*.

18 Nicolaas W. Posthumus, *Nederlandsche Prijsgeschiedenis*, vol. 1 (Leiden: E.J. Brill, 1943).

this hypothesis holds.[19] The prices are published in Dutch guilders though, so they evidently had to be converted to Brabantine guilders.[20] Lastly, data from the French trade statistics, which contain both volumes and prices, can also be used. This source includes the destinations and origins of traded goods, and so the bilateral trade flows between both regions can be filtered out. The ongoing digitisation of these statistics – a project led by Guillaume Daudin and Loïc Charles – remains in its early stages, and so, unfortunately, we cannot yet use this trove of information.

In the end, the trade balance can be calculated on the basis of data for 272 goods, including wool, wine, salt, cotton, spices, dyes, grain, linen, flax, coal and luxury goods such as fine decorations (for the complete overview, see Appendix, Table A.2). In terms of volume these commodities definitely accounted for over 50 percent of total international trade (not surprisingly, goods for which prices have been published are goods that were traded most frequently); in terms of value they likely accounted for an even larger share, as they include a large portion of the most expensive goods (such as silk and spices). To be sure, extra price data would allow for inclusion of more goods and would thus greatly increase the accuracy of these estimations. The current selection, however, unquestionably offers an extensive enough sample of international trade in the eighteenth century to expose accurate trends.

Before examining the results, a few remarks on missing prices are in order. For some products, prices are not available for each year, but only for a few years within the timeframe covered in this study. Initially, in cases of the goods for which no annual prices are available, the annual volumes from the customs statistics were combined with the price from the closest available preceding year. Prices were thus kept constant over several years, as the annual prices on hand suggested that inflation remained negligible during these 33 years. This is also confirmed by the – highly disputed – work of Robert Allen.[21] However, because a number of the available annual prices were found to have fluctuated greatly – both upwards and downwards – I thought it important to see to what extent the initial result would prove robust when prices varied. Consequently, I recalculated the result, using weighted averages of the nearest two prices. For most

---

19 Materné, *De Prijzenadministratie*.

20 1 Amsterdam guilder = 1,1 Brabantine guilder: C. Verlinden and E. Scholliers, *Dokumenten voor de Geschiedenis van Prijzen en Lonen in Vlaanderen en Brabant* (Bruges: 1959–1973), 14.

21 Robert Allen, "The Great Divergence in European Wages and Prices from the Middle Ages to the First World War," in: *Explorations in Economic History* 38 (2001) 411–447, Allen, "Wages, Prices & Living Standards: The World-Historical Perspective," http://www.iisg.nl/hpw/data.php 2009, Verlinden and Scholliers, *Dokumenten*, xvii.

years the deviations from the initial result are small (with a difference of around one percent). Yet it seems incautious not to take into account the price fluctuations, since in some years the discrepancies are quite large. For example, in 1788 the first result (with prices mostly from 1785) differs from the weighted average by 40 percent. This is not surprising, as during the advent of the Brabantine Revolution – which thoroughly disrupted economic life (and everything else) – a major price increase occurred. In 1773, 1778 and 1781 the differences compared to the first calculation are also considerable, although it makes little difference to the overall trend. It might thus be safe to say that inflation was absent (except perhaps at the very end of the period and then mainly for grains and other agricultural products), but that there were definitely occasional spikes in the price movements – both upwards and downwards – because of several factors (harvest failures, supply and demand, quality differences, political turmoil that led to insecurity, etcetera). However, due to the irregularity of these fluctuations I could make no general estimations about the relative heights of the missing prices. It should be kept in mind that this contributes markedly to the uncertainty of the results in the final two or three years of the period, when prices of some commodities may have risen strongly.

3 Results

A first look at the balance of trade primarily munitions the more pessimist economic historians from our introduction. Even though the balance shows large fluctuations between 1759 and 1791 (Chart 1 and Tables 1 and 2), for most years it was clearly unfavourable. And after 1788 it even caved in entirely. However, for these last years we should take into account the abrupt political changes that took place, which make it difficult to draw conclusions regarding international trade. What is particularly strange is that the balance did not become positive during the four year's war between Britain, France and the Republic (except during the year 1782), while that war had presumably created an opening for the Austrian Netherlands to enter the European market without too much hindrance from the larger surrounding nations. Michielsen wrote that 1781 was the best year for trade during the entire eighteenth century, but he appears to have been mistaken.[22] Given the large deviations between successive years, we obviously have to be prudent. We must also note that because of the higher taxes the incentive to smuggle was larger in the case of

22 A. Michielsen, "Het Volume van de Belgische Handel in de 18e Eeuw," *Tijdschrift voor economie en sociologie* 5 (1939): 216.

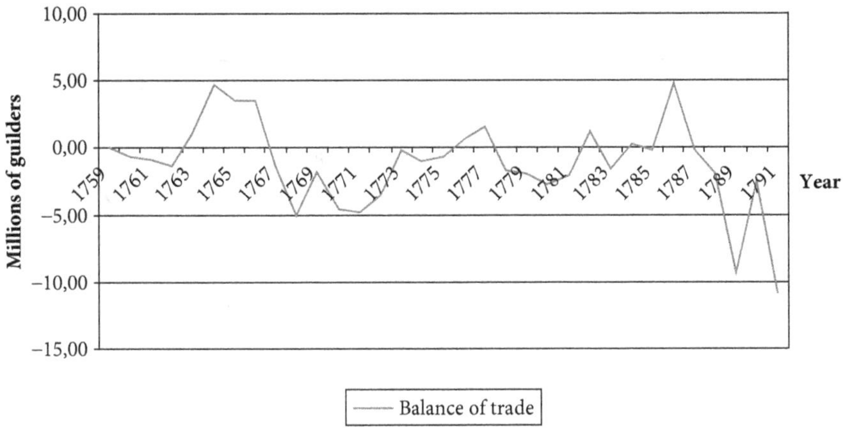

CHART 1 *The balance of trade, 1759–1791*
SOURCE: RÉLÉVÉ GENERAL, NATIONAL ARCHIVES BRUSSELS, FINANCE COUNCIL, 5748–5805.

imports (so these might have been even higher than the source suggests). During the first five years (1759–1763) of the customs statistics all traded amounts were relatively small and the categorization of the *Relevé* was frequently altered, what unfortunately renders the figures from these years less reliable than in the rest of the period.

Yet at the same time these results also surpass the expectations of some of the discussed authors, namely those who assume that the balance could have never become positive nor even have reached equilibrium. Except for the last years, it actually did. Ten out of 33 years had a positive balance and for nine more years the value was only slightly negative (with a deficit of less than one and a half million guilders, or about ten per cent). At any rate the peak around 1765 coincides with the pattern of eighteenth-century industry that was described by Herve Hasquin.[23] Below we will see that the categories of goods which comprise the largest proportion of the balance were always the same. So there is a fairly regular pattern behind this result, which lends support to the accuracy of these trends. In a nutshell: at least for the sum of 272 goods hidden behind this graph we can assume that international trade was more or less at equilibrium. Later on, we will go into the meaning of that assessment for the eighteenth-century economy.

More important than knowing the general movement of the trade balance – which is nothing more or less than an abstract tool to make some general

23 Hasquin, "Nijverheid," 158.

TABLE 1 *The balance of trade, 1759–1791*

Year	Import (in Brabantine guilders)	Export (in Brabantine guilders)	Transit (in Brabantine guilders)	Balance of trade
1759	7.041.561,89	7.132.528,98	–	90.967,09
1760	9.038.259,20	8.378.728,24	–	-659.530,96
1761	8.707.197,14	7.787.227,34	3.426.761,60	-919.969,80
1762	9.710.286,46	8.365.005,86	2.633.220,93	-1.345.280,60
1763	8.201.766,06	9.306.192,17	3.383.663,27	1.104.426,11
1764	13.690.842,96	18.385.831,34	3.977.670,35	4.694.988,38
1765	15.595.079,64	19.147.821,96	5.011.898,54	3.552.742,32
1766	14.625.841,72	18.164.664,70	2.390.013,48	3.538.822,98
1767	16.966.965,54	15.613.291,35	3.339.909,66	-1.353.674,19
1768	15.156.450,94	10.084.039,13	2.671.327,47	-5.072.411,82
1769	14.419.389,35	12.578.795,22	3.271.884,30	-1.840.594,13
1770	15.764.868,64	11.182.633,86	4.549.189,53	-4.582.234,78
1771	14.722.905,66	9.946.385,54	4.868.593,04	-4.776.520,12
1772	13.619.867,59	10.055.583,52	4.271.515,10	-3.564.284,07
1773	13.177.673,93	12.999.191,41	4.541.556,03	-178.482,52
1774	13.933.702,06	12.961.716,36	4.815.156,67	-971.985,70
1775	15.715.752,12	15.040.474,45	5.240.604,36	-675.277,67
1776	16.020.418,87	16.670.349,56	8.155.803,38	649.930,69
1777	16.024.055,83	17.572.564,58	8.609.369,30	1.548.508,75
1778	16.753.151,61	15.067.173,20	9.764.290,03	-1.685.978,41
1779	17.914.733,98	16.031.346,02	17.987.906,32	-1.883.387,96
1780	19.138.835,41	16.448.087,09	20.933.434,63	-2.690.748,32
1781	18.845.174,30	16.802.480,57	27.497.575,67	-2.042.693,73
1782	20.219.486,77	21.408.051,88	22.932.540,72	1.188.565,11
1783	16.063.321,78	14.487.479,08	20.466.631,10	-1.575.842,71
1784	16.187.679,62	16.510.436,70	15.913.691,04	322.757,08
1785	15.365.292,76	15.210.823,69	16.226.820,63	-154.469,08
1786	18.612.450,36	23.353.699,56	16.521.739,34	4.741.249,20
1787	22.449.973,02	22.290.684,42	14.521.239,39	-159.288,60
1788	20.170.596,85	18.284.763,84	16.770.676,86	-1.885.833,01
1789	22.744.295,21	13.386.134,83	15.253.630,96	-9.358.160,38
1790	17.151.886,58	14.625.287,12	15.755.730,52	-2.526.599,46
1791	25.307.124,26	14.458.768,81	16.870.846,02	-10.848.355,45
Average	*15.728.996,61*	*14.537.522,50*	*10.405.641,62*	*-1.191.474,11*

SOURCE: RÉLÉVÉ GENERAL, NAB, FC, 5748–5805.

TABLE 2 *General and five-yearly averages (in Brabantine guilders)*

	Balance of trade	Average Import	Average export	Deficit/surplus as percentage of imports	Deficit/surplus as percentage of exports
1759–1791	-1.191.474,11	15.728.996,61	14.537.522,50	-0.08	-0.08
1761–1765	1.417.381,28	11.181.034,45	12.598.415,73	0.13	0.11
1766–1770	-1.862.018,39	15.386.703,24	13.524.684,85	-0.12	-0.14
1771–1775	-2.033.310,02	14.233.980,27	12.200.670,25	-0.14	-0.17
1776–1780	-812.335,05	17.170.239,14	16.357.904,09	-0.05	-0.05
1781–1785	-452.336,66	17.336.191,05	16.883.854,38	-0.03	-0.03
1786–1788	898.709,20	20.411.006,74	21.309.715,94	0.04	0.04
1786–1791	-3.339.497,95	21.072.721,05	17.733.223,10	-0.16	-0.19

SOURCE: RÉLÉVÉ GENERAL, NAB, FC, 5748–5805.

claims about the evolution of trade, and not about its significance or impact – is knowing what was hidden behind the total figures and what caused them. Was there a decrease in exports or imports? Which goods were traded? Did we mainly import resources and export finished goods, or was it the other way around? In the first case, the negative balance would not have necessarily pointed at a worsening economic environment and even in the second case we must dig deeper before making such an assumption (which would be the mercantilist's conditioned evaluation).

One look at Chart 2 first of all shows us that the unfavourable balance in the majority of the investigated years can not be ascribed to a decrease in exports. On the contrary, both exports and imports increased at a comparable pace. It therefore appears that while the Austrian Netherlands did not generally succeed in keeping down foreign imports, they definitely were able to boost the trade of their domestic produce (or they managed to export more expensive goods). One of the reasons for the increase in exports could have been the relatively low wages, especially for labour-intensive sectors such as textiles, which implies that England, France and the United Provinces were becoming relatively less competitive.[24]

Strangely, whereas imports where on a fairly steady upwards course, exports fluctuated considerably. Striking is the sharp plunge in 1783. The explanation may lie in the aforementioned four year's war, although that was already drawing to a close. However, the war is usually attributed with positive effects

24 Allen, "Wages," Vandenbroeke, "The Regional Economy," 165.

for this region, since it remained politically neutral and was therefore an uncontested trading partner. It is possible that the increase in exports in the decade (1772–1782) preceding the war had been 'artificially' driven up by exogenous factors, in particular by the American War of Independence and the following four year's war. During that period France supported the American rebels, what provoked trade sanctions by England. The boost that this had possibly given to the trade of the Southern Low Countries fell away after the declaration of American Independence. Furthermore, it is still very difficult to determine what the other contingent sharp corrections in the balance of trade infer. Chances are that measurement errors are involved (especially in the first years where the figures are very low), that unexpected events on trading partners' soil exerted an influence or that automatic adjustments such as Hume's specie-flow mechanism played a role.[25] The only thing that is clear is that the oscillations were mostly determined by export.

It still interests us to know whether the trade flows would evolve differently when we would include the products that were excluded because of lacking

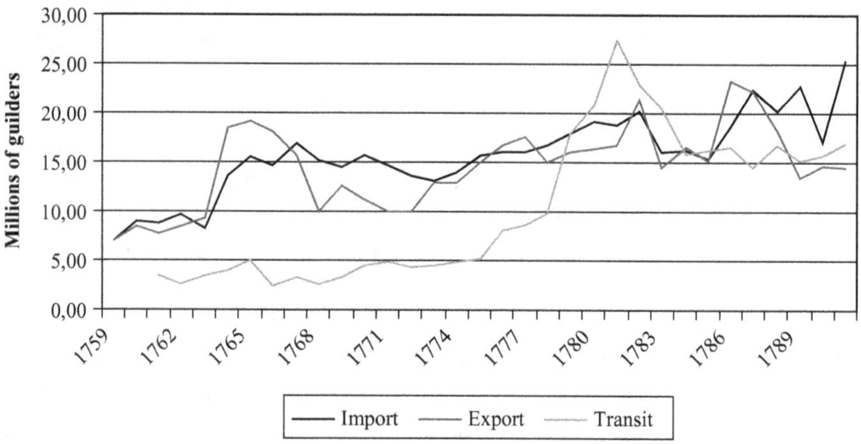

CHART 2 *Import, export and transit, 1759–1791*[26]
SOURCE: RÉLÉVÉ GENERAL, NAB, FC, 5748–5805.

25 This mechanism implies that in case of a positive balance of trade prices will rise so that exports will decrease and imports will increase, and vice versa in countries with a negative balance. This is an argument against mercantilism, given that in the long run only an equilibrium can exist.

26 One of the aspirations of the Habsburg authorities was to turn the Netherlands into a hub in the international transit trade network. However, I will go into the results of that attempt separately in Chapter 5, precisely because there was a very active policy

prices. There is unfortunately no straight-forward manner in which we can add these heterogeneous goods together in a way that takes into account their relative weight within the trade flows. For example: differentiate between the value of one traded pound of butter and one copiously decorated coach. Without some indication on the relative worth for each commodity in the customs statistics, there is no mathematically sound way to calculate a total figure based on the different measurements (while also taking into account the shortcomings of volume data for the study of dynamic (i.e. spanning more than one year) subjects). However, merely by way of exemplification, I will formulate two hypotheses on the evolution of the missing products: firstly, by plainly adding the figures for these 800 categories together without estimating their relative worth, and secondly, by converting each product into an index and calculating the average. Especially in the first case we see that the evolution of the trade flows (Chart 3) does not substantially differ from our original result. Both export and import volumes increased, but in both methods the rise in exports had a clearly slower pace and could never surpass imports. The same holds true when we add up the original (volume) data on the goods with which we have calculated the balance of trade in value (Chart 4) and compare them with the result in Chart 2. This implies that there was likely a steady shift

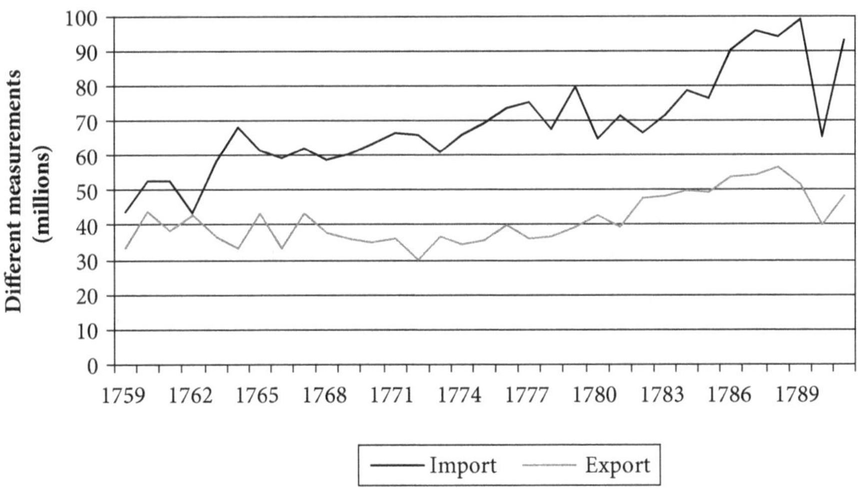

CHART 3 *Import and export of missing goods (in volumes)*
SOURCE: RÉLÉVÉ GENERAL, NAB, FC, 5748–5805.

regarding this transit trade and because the government probably has not been able to keep its promises in this case, since the graph shows that transit only started to grow towards the end of this period and experienced a relapse at the very end.

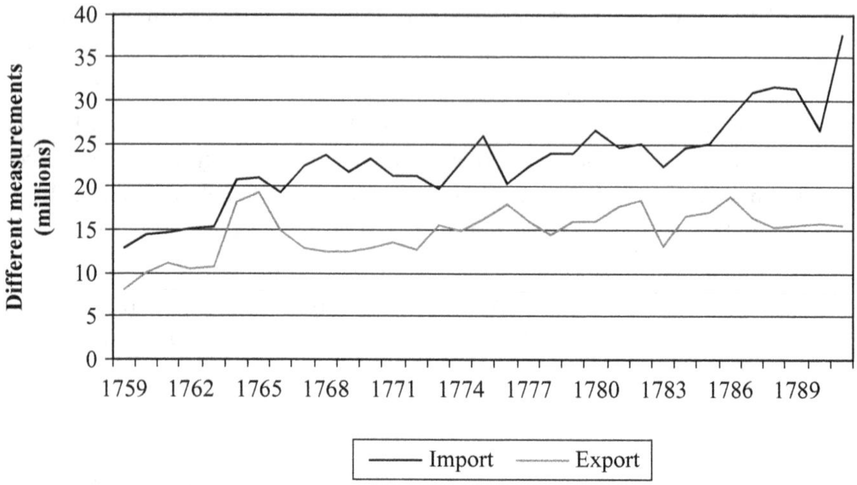

CHART 4 *Import and export of the 272 known goods (in original volumes)*
SOURCE: RÉLÉVÉ GENERAL, NAB, FC, 5748–5805.

to exporting more expensive – and thus probably further processed – goods. Because the balance of trade was markedly negative for the added missing goods (in different measurements) there is an increased likelihood that the trade balance was less favourable than our primary results suggest, but on the other hand it is also possible that some of the excluded exported commodities were relatively expensive, so that the trend of the balance (exports minus imports) remains the same. Lastly, the estimated evolution based on indices shows that imports were relatively huge in 1783 (see Chart 5).

Thirdly, we can also have a look at the evolutions in the composition of the missing goods. This is especially interesting in those cases where the annual balance of trade of separate products shows large deviations from the calculated average. First, a number of goods show distinctly positive results, with relatively large exported volumes. The most striking ones are meat, chalk, oak bark for tanning, different kinds of tooled wood, iron, whetstones, powdered tobacco (*karotten*), livestock, silverware, paintings and coaches. The last four of these were relatively expensive, but all in all the sums they represented were most likely not as huge as the ones represented by the goods that were imported in large quantities. Among those, we find weaponry, steel, alum, slate, saltpetre, cocoa, crude hemp and cotton, exotic drugs, tin, tin-plate, citrus fruits, honey, pottery, feathers for writing, grey salt, seeds, unrefined sugar, tobacco leaves and dyestuffs. This implies that it is indeed probable that the balance of trade was more unfavourable than initially assumed, but the fact remains that the trends in imports and exports did not look too bad. While we must handle

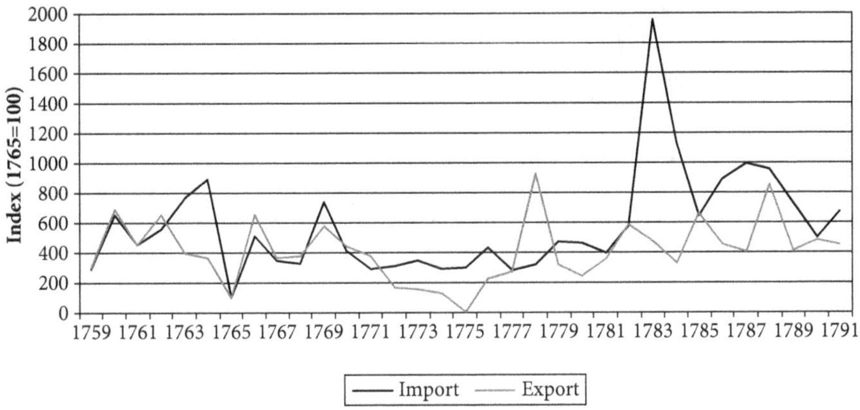

CHART 5 *Import and export of all goods in indices (with base year 1765)*[27]
SOURCE: RÉLÉVÉ GENERAL, NAB, FC, 5748–5805.

the partial calculations of the trade flows with a lot of care and although the precise values of the three categories are inevitably not exact (even though the sample is definitely rather wide), the quality of the sources and the quantity of goods comprised so far make it the most accurate estimate available.

Since we may not fall into the trap set by mercantilist discourse that has always argued the importance of a strictly positive trade balance, we must look deeper into the composition of the Habsburg trade. After the breakdown of the trade balance in import, export and transit flows we can also include the trade values for individual goods in the analysis. Although there are large differences between the absolute value of the trade balance in consecutive years, it seems that the chief bites out of the budget were always the same. Wine, Spanish wool and cotton fabrics were introduced in exchange for the greatest number of guilders (Chart 6), while linen was by far the largest category among exports (Chart 7). Corluy already wrote in his work on the years 1792–1794 that the latter commodity indeed determined the final result to a very large extent.[28] According to literature, broadcloth and other woollen fabrics were also exported abundantly during the eighteenth century; unfortunately there are too few prices to draw any definite conclusions on this matter. Purely woollen fabrics were in any case mostly imported, so this historiography has likely been based mainly on mixed fabrics.

---

27 I have chosen 1765 as base year since from that year onwards the composition of the customs statistics had stabilized.

28 Corluy, "Een Metodologische Poging," 219.

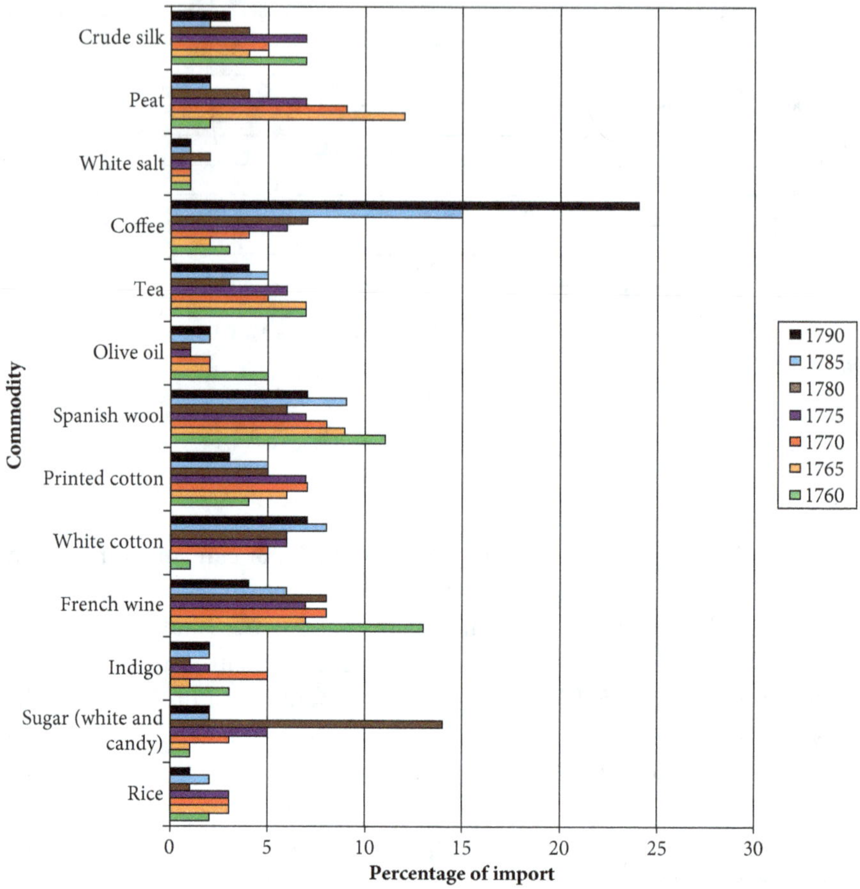

CHART 6 *Main imported commodities*
SOURCE: RÉLÉVÉ GENERAL, NAB, FC, 5748–5805.

What do these goods tell us about the economic situation of the Austrian Netherlands? The largest import categories were primarily resources for manufactories. Of course French wine, coffee, tea and olive oil were intended purely for consumption, but Spanish wool was used for further processing in the textile industry, in particular for production of cloth and mixed fabrics like flannel.[29] In the case of cotton imports we should distinguish between white and printed cotton fabrics. The white fabrics were the main raw material for a new

29 Lis and Soly, *Een Groot Bedrijf*, Alfons K.L. Thijs, *Van "werkwinkel" tot "fabriek." De Textielnijverheid te Antwerpen* (*Einde 15de-Begin 19de Eeuw*) (Brussels: 1986).

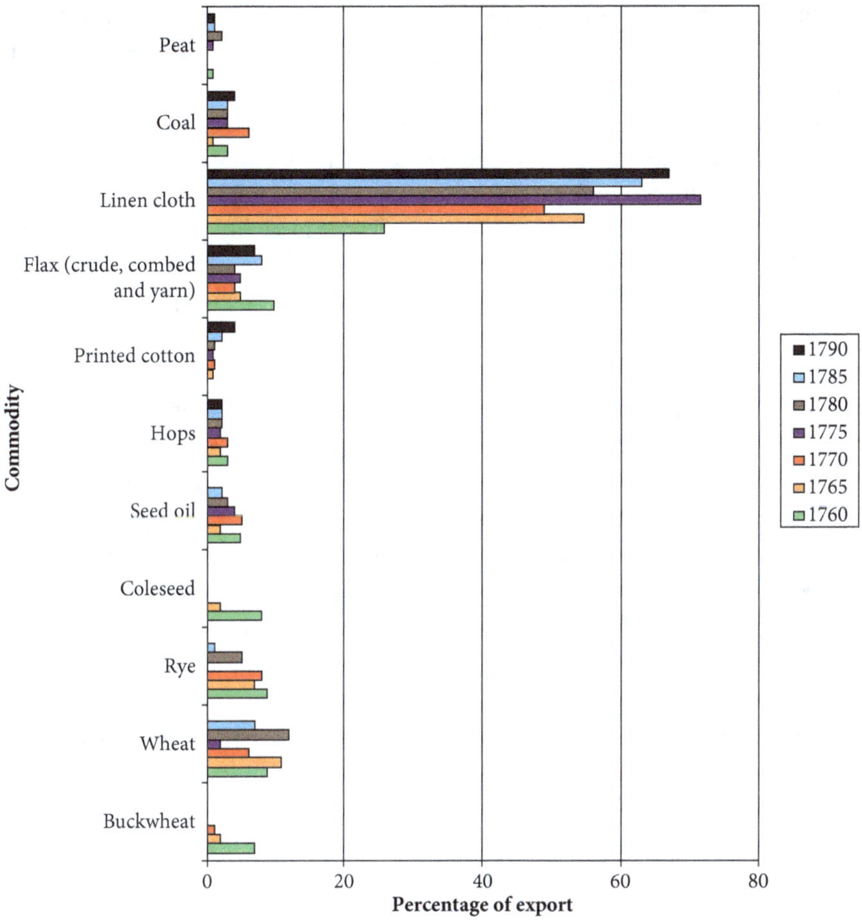

CHART 7 *Main exported commodities*

SOURCE: RÉLÉVÉ GENERAL, NAB, FC, 5748–5805.

industry: that of the cotton printers. Printed fabrics on the other hand required no further processing. The customs statistics show that the quantity of imported printed fabrics throughout the period decreased, so that white cotton – a resource – accounted for the lion's share of cotton imports from 1778 onwards. The value of imports was furthermore determined by various dyestuffs such as indigo, which were also needed as a raw material for the textile industry. This raises suspicion that it was especially the demand from the home market that pushed some industries forward, since exports of textiles did not improve much but the production definitely appeared to have been on the rise. Below we will see whether this hypothesis stands the test. On the other hand, colonial commodities such as coffee experienced a sturdy rise in imports, what gives us a nice image of the changing consumption patterns during the eighteenth century.

Among exports linen yielded by far the highest income and this was, in contrast to some of the main imported goods, a finished product. In the Austrian Netherlands, flax was mostly processed into linen by peasants at home to provide them with a supplementary income.[30] The large linen exports underpin the view that the Flemish proto-industry was essential for the economic development of this region.[31] However, these positive results for linen should not lead us to conclude that a thriving export industry had developed in this region in the second half of the eighteenth century. The export surplus was almost entirely due to the proto-industry and to the trade in agricultural goods, such as grains. Grains and hops clearly played a prominent role in international trade, albeit on a much less regular basis than linen. They draw our attention, because the balance for grains was very positive at the beginning of the period, but later on started to struggle and even became negative in the end. In 1760 buckwheat, wheat and rye each accounted for a share of more than half a million guilders in total exports, what falls in line with the image of the highly productive Flemish husbandry.[32] Between 1765 and 1770 the figures for wheat and rye were still high, but in 1775 and 1780 the balance for grains had become modest and even negative in the case of rye. Nonetheless, in spite of the large disparity between subsequent years, grain makes up at least one million guilders of the total export value.[33] The data for other agricultural products such as hops, seed oil and flax always remained high, but it is linen in its many forms, that was the absolute winner among exports. Thus, even though coal and peat

30 Joseph Vermaut, "De Textielnijverheid in Brugge en op het Platteland in Westelijk Vlaanderen voor 1800" (RUG, 1974), 269–270.

31 For an introduction, see for example: Franklin F. Mendels, *Industrialization and Population Pressure in Eighteenth-Century Flanders* (New York: 1981), Sheilagh C. Ogilvie and Markus Cerman, *European Proto-Industrialization* (Cambridge: Cambridge University Press, 1996), Reinoud Vermoesen, *Markttoegang en 'Commerciële' Netwerken van Rurale Huishoudens: de Regio Aalst, 1650–1800, Doctoraatsverhandeling* (Antwerp: Universiteit Antwerpen, 2008).

32 Adriaan Verhulst and Christiaan Vandenbroeke, *Landbouwproduktiviteit in Vlaanderen en Brabant 14de-18de Eeuw*, vol. 56, *Belgisch Centrum voor Landelijke Geschiedenis* (Ghent: 1979), i.

33 The reasons for these fluctuations may lie in the changing trade policy, but variations in the success of harvests might have also played a part. Christiaan Vandenbroeke, *Agriculture et Alimentation dans les Pays-Bas Autrichiens*, vol. 49, *Belgisch Centrum voor Landelijke Geschiedenis* (Ghent: 1975), 159–196.

were also much exported, stating that the region was exporting only raw materials, such as Blomme thought, does not hold.[34]

Our hypothesis so far is that the Austrian Netherlands were able to achieve a rather high degree of import substitution for a number of key economic sectors, since exports of manufactured goods (at least the few included above) did not rise, but imports dropped during the period. At the same time, imports of primary resources (wool, coal, crude salt and sugar) kept rising, possibly to feed the growing industry. Of course, the Southern Netherlands also remained dependent on imports for a lot of other foreign commodities and especially for colonial goods. Anyhow we should not be swept away by the overall trade figures from the beginning of this chapter. Below the surface, the trade statistics reveal a very multi-faceted story.

4 What Did It Mean?

Even now that the part on the value of trade and the large trends in trade flows and in the balance of trade is no longer missing from the picture, the question about the impact of trade on economic development, posed in the international debates mentioned above, still can not be answered thoroughly. In order to go beyond large-scale theoretical considerations about what its international trade could mean, it would be interesting to first of all place the numbers on the Austrian Netherlands in a broader perspective by making an international comparison. We know that throughout the eighteenth century agriculture remained the most important sector all over Europe, towering far above trade or industry, just like in Flanders and Brabant. However, previous attempts to calculate trade balances or the value of those trade flows for other countries or periods were usually based on a much thinner corpus of sources and often did not include an explicit, quantifiable result. It is therefore difficult to compare them with the results on the Southern Netherlands and determine what the relative magnitude of the figures was, even more so because our own absolute figures are also not correct. However, while the calculated data understates the actual trade flows (because of missing goods), the trend we observe does lay claim to credibility.

To date, an exact value of imports and exports has been estimated only for England. Unsurprisingly the British figures were much higher than ours. Ralph Davis calculated that the value of English imports around 1773 was about

34 Blomme and Van Der Wee, "The Belgian Economy," 9.

12,735,000 pound sterling, exports £15,671,000 and the balance of both was a surplus of a little below three million pounds.[35] When we convert the imports from the Southern Low Countries during that year (13,619,867 Brabantine guilders) to eighteenth-century British pounds it corresponds with approximately 1.26 million pounds. Export matches up to around 1.22 million.[36] The population figures for both regions observed, the Southern Netherlands exported four times less (0.55 pounds per person versus 2.2).[37] Even with a large margin of error (assuming that the Habsburg calculation is about 30 per cent lower than the actual trade value), the disparity is abundantly clear. Yet England was considered to be the main commercial player of the age, so it would be more interesting to compare with values of other eighteenth-century regions. Regrettably, we mostly hold indirect estimates of the value of trade for other countries.[38]

Certainly, just as interesting as comparing with foreign figures would be to weigh the evolutions of the trade balance against the growth and value of Gross Domestic Product – however contested this indicator is. Research into the eighteenth-century GDP has not yet come to a conclusion, but for the Southern Low Countries, the lack of understanding of the region's GDP has been taken to heart by among others Erik Buyst.[39] Recently, Stephen Broadberry and Bruce Campbell compiled the main estimates on European GDP and

35 Davis, "English Foreign Trade, 1700–1774," 300–302, John J. McCusker, "The Current Value of English Exports, 1697 to 1800," *The William and Mary Quarterly* 28, no. 4 (1971), E.B. Schumpeter, *English Overseas Trade Statistics 1697–1808* (Oxford: 1960).

36 The Marteau Early 18th-Century Currency Converter, 2008, Pierre Marteau, http://pierre-marteau.com/wiki/index.php?title=Great_Britain:Money (April 23rd 2010).

37 The Austrian Netherlands counted 2.272.962 inhabitants in 1784. England had about 7 million. Christiaan Vandenbroeke, "De Landbouw en Levensmiddelenpolitiek in de Oostenrijkse Nederlanden" (RUG, 1970–1971), 380, E.A. Wrigley and R.S. Schofield, *The Population History of England 1541–1871: A Reconstruction* (London: Edward Arnold, 1981), 528.

38 For example it is estimated that foreign trade was worth 11.6 per cent of the Dutch GNP in 1807 and around 12 per cent in France at the end of the Early Modern Period. Daudin, *Commerce*, 156, Jan-Pieter Smits, Edwin Horlings, and Jan Luiten Van Zanden, *Dutch GNP and Its Components, 1800–1913, Groningen Growth and Development Centre Monograph Series No.5* (Groningen: 2000), 50.

39 Buyst's findings are yet to be published, but some numbers on growth and welfare have also been assembled by Bob Allen for the city of Antwerp in specific: Allen, "Wages." However, Allen has collected urban wages which might not be so interesting to track growth based on rural industry. More on this line of research (since March 2010 often referred to as the "Maddison Project"): Maddison, *Contours*. http://www.ggdc.net/maddison/publications/wp.htm.

growth between 1300 and 1850. Unsurprisingly these estimates vary widely.[40] To sum their findings up, some GDP-growth definitely took place in the Austrian Netherlands during the second half of the eighteenth century (around 1 per cent annual real GDP-growth) which is somewhat slower than in Great Britain and the Northern Netherlands.[41] This is thus in line – albeit the former was probably slower – with the growth in international trade (with an average annual growth of 5.46 per cent for imports and 4.74 per cent for exports). There are no published estimates of eighteenth-century GDP figures for the Southern Netherlands, but following Buyst it was worth about 450,000,000 BEF in 1765 (which would equal about 12,500,000 Brabantine guilders).[42] That would mean that the average trade deficit was worth about 10 per cent of the GDP (in comparison: the Belgian trade deficit in 2011 was worth €7.7 billions or about 2 per cent of its GDP).[43] However, this calculation is probably incorrect since GDP is now lower than the value of imports into the region. The relative deficit must have been much lower, as is shown by looking at average earnings.

When one looks at the worth of the balance of trade per capita, the overall results of this chapter are indeed very much humbled; even while keeping in mind the underestimation. On average the trade deficit (leaving out benefits that flowed from intermediary services in the transit trade) cost an inhabitant of the Austrian Netherlands less then one guilder (0.54). In a very good year such as 1786 the surplus embodied a profit of a little over two guilders per person, and during the perils of the Brabantine Revolution a net five guilders per head yearly went to foreign imports. Despite the fact that estimates of yearly incomes in the eighteenth century are also preliminary, it is likely that for most people (except for those actively involved in trade) this caused little nuisance nor advantage. It is certainly much less than what is spent on international trade per capita today.[44] Even more so since the trade deficit could probably be

---

40 Stephen Broadberry and Bruce Campbell, "GDP Per Capita in Europe, 1300–1850," *World Economic History Congress* (2009).

41 I am very grateful to Professor Buyst for sharing his most recent estimates with me. See also: Jan Luiten Van Zanden, *The Long Road to the Industrial Revolution. The European Economy in a Global Perspective, 1000–1800*, ed. Maarten Prak and Jan Luiten Van Zanden, vol. 1, *Global Economic History Series* (Leiden: Brill, 2009).

42 Assuming that 1 Brabantine guilder was worth 0.726 grams of gold. Posthumus, *Nederlandsche Prijsgeschiedenis*, CXIX.

43 In 2011 Belgian exports valued €236,7 billion and imports €244,4 billion. Its GDP was worth €412 billion. Nationale Bank van België, *Statistiek buitenlandse handel* (Brussels 2011), http://www.nbb.be/doc/DQ/N/DQ3/HISTO/ENM1112.PDF (accessed December 1st 2012).

44 Based on the figures above, a net €700 per person was spent on imports (i.e. a deficit of 7.7 billion) in 2011.

financed by the surplus on the balance of payments that – based on Karel Degryse's data for Antwerp – sprung increasingly from foreign investments.[45] On the other hand, we will see in the following chapters that the changes international trade has brought about in the features of the eighteenth-century economy are much more exciting than its value.

5 The Pitfalls of the Balance of Trade

All in all these calculations can only lead to a preliminary conclusion, since it is based on the macroeconomic image. Also, a number of critical considerations are in place. First of all, the balance of trade provides only one way to look at international trade and in my view not the most important one. Since specialization seems much more revealing than a deficit or surplus, we should look into the contribution of individual economic sectors to international trade (as I will do in the following chapter) and, as said, to the effects of trade on specific products. Only then can we also establish the real significance of international trade for concrete stakeholders and determine whether the home market indeed played a crucial role (what we could already guess when looking at the increasing imports of several resources in the charts above). Focusing purely on international trade can cloud our vision on other factors such as internal demand.

Secondly, we must bear in mind the dissimilar impact of international trade on different actors (merchants, producers and consumers, the government,...) and on different areas (rural versus urban for example). This has been missing from the story so far. The sources have shown that the Austrian Netherlands were probably able to reach a nearly or entirely favourable trade balance at different points during the eighteenth century. However, more important than knowing these data, is finding out whether its inhabitants were able to use this possible surplus to their advantage and convert it into investments and in other words into capital accumulation. That the government pursued a mercantilist ideal and therefore tried to design a sound trade policy, is insufficient in itself. Indeed, even years with a structural trade deficit may represent years

45 Up to 70 per cent of an investor's fortune was invested abroad. Karel Degryse, "De Antwerpse Fortuinen: Kapitaalsaccumulatie, –Investering en -Rendement te Antwerpen in de 18de Eeuw," *Bijdragen tot de Geschiedenis* 2005, no. 1–4 (2005): 251, Janssens, "Het Geldwezen," L. Michielsen, "Het Kapitalisme te Antwerpen in de XVIIe en XVIIIe Eeuwen," *Nederlandsche Historiebladen* II (1939): 254.

of strong economic growth in key sectors. Trade policy should thus go hand in glove with a thought through industrial policy.

Lastly, we must be very careful when drawing conclusions on economic development. That the trade in for example linen was flourishing did hardly mean that the producers and the inhabitants of the producing regions were doing well. On the contrary, one of the reasons that trade flourished was because of the very low wages they were given. Conversely, rising imports (even when going together with trade deficits) can pinpoint at flourishing industries or sectors, even though these were probably working for the home markets!

6 Revealed Comparative Advantages Through International Trade Contributions

Another possible approach to provide a macroeconomic framework to the eighteenth-century trade flows starts from a different angle than traditional national accounts calculations. The research presented below is still ongoing, in co-operation with Guillaume Daudin and Loïc Charles, but it already enables us to look to what extent trade in different sectors has contributed to the balance of trade in different places.[46] By comparing the customs statistics to trade data from other countries or regions, the method provides a sort of proxy for revealing comparative advantages within an economy. By exposing in what type of commodities the biggest contribution was made (and also which sectors were still relatively weak), it is possible to draw up a more insightful image of the early modern Habsburg economy. And by looking at the results in comparison with other eighteenth-century nations we can see whether this type of specialization was unique in Europe at the very early stages of the industrial revolution or not.

We have used an indicator of comparative advantage (Revealed Comparative Advantage or RCA) for three countries/regions: the Austrian Netherlands, England and France.[47] England is hereby used as a sort of yardstick, being the example of an early industrializing economy. We believe that this indicator

46 The first results have been presented at different venues: Firstly in Lille (Workshop on European external trade statistics, March 2011), next in London (ENIUGH, April 2011), followed by Dublin (EHES, August 2011), Glasgow (ESSHC, April 2012) and finally Stellenbosch (WEHC, July 2012).

47 G. Lafay, "The Measurement of Revealed Comparative Advantages," in *International Trade Modelling*, ed. M.G. Dagenais and P.-A. Muet (London: Chapman and Hall, 1992).

might tell an interesting story about the relative pace and nature of the economic development of these three regions. There are a few points in choosing to compare France, Britain and the Austrian Netherlands that might make the results particularly worthwhile – besides the fact that for each of them we have more or less complete series on international trade over the second part of the eighteenth century. First, they are geographically quite close to each other, and two of them even had a land frontier, hence transport costs were not a very significant factor limiting the intensity of their trade. The second point is that the comparative study of the external trade of these three countries poses the very interesting historical riddle: if England was the first to enter the industrial revolution, and Belgium was second, is it possible to detect a similar evolution in their international trade as early as the 1780s?

To use the method we have used, it was necessary to categorize the traded goods, instead of looking at individual goods that accounted for the largest shares of the trade flows as we have done above. The main reason to classify the goods in categories is the fact that the early modern sources for different countries do not use exactly the same terms for commodities and have different compositions. Categorization makes it nonetheless possible to compare their economies. In our aim to find an existing encoding that reflects the materials used during production, the stage of processing, the intended use of the products, their importance in terms of world trade and technological changes, we started to classify the goods according to the nine categories of the most aggregated level of the Standard International Trade Classification (SITC, see Table 3). To study the eighteenth-century evolution in greater detail and take into account especially questions concerning the industrial revolution, we have added some more specific categories that are particularly pertinent for the economic development of manufactures and the consumer revolution – i.e. a division between colonial and domestic foodstuffs and a differentiation among textiles (silk, cotton, linen and woollens).

In basic terms, the RCA method compares the sectorial balance of trade with the total trade balance, adjusting by the size of the trade in that sector:

$$CTBi = (\frac{1000}{X_t + M_t}) * [(X_i - M_i) - \frac{(X_t - M_t) * (X_i + M_i)}{(X_t + M_t)}]$$

In the formula X_i and M_i represent respectively the exports and imports of one sector/category, and X_t and M_t represent the total exports and imports of one country. The indicator thus signals the difference between the expected performance of one good, industry or sector's external trade, which is obtained

TABLE 3 *SITC categories*

SITC code	SITC description	Adapted to 18th-century trade
0	Food and living animals	–
0a	–	European foodstuffs
0b	–	Colonial foodstuffs
1	Beverages and tobacco	–
2	Crude materials, inedible, except fuels	–
3	Mineral fuels, lubricants, and related materials	–
4	Animal and vegetable oils, fats and waxes	–
5	Chemicals	–
6	Manufactured goods, classified chiefly by material	Not otherwise classified
6a	–	Out of linen
6b	–	Out of wool
6c	–	Out of silk
6d	–	Out of cotton
7	Machinery and transport equipment	–
8	Miscellaneous manufactured articles	–
9	Miscellaneous transactions and commodities, not specified elsewhere	–

SOURCE: UNITED NATIONS STATISTICS DIVISION (http://unstats.un.org/unsd/cr/registry/regcst.asp?cl=14).

when the indicator is equal to 0, and its actual performance (Contribution To Balance of trade, or CTB). A positive value indicates a comparative advantage. This indicator is interesting since contrary to most comparative advantage indicators it does not need either the value of GDP or the total world trade, which are both very difficult to estimate within a reasonably exact range for this time period. By computing the RCA measure for the Austrian Netherlands, France and England in different years, it allows us to see the 'moving' comparative advantages of those three regions.

The first coarse results of our inquiry for Britain reflected the image that is presented in the bulk of historical literature: a crisis in the wool industry and already more 'action' in metal wares than in cotton. In short: the image of an already mutating industrialized nation. France, on the other hand, did not show many signs of specialization, but does show some elements of a 'mature' industrialized nation: importing especially raw materials and exporting some manufactured goods, but also a large amount of beverages. Finally, we reached the subject of interest for this volume. In the Austrian Netherlands manufactured goods seem to have had the highest RCA and the relative importance of agricultural exports is declining (Charts 8 and 9). However, it is the linen

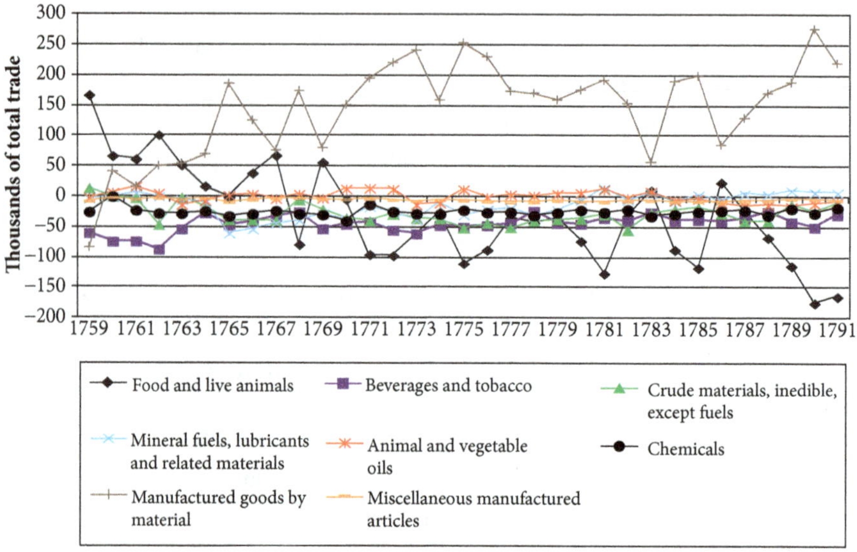

CHART 8 *RCA results for the Austrian Netherlands (1759–1791)*
SOURCE: RÉLÉVÉ GENERAL, NAB, FC, 5748–5805.

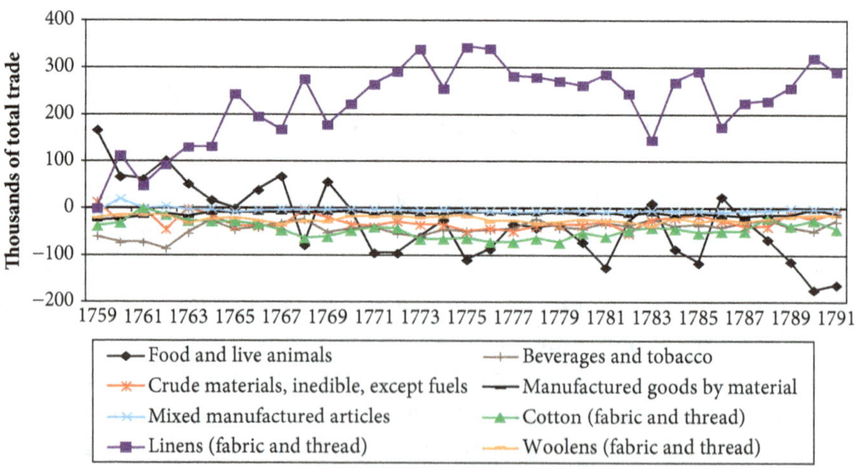

CHART 9 *RCA results for the Austrian Netherlands, with detailed categories for textiles (1759–1791)*
SOURCE: RÉLÉVÉ GENERAL, NAB, FC, 5748–5805.

proto-industry which accounts mostly for this outcome, and not the urban manufactures based on for example cotton or metal (although these were on the rise as well).

This attempt at examining comparative advantage through assessment of international trade remains in an early stage and so requires much further analysis, yet it definitely adds to an international contextualisation that is vital for the following chapters. Each of the categories included in this analysis will be represented to some degree in those chapters, and so I will often return to the results from this section.

7 Conclusion

Based on the Habsburg customs statistics, we can safely assume that commerce in the Austrian Netherlands was faring rather well during the time period in question. Even though earlier historiography was not incorrect in claiming that the balance of trade remained unfavourable for much of the second half of the eighteenth century, the evolution of exports was nonetheless developing favourably. Moreover, in a contemporary point of view, the deficit per capita was actually very small. Indeed, we will see that for a number of highly important bulk commodities (salt, coal and grains) the Austrian Netherlands were nearly autarkic. Also, in moving beyond macroeconomic instruments such as the trade balance, we see that the composition of the trade flows was quite promising from the viewpoint of the government. The key guidelines of a mercantilist policy appear to have been taken to heart, especially on the matter of attracting resources. However, this did not appear to have been accompanied by strong development of industrial exports, since in general only few manufactured items were exported besides linen cloth. Likewise, the fact that few 'industrial' goods were being exported even as the resources for industry continued flowing in may indicate that the true seed of the later economic developments was mainly in growing domestic demand for these goods. This is for example evident from the fact that imported white cotton was not exported in its printed, finished form. On the contrary: a great amount of additional printed cotton was imported alongside the domestic produce. The product would thus have to have been increasingly purchased by local consumers. International trade thus did not pose a threat and the flourishing trade flows must have brought more benefits than merely feeding the Treasury through taxes, even though export gains were still limited to sectors such as linen and grains.

There should be no doubt that the results presented in this chapter are but a start for more comprehensive investigations. It was necessary to make certain assumptions and estimates, and it is clear that additional commodity prices, and also specific prices for each year, would render more accurate results. Yet it seems unlikely that the results will be entirely thrown asunder, since the trade balance included most of the goods which contemporary authors and present-day historians all agree were crucial for international trade. We can therefore conclude that the position of international trade in the region was far more prosperous than hitherto assumed. If the government was able to combine these circumstances with a well considered and effective industrial policy, international trade might well have offered a seed for growth, but whether this was the case will become clear in the following chapters.

PART 3

International Trade in the Austrian Netherlands, a Study of Five Key Sectors

In the following chapters I will look into the nature of the relation between international trade and economic development in five specific sectors. Firstly, the data on import and export of individual commodities (transit will only follow in Part Four), can reveal which sectors were flourishing and which were withering away (both on the international and the domestic market), but will also shed light on other kinds of changes that were brought about by international trade flows. Finally, the micro-perspective of individual commodities and industries will allow us to highlight the role of the government and its trade policy for these different sectors and its impact on the different stakeholders involved, such as merchants, producers, manufacturers and consumers.

The selected sectors span a very large part of the eighteenth-century economy in the Southern Low Countries. They include the vital primary sector with both its traditional agricultural and its proto-industrial activities, shed light on some well-known traditional urban sectors such as wool, lace and silk manufacturing, on new 'industrial' sectors like cotton printing, sugar refining and large-scale coal mining, they unveil the influential trade in exotic commodities from the New World, but the selection also does not neglect everyday – but highly necessary – manufacturing sectors such as salt refining. They enable us to give the necessary differentiations to the history of international trade.

The latter sector will be discussed first, because it is actually a near to inexorable pick when studying international trade. Without any crude salt resources of their own, salt was very much subject to international trade in the Austrian Netherlands. Moreover, salt had an intriguing dual character because it was at the same time a consumer good (the finished product of the growing salt refining industry) and an industrial resource, for example in textile bleaching. The success of the salt sector is thereby also a prelude to the second chapter, which focuses on textiles. The textile sector was by far the most important manufacturing sector at the time and was – as we will see – undergoing major changes during the second half of the eighteenth century, among others because of the effects of international trade. While domestic textile producers did their best to adapt to changing fashions triggered by trade, it will be very exiting to see what happens in cases where the Low Countries were not able to provide a decent alternative for imports; indeed, when a substitute was entirely out of the question and consumer demand roared. Coffee, sugar and other colonial commodities will complete that part of the story in section 3. Finally, we will go to the large resource industries: namely coal mining and agriculture (in particular grain production). For these sectors, relatively little has been said on international trade, but as these goods formed – or would form in the case of coal – the very basis of the economy, the conclusions reached here have a very broad scope.

CHAPTER 6

The Salt Trade

The Flavour of Progress

1 "The Salt of Life"

The major debates in historiography have tended to focus – as I will as well in large parts of the following chapters – on changing and allegedly innovative products, like cotton, coal or colonial commodities. Presumably 'common' or 'old' commodities have been marginalised in such discussions, in large part, doubtlessly, because such *histoire immobile* stimulates negligible passion in the average historian. Yet this chapter will show that precisely these goods afford us significant aid in tracing and assessing the major shifts in economic history. Although discussions addressing traditional products have rarely occasioned noteworthy stir in the wider debates concerning economic growth, such products are often the ones which in fact exerted the broadest influence, as they were deeply embedded in society and flowed in huge volumes. Salt clearly is one such product. Unlike the previously noted innovative, industrial commodities, salt had been in common use for thousands of years. This product thus offers the perspective of an everyday commodity, a perspective which is addressed too little in larger economic investigation.

The importance of salt in the history of human civilization is well known. As a product it has always been highly coveted, not only as a foodstuff and preservative, but also for its myriad other uses. For much of history common salt was very expensive and therefore often regarded as a symbol not just of prosperity but of the mere possibility of living a fulfilling life. Governments often seized upon the high value of salt to employ it as a fiscal instrument or as legal tender in areas where it was most scarce.[1] Salt was long so costly, because crude salt was found only in sediments or in seawater and needed to be refined via mining and evaporation, respectively. Both were highly complex and costly processes. In the eighteenth century, however, salt had become well integrated in everyday life and offered even more uses than it had before. It was of course

1 The case of France is much debated. For example in: S.A.M. Adshead, *Salt and Civilization* (Basingstoke: Macmillan, 1992), Mark Kurlansky, *Salt, a World History* (London: Jonathan Cape, 2002), 225–228, Michel Mollat, *Le Rôle du Sel dans l'Histoire* (Paris: Presses universitaires de France, 1968), Robert P. Multhauf, *Neptune's Gift: A History of Common Salt*, vol. 2, *Studies in the History of Technology* (London: Johns Hopkins University Press, 1996).

 | DOI 10.1163/9789004272606_008

first and foremost a preservative and a food seasoning – indeed, salt literally flavoured life – yet it was also used as a resource in various manufacturing processes, including bleaching and dying of textiles, production of soap, the melting of ice, and cleaning processes. Moreover, various new chemical industries requiring salt (e.g. production of ammonia and sulphuric acid) had begun to emerge.[2]

It is however not the immense importance of salt throughout history that has urged me to include it in this work. In the instances where salt is used as relate to human consumption the demand for salt was largely income inelastic: "The poorest consumed at least as much as a millionaire."[3] In the latter instances, however, demand for salt mirrored the success of numerous old and new industries. Indeed, salt offers a parameter for the evolution of the eighteenth-century economy in Western Europe, and it will enable us to trace some of the motors for growth during this era. Moreover, as suitable crude salt was highly rare in the Austrian Netherlands and because salt refining developed very slowly in the region, we can thus fairly easily track the history of this commodity and its consumption through the customs statistics. In other words: foreign importation of (crude) salt was nothing less than vital for the Southern Low Countries and salt, far more than the other commodities mentioned in the introduction, was inescapably subject to international trade.[4] Because of these two reasons the Habsburg customs statistics are thus immensely revealing not only about local demand for salt but also, and consequently, for the early industrial development of the region. This touches directly at the heart of the questions related to international trade and economic development.

2 The Salt Sector in the Austrian Netherlands

In light of its innumerable uses as an industrial resource and as a commonplace if not universal consumer good, it is hardly surprising that salt accounted for a sizable share of the trade flows into and out of the Southern Netherlands. As Wilfrid Brulez has detailed, salt was one of the main imported commodities

2 Annette André-Félix, *Les Débuts de l'Industrie Chimique dans les Pays-Bas Autrichiens* (Brussels: Institut de sociologie, 1971), Hilda Coppejans-Desmedt, *Bijdrage tot de Studie van de Gegoede Burgerij te Gent in de XVIIIe Eeuw* (Brussels: 1952), 19.

3 "le plus pauvre en consume pour le moins autant qu'un millionaire," NAB, FC, 5225, request by Antwerp magistrates and the States of Brabant, October 29th 1764.

4 Hasquin, "Nijverheid," 152.

for the Southern Netherlands during the fifteenth and sixteenth centuries.[5] My research confirms that it retained this position during the second half of the eighteenth century (Chart 10), when it represented about one and a half per cent of total imports. This share appears to have decreased slightly during this 33-years period, primarily because the value of total imports rose faster than the import of salt, which also increased. In any case, it remained an important category among internationally traded commodities until at least 1791. The share of salt in exports never amounted to more than a half percent – with its peak towards the end of the period, in the years 1789–1790 – and has not been included in the graph.

Despite the considerable share of salt in the overall import trade of the Southern Low Countries, we know little about the history of the product in the region. In the sixteenth century salt, in both its crude and refined forms, was imported primarily from Portugal, Spain and the French Brouage region.[6] Its market origins are somewhat less clear for the eighteenth century. The customs statistics note the origins for only a small portion of the salt trade and only over a short period. In the first three years they offer separate figures for Spanish and Portuguese salt; subsequently, however, they discriminate only

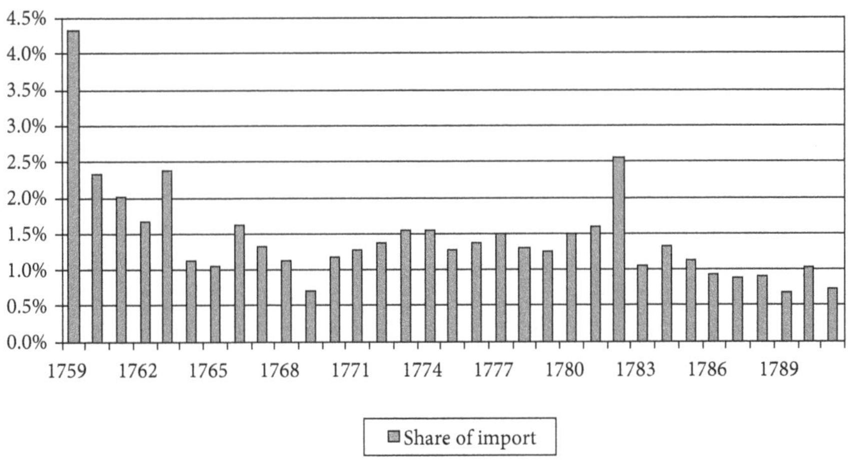

CHART 10 *Salt imports as a share of total imports (in value), 1759–1791*
SOURCE: RÉLÉVÉ GENERAL, NAB, FC, 5748–5805 AND VERLINDEN (1959–1973) 834–835.

5 Wilfrid Brulez, "De Zoutinvoer in de Nederlanden in de 16de Eeuw," *Tijdschrift voor Geschiedenis* 68, no. 2 (1955): 181.

6 Ibid.: 182.

between white (i.e. refined) and grey (i.e. crude) salt.[7] It is probable that from 1765 onwards Great Britain became a large supplier to the Southern Netherlands, as a new customs policy favoured English rock salt. There had been health-related concerns about the safety and suitability of this mineral, but in 1764 a scientific report ordered by the Habsburg government had approved the use of this "*sel de roche*."[8] Hasquin contended that the new kind of crude salt from England eventually surpassed imports from Spain, Portugal and France after 1777.[9] Christiaan Vandenbroeke, however, has claimed that imports of Iberian salt retained their position but that imports of French salt fell after 1764.[10] Luk Corluy presented further information about the origin of these commercial salt flows; like Vandenbroeke, he held that Spain was, until 1765, the main provider of grey salt and that England, owing to English rock salt being much cheaper, had overtaken that position by the final quarter of the eighteenth century.[11] Nothing about the origins of refined salt imports is indicated in the registers; however, besides the partial clues offered by the customs statistics, we can identify the largest salt-producing and exporting nations at that time. France was by far the principal producer around 1800, but the country probably consumed most of its own salt production. Its estimated annual output according to Adshead, amounted to 225,000 tons, followed closely by England (and Russia), with 200,000 tons.[12] The Dutch Republic – in particular, the province of Zeeland – was also an important player in the salt trade and likely supplied white salt to Flanders and Brabant.[13] Below, we will see – through the detailed trade data for the separate departments – if the location of those customs bureaus via which salt usually entered the Southern Netherlands, reveals more about the product's origins and suppliers.

As noted, crude salt was quite rare in the Austrian Netherlands and the climate unfit for producing it via seawater evaporation. A 1781 memorandum from the customs bureau, in response to a request by the merchant Henri Moriau concerning the possibility of extracting crude salt in the region, dismisses the idea. Moriau wished to establish a salt refinery near Ostend, yet

7 NAB, FC, 5748–5805: *Sel blanc* and *Sel gris*.

8 NAB, FC, 5225, Report on English rock salt (*sel de roche*), prepared by the faculty of medicine and chemistry at the University of Louvain, (ordered in 1763). Some refined salt was also imported from England, more specifically from Liverpool at the end of the eighteenth century. NAB, FC, 5243 and 5245 mention salt imports from Liverpool.

9 Hasquin, "Nijverheid," 152.

10 Vandenbroeke, *Agriculture*, 474.

11 Corluy, "Een Metodologische Poging," 48.

12 Adshead, *Salt*, 114.

13 Hasquin, "Nijverheid," 152.

admitted that rainfall in the Austrian Netherlands precluded obtaining salt through evaporation, for the process required a hot, dry climate.[14] Boiling seawater was likewise not an option "In a country where heating is expensive".[15] However, Moriau and his associates hoped someday to produce crude salt in the Austrian Netherlands; in the meantime Moriau requested exemption from import duties on English rock salt. The bureau did not share his optimism and rejected the request.

In contrast, the manufacturing of refined, white salt was common in the region. It is unsurprising that entrepreneurs were highly interested in domestic production of this vital commodity. In his report on the eighteenth-century industry, Briavoinne included salt refining amongst such important sectors as cotton printing, sugar refining and silk manufacturing.[16] However, his list likely expressed more a desire rather than a true description of profitable undertakings from the time, not least because although the region counted many salt refineries most of these were very small, employing just one or two workers.[17] In 1764, according to Julin, only two refineries – in Ostend and Menen, respectively – were somewhat larger yet even they included only eight and twelve employees respectively.[18] One person in Antwerp succeeded in considerably enriching himself through the salt trade.[19] But this particular merchant-entrepreneur – one Joseph Pieters – appears to have been a rather dubious character, who was not deemed very trustworthy by the administration, as we will see in the following paragraph. Thus, unsurprisingly, a few years later the same Briavoinne expressed concern about the salt-refining sector in the eighteenth century. The greatest threat, he reasoned, had been that the thirteenth article of the Treaty of Munster had forbidden the government to levy higher import duties on white salt than on grey salt: "Boiled white salt

14 NAB, FC, 5239, September 1st 1781, report signed by Libeau: "On à déjà reconnu lors des représentations antérieurs, que la chaleur et la sécheresse du climat sont absolument nécessaires à la cristallisation du sel: que les pluies y sont tellement contraire (…) notre climat, sujet à des pluies fréquentes présente un grand inconvénient de ce chef."

15 "dans un pays ou le chauffage est cher," Ibidem.

16 Briavoinne, *De'Industrie*, 83.

17 This is derived from the industrial census of 1764. The original source is in NAB, FC, 4392–4393, but it has been published by Philippe Moureaux, *La Statistique Industrielle dans les Pays-Bas Autrichiens à l'Époque de Marie-Thérèse. Documents et Cartes*, 2 vols. (Brussels: 1974–1981). The source is far from complete, but offers an approximate image of industry in the Southern Netherlands: Moureaux, *Les Préoccupations*, 387.

18 Armand Julin, *Les Grandes Fabriques en Belgique vers le Milieu du XVIIIe Siècle, Académie Royale de Belgique* (1902), 66. Moureaux, *La Statistique*.

19 Degryse, "De Antwerpse Fortuinen," 126.

from the United Provinces will be admitted by the provinces of Her Majesty, without being charged higher than crude salt."[20] This provision had served to assure suppliers from the Dutch Republic that import tariffs on their refined salt would remain moderate.

The sources (various letters, decrees and requests) compiled by the customs bureau also suggest that the situation was fairly grim for the salt-refining industry in the Austrian Netherlands. First, the quality of domestically refined salt was allegedly quite poor, and was definitely so at the beginning of the period studied here. Even before 1759 salt was being refined in various cities throughout the region; however, according to Antoine Desenfans, a merchant from Mons, the quality was almost always highly questionable.[21] He pleaded in favour of establishing new salt refineries so as to be able to compete with foreign – in particular, Dutch – salt. Finance Councillor Van Heurck, who appears to have been an expert on matters related to salt, vigorously criticized local refiners who invested insufficient time in salt preparation (in other words: who boiled their salt too briefly) and consequently sold salt of inferior quality.[22] According to Van Heurck – who is known as a rather moderate mercantilist or even a *préliberal* – this was the main reason why the Habsburg Netherlands needed to import white salt.[23] Elsewhere, he was especially harsh towards the previously mentioned merchant-entrepreneur Joseph Pieters, accusing, with unconcealed irony, this "self-appointed loyal servant of her majesty" of seeking to keep the small refineries in the country's centre under the whip and of acting solely for his own benefit. Van Heurck also suspected Pieters of fraud.[24] In the same report, Van Heurck widens his criticism so as to include most of the other salt merchants. The piece offers a spirited description of the customary manner in which traders and producers of the time appealed to their government.

> For over thirty years I have frequented our merchants and I gained some knowledge of public affairs, I have always noticed that those who

20 "le sel Blanc bouilli venant des Provinces Unies en celles de S.M. y sera reçu et admis, sans y etre chargé de plus hautes impositions que le gros sel." NAB, FC, 5228, letter by the States of Brabant, May 14th 1765: citation from article 13 of the Treaty of Munster. Briavoinne, *Mémoire*, 58.

21 NAB, FC, 5220, letter on "*Transit du sel*," presented to De Nény, January 21st 1754.

22 NAB, FC, 5223, Van Heurck mentions fraud in Hainault, in light of salt that was too moist and hence too heavy, July 11th 1761.

23 Bernard, *Patrice-François de Neny*, 114.

24 NAB, FC, 5220, January 29th 1755, report on the request by Joseph Pieters in December 1754. Pieters had requested – among other things – that he be granted the exclusive right to import grey salt into the Austrian Netherlands.

> introduce large projects usually begin their writing by a pompous array of benefits that should result to Her Majesty and to the welfare of her subjects, while it is only the personal interest that guides them, to the detriment of other traders.
>
> And they never fail to insist that they are zealous and faithful subjects of Her Majesty, knowing perfectly the trade in general and in particular, adding, however, that the inventor of the project should also be the executor.
>
> This is exactly what occurs in the memorandum by Pieters.[25]

Second, the sources abound with complaints submitted by salt refiners concerning their pitiable situation. Refiners from Ypres and Charleroi submitted such complaints numerous times.[26] These complaints generally served as a bolster when refiners were requesting some kind of privilege, for example a tax cut or some form of government support (see Table 4). Another recurring motif in their grievances is the ruinous competition from other countries. A memorandum by the States of Flanders pleaded for higher import rights or even a partial import ban because 'Belgian' refined salt was far surpassed by that from Holland. This memorandum noted that a positive balance of trade was vital in preventing currency outflow: "Having neither gold nor silver, all of our wealth has to come from or factories and production."[27] The refiners from Namur and Charleroi were more concerned about competition from Liège and advised the customs bureau to impose additional tax on salt exports to the Prince-Bishopric.[28]

---

25 NAB, FC, 5220, January 29th 1755, report on the request by Joseph Pieters in December 1754. "Depuis plus de trente ans que j'ai fréquenté nos commerçans et que j'ai eu quelque connoissance des affaires publiques, j'ai toujours remarqué, que ceux qui produisent de grands projets commencent ordinairement leurs écrits par un étalage pompeux des avantages qui doivent en résulter au profit de Sa Majesté et au bien être de ses sujets, tandis que ce n'est que l'intérêt particulier qui les guide au détriment des autres commerçans.

Et qu'ils ne manquent jamais de protester qu'ils sont zèles et fideles sujets de sa majesté, connoissant parfaitement le commerce en général et en particulier, en ajoutant cependant que l'inventeur du projet devroit aussi en être l'exécuteur.

C'est ce qui se rencontre exactement dans le Mémoire de Pieters."

26 NAB, FC, 5222, letter by five refiners from Ipres, December 15th 1761.

27 "N'ayant ni or ni argent chez nous, toute notre richesse doit venir de nos fabriques et productions," NAB, FC, 5226, "*Memoire additionel sur le surhaussement des droits sur le sel*," December 1764.

28 NAB, FC, 5242, requests by refiners from Namur and Charleroi, June 17th and December 7th 1785. Their advice was adopted by the bureau.

TABLE 4 *Requests by salt refiners*

		Ruling				Total
		Approved	Rejected	Unknown	Partially approved	
Nature of request	Warehouse access[29]	4	0	1	1	6
	Exemption of import duty	2	1	0	0	3
	Higher import duty on foreign refined salt	1	2	0	0	3
	Moderation of import duty	0	0	1	0	1
	Establishment of a refinery[30]	2	6	5	1	14
	More rapid handling by customs	3	0	0	2	5
	Supportive measures[31]	2	5	8	2	17
	Unknown	0	2	1	0	3
Total		14	16	16	6	52

SOURCE: NAB, FC, 5221–5243.

Although from 1749 onwards the government had far more manoeuvrability in respect to trade intervention, it had undertaken no major steps towards import substitution in the salt sector. Several protectionist measures – including higher import tariffs on white salt – had been adopted in 1699 to support salt refining, but these had been undone during the War of the Spanish Succession (1701–1714).[32] The unfavourable excise treatment imposed by the Barrier Treaty

29 In an attempt to reduce smuggling and fraud, merchants were obliged to request permission to store their goods in a warehouse.

30 Entrepreneurs were obliged to request permission to start a factory. Such requests were often rejected, usually because the government considered the project infeasible or, as was the case in the first years of the period under examination, felt that the project could potentially hinder the royal refinery.

31 These included various benefits inquired about by the actors, such as exemptions from local taxes, loans and allowances, aid against smugglers, use of government territory and modification of the mandatory salt weight. In some cases the source stated "support," without further details.

32 Coppejans-Desmedt, "Aspecten," 74, Hasquin, "Nijverheid," 126.

of 1715 was revoked in 1749, so the Habsburg rulers were (to a certain degree) free to choose tariffs.[33] However, the following years saw continuation of the equally high taxes on both kinds of salt, owing to the fiscal gains facilitated by these continuous imports. It was not until well into the 1760s that the customs administration would begin taking the needs of the salt refiners slightly more seriously, such as by liberating the export of refined salt. According to Hasquin this led to a rapid increase in the number of salt operations from 1760 onwards, especially in the region around Charleroi.[34] Yet, as we have seen, these ventures were perpetually seeking support from the government and never seemed to grow beyond their embryonic stage.

The salt industry in the Southern Netherlands included not only these small, struggling companies but also at least one other – very particular kind of – enterprise, that of the state. Midway through the eighteenth century customs policy indeed remained bound by heavy restrictions; however, such restraints certainly did not result in an absence of governmental intervention in the salt trade. Indeed, unlike as with the other industries that will be considered in this study, the administration opted to become actively involved in salt refining, even establishing an official state enterprise: namely, the royal salt refinery in Ostend. This company was founded by Count de Cobenzl, in 1756, and was fully financed by the government.[35] Management was entrusted to Levasseur, a merchant from Tournai, who collaborated with the brothers Deloose, well-known traders from Ghent. Despite the large sums of government money invested in the company (97,833 guilders and 6 stivers between 1756 and 1758) and the fact that Levasseur's operation was the sole enterprise exempted from all import duties since 1765, the company never managed to become profitable.[36] It closed in 1770 and Levasseur was granted an annual pension of 600 guilders.[37] Indeed, not only did the royal refinery fail, even with the various

33 Robert S. Duplessis, *Transitions to Capitalism in Early Modern Europe* (Cambridge: Cambridge University Press, 1997), 236.

34 According to Hasquin, Charleroi accounted for half of the salt exports in the years 1766–1785. Hervé Hasquin, *Une Mutation: Le 'Pays de Charleroi' Aux XVIIe et XVIIIe Siècles. Aux Origines de la Révolution Industrielle en Belgique* (Brussels: 1971), Hasquin, "Nijverheid," 152.

35 Hasquin, "Nijverheid," 131.

36 NAB, FC, 5248, correspondence between the Bureau and Levasseur 1764–1770, accounts of the royal refinery; 5249, memoir by the Finance Council, April 19th 1766.

37 NAB, FC, 5249, Consult of May 9th 1770, the Finance Council advises Her Majesty to close the royal refinery because it is unprofitable and suggests granting Levasseur an annual pension of 600 guilders; letter in the name of the empress, August 2nd 1770, ratifying the former suggestions.

governmental aid and tax exemptions it had received; it was also accused of being responsible for raising prices instead of lowering them.[38] Tania Van Moorhem suggests that the administration had retained the unfavourable tariffs in an attempt to foster the state monopoly and eliminate the small refineries.[39] Van Moorhem's account is corroborated by a memorandum from Finance Councillor De Müllendorf that summarizes various reasons for establishing the Ostend refinery. He notes that not only was salt an interesting means of government revenue, but that (in his view) it should be produced cheaply, so as to benefit other industries. De Müllendorf felt that this could be brought about by weakening the existing local businesses through high import taxes and establishing a government monopoly, both of which fit seamlessly into Colbertist policy.[40] The consequences are revealed in a letter from the director of the refinery himself. Writing, in a plaintive yet scholarly tone, Levasseur relates how his reputation had been befouled. "In my country I am subject to sovereign contempt, the great as well as the small, the poor and the rich blame me of being the author of the expensiveness of salt, all that holds my name has become odious, nothing can erase the sinister impressions people have drawn up against me."[41]

Even after the failure of the monopoly, private salt refiners apparently remained a matter of lesser concern to the government. This was already evident in Van Heurck's report and was corroborated by an anonymous note concerning complaints about the tariff increase of 1764 (the complaints had questioned whether the local refineries merited government support).[42] The political clout of these small enterprises was probably too slight to raise a significant lobby and the government apparently did not think them capable of

---

38 NAB, FC, 5229, complaint by the city of Namur about the increasing price of salt; however, the government disagreed, May 14th 1765; 5234, observation of the increased salt price, November 1770. The prices presented by Verlinden do not evidence a severe increase, save perhaps for the years 1765–1766.

39 Jan Van Houtte, *Economische Geschiedenis van de Lage Landen 800–1800* (Haarlem: Fibula-Van Dishoeck, 1979), 216, Tania Van Moorhem, "Sociaal Economisch Survey van een Aantal Nieuwe Nijverheden te Gent, 1750–1830 Inzonderheid de Suiker-, Tabaks-, Zeep- en Zout-, Papierindustrie, de Speelkaartenfabricatie en de Jeneverstokerijen" (RUG, 1988), 124–125.

40 NAB, FC, 5229, Memoir by De Müllendorf to Kaunitz, end of 1764.

41 "Je suis dans mon pays l'objet du souverain mépris, le grand comme le petit, le pauvre et le riche m'inputtent être l'autheur de la chèretée du sel, tous ce qui porte mon nom est devenu odieux, rien n'est capable d'effacer les sinistres impressions que des gens en place ont tracés contre moy." NAB, FC, 5248, letter by Levasseur to Baudier, end of December 1765.

42 NAB, FC, 5231, memoir, s.n., s.d.

producing affordable and qualitative salt. Therefore, the supportive measures at the government's disposal, including simpler customs procedures and loans, were awarded with great reservation. Tables 4 and 5 show that salt refiners rarely benefited from tax cuts, whereas consumers and other manufacturers generally did.[43] Unlike requests by public institutions (usually city officials) or the various eighteenth-century manufacturers who needed salt, either for consumption or for production processes, salt refiners were less often successful in seeing their claims granted (see Table 5). However, this difference, while indeed significant (see Table 6) shows a rather weak correlation and it possibly also stems from the fact that a sizable proportion of the rulings on salt refiners' petitions remains unknown. Especially surprising is that even after the demise of the royal refinery in 1770 the government still frequently forbade establishment of new refineries and remained notably fastidious in granting other sorts of appeals. In short, it appears that the government was acutely concerned towards mitigating the effects of high import duties for its subjects (ordinary consumers and manufacturers) and much less so with bolstering its domestic salt industry, what is very different from what we will see in other industries. To conclude, the last category of applicants' (i.e. salt merchants) appeals to the administration garnered mixed results, for various kinds of requests (moderation of import taxes, restitution of wrongly paid duties, swifter handling of cargo by customs officials, etc.).

The salt-refining industry in the Austrian Netherlands thus appeared to cope quite poorly according to the sources and, as Chart 10 demonstrated, foreign salt (both crude and refined) imports remained voluminous for the Southern Low Countries. However, the sources are – predictably – much coloured by the various aspirations of salt refiners and public servants, and much less by consumers and other buyers of salt. The Habsburg customs statistics enable us to better examine the actual evolutions within the salt sector and to evaluate the government's interferences in the industry. In this way we can determine whether import of crude salt or export of refined salt indeed mirror the rather gloomy story of salt refiners recounted thus far, and what that infers for other stakeholders of the trade, especially consumers. Moreover, available research into salt allows for comparing estimates of production and consumption, and for placing this particular trade into international perspective. In the end this data will enable us to unravel the effects of the international salt trade on wider economic developments.

43 For details about the requests regarding moderation of duties, see Appendix A.4.

TABLE 5 *Percentage of granted applications, per applicant category*

			Ruling				Total
			Approved	Partially approved	Rejected	Unknown	
Applicant's occupation	Institution	Count	6	0	4	0	10
		% within applicant	60%	0%	40%	0%	100%
	Manufacturer	Count	6	0	2	1	9
		% within applicant	67%	0%	22%	11%	100%
	Merchant	Count	57	15	30	3	105
		% within applicant	54%	14%	29%	3%	100%
	Merchant and manufacturer	Count	4	0	1	2	7
		% within applicant	57%	0%	14%	29%	100%
	Salt refiner	Count	14	6	16	16	52
		% within applicant	27%	12%	31%	31%	100%
	Unknown	Count	3	2	1	2	8
		% within applicant	38%	25%	13%	25%	100%
Total		Count	90	23	54	24	191
		% within applicant	47%	12%	28%	13%	100%

SOURCE: NAB, FC, 5221–5243.

TABLE 6 *Percentage of granted applications, per applicant category, with aggregated actor categories*[44]

			Ruling				Total
			Approved	Partially approved	Rejected	Unknown	
Applicant's occupation	Salt refiner	Count	14	6	16	16	52
		% within applicant	26.9%	11.5%	30.8%	30.8%	100%
	Other	Count	73	15	37	6	131
		% within applicant	55.7%	11.5%	28.2%	4.6%	100%
Total		Count	87	21	53	22	183
		% within applicant	47.5%	11.5%	29%	12%	100%

Chi-Square Tests

	Value	df	Asymp. Sig. (2-sided)
Pearson Chi-Square	27,815[a]	3	0000
Likelihood Ratio	25,844	3	0000
N of Valid Cases	183	–	–

-a. 0 cells (0%) have expected count less than 5. The minimum expected count is 5.97.

Symmetric Measures[45]

		Value	Approx. Sig.
Nominal by Nominal	Phi	0.132	0.095
	Cramer's V	0.132	0.095
N of Valid Cases		161	–

a. Not assuming the null hypothesis.
b. Using the asymptotic standard error assuming the null hypothesis.

SOURCE: NAB, FC, 5221–5243.

44 The category "unknown" has been omitted here, so as to allow for significance testing (Pearson chi-square).

45 To facilitate interpretation, this Cramer's V has been based only on the requests with known rulings and thus on a simplified 2x2 table (with applicant category's salt refiners and other, and ruling category's (partially) approved and rejected).

3 The Salt Flows

We must first take into account an important methodological issue: namely, that in the salt sector, more so than in other commodities, contraband was a major problem. Indeed, about one fourth of total imports into the Southern Netherlands were believed to be unreported.[46] Pricken blamed this on the high taxes: "The elevated import duties, in particular on salt and tobacco, have led to huge fraud."[47] The many lawsuits in their archives suggest that the customs authorities regularly apprehended smugglers, but there is no way of knowing how many others escaped undetected.[48] Yet it seems clear that customs officials were waging a concerted campaign against smugglers, especially between 1765 and 1771. Nearly half the documents in the customs archives from these years are apprehension reports by customs officers.[49] Unlike fraud efforts that will be described in other chapters, salt smuggling was not limited to casual attempts by traders to tweak particular declared amounts. A sizable group of people, including many paupers, women and even children, specialized in smuggling salt.[50] The steady worsening of the issue led to a decree, in 1765, that allowed customs officers to imprison smugglers until they agreed to pay the required duties and which granted the arresting officer a bonus worth

46 Corluy, "Een Metodologische Poging," 48.

47 "L'élévation des droits d'entrée, notamment sur le sel et le tabac [...] donnaient lieu à de vastes fraudes." Pricken, *La Douane*, 108. NAB, FC, 5226, "*Memoire additionel sur le surhaussement des droits sur le sel*," the States of Flanders estimate that 20.000 quarters of refined salt are being smuggled due to the elevated import duty.

48 NAB, FC, 5215, court extracts from 1731 on fraudulent imports in Turnhout and Malines; these mention contraband problems in Brabant dating to the second half of the 17th century; 5216, various small lawsuits, 1738–1740; 5218, „*Réflexions sur la consommation du sel, dans la Province de Flandres*", memorandum on fraud, etc; 5220: "Transit du sel, présentée le 21 jan 1754, à monseigneur De Neny," mentions fraudulent import of refined salt from Holland to Brabant and the Campine area; 5222, various pieces from 1761 about the lawsuit against Jean Nicolas Olinger from Rémich, a matter in which 19 tons of salt had been confiscated; NAB, FC, 5227, various lawsuits concerning fraud; 5228, various lawsuits on fraud; 5229–5231, idem; 5232, "Placard concernant les frauds," August 27th 1766; various lawsuits; 5233, 1768–1769, frequent mentions of imprisonment in case of fraud; 5234, 1770–1771, various lawsuits.

49 Namely, in boxes NAB, FC, 5226 to 5234.

50 NAB, FC, 5226, smuggling by children in March and May 1765; 5227, salt smuggling children mentioned in February 14th 1765; pregnant woman arrested on February 21st 1765; 5231, poor smugglers released from prison December 5th 1765; 5232, idem on April 28th 1766 and June 17th 1767.

one *pistole* (ten and a half guilders).[51] Not surprisingly, this high premium led to a number of escalations, including arguments between bureaus over who could claim an arrest, and even to fatalities during apprehensions.[52] From 1777 onwards the number of reported smuggling cases decreased. All of this strongly suggests the possibility that fraud increased due to heightened import duties but later diminished.[53] However, it is also possible that customs brigades had more luck in intercepting illegal trade after 1765. The customs officials had certainly anticipated the reality of illegal trade, for when they adjusted the duties they also mandated establishment of several new customs offices and the hiring of supplementary staff and brigades.[54] Clearly, we must keep in mind that the statistics likely understated the actual import figures, not least, as one report noted, because "From all corners it becomes clear that the salt smuggling is becoming immense."[55]

Secondly, there was also much tampering – sometimes inadvertent; sometimes deliberate – with the weight of salt consignments. Such manipulation was not always due to malice or deceit; often it was a consequence of the great confusion surrounding the exact value of a quarter (*rasière*), confusion that was exacerbated by differences between cities and between types of salt.[56] These circumstances led to various decrees imposing a weight of at least 270 pounds (which equals about 126 kilograms) for a quarter (this is the official "*razière d'Ostende*" or "*sac de Malines*"). Selling salt of lower weight was illegal and punishable by law.[57] Nonetheless, problems continued being reported through the end of the period examined here. It is thus rather precarious to estimate the exact volumes of salt that were traded. That such figures should be 'taken with a grain of salt' is, as salt traders of the time would surely agree, not idle advice.

An initial look at the trade volumes registered in the Habsburg customs statistics makes clear that the general situation of the salt sector in the

51 NAB, FC, 5227, decree of February 23rd 1765.

52 NAB, FC, 5226, Doctor's report on the death of a smuggler, March 23rd 1765; 5232, argument between two customs bureaus, January 27th 1766.

53 Pricken, *La Douane*, 108.

54 NAB, FC, 5225, protocol by de Müllendorf, October 17th 1764.

55 "il nous revient de tout coté que la fraude du sel devient immense." NAB, FC, 5231, lawsuit, department of Ghent, November 21st 1765.

56 NAB, FC, 5218, a report from 1752 for example mentions "*rasières*" of 304, 228 and 253 pounds; 5242, Note on measuring differences, December 7th 1785. 1 pound equals 467.7 grams.

57 NAB, FC, 5229, June 1765; 5230, "avis au public," Namur, May 25th 1765.

Austrian Netherlands was probably far less univocal than the complaints from the refiners suggested. Indeed, the import duties on white and grey salt officially remained equal, yet they certainly did not produce equal effects. Imports of crude or grey salt were clearly rising, even when rock salt is not included in grey salt (Chart 11). (The statistics for the first three years had, rather oddly, labelled rock salt a type of white salt.) The remarkable peak of 1766 was likely an after-effect of the Seven Years' War (1756–1763), but the customs sources make no mention of the war. These trends suggest a fairly marked advance in the eighteenth-century salt refining sector. Apparently, the number of salt refineries or their size increased, since demand for resources necessary for this type of business soared. Also, this suggests that demand from other industries requiring salt was probably on the rise as well. Unsurprisingly, exports of crude salt remained negligible, as such salt was scarce in the Southern Netherlands.

For white, refined salt, on the other hand, the trends are quite different, especially for imports (see Chart 13). Exports of domestic finished salt increased slightly over the period, despite the quality of such salt likely being fairly low and with high import duties in the surrounding countries.[58] If the first three years are overlooked, imports of the commodity appear rather stable, save for a peak during the four years' war around 1780–1783, and two drops during the 1760s.[59] Moreover, comparing the import of white salt with the estimated annual domestic consumption

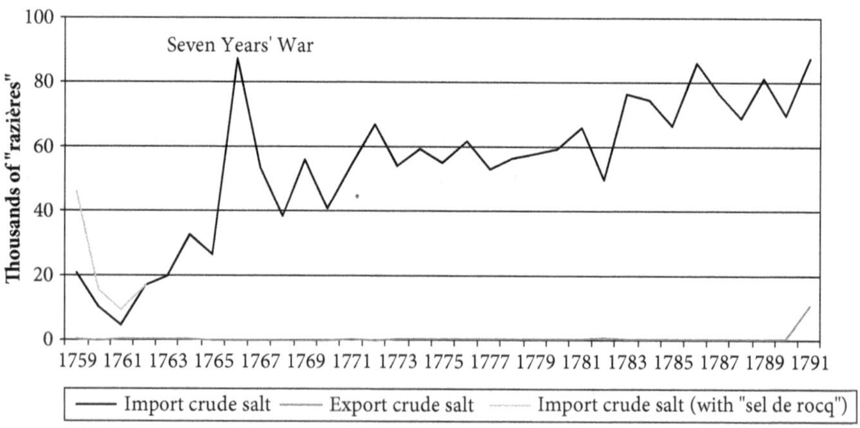

CHART 11 *The trade in crude salt, 1759–1791*
SOURCE: RÉLÉVÉ GENERAL, NAB, FC, 5748–5805.

58 Moureaux, *Les Préoccupations*, 372.
59 The problem in the first years has been discussed in the methodology.

shows that the share of foreign imported supply was quite modest. As noted in the introduction, the number of sectors that required salt was increasing during the eighteenth century; even before the beginning of the industrial revolution demand for salt had risen sharply throughout Europe. According to Adshead, by the end of the eighteenth century demand for salt amounted to 15 pounds (almost 7 kg) of refined salt per capita, a fifty per cent increase since 1500.[60] This matches Vandenbroeke's estimation for the period 1759–1791.[61] The increase stemmed from the fact that the average person now enjoyed a richer diet; and it was also strongly linked with the emergence of new branches of manufacturing, especially development of the chemical industry. With the Austrian Netherlands being home to 2,272,962 inhabitants in 1784, each of whom consumed an average of 15 pounds of salt annually, a total of 34,094,430 pounds of salt would have been needed to meet national demand.[62] The same year, imports of salt in finished form amounted to approximately 5,162,400 pounds (approximately, because the exact weight of a quarter was, as said, imprecise), or about fifteen per cent of the country's salt consumption. The other 85 per cent had to be produced locally, using imported grey salt. According to the customs statistics, the quantity of grey salt yielded approximately 23 to 36 million pounds of refined salt; if this figure is added up to that of imported white salt, the total figure closely approaches the estimated amount (i.e. 34,094,430 pounds) of consumption calculated by Adshead (and also by Vandenbroeke, but this is obvious since he already based his estimation on the customs statistics).[63] This bolsters the assumed reliability of the customs statistics; even though the estimates developed by Adshead and Vandenbroeke were fairly rough.

60 Adshead, *Salt*, 114.

61 Vandenbroeke, *Agriculture*, 476–477.

62 Ibid., 380.

63 It is somewhat more difficult to compare the quarters of grey salt recorded in the customs statistics with the required pounds of white salt. For the weight of a quarter (*rasière d'Ostende*) we used 270 pounds, which had been the legally imposed minimum weight since August 23rd 1764 (NAB, FC, 5228). We also assumed that the refining of crude salt into white salt inflated the volume of grey salt by a factor of 1.666 (since three quarters of grey salt yielded five quarters of refined product, NAB, FC, 5226, *Memoire additionel sur le surhaussement des droits sur le sel*, States of Flanders, December 1764; 5248, *Correspondance de Levasseur, 1764–1770*, letter of June 13th 1766: the royal refinery imported 20.028 quarters of crude salt in 1764 to produce 32.413 quarters of white salt). However, this ratio varies according to the kind of crude salt used in refining. For some estimates, see Ibid., 474.

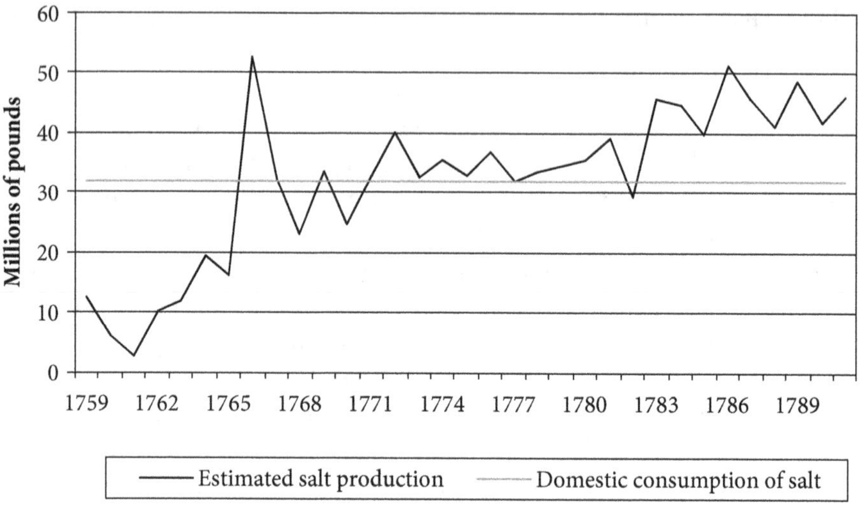

CHART 12 *Estimates of domestic production and consumption of salt, 1759–1791*
SOURCE: RÉLÉVÉ GENERAL, NAB, FC, 5748-5805 AND ADSHEAD (1992) 114.

Until 1766, the import figures for white salt appear to have been far less stable and there seems to have been a marked decrease of imports in the categories listed as *sel blanc*. Protectionist tariffs may have impacted imports of refined salt, thereby creating more opportunities for inland salt refiners; however, Van Heurck feared that the high tariffs mostly resulted in increased levels of contraband. More importantly, there is great uncertainty about the nature of the white salt included for the first three years in the customs statistics. In 1759, 1760 and 1761 white salt was subdivided into four categories: namely, *sel blanc, sel blanc de rocq, sel blanc d'Espagne* and *sel blanc de Portugal*. These have been combined in Chart 13. However, since the title of the largest category among them (namely, *sel de rocq*) is usually attributed to British grey salt, a separate – and considerably lower – curve is presented for *sel blanc* during these years. Since it is impossible to know whether customs officials were mistaken in these classifications of white salt, these first three years are not taken into account for this analysis.

By way of a short sidestep, I will remedy some of the historiographical uncertainty – mentioned in the introduction – on the origins of imported salt, by examining the departmental figures from the customs statistics for the years 1764–1781. Imports of crude salt entered the Southern Netherlands almost exclusively via bureaus in Ghent and Ostend (between 81 and 99 per cent in the period 1764–1781); the remainder entered through Newport and Bruges. This does not necessarily entail that most of the imported crude salt was from the British Isles – some may still have been coming from the Iberian Peninsula or even France – although a large part likely did, as imports from France are thought to have entered primarily through mainland bureaus rather than ports. This is peculiar, for the Brouage region, one of the main salt trade centres, is located on the Atlantic shore, yet sources agree that Britain overtook it as the leading source for salt imports to the Southern Netherlands.[64] The departmental data also confirm that Charleroi was the point of departure for much of the refined salt exports (almost 70 per cent, and even higher in some years), as Hervé Hasquin had presumed. White salt appears to have been imported mainly through the customs offices of Luxemburg and Marche; this suggests that the commodity was supplied by France – specifically, by Lorraine – and perhaps by Liège (in the case of Marche imports).

The total importation of salt (refined and crude salt, collectively; see Chart 14) into the Austrian Netherlands thus rose continuously, in-line with possible increasing demand, and the bulk of imports was crude salt. Even when we follow the assumption that about one fourth of refined salt imports was smuggled, its volume remains well below that of crude salt. Only fifteen per cent of the need for refined salt was not fulfilled domestically (or about twenty per cent including estimated contraband). Moreover, some white salt

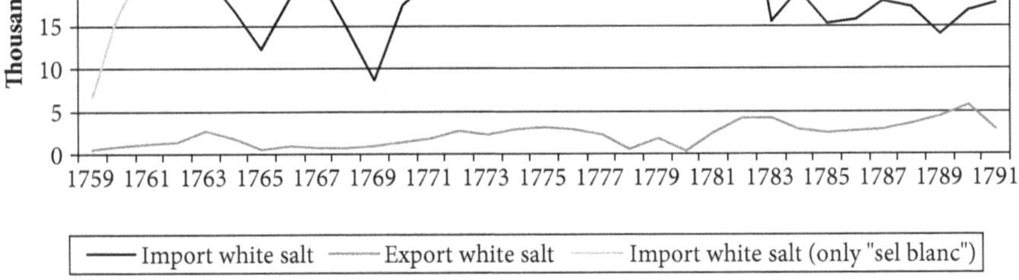

CHART 13 *The trade in white salt, 1759–1791*
SOURCE: RÉLÉVÉ GENERAL, NATIONAL ARCHIVES BRUSSELS, FINANCE COUNCIL, 5748–5805.

64 Vandenbroeke believed that some salt imports still came from Spain, but that most of it was in the form of rock salt. Ibid. He is supported by some sources that mention imports of grey salt *d'allematte* (meaning from Spain): NAB, FC, 5231; 5248, *Correspondance de Levasseur, 1764–1770*, accounts, the royal refinery used British salt and *'allemate'*.

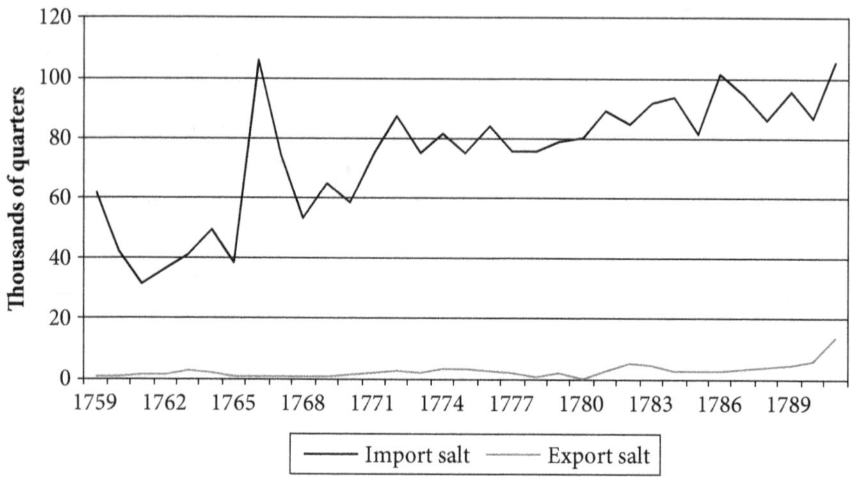

CHART 14 *Total volume of the salt trade, 1759–1791*[65]
SOURCE: RÉLÉVÉ GENERAL, NATIONAL ARCHIVES BRUSSELS, FINANCE COUNCIL, 5748–5805.

was even exported. Although crude salt was cheaper than refined salt, the balance of trade was evidently highly unfavourable, even in estimated nominal value (Chart 15); but since crude salt was an important resource, this imbalance did not cause concern for the government. The closure of the royal salt refinery in Ostend, in 1770, apparently had no influence on overall trade trends; this confirms that the refinery never managed to produce any significant amount of refined salt, notwithstanding the government's sizable financial efforts.

These figures can be compared with available data on the international trade and production of salt. As noted in the introduction, around 1800 France was by far the principal producer of salt, with an estimated annual output of 225,000 tons. England followed closely, with 200,000 tons.[66] The Austrian Netherlands, as I calculated in this chapter, produced annually a potential amount of 23 to 36 million pounds of refined salt – as based on the quantity of grey salt that was imported – plus some 4000 quarters that were exported from the region (see Chart 12). Tania Van Moorhem has provided production estimates for Ghent. Based on the *recensement industriel* (industrial census)

65 Since I have not found prices for crude salt, I used the 3:5 ratio (three quarters of grey salt yielded five quarters of refined product, NAB, FC, 5226 and 5248) to estimate the price of grey salt.

66 Adshead, *Salt*, 114.

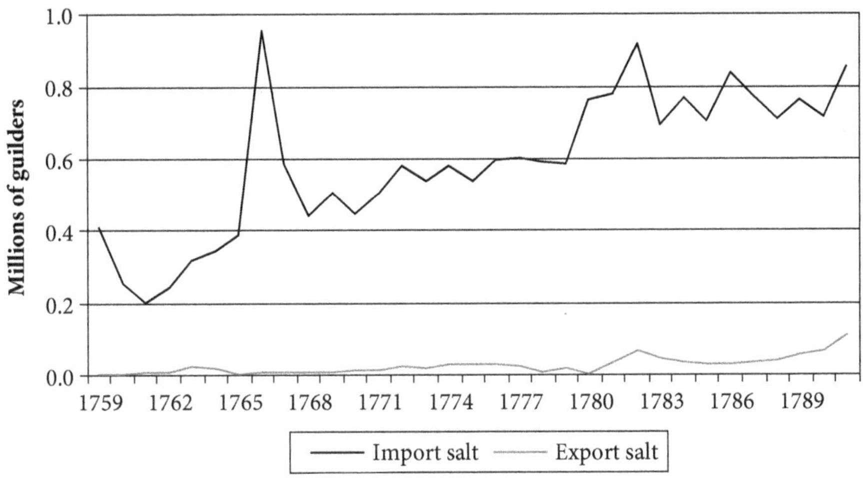

CHART 15 *Total value of the salt trade, 1759–1791*
SOURCE: RÉLÉVÉ GENERAL, NATIONAL ARCHIVES BRUSSELS, FINANCE COUNCIL, 5748-5805 AND VERLINDEN, 1959–1973, 834–835.

of 1764, the city produced 20,000 quarters (2500 tons) of refined salt in 1763, most of which was sold in surrounding areas. The city's refiners even claimed to be capable of producing double this amount, had there been sufficient sale potential.[67] Calculating, based on the records of 1764, the total production yields a minimum of 73,987 quarters (almost 20 million pounds) of refined salt.[68] This comes sufficiently close to the figure (23 to 36 million pounds) that was estimated based on grey salt imports, especially as some imported crude salt went directly to other manufacturers rather than to refineries.[69] Based on these figures, the produced amount would thus have been 11,000 to 17,000 tons, not even ten per cent of either French or English output. France and England, of course, were much larger nations and could benefit from domestic crude salt supplies. Moreover, the size of its production indicates that the Habsburg region was close to being self-sufficient. Salt production was likely even somewhat higher than the previously mentioned figure (based on the trade statistics) would suggest, for the customs statistics and the *recensement industriel* suffered from under-registration of salt figures, due both to smuggling and inaccuracy. For a small country with no domestic salt resources, these figures for the salt industry of the Southern Netherlands are quite impressive.

67 Van Houtte, *Economische Geschiedenis*, 216, Van Moorhem, "Sociaal Economisch Survey," 124–125.

68 Moureaux, *La Statistique*. See Table A.3 in Appendix for the figures per city.

69 See below.

4 Contradicting Histories?

After reviewing the qualitative sources on the eighteenth-century salt trade, the picture provided by the customs statistics and by previous historiography on the salt industry comes as a surprise. Similarly, it raises the question of why salt refiners were so dissatisfied, as evidenced by their appeals to the government. An initial part of the answer follows from the dual nature of the product. Salt, besides being a finished foodstuff provided by the refineries, was also a resource for various other industries. As such, the import levels of salt are actually an indicator of overall industrial growth. It is not known how much salt was used for human consumption; it is highly unlikely, however, that the marked increase in imported salt was attributable to everyday use in private kitchens, as such usage remained fairly stable and inelastic. Therefore, the rise in demand would have stemmed mostly from the growth of other industries and not from the salt sector itself. For example, crude salt was imported by, among others, Lemerel, a producer of ammonium salt, and by dyestuff producers Joseph de Leye and Pierre Allaire.[70] Both parties' products were used almost exclusively in the textile industry (ammonium salt for bleaching; dyestuffs for treating fabrics). The salt trade thus provides a compelling argument that both the chemical sectors linked to it and the (internal) market for textiles were flourishing.[71] The latter hypothesis will be elaborated in the next chapter.

However, there remains a degree of inconsistency, if not contradiction, between the story in the sources from the refiners and the calculated figures. The modest imports of refined salt suggest that the region was nearly self-sufficient in meeting domestic demand for the product; thus, the overall salt sector was likely not in any particularly deficient condition. Indeed, some of the sources underscore the image presented from this chapter's charts. For example, in 1782 three salt refiners from Termonde, in their request to the Finance Council, noted with satisfaction that their high-quality salt had

70 NAB, FC, 4514, exemption for crude salt imports by Lemerel, October 2nd 1771; 4516, de Leye receives a general exemption for establishing a factory, August 25th 1773; 4517, *apostille pour le medecin Lemerel*, May 19th 1774; 4528, Allaire is exempted from all duties on crude salt imports, January 15th 1783.

71 The aforementioned Lemerel could rely on ample government support, as A.4 (appendix) shows. This was because the administration was probably quite aware that ammonium salt was becoming a highly important resource and also possibly emerging as an import substitution since it was also imported, for example by cotton-printer Devisser, NAB, FC, 4523, May 12th 1781; 4510, March 5th 1767, memorandum by the States of Hainaut regarding the importance of ammonia.

replaced some of the foreign imports, in particular that from Zeeland. However, they attributed this success to circumstances stemming from the four years' war between France, Britain and the Republic, and so, according to the refiners, it remained most necessary to impose restrictive import duties on foreign white salt.[72] The customs archives also contain several requests that demonstrate that import duties were in fact not especially equal. The Treaty of Munster had imposed unified trade duties on white and grey salt, and even after 1748 the government officially adhered to these restrictions. In 1764 rather than opting for differentiation, the government increased both duties to ten guilders per quarter.[73] After a barrage of complaints, the duties were lowered the next year.[74] Yet the government had meanwhile secretly begun imposing tariffs of three guilders (instead of four and a half guilders) per quarter on crude salt imports.[75] Import duties on crude salt were, in numerous cases, lowered for particular manufacturers (who, not uncommonly, were represented by their municipal or provincial officials) and salt refiners that required it, as was also generally happening with coal imports.[76] The most likely reason the government never proceeded to a general ruling was that not doing so would foster a smokescreen that would divert any suspicions that might arise from neighbouring countries. In 1749 the Finance Council issued a note concerning the new customs policy, stating that duties should indeed be lowered on all goods which furthered domestic industries. Crude salt was explicitly included.[77]

That the measure was never formalized entails that it is often difficult to establish the exact extent of customs duties during the last third of the eighteenth century. In fact, since the mid-1760s the administration had actually

---

72 NAB, FC, 5239, request to the Finance Council, July 17th 1782. The request was rejected.

73 NAB, FC, 5224, anonymous note from 1765 (s.d.) referencing the decree of October 6th, 1764. Unfortunately, the original decree is not present in the documents.

74 To four and a half guilders per quarter: NAB, FC, 5231, decree of December 6th, 1765; 8874, tariff book, handwritten note of December 6th, 1765 on "sel gris et blanc par rasière d'Ostende." The export duty was 2 stivers and 6 pennies. The heavy duties were said to make prices escalate, since the import duty accounted for over one third of the price: white salt cost approximately 12.5 guilders and the official tariff was 4.5 guilders per quarter. Van Moorhem, "Sociaal Economisch Survey," 125, C. Verlinden and J. Craeybeckx, *Documents Pour L'histoire des Prix et des Salaires en Flandres et en Brabant*, vol. II (Brussels: 1959–1973), 834–835.

75 Coppens, "De Financiën": 104, Vandenbroeke, *Agriculture*, 482.

76 See Appendix, A.4 for details on these requests. As we will see there are many parallels with the international coal trade, but these are detailed within the chapter on coal, see below.

77 NAB, FC, 5219, «Sel et la régulation de 1749», December 8th, 1749.

chosen to keep secret, as much as possible, favours and changes in the tariff regime (including the practice of imposing three rather than four and a half guilders on crude salt).[78] Local officials maintained the arrangement as well. Indeed, city governments were sometimes as zealous as the central government in producing different tariffs and measures. Henri Delplancq, under whose supervision the customs bureau developed into a genuine ministry for economic affairs, admitted that, as he could not keep track of all the changes, only the chief modifications were included in the tariff books.[79]

The second, and more important, consequence of this *ad hoc* approach was that success in obtaining privileges was significantly dependent on political influence and the power of lobby groups. As discussed earlier, refiners' petitions to the administration rarely garnered positive or successful responses. This surely resulted in no small degree of cynicism and frustration towards such matters among this group. Moreover, establishment of a state refinery was likely regarded as an affront by the sector's established entrepreneurs. Such refiners may not have truly required government support, seeing as they were already gaining ground on the Dutch refiners (as noted previously); however, from their perspective it was highly necessary to persuade the government to reshape policy in favour of existing refineries.[80]

In this endeavour they met with little success, for the ruling objective within the *bureau de la régie* appears to have remained one of maintaining low salt prices, which was likely a wiser course for the economy as a whole (both for regular consumers and for different kinds of manufacturers). There was thus no need to further curb the already modest import figures of refined salt since the threat they posed was small and the imported salt was mostly cheaper and of a higher quality. Another possible reason for the refiners' lack of political leverage lies in the fact that the salt sector was, far more than other traded commodities, associated with criminality. The salt refiners were frequently accused of deliberately producing salt of inferior quality, and the regular commerce in salt operated alongside widespread illegal trading activity. Such a situation would surely have been regarded by administrators as an obstacle rather than an opportunity for development. Nonetheless, we should not discard all of the complaints as mere persuasive discourse: the government's price policy – while favourable to its other subjects – might have rendered it quite difficult for some salt refiners to earn reasonable returns and may have

78 Coppens, "De Financiën": 104, Vandenbroeke, *Agriculture*, 482.

79 Pricken, *La Douane*.

80 Van Houtte, *Economische Geschiedenis*, 216, Van Moorhem, "Sociaal Economisch Survey," 124–125.

engendered discrepancy between macroeconomic trends and the actual living conditions of salt refiners. Their companies were small and they frequently encountered difficulties in providing salt of decent quality; as such, their revenues were likely quite low. Moreover, some refiners still had to pay high import duties for their resources, as not all reductions were approved. As was the case with the linen industry (what we will see in the following chapter), optimistic trade figures for the salt trade point at a flourishing economy, but did not necessarily mean that all refiners benefited from their involvement in the industry.

5 Conclusion

Economic history has often overlooked salt, in large part because of the commonplace nature of the commodity. Yet the salt trade held several remarkable characteristics not generally present in other Early Modern sectors and trades. Such historical factors and developments as the Habsburg government's attempts to establish a government monopoly over the salt industry, the enormous problems ensuing from contraband, the passionate involvement of various Finance Councillors and, in particular, the salt trade's influences on and linkages with other sectors (such as textiles) establish that the story of this resource in the Austrian Netherlands is indeed far more complex and engaging than one might expect. It is surely not an exaggeration to note that the subject should be appreciated as such by any historian worth his salt.

Despite these innovative and very peculiar aspects of the salt trade, the history of this sector brings to the fore some findings about the development of the eighteenth-century Austrian Netherlands that will turn out to be the connecting thread throughout this volume. Despite various difficulties, such as the absence of a firm customs policy, there is evidence of some actual home-spun growth in the salt sector. Although the Southern Low Countries' salt refineries were customarily small enterprises, the customs statistics bolster the view of Jan Van Houtte that the refineries were gaining ground on Dutch refineries. Exports of white salt barely increased, but the low, stagnating levels of imports of white refined salt and growing imports of crude salt show that the sector was hardly faring poorly. The industry might have performed even better had the government taken stronger interest, yet the administration preferred a broader industrial approach – keeping salt prices low. International trade in refined salt – albeit its relatively modest volume – might have even aided in this by offering competition of a higher quality. And indeed, particularly as the overall trend in the salt trade indicates rising demand from the home market and therefore a steadily developing and expanding local industry, the approach was likely successful. Whether government policy was indeed the main cause for these developments remains doubtful and will be discussed in the following chapters, especially that on textiles. In any case, salt gave us a first impression of the possible engines for growth in the second half of the eighteenth century. In short, examining the salt industry illuminates wider economic developments, not least as increasing imports of salt already offer circumstantial evidence for a higher degree of domestic production of certain finished goods requiring this resource, in particular textile goods, and for the semi-finished goods (bleach) needed within this sector.

CHAPTER 7

The Textile Trade

A Tradition in Decay?

1 The Eighteenth-Century Textile Sector

Textiles are generally considered to have been the most important 'industrial' sector within the economy of the Southern Netherlands. Since Medieval times the region had played a leading role in the production of textiles and had become a major supplier to the rest of Europe and its hinterland. In the eighteenth century, however, developments in the international textile trade, in particular the arrival of new types of cotton-based fabrics, caused a wholesale shift in textile sales. Imports of calicoes, which had begun in 1720, triggered a revolution in European fashion and led to soaring demand for light, colourful fabrics.[1] Meanwhile, the traditional strongholds of the Austrian Netherlands' export trade (i.e. broadcloth, lace and silk) were presumably withering under international competition.

Despite the weight of textiles within the local early modern industry, historiography seems to have lost interest for their history in the eighteenth century. More than 35 years ago, historian Joseph Vermaut, in his dissertation, lamented the deplorable dearth of academic work on the early modern textile industry in the Southern Netherlands. This was in 1974; a year later, Chris Vandenbroeke made the same observation.[2] Unfortunately, the situation has improved little since then. Although we now have the highly enlightening works of Alfons Thijs, Hugo Soly, Catharina Lis, and Etienne Sabbe, as well as those of Vermaut and Vandenbroeke, it remains difficult to gather extensive and reliable information for textiles during this period.[3] In particular, as regards textiles, the history of the eighteenth century (excepting – not surprisingly – the omni-present Flemish proto-industry in linen and the burgeoning cotton industry) remains shrouded in indeterminacy, particularly in respect to the international trade of

1 For recent insights into this fashion change, see Giorgio Riello and Peter McNeil, eds., *The Fashion History Reader: Global Perspectives* (London: Routledge, 2010).

2 Vandenbroeke, *Agriculture*, Vermaut, "De Textielnijverheid," 1.

3 Lis and Soly, "Restructuring," Etienne Sabbe, *De Belgische Vlasnijverheid*, 2 vols. (Kortrijk: Nationaal Vlasmuseum, 1975), Alfons K.L. Thijs, "De Textielnijverheid," in *Industriële Revoluties in de Provincie Antwerpen*, ed. Roland Baetens (Antwerp: Standaard, 1984).

 | DOI 10.1163/9789004272606_009

the sector's products. Attention to the industry's early modern history probably waned because of the presumption that the sector was perishing.

However, as evidenced by the balance of trade, and as the previous chapter already suggested, significant developments were unfolding within the early modern textile industry. Indeed, contrary to historiography's relatively Cinderella-like assessments of it (compared to the study of textiles in previous centuries), the textile sector of the Austrian Netherlands was still extremely successful throughout Europe during this period, just as it had been earlier. The sector accounted for a considerable proportion of employment in both urban and rural areas.[4] The remarkable scale of this production did not escape contemporary observers. For example, James Shaw, in the chapter "Manufactures" in his 1788 work on the 'Belgian' economy, focuses almost exclusively on the textile sector.[5] And even cursory examination of the customs statistics makes clear the predominance of textiles for the economy of the eighteenth-century Austrian Netherlands. In fact, of the roughly three thousand categories defined by the customs authorities, hundreds are for textile articles. The most prevalent commodities can be grouped under the labels of unprocessed wool, *draps* (broadcloth) and *toiles* (linen cloth). Besides the dozens of subcategories into which woollens and linens are divided, this source contains data for myriad kinds of mixed fabrics in which wool, linen, silk and cotton were used to varying extents. Just like on salt, the archives of the customs bureau also include a number of series on the international trade in textile products; these series are in fact larger than any other in the bureau's collections.[6] Of course, from a present-day perspective, the importance of the eighteenth-century textile industry should not be overestimated. Even in 1812, agriculture still constituted 47.6 per cent of the gross regional product of Flanders and Brabant, whereas the industrial sector as a whole accounted for only 22.8 per cent. Nonetheless, within this rather confined early modern industry, textiles held by far the most prominent place.[7]

---

4 As regards employment, it was by far the largest industrial sector. Erik Aerts, "De Zuidnederlandse Textielindustrie C. 1600–C. 1850," *Alumni Leuven* 13, no. 1 (1982): 18, Hasquin, "Nijverheid," 147.

5 Shaw, *Essai*, section VI.

6 The main pieces on textiles are: NAB, FC, 5319–5339: Toiles; 4556–4560: Etoffes de laine, d'or, de soie et toiles de coton en généralité; 4563–4596: Etoffes de laines de toutes espèces; 4597–4598: Draps faits de queue et penne; 4599–4607: Etoffes d'or, d'argent, de soie, velours de soie et soie crue et filée; 4610–4637: toiles de toutes genres; 4638–4644: Imprimeries de coton; 4688–4689: Gazes et crêpes de soie, de fil, marli, treilli, etc; 4856–4890: Laines; 4892–4899: draperies de Limbourg.

7 Blomme and Van Der Wee, "The Belgian Economy," 5.

However, as said, the available information remains fairly approximate. Nonetheless, a sector of this size, which linked to and affected numerous other industries, certainly merits more thorough analysis. Interestingly, authors such as Van der Wee and Vermaut have explained that the textile production of the Southern Netherlands in the second half of the eighteenth century was primarily destined for export. As such, investigating the real trade flows offers an excellent means to gain insight into the experiences of and the shifts in the textile industry. Moreover, it suggests that international trade significantly impacted the most important industry within the Austrian Netherlands, and thus possibly the economy as a whole. As such, the textile industry is a particularly useful research complement to several less prominent economic sectors. Also, the case study enables us to explore how the Austrian Netherlands responded to economic pressures caused by shifting international consumer preferences and how its textile market was influenced by the introduction of new types of textiles. Finally, it will also place some heavy question marks regarding the role of the eighteenth-century trade policy.

2 The Economic Weight of the Textile Branches

Although macroeconomic studies on the textile sector are scarce, previous researchers have identified important elements in the history of textiles. However, since this – primarily Anglo-Saxon – literature has concentrated mostly on cotton, a product generally linked to accelerated growth, there is risk both of losing sight of the actual structure of the local textile sector and of overestimating the share of cotton in it. The economic weight of the urban industries, including cotton, was limited in the Austrian Netherlands, and certainly so in comparison to neighbouring countries such as England and even the Northern Netherlands.[8] During the second half of the eighteenth century the urban textile industry employed decreasing numbers of people, while the activity of much cheaper labour in the countryside expanded dramatically, particularly in the linen industry.[9] This industry alone accounted for 56 per cent

8 For the exact figures, see below in the chapter on the cotton sector. Stephen Broadberry, Rainer Fremdling, and Peter Solar, "Industry, 1700–1870," in *Unifying the European Experience: An Economic History of Modern Europe*, ed. Stephen Broadberry and Kevin H. O'Rourke (2008), C.K. Harley and N.F.R. Crafts, "Cotton Textiles and Industrial Output Growth During the Industrial Revolution," *The Economic History Review, New Series* 48, no. 1 (1995): 141, Edwin Horlings, *The Economic Development of the Dutch Service Sector 1800–1850* (Amsterdam: NEHA, 1995), 50.

9 Hasquin, "Nijverheid," 147.

of industrial employment by century's end.[10] With the focus of the existing literature threatening to lead further analysis in an unproductive or even misleading direction, the figures from the Habsburg Customs statistics are thus especially valuable, as they contribute to establishing the true market proportions of the various materials within the textile sector. Focusing on the real economic centres of gravity will clarify the larger picture.

The export figures presented in these four graphs (Charts 16–19) leave little to the imagination: even a cursory glance makes clear that linen was, by far, the Austrian Netherlands' leading textile export – in line with the RCA-analysis. Linen exports throughout this 33-year period averaged about fourteen million ells annually. That of tick – a sturdy linen fabric which, unlike regular linen, was manufactured in city centres – amounted annually to almost two million ells on average. Along with the required raw materials (crude flax) the linen industry thus represented no less than 95 per cent of exports between 1759 and 1791.

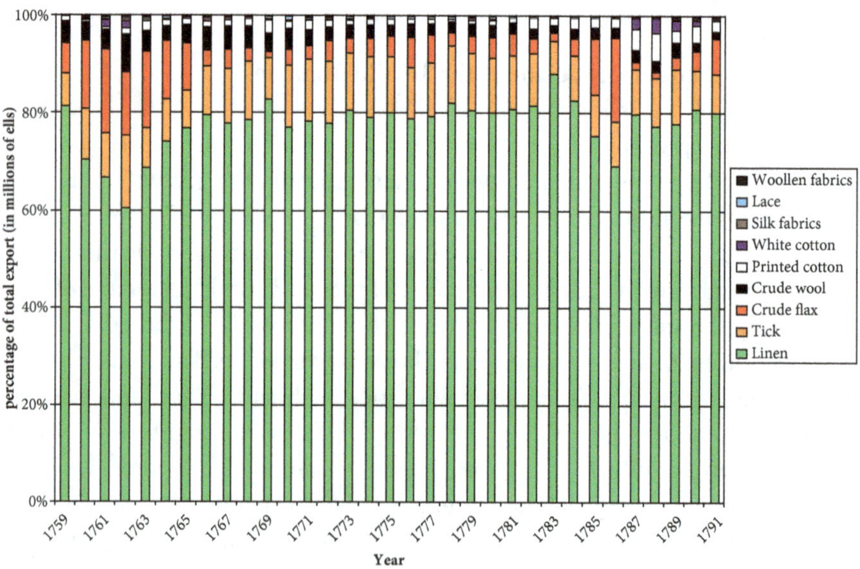

CHART 16 *The percentual composition of textile exports, in volume (number of ells), 1759–1791*[11]
SOURCE: RELEVÉ GÉNÉRAL, NATIONAL ARCHIVES BRUSSELS, FINANCE COUNCIL, 5748–5805.

10 Blomme and Van Der Wee, "The Belgian Economy," 5.

11 Crude wool and flax are recorded in the customs statistics in weight (number of pounds) but have been converted into the number of ells that this amount could produce in finished fabric.

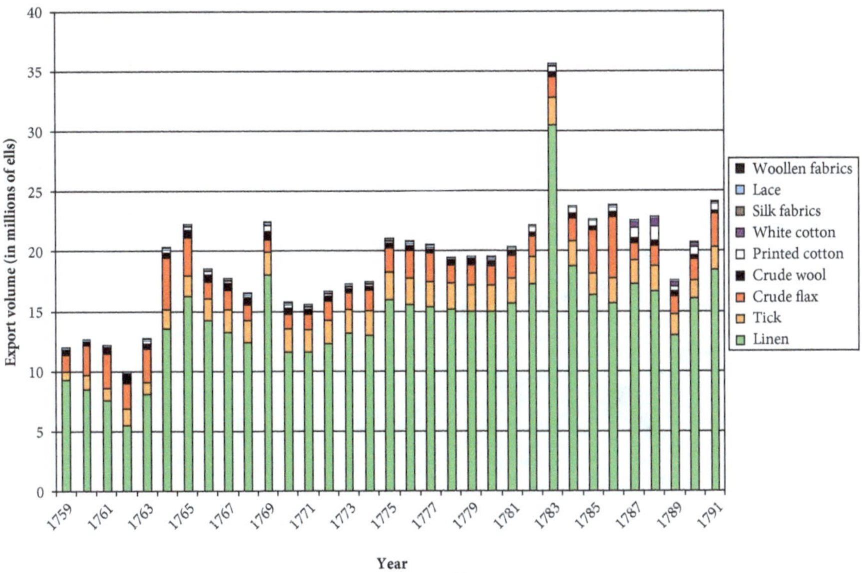

CHART 17 *The composition of textile exports, in absolute value (number of ells), 1759–1791*
SOURCE: RELEVÉ GÉNÉRAL, NAB, FC, 5748–5805.

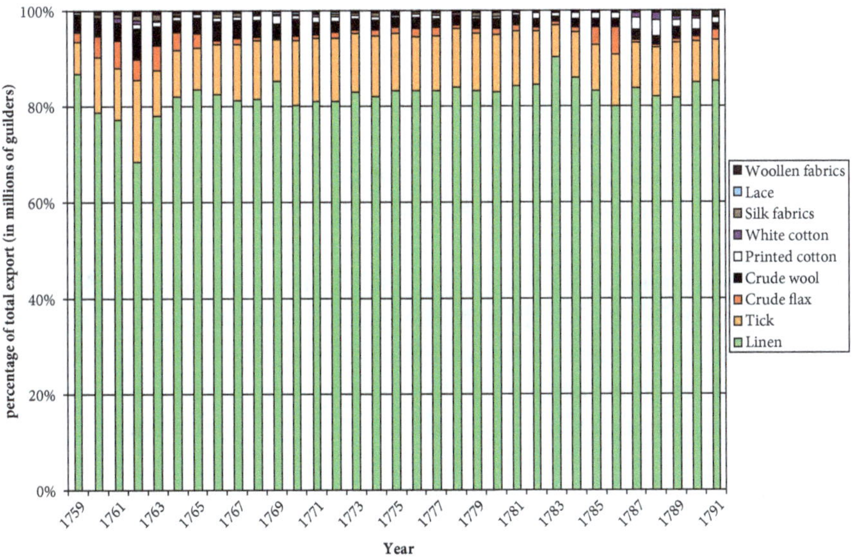

CHART 18 *The percentual composition of textile exports, in monetary value (Brabantine guilders), 1759–1791*[12]
SOURCE: RELEVÉ GÉNÉRAL, NAB, FC, 5748–5805.

12 The sources for the prices used can be found in the chapter on the balance of trade, Appendix, Table A.2. In the case of silk fabrics, it is an estimate, see below.

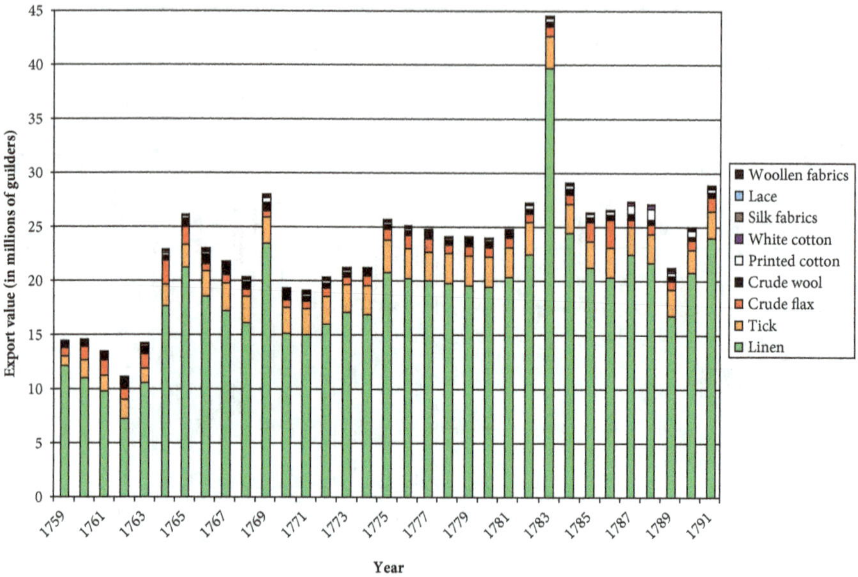

CHART 19 *The composition of textile exports, in absolute value (Brabantine guilders), 1759–1791*
SOURCE: RELEVÉ GÉNÉRAL, NAB, FC, 5748–5805.

This renders the shares of other fabrics almost negligible, both in volume and in value.

Totalling the exports of printed cotton fabrics – the 'buzz product' of the eighteenth century – with the various mixed cotton fabrics in a relatively good year – in this case, 1781 – yields a total of only 347,614 ells. This number is dwarfed by that for linen exports, even when the prices of the goods are taken into account. However, it would be premature to assume that the share of cotton exports in foreign trade was thus far smaller than in Britain or the Northern Netherlands. Unlike the Southern Netherlands these areas possessed overseas colonies and were home to large trading companies, and so it would certainly be expected that their absolute cotton exports were much larger. For Great Britain the export of cotton accounted for two per cent of total exports in 1774 (while wool still accounted for nearly 50 per cent), and this proportion continued rising, to about fifteen per cent in the 1790s.[13] In the Southern Netherlands

13 This figure comprises both finished fabrics and raw materials. N.F.R. Crafts, *British Economic Growth During the Industrial Revolution* (Oxford: Clarendon Press, 1985), 22, Davis, "English Foreign Trade, 1700–1774," 302, Harley and Crafts, "Cotton Textiles," 141, Herman Van der Wee, "The Western European Woollen Industries, 1500–1750," in *The Cambridge History of Western Textiles, Part 1*, ed. David Jenkins (Cambridge: 2003), 461.

cotton exports, even at their peak, around 1788, represented only seven per cent of textile exports. However, since textile exports likely constituted almost half the value of total exports, the share of cotton should be estimated at 3.5 per cent and possibly even five per cent for the following years.[14] In previous years it had probably amounted to just one per cent. However, in 1802, cotton exports also, surprisingly, represented only 3.4 per cent of total export value for the Dutch Republic. In international comparison the share of cotton exports was thus definitely not that low. Yet, with Dutch imports totalling 1,369,000 Amsterdam guilders and exports almost double that, totalling 2,629,000 guilders, in value the Dutch cotton exports thus – like the British – indeed far surpassed those of the 'Belgians', which had an estimated average value of about half a million Brabantine guilders (or 0.55 million Amsterdam guilders) in the period 1759–1791.[15]

Also compared to some fabrics that had been around much longer the levels of cotton exports were not especially low. Indeed, they easily surpassed the exports of woollen cloth and silk during the second half of the eighteenth century. The export of broadcloth, once the showpiece textile of the region, fluctuated around a meagre average of 17,853 ells. Exports of silk are more difficult to compare with that of other fabrics, since the value of an ell of silk was several times that of an ell of ordinary cotton. In any case, silk exports peaked in 1779, with about 50,000 ells, but in other years were at the same level as broadcloth. The wool and silk manufacturers possibly had to cope with the harsh reality that their sectors were no longer able to play any significant role in international trade, but we will see what that actually meant for their economic viability later on.

It is also worthwhile to examine the commercial centres of gravity within import flows (Charts 20–23). Indeed, the evolution of imports is certainly as revealing as that of exports in regards to the shifts in and the fortunes of the industrial branches of the Habsburg economy. Certainly in the highly mercantilist era on which this research focuses, the government was essentially terrified to increase imports of finished goods (and welcomed incoming industrial resources), whereas consumers generally embraced the increasingly diversifying supply of fabrics.

---

14 See chapter on the balance of trade; Blomme and Van Der Wee, "The Belgian Economy," 5. For the rest of Europe, the production of textiles and clothing was also the largest economic activity during the eighteenth and nineteenth centuries, after agriculture and food processing. Around 1870 it accounted for about five per cent of the GDP in most countries and 15 to 30 per cent of manufacturing output. Around 1700 its share in the much smaller manufacturing sector was probably much higher; perhaps even 40 to 50 percent.

15 Horlings, *The Economic Development*, 351, 376.

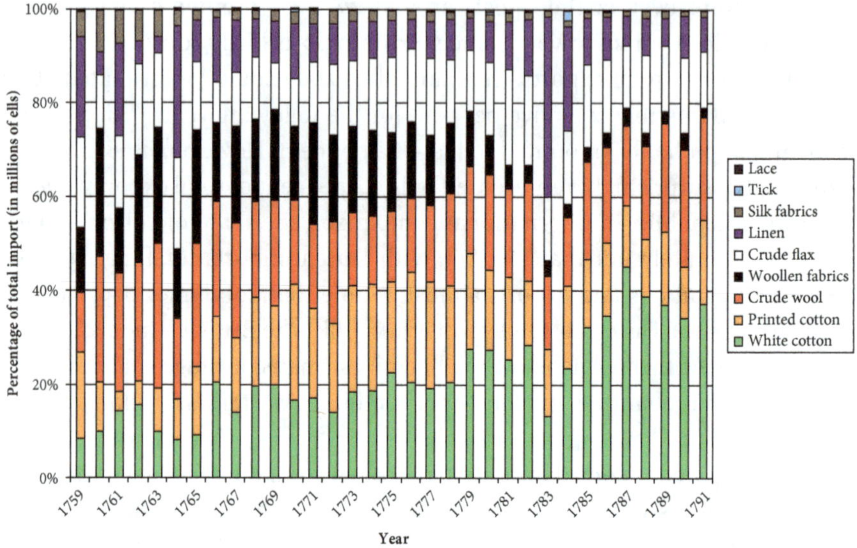

CHART 20 *The percentual composition of textile imports, in volume (number of ells), 1759–1791*
SOURCE: RELEVÉ GÉNÉRAL, NAB, FC, 5748–5805.

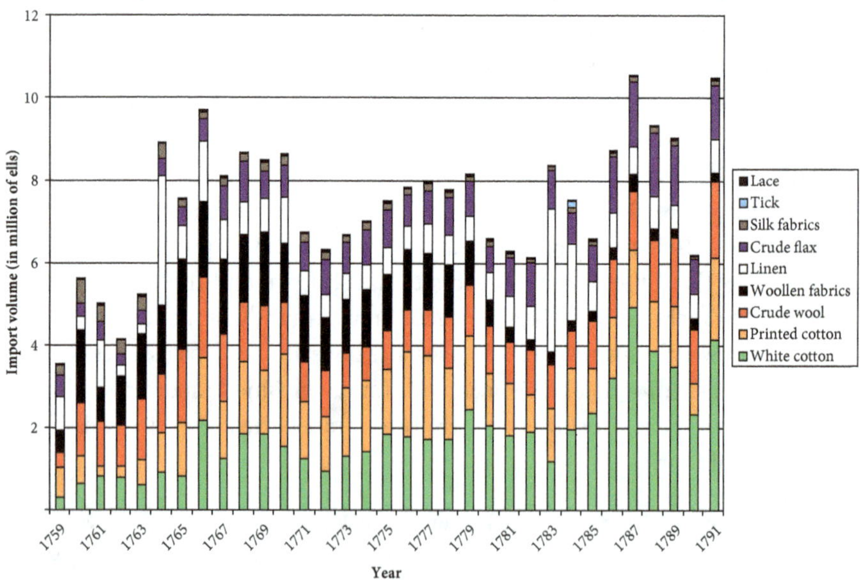

CHART 21 *The composition of textile imports, in absolute value (number of ells), 1759–1791*
SOURCE: RELEVÉ GÉNÉRAL, NAB, FC, 5748–5805.

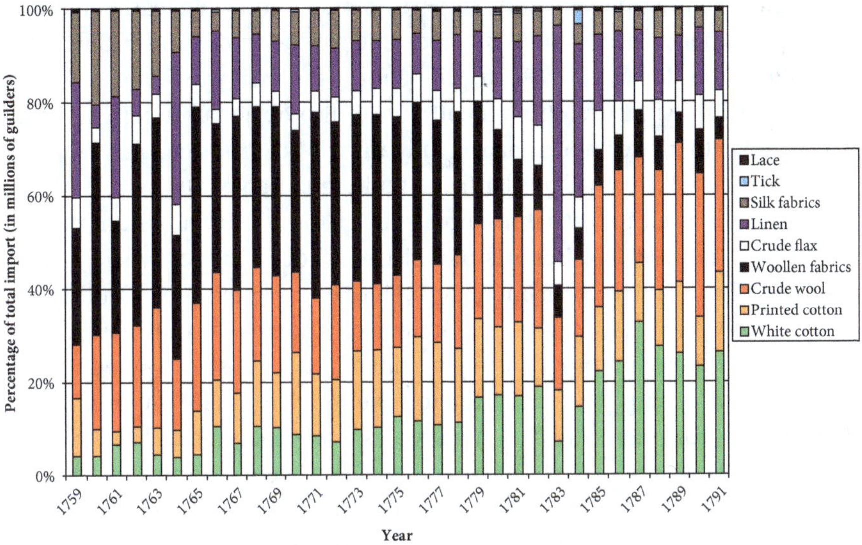

CHART 22 *The percentual composition of textile imports, in monetary value (Brabantine guilders), 1759–1791*
SOURCE: RELEVÉ GÉNÉRAL, NAB, FC, 5748–5805.

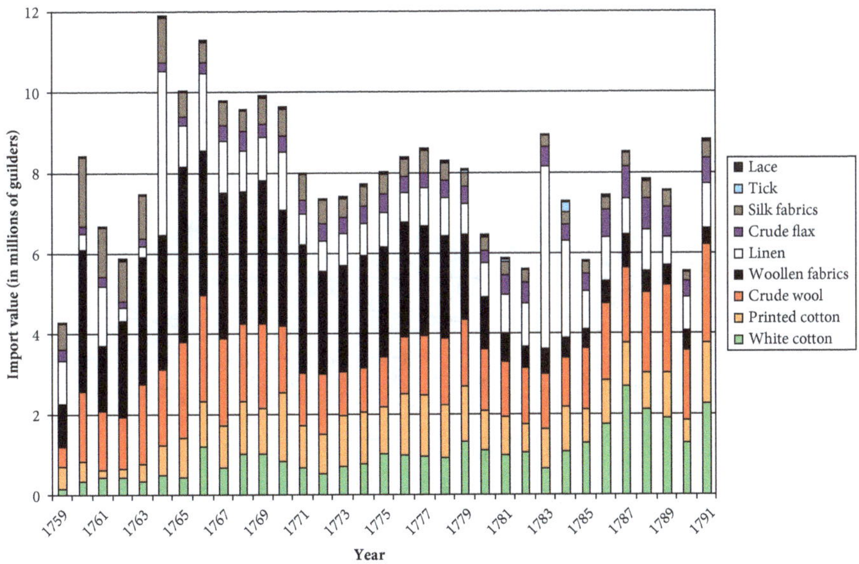

CHART 23 *The composition of textile imports, in absolute value (Brabantine guilders), 1759–1791*
SOURCE: RELEVÉ GÉNÉRAL, NAB, FC, 5748–5805.

In these four graphs detailing imports, cotton and wool clearly hold a far more prominent place than in the preceding graphs. In particular, the import of white, unprinted cotton rose steadily throughout the 33-year period covered by the customs statistics. Printed cotton was also obviously a highly popular fabric, yet in this case imports had already, in 1778, begun to stagnate. What this development inferred will be clarified later in this chapter. Raw wool – which, like cotton, was an industrial resource – also assumed an important place in the import flows, while imports of finished woollen fabrics where steadily declining. In considering the monetary values of imported goods, the value of silk, a prototypical luxury good, is immediately notable as well, even though imports of silk fabrics progressively declined in both absolute amounts as in relation to other imports. Finally, the relatively high levels for imports of linen fabrics are surprising, as this commodity was also being exported in significant quantities. However it is rather logical, as there were countless varieties of linen, not all of which were fabricated within the Austrian Netherlands.

Before assessing how international trade affected the textile sector and how well the existing historiographical assumptions correspond to the actual changes in the sector for each type of commodity, I will first return to the sum of the textile flows. This macro overview offers fresh insight into the eighteenth-century economy. As shown in the earlier chapters, the accumulated trade balance for textile products (Chart 24) was extremely positive; this was a

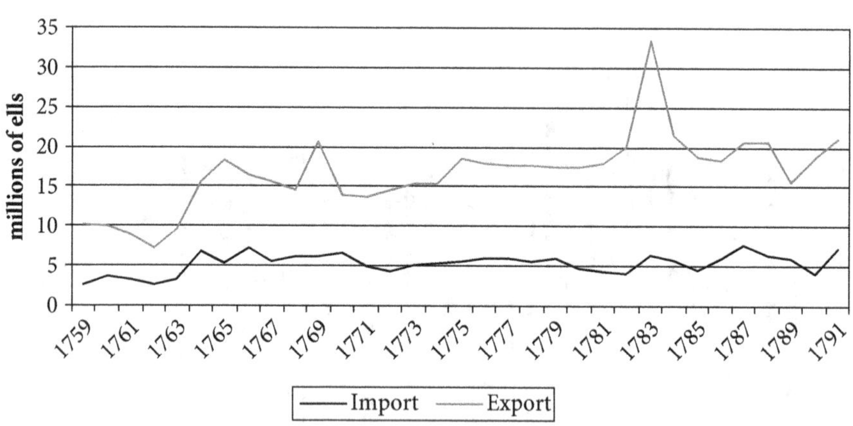

CHART 24 *The total trade in textiles, 1759–1791*[16]
SOURCE: RELEVÉ GÉNÉRAL, NAB, FC, 5748–5805.

16 The raw materials included have been converted into the number of ells that they can produce.

logical consequence of the enormous preponderance of linen within the international trade flows. Even when taking into account the monetary value of the fabrics (Chart 25) the balance of trade remains strongly positive; a modest decline in textile imports is even noticeable. In fact the export of textile fabrics was the main reason why the trade balance had not been disadvantageous during the entire second half of the eighteenth century, but only during some of the years. Based on my estimate of the eighteenth-century trade, the export of textiles was valued at about eight million Brabantine guilders more than imports – even as the total value of exports rarely surpassed total imports, such that the balance of trade was thus only slightly negative or even positive. In short, the trade in textiles was potentially the greatest source of income within the overall commercial sector of the Austrian Netherlands. The relevance of this trade for the Early Modern 'Belgian' economy as a whole was therefore probably high. Contrary to what many scholars have suspected, during this period the international trade in textiles – at least in linen – continued to play a vital role in the economic development of the Austrian Netherlands.

However, these observations do not refute the view that a part of the traditional textile industry might have quietly withered (at least on the international scene) and that international trade could threaten its already weakened position. Indeed, if flax and linen fabrics are omitted (Chart 26), the trade balance becomes strongly negative. Nonetheless, two positive developments about the situation of the textile industry are already discernible in this rough overview. First, overall exports of textiles during this period increased moderately. Second, linen, the main export product in this list, was a finished product, whereas the main imported commodity, crude (Spanish)

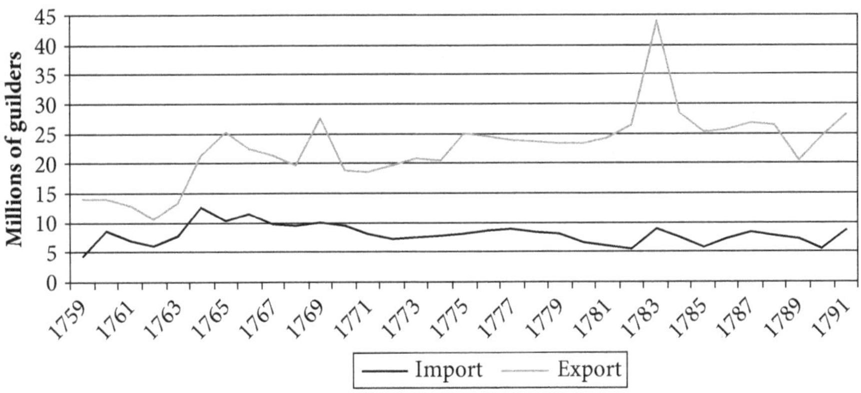

CHART 25 *The total trade in textiles, in monetary value, 1759–1761*
SOURCE: RELEVÉ GÉNÉRAL, NAB, FC, 5748–5805.

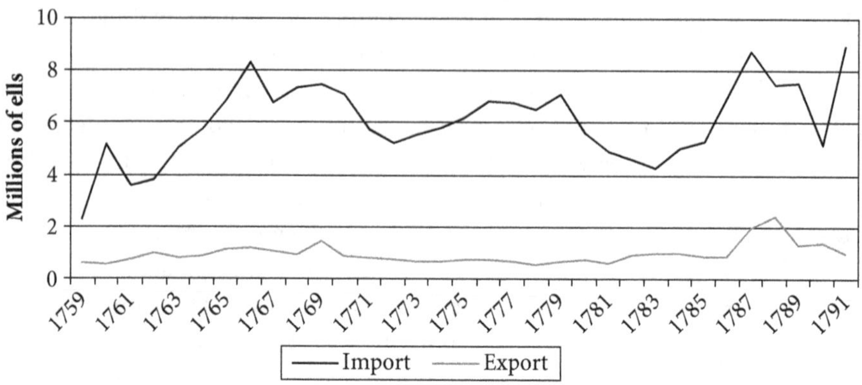

CHART 26 *The textile trade without flax and linen, 1759–1791*
SOURCE: RELEVÉ GÉNÉRAL, NAB, FC, 5748–5805.

wool, was a raw material. Furthermore, high levels of imports were also due largely to imports of white cotton and flax, both of which were industrial resources as well (Chart 18). All of this thus confirms the image of a relatively matured industrializing region, suggested in the RCA-analysis. Most importantly, the overall imported quantities of finished fabrics decreased, although they never fell below the volume of exports, what gives a first hint that import substitution may have been taking place within the textile sector. At least in a mercantilist perspective, trade in the Southern Netherlands was not faring all that poorly.

Still, the provided macro-image cannot answer the questions about how the textile sector in the Austrian Netherlands responded to the introduction of new fabrics and about the specific changes that were occurring during the eighteenth century, since it is prone to simplistic balance of trade arguments. Therefore we need to look to the existing branches separately. Moreover, to effectively draw up the balance sheet on the impact of eighteenth-century international trade on these transformations within the Southern Netherlands, it is important to examine, via the customs statistics and various other qualitative sources the various players involved and the characteristics of the various merchandise.

3 A Textile Landscape in Evolution

3.1 *Old Glory: The Wool Industry*

Wool, especially in the form of broadcloth (*laken*, in Dutch; *drap*, in French), had been the region's commercial flagship during its glory days. However, as detailed previously in this chapter, the once illustrious wool trade of the Southern Low Countries had declined markedly by the second half of the eighteenth century, by which time it accounted for a miniscule part of the nation's trade flows. This was accompanied by a decline in the numbers of active looms.[17] Yet, even despite such decline, it remained a significant branch of the manufacturing sector, especially for cities, and this type of small-scale yet labour-intensive type of enterprise would continue to determine the face of the economy in the Southern Netherlands until deep into the nineteenth century. Consequentially, in the archives of the customs bureau the sources on the wool trade are as numerous as those on linen and flax, which formed a far larger sector. There are also striking parallels as regards the content of these sources and that of the related historical literature, despite the two industries' differences in scale. The government treated both goods almost identically, and contemporary historians have often labelled each as having been a typical traditional product. Nevertheless, manufacturers from the Southern Netherlands processed wool and linen in an extensive range of fabrics, ranging from commonplace cloth to luxurious, exorbitantly expensive tissues and from ancient to innovative fabrics.

Among (partially) woollen fabrics the most vibrant trades were those in broadcloth, serge (*saye*), baize, camel cloth (*Camelot*), ratteen, kersey, frisade and flannel.[18] The most frequently traded product of this sector was unprocessed wool. Even before the period covered in the customs statistics, French traders had been purchasing huge amounts of wool in the Austrian Netherlands; moreover, during the years examined here, the market for unprocessed wool included many customers. Broadcloth and serge, originally mass produced in the Southern Low Countries, were – according to Blomme and Van der Wee – during the sixteenth and seventeenth centuries also intended for export; however, by the eighteenth century the traditional urban wool sector had been decimated, primarily by changing fashions and competition from British manufacturers.[19] The so-called light drapery fared somewhat better, but likewise suffered from foreign competition, as evidenced by the declining figures for serge production in Bruges.[20] Besides the products from the English and

17 Hasquin, "Nijverheid," 141–143.

18 A description of these fabrics is included in the Glossary.

19 Blomme and Van Der Wee, "The Belgian Economy," 8–9.

20 Vermaut, "De Textielnijverheid," App. 5B. Unfortunately, these are the only available production figures for woollen fabrics. Emile Coornaert, *Un Centre Industriel d'autrefois: la Draperie-Sayetterie d'Hondschoote (14e-18e Siècles)* (Paris: 1930), 68–69, Roger De Peuter, *Brussel in de Achttiende Eeuw* (Brussels: VUB Press, 1999), 253.

French wool industries, cheap broadcloth from the prince bishopric of Liège also inundated the region, especially the duchy of Limburg, rendering it commercially safer to switch to production of mixed fabrics such as flannel.[21] Hilda Coppejans-Desmedt's succinct overview of the wool sector leaves little doubt that by the end of the eighteenth century the sector had ebbed drastically. Production was significant only on a local scale, and the international trade relations of the Southern Netherlands were principally a threat to the region.[22] The overall image of traditional textiles, both in the cities and in rural areas, as presented in academic literature, appears grim. From such a perspective it is little wonder that policy makers opted for a strongly protectionist policy in which both the import of resources – unprocessed wool – and the export of finished tissues were exempt from trade duties, while the tariff on the import of woollen fabrics amounted to at least five per cent of its value.[23]

The duchy of Limburg plays a peculiar role in the sources on wool. In this region the rural broadcloth industry was still crucial and thus there were significant fear and apprehension about foreign imports. This is unsurprising, given that the region's cloth manufacturing provided employment to 30,000 persons, according to Briavoinne.[24] Limburgers especially suffered from competition with the nearby city of Verviers (Liège). The Habsburg rulers therefore tried – after receiving a long list of complaints about the difficulties that the sector had been encountering – to support Limburg broadcloth manufacturers, at Verviers's expense.[25] This entailed granting the manufacturers various privileges, including exemption from import duties on wool and other resources and allowing loans so as to support new factories in Herve, Hodimont and Eupen.[26] The producers also pleaded for a ban on imports of woollen fabrics from France and England to replace the existing import duty of six per cent. They argued that their factories were (as Briavoinne has confirmed)

21 Lis and Soly, *Een Groot Bedrijf*, 18, Van Houtte, *An Economic History*, 258.

22 H. Coppejans-Desmedt, "Pogingen tot Opbeuring van de Gentse Wolnijverheid Bij de Aanvang van de XIXe Eeuw," *Handelingen der maatschappij voor geschiedenis en oudheidkunde te Gent* XXI (1967): 163.

23 NAB, FC, 8874 and 5606, tariff lists.

24 Briavoinne, *De L'industrie*, 83, Hilda Coppejans-Desmedt, "De Belgische Textielnijverheid op Nieuwe Wegen door een Nieuwe Mentaliteit. Schets van een Historisch Ontwikkelingsproces," in *Vijfde Nationaal Kongres voor Industriële Archeologie: Textiel* (Ghent: Werkgroep voor industriële archeologie, 1977).

25 NAB, FC, 4564; 4574, complaint from April 15th 1764; 4589, complaints from 1770 and April 4th 1778.

26 NAB, FC, 4565, 4875, 4619, 4899, 4592–4593, « *dispositions favorables pour les fabriques de draps de la province de Limbourg.* »

doing well but that England and France had, for some time already, barred the sale of their products.[27] However, there are no indications that such restrictions had been implemented, and the government never responded to the producers' request. Of course the inhabitants of Liège were also wary of competition from Limburg and took precautions, such as prohibiting the export of unprocessed wool to the Austrian Netherlands.[28]

What were the actual reasons for the decline of the wool trade in the Austrian Netherlands? First, the fact that crude and combed wool exports from the country (Chart 27) were relatively small is not surprising: in fact, the sources reveal that such exports were often simply forbidden. Already in 1744,

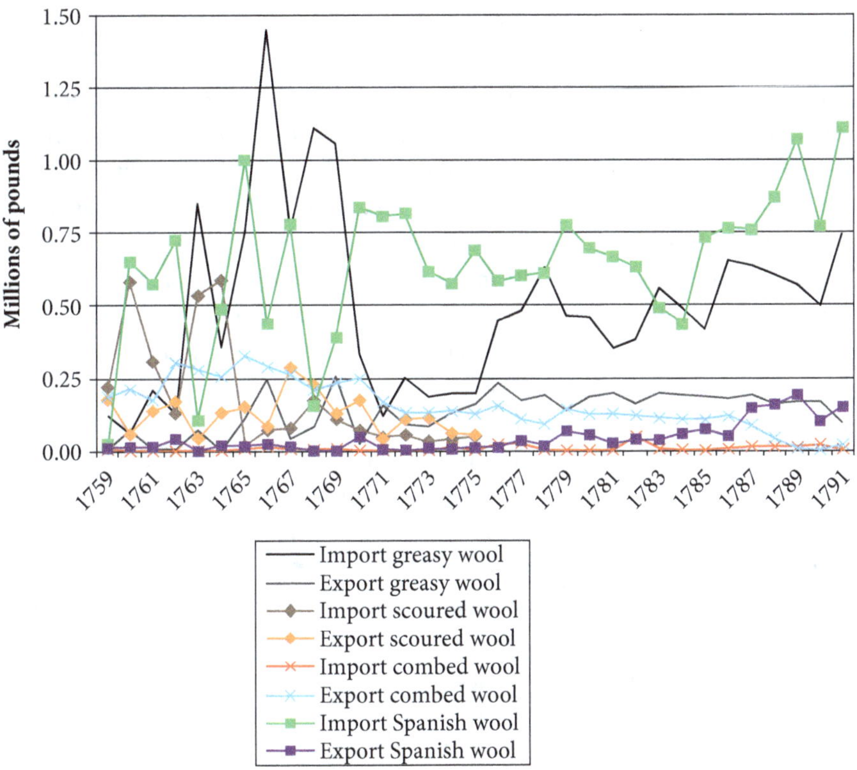

CHART 27 *The trade in unspun wool, 1759–1791*
SOURCE: RELEVÉ GÉNÉRAL, NAB, FC, 5748–5805.

---

27 Briavoinne, *De L'industrie*, 83. NAB, FC, 4593, request, March 18th 1787.

28 NAB, FC, 4565, compilation of letters on the relations with Liège. Laurent Dechesne, *Industrie Drapière de la Vesdre avant 1800* (Liège: 1926), 58.

spurred by fears that domestic serge weavers would face a short supply of wool, exports were prohibited; they were allowed again soon after.[29] During the 1750s export duties on wool were raised more than once to a nearly prohibitive rate.[30] This soon elicited complaints from the *Provinces de Flandres* and from individual merchants and wool producers, all of whom argued that there was in fact a sizable wool surplus and that, owing to the increased export duties, the domestic oversupply was now so large that wool producers could not pay their taxes with the meagre prices their wool fetched. Their argument was, in other words, that the government should encourage export of wool instead of hindering it.[31] The reactions to the requests from Flanders more than once confused wool with linen (that is, *laine* with *lin*), because, as will be seen in the chapter on linens, both sectors faced the same type of conflict between the producers of the resource and the manufacturers of fabrics. It is possible that there was indeed a domestic wool surplus but that only wool of poor quality remained in the Austrian Netherlands, with the rest being sold abroad. For example, long combing wool, which was needed in the production of fine serge, was exported, whereas short combing wool, which was suited only for broadcloth, was retained.[32] And since broadcloth was rather old-fashioned and not much sought-after, this was not a sector where high profits could be made. This may explain why during the years 1760 the government appeared to be strongly inclined towards the industry's side of the quarrel and barred several merchants from selling their wool over the border.[33] Also, a general export ban on wool yarn to be processed in Liège was imposed in 1762, just as the Prince-Bishopric had done in 1741.[34]

Despite these efforts cloth producers remained dissatisfied and during the following decennia continued requesting further increase of export duties or – more preferably – a general export ban. They argued that not only had crude wool prices risen strongly because of exports to France and other countries, but that the continuing export had actually forced them to import foreign wool.[35]

29 NAB, FC, 4859, printed decree, 1744. Vermaut, "De Textielnijverheid," 265.

30 NAB, FC, 4864, decree, July 10th 1756, s.n.

31 NAB, FC, 4863, memoir by the *Provinces de Flandres*; 4869, memoir on wool exports, s.d., copy for Van Heurck, councillor for commerce.

32 To clarify this point we would need production figures for wool, which are unfortunately unavailable.

33 NAB, FC, 4874, letter, November 20th 1765 (signed by Paradis); note by Baudier, September 25th 1765; letter, September 21st 1765; 4875; 4876.

34 NAB, FC, 4571, decree, August 23rd 1762, s.n.

35 NAB, FC, 4571; 4879; 4880, letter by Cornelius t'Kint on the dearness and scarcity of wool, October 8th 1771.

Lebrun's work confirms that wool prices had indeed increased during the second half of the eighteenth century, and the customs data shows that more wool was imported than exported during this period.[36] However, this may well have been a consequence of the many restrictions on wool exports or the fact that Spanish wool was a highly esteemed resource, and neither does it prove the existence of a wool shortage. Nonetheless, the idea that wool exports should be kept low was perfectly in-line with mercantilist thought and so it continued to be applied. On November 18th 1787 the Finance Council again forbade the export of crude and combed wool. The ban was lifted on May 28th 1790, but some departments appear to have retained it in later years.[37]

The fact that crude wool exports, according to the figures from the customs statistics (Chart 28), never really ceased – not even during periods when prohibitions were in effect – is explained by the many exceptions that traders were able to obtain. Of course imports of wool, which came primarily from Spain, remained greater than exports throughout the entire period. Imports were never restricted, save for one exceptional case, in

CHART 28 *The trade in unspun wool, in total*
SOURCE: RELEVÉ GÉNÉRAL, NAB, FC, 5748–5805.

36 Pierre Lebrun, *L'Industrie de la Laine a Verviers pendant le XVIIIe et le Début du XIXe Siècle* (Liège: Faculté de Philosophie et Lettres, 1948), 301.

37 NAB, FC, 4889, memorandum concerning the danger of wool exports, December 27th 1791, s.n.

response to epizootic disease.[38] As noted, it is possible that textile producers often preferred foreign wool over domestic varieties. The domestic wool production probably did not meet the quality requirements that Spanish merino wool did. In any case, the high imports of especially high quality Spanish wool, combined with falling crude wool exports, point to increased processing of the raw material on the domestic front, which was the ultimate aim of the strict export regulations. From this perspective, the trade flows for raw wool likely evidenced a flourishing domestic industry.

Before examining whether the processing industry was indeed advancing, one particular resource for the wool industry merits note. It was possible to manufacture broadcloth without using crude wool, applying instead scraps and bits of wool left over from the customary production process. This technique of producing *draps faits de queues et de pennes* was used mostly in the duchy of Limburg, at a town called Dison. The trade in these so-called *queues et pennes* (wool tailings) followed a notably peculiar evolution (Chart 29).

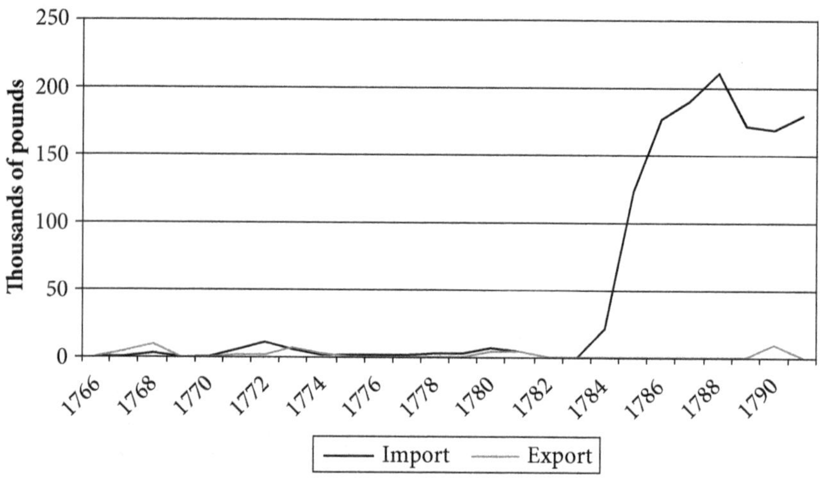

CHART 29 *The trade in wool tailings, 1766–1791*
SOURCE: RELEVÉ GÉNÉRAL, NAB, FC, 5748–5805.

38 NAB, FC, 8874, handwritten remark in the tariff book; 4879, decree of June 26th 1770; 4892, September 3rd 1770; 4890, August 9th 1792. The epizootic may have been used as an excuse for taking protectionist measures, since nonliving material such as wool could not transmit the disease; however, research into the subject shows that there was genuine concern from the government. René De Herdt, "Het Uitroeien van de Runderpest in Vlaanderen (1769–1785). Regeringsmaatregelen en Oppositie ertegen," *Tijdschrift voor industriële cultuur* 23, no. 3 (2003): 75 en 84.

The balance of trade became markedly negative only after 1784. The reason for this was that broadcloth made with wool tailings was sometimes sold under the guise of normal Limburg broadcloth, yet its quality was much lower.[39] The government feared that such broadcloth was discrediting regular draperies and that the use of used wool could threaten local wool producers. The government had, at the beginning of this period, therefore forbidden any import or use of *queues et pennes*, despite objections from Limburg manufacturers.[40] Only in 1784 did Joseph II again permit this industry.[41] From that moment, wool tailings were imported in significant amounts from Verviers (where their use was also prohibited), Aachen, Northern France and Portugal.[42] This again points to a flourishing wool processing industry, or at least the part based on wool tailings. Also notable is that the revised policy was immediately translated into the customs statistics, a fact that further undergirds the reliability of this source.

We now have some impression about the developments regarding woollen resources, but what had befallen the manufacturers of woollen fabrics? As the overview of the textile trade showed, the international trade in finished products from the wool industry accounted for very little, both for exports and for imports. While this sector had once been tremendously important for urban employment, many authors agree that its prospects seemed bleak.[43] As such, it is worthwhile to see how the separate trade flows of woollen fabrics evolved, not least as the trade in unprocessed wool suggested that the industry was not in fact faring so badly.

In the case of the best-known woollen fabric, broadcloth, a rather clear-cut evolution was occurring (Chart 30). Imports of foreign broadcloth were decreasing, which may have indicated rising broadcloth production in the Southern Netherlands. However, since exports remained at very low levels during most of the period, import substitution would not have been the only possible explanation. It is just as likely that demand for this type of fabric had waned. Especially in the case of broadcloth, the traditional fabric par excellence,

---

39 NAB, FC, 4597, printed decree by the Finance Council, April 25th 1765.

40 NAB, FC, 5606, *Tarif pour la levée Des Droits sur les marchandises, manufactures & denrées entrantes ou sortantes le Royaume de France, Pays cedé & autres*, July 18th 1670; 4597, printed decree by the Finance Council and a response by Limburg manufacturers, April 25th 1765.

41 NAB, FC, 4598, imperial decree, June 14th 1784. D. Brouwers, *La Fabrique des Queues et Pennes dans le Duché de Limbourg en 1766*, 290, Dechesne, *Industrie*, 62.

42 Hasquin, "Nijverheid," 142.

43 Blomme and Van Der Wee, "The Belgian Economy," 9–10.

CHART 30 *The trade in broadcloth, 1759–1791*
SOURCE: RELEVÉ GÉNÉRAL, NAB, FC, 5748–5805.

dwindling consumer interest should be considered as a possible factor, even though at the end of this period there was still a noteworthy increase in exports.

However, as would be expected for such a diversified sector, the trade figures do not present a homogenous image. It is true that nearly all purely woollen products were being imported and were almost not being exported. However, for some of these products the import figures show drastic fluctuations throughout the second half of the eighteenth century, whereas others charted a more one-directional downwards course. Without doubt, for many wool-based fabrics the economic situation was looking distinctly gloomy. Ratteen, kersey, baize and serge (Charts 31 to 34) were no longer leaving the country; and, though imports saw occasional upward fluctuations, they no longer seemed subject to any significant international trade.

One reason for the very limited exports of woollen fabrics was the fact that surrounding countries were likewise adhering to protectionist trade policies. Manufacturers from the wool sector often expressed trepidation about ruinous competition from woollen tissues from France, from camel cloth from England, Holland and Prussia, and from the softer and whiter woollens produced in England. Yet they nonetheless stressed that the quality of their own goods surpassed those of foreign equivalents.[44] The mercantilist adage that "the best way to make a country's factories flourish is to hinder the products of

44 NAB, FC, 4572, letter by Cornelius t'Kint, October 7th 1763; 4564, letter by Huygh and Jacobs, September 30th 1752.

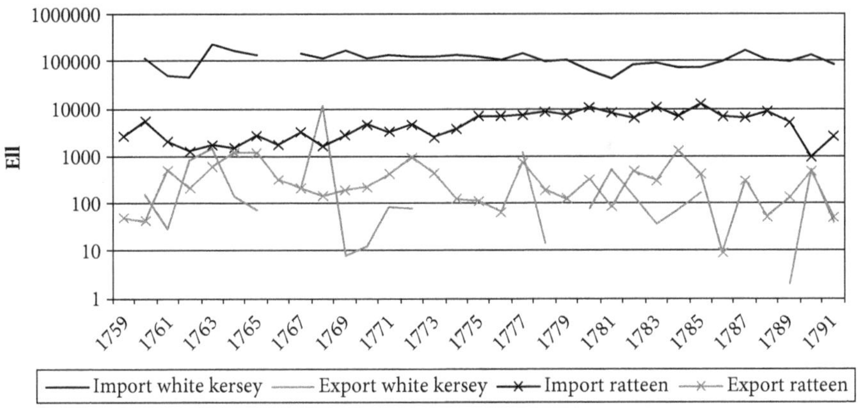

CHART 31 *The trade in ratteen and white kersey, 1759–1791 (semi-logarithmic)*
SOURCE: RELEVÉ GÉNÉRAL, NAB, FC, 5748–5805.

CHART 32 *The trade in baize, 1759–1791*
SOURCE: RELEVÉ GÉNÉRAL, NAB, FC, 5748–5805.

foreigners" was thus put into practice in this sector.[45] In 1699 the Perpetual Edict had forbidden the import of almost all types of finished textiles, yet the measure had to be withdrawn the same year, in response to international

45 NAB, FC, 4566, memoir from 1757, "Un des meilleurs moïens de favoriser les manufactures et fabriques du Païs, est de gêner et rendre difficile le débit des fabriques étrangères."

CHART 33 *The trade in serge* (saye), *1759–1791*
SOURCE: RELEVÉ GÉNÉRAL, NAB, FC, 5748–5805.

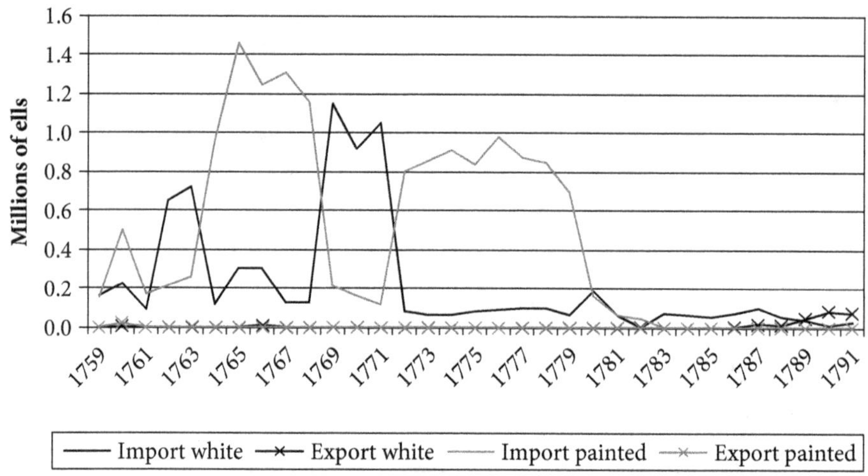

CHART 34 *The trade in white and printed serge* (saye), *1759–1791*
SOURCE: RELEVÉ GÉNÉRAL, NAB, FC, 5748–5805.

pressure.[46] Import taxes on woollen fabrics remained relatively high, but manufacturers remained discontented. They usually pleaded for further increase of import duties on several woollen tissues such as kersey, white broadcloth,

46 Coppejans-Desmedt, "Aspecten," 73.

woollen blankets, baize and serge.[47] English, French and Dutch competition remained particularly vexing to the manufacturers, some of whom continued to seek a complete ban on woollen imports.[48] According to local manufacturers, all imported foreign fabrics should be sealed (and the importers obliged to pay a stamp duty for them) "To shelter our nation's manufacturers from the difficulties posed by the fraudulent imports of foreign woollens."[49] However, the customs bureau feared that higher tariffs would incite smuggling.[50] Other motives, which had little if any apparent purpose towards contributing to the prosperity of the Austrian Netherlands and its wool industry, played a role in the Habsburg international trade policy as well. For example, import duties on fabrics from the Habsburg hereditary lands were often reduced, even though such fabrics competed against products from the Southern Netherlands.[51]

The historical sources offer no evidence that the government yielded to the calls for higher duties. The graphs present a decline in the imports of baize and serge, but this followed much later, long after the requests from manufacturers, and was thus probably due to competition from other (cotton or mixed) fabrics and – consequently – a change in demand. As will be discussed later in this chapter, it is probable that mixed fabrics and cotton gradually replaced the woollen fabrics, as production of domestic serge in Bruges had been declining since the middle of the eighteenth century.[52] The hypothesis is particularly

---

47 NAB, FC, 8873, tariff book; 4576, letter by manufacturers from Malines, Antwerp, Leuven and Ghent, February 13th 1766: the import duty of 10 per cent on blankets and frisades was not high enough to avoid the large importation, leaving factories without work. Delplancq replied that this had to be verified before their request could be granted. FC, 4586, August 30th 1775: manufacturers of serge and woolen blankets from Brussels, Malines, Leuven and Ghent found the tariff of 1768 (8 guilders 12 stivers for every 100 pounds) still too low. Delplancq recommended in his response an import duty of 13 florins and 15 stivers. FC, 4569 (1761) and 4880 (1771), petitions on raising the import duty on baize, serge and kersey. FC, 4569, April 18th 1761, request by Cornelius t'Kint to increase the import duty on kersey and frisades; idem, April 29th, circular on the increasing duties for white blankets.

48 NAB, FC, 4861, request to the Finance Council in which wool manufacturers from Brussel, Antwerp, Malines and Ghent asked to forbid imports from woollen fabrics from England, Holland and Germany, June 27th 1752.

49 "pour mettre les fabriquans du pays à l'abris du préjudice que l'importation frauduleuse des lainages etrangères leur causeroit." NAB, FC, 4572, September 10th 1763, reaction to the request from manufacturers from Herve, signed by de Beelen.

50 NAB, FC, 4581, letter as a result of the increased import duty on September 4th 1769, s.d., s.n.

51 NAB, FC, 4278, 4604, 4581 and 4596. Österreichisches Staatsarchiv, Finanz- und Hofkammerarchiv, Neues Hofkammerarchiv, Kommerz Litorale, Akten: "Kommerz der österreichischen Niederlande mit den Erbländern," 1003.

52 Vermaut, "De Textielnijverheid," App. 5B.

plausible in light of the final decline of serge and baize imports, which began in 1778. In that year, the monopoly of the cotton printing mill at Dambrugge ended and the number of cotton printers spiked significantly.[53] Suddenly, producers were able to meet the sharply increased demand for light fabrics to a much greater extent. Most likely, the monopoly had probably for years maintained the import of lighter wool fabrics and cotton fabrics from abroad at artificially high levels, because one company was unable to satisfy the entire need for such goods. The Finance Council even admitted as much.[54]

A short digression is necessary in regards to one of these woollen fabrics. The remarkable horizontal mirroring of the import flows in the third graph below, in which white and printed serge (*saye*) are presented separately (Chart 34), raises questions. When dyed serge imports were high, white serge imports were low, and vice versa. At least until 1779, when imports for both fabrics plummeted – as did baize imports – probably due to competition from other light fabrics mentioned (especially those noted in the previous paragraph). However, the explanation for this seemingly odd pattern is in fact quite simple. Manufacturers were able to dye white serge and therefore did not need to import dyed serge after enough white serge had been imported – and when sufficient amounts of dyed serge were coming in, no white serge was needed. This intercommunion occurred almost immediately, so there was virtually no delay in the trade movement. The reason manufacturers in the Southern Netherlands were not constantly dyeing the serge themselves is not found in the available sources. The answer may lie partly with events that were affecting the foreign providers of serge, such as those from the Dutch Republic, where a large number of serge-producers who had left Hondschoote for Antwerp had found yet a new home.[55]

Camel cloth, the final fabric I examine within the wool industry, shows patterns of exports and imports that progressed in a more direct way than did the previously discussed fabrics (Chart 35). In the case of camel cloth, the balance of trade was again clearly negative, but imports decreased markedly and persistently. At the same time, exports remained at a relatively consistent, albeit very low, level. As with broadcloth it can perhaps be assumed that import substitution occurred, or, in other words, that the Southern Netherlands gradually became able to meet their own needs. However, it is again just as likely that demand for this fabric waned due to changing textile fashions.

53 Alfons K.L. Thijs, "Schets van de Ontwikkeling der Katoendrukkerij te Antwerpen (1753–1813)," *Bijdragen tot de Geschiedenis van het Oud Hertogdom Brabant* (1970).

54 NAB, FC, 4641, July 10th 1777.

55 Coornaert, *Un Centre*, Alfons K.L. Thijs, "Hondschootse Saaiwevers te Antwerpen," *Bijdragen tot de Geschiedenis* 54, no. 3–4 (1971).

CHART 35 *The trade in camel cloth (semi-logarithmic)*
SOURCE: RELEVÉ GÉNÉRAL, NAB, FC, 5748–5805.

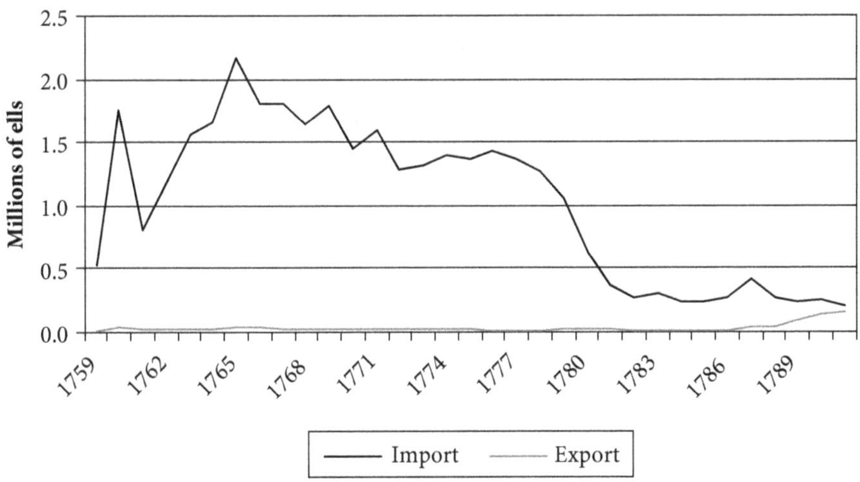

CHART 36 *Total trade in finished woollen fabrics, 1759–1791*
SOURCE: RELEVÉ GÉNÉRAL, NAB, FC, 5748–5805.

In totalling the trade figures for all finished woollen fabrics (Chart 36), the general image that emerges is quite similar to that for camel cloth: strongly declining imports (at least from 1765 onwards, when the composition of categories in the trade statistics had been finalized) and stable – by the end of the period even slightly increasing – exports. The possible cases of import substitution that can be inferred from these falling imports combined with stable crude wool imports in the end outnumber other cases, and this is an indication that the wool industry had certainly not been reduced to an immobilized victim of international trade competition, even though some of the purely woollen fabrics had clearly lost their appeal abroad and – according to partial data on production – at home. The argument is supported by evolutions of the baize and serge trade, where import substitution was probably delayed until 1778 by the cotton printing monopoly of Dambrugge. The chapters on the cotton and mixed fabrics sector (which also accounted for a portion of the crude wool imports, as we will see) will present further evidence, but analysis of the wool trade has shown that the home market in the Southern Netherlands was likely strong enough to produce its own substitutes for out-of-fashion commodities, even though the country's international trade policy was apparently doing relatively little to assist wool manufacturers.

3.2 *Ancient Luxury: The Silk Industry*

The second so-called traditional textile sector in the eighteenth-century Southern Low Countries was the silk sector. Like the wool industry, silk processing was a primarily urban activity, but compared to other sectors it was always quite small. Even compared to the local cotton industry, which had emerged in the region much more recently, the traded numbers for silk are small. This likely explains to some degree why silk has received far less attention from historians than have the other types of textile discussed in this chapter.

What literature there is has always labelled silk to have been solely a luxury product, in contrast to wool and linen for example, which have garnered a more diverse image. Manufacturers in the Austrian Netherlands processed silk yarn in exquisite tissues such as bourat, satin, damask, Caffa, velvet and plush. They also used crude silk in different kinds of semi-silk fabrics, silk yarns and so-called blond lace (lace made of silk instead of linen). These were each highly valuable products, yet they were disappearing because of dwindling popularity and the protectionist measures taken by neighbouring countries.[56] Still, in Antwerp and Brussels, considerable sums continued to be invested in the luxury goods industry, for which silk weaving was the most important branch. Silk manufacturing also remained significant in Ypres.[57] Unfortunately, the companies involved were small and – according to Pierre Lebrun – ill-suited to the requirements of industrialisation.[58] Because of that, and especially because of changing fashion, literature believed the silk sector was fated to disappear.

---

56 Degryse, "De Antwerpse Fortuinen," 121, Hasquin, "Nijverheid," 146.

57 Briavoinne, *De L'industrie*, 83.

58 Lebrun et al., *Essai*, 76, Michielsen, "Het Kapitalisme," 255.

CHART 37 *The trade in silk and semi-silk fabrics, 1759–1791*
SOURCE: RELEVÉ GÉNÉRAL, NAB, FC, 5748–5805.

Indeed, as Chart 37 demonstrates, the popularity of silk fabrics on the international market was withering even faster than other authors have suspected.[59] On the other hand, Michielsen's claims, in his argument that silk manufacturers in the Austrian Netherlands manufactured their products only in small companies, are without foundation. According to the industrial census of 1764, there were silk manufactories of considerable size in Antwerp, Brussels and Tournai.[60] The Tournai factory of Audibert Carré employed thirty people; the silk factories in Antwerp and Brussels employed no less than 1800 and 440 people, respectively. These three companies were together exporting silk fabrics worth at least 100,000 guilders annually to Germany, Holland and Liège; this value has been estimated, based on the customs statistics, to represent two-thirds of total exports in the year of the industrial census.[61] Notable in this respect is the story of Joseph Maroteau, who claimed to have founded the first factory for silk gauze in the Austrian Netherlands. He maintained that after his

59 Lebrun et al., *Essai*, 76.

60 Moureaux, *La Statistique*.

61 The value of the exported ells in the 1764 customs statistics equalled 142,089 guilders. However, this figure is very uncertain, since the fabrics mentioned in the statistics were largely listed in ells. It is known, from the industrial records, that a piece of silk cost 50 guilders and probably measured no more than 15 ells. This brings the value of an ell silk to at least 3 ells guilders.

business opened, at least 360 other factories for silk gauze were established, putting 300 looms at work. According to Maroteau, these businesses, along with his own, each year produced gauze worth a thousand guilders, of which half was exchanged for raw materials abroad.[62] Given the high cost of silk and based on the *Relevé général*, a figure of a thousand guilders for total exports of silk gauze would seem entirely realistic.[63]

However, other sources contradict these aforementioned success stories. As early as 1753, silk manufacturers from Antwerp were lamenting the gloomy condition and prospects of their businesses due to the moderate import duties on foreign fabrics.[64] They were anxious, about, among other things, the import of *velours de coton et fil* (cotton and yarn velvet), which had indeed been increasing exponentially, according to the customs statistics. From an annual average of 5000 ells during the first ten years, it rose to 50,000 in the years 1770–1785 and even surpassed 100,000 ells over the final years. Even Audibert Carré admitted that his factory was threatened by the increasing use of cotton and the rising costs of crude silk.[65] When import duties on cotton fabrics were raised in September 1762 one of the arguments for doing so was concern that cotton imports would harm the silk velvet manufacturers in Antwerp.[66] Moreover, imports of various foreign silk tissues (mixed fabrics, muslin and plush) were heavily taxed, while crude silk imports were exempt from duties.[67] This indeed led to declining imports, as noted above; but, unfortunately for the silk industry of the Southern Netherlands, neighbouring countries – particularly France – were pursuing the same tactic, resulting in declining exports of silk fabrics exports.[68] The silk industry thus seemed fated to perish or at least to limit its sales to the local market.

The trade in crude silk (Chart 38) tells a slightly different story. The raw material that entered the region came mainly from Italy. According to at least one Antwerp textile manufacturer, the spinning of silk yarn did not occur within the Austrian Netherlands; but in fact, according to the customs statistics, a considerable amount of raw silk was imported (50,000 pounds), and was

62 NAB, FC, 4689, petition by Maroteau, June 10th 1782.

63 For 1764 there are no separate figures on silk gauze, but in 1765 387 ells of silk gauze were being exported. Assuming that an ell again cost 3 guilders, the export would have been worth 1161 guilders.

64 NAB, FC, 4599, request by Antwerp silk manufacturers, February 1st 1753.

65 Moureaux, *La Statistique*, folio 742.

66 NAB, FC, 4556, note by the customs bureau, October 20th 1762, signed by Vanoverloope.

67 NAB, FC, 8874, tariff book.

68 Hasquin, "Nijverheid," 147.

CHART 38 *The trade in crude silk, 1759–1791 (semi-logarithmic)*
SOURCE: RELEVÉ GÉNÉRAL, NAB, FC, 5748–5805.

likely intended to be spun into thread by domestic yarn producers.[69] Moreover, the customs statistics show that more silk yarn was being exported than was being brought into the Habsburg Netherlands. There had also been several attempts to cultivate crude silk domestically. Occasionally, these were successful, for example in the case of Flamen van Lerberghe, but more often they garnered little if any success. The attempts by Antoine Leva, Jacques Dupont, Jacques Daussez and Daussez's sons to plant mulberry trees for the breeding of silkworms ended ingloriously.[70] Since there was thus virtually no domestic silk production, the import of crude silk represents the complete resource supply; this apparently remained remarkably stable, excepting some temporary declines around 1772 and after 1785. This indicates that silk production possibly could have been maintained at a sustainable level, but likely increasingly in the form of mixed rather than entirely silk fabrics.

The sudden outlier in the export of raw silk in 1781 is difficult to explain but may be due to an error by one of the customs offices – the office in Bruges, in particular, recorded a strikingly high output for that year.[71] It is possible that the officials confused the categories and that the amounts did not belong to exports but were in fact being transited, since for a large number of colonial

69 NAB, FC, 4605, July 15th 1782. The manufacturer at issue, a certain Molijn, uses this as an argument to import silk yarn tax-free, which was allowed.

70 NAB, FC, 4608, January 19th 1766; 4609, July 20th 1786. A. Viaene, "Proeven van Zijdeteelt in de Vlaanders, 1606–1840," *Biekorf* 58, no. 8 (1957).

71 NAB, FC, 5791, folio 20 verso.

CHART 39 *The trade in silk yarn, 1759–1791*[72]
SOURCE: RELEVÉ GÉNÉRAL, NAB, FC, 5748–5805.

products transit rose sharply in the last four years of the American war for independence, as we will see in the final chapter of this work. Also remarkable is the identical peak in the import of silk yarn (Chart 39). It is possible that these changes were related, but since the import of raw silk saw a modest peak at exactly the same time it would seem more plausible that these phenomena were attributable to external factors, more specifically: the war between the major maritime powers.

It is interesting to compare the import of raw silk and silk yarn to the exports of the silk fabrics into which they were processed. Such a comparison clarifies the extent to which producers had to rely on imports of raw materials; it also broadens the limited knowledge on the eighteenth-century silk production. If more crude silk was indeed being imported than the amounts of finished silk fabrics that were being sold abroad, then there would have still existed a fairly substantial domestic market. Unfortunately, there are many difficulties in making this estimate. It is known that seven to nine pounds of raw silk were needed to produce one pound of silk fabric (the ratio of yarn to fabric was obviously one to one), but estimating how many ells corresponded to one pound of silk is problematic.[73] After all, this correspondence depended on the density of the fabric and the share of other yarns (cotton, wool, linen) with which silk was combined. It is clear from the customs records that fewer pure silk fabrics were traded than mixed ones, but otherwise many assumptions

72 This graph contains the sum of the figures for "coarse silk thread" and "sewing silk."

73 H.F.J.M. Van den Eerenbeemt, *Op Zoek naar het Zachte Goud: Pogingen tot Innovatie via een Zijdeteelt in Nederland, 17de-20de Eeuw* (Tilburg: Gianotten, 1993), 30.

needed to be made.[74] The resultant estimation (Chart 40) shows that from 1781 onwards the silk production probably found an outlet almost exclusively on the domestic market, since the number of exported ells was an amount less than ten per cent of the quantity of raw material that was entered (and therefore of the potential output), whereas the shares of earlier years had hovered around twenty per cent. That the state of exports from 1781 onwards was tenuous was already evident from Chart 37. Yet, the declining imports of foreign finished silks and the fact that the import of raw silk was maintained while that of yarn even slightly increased, illustrate that it was again not international competition that crippled the silk sector. It suggests that domestic demand remained fairly stable, though this was perhaps mostly due to demand for mixed fabrics than for classic silk fabrics. It thus also hints – again – at the possibility of import substitution by other – cotton and mixed – fabrics.

We can again conclude that overall exports for this branch of the textile industry had been reduced to a marginal factor in international trade during the 33-year period studied here. The silk manufacturers could certainly not rely

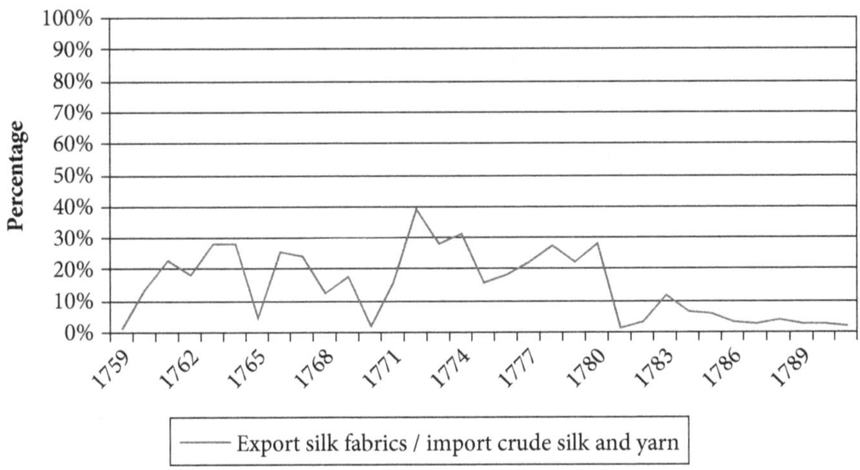

CHART 40 *Proportion of exported silk fabrics compared to the import of resources for the silk industry, 1759–1791*
SOURCE: RELEVÉ GÉNÉRAL, NAB, FC, 5748–5805.

74 Based on contemporary silk fabrics I have assumed an average density of 0.108 pounds per square ell silk (100 grams per square meter). To convert crude silk and yarn into the number of ells that could be woven with them, this figure was again reduced by two-thirds, so as to reflect the share of other raw materials used in the tissues. Finally, the export of yarn was subtracted from the import of crude silk, as production of yarn also required crude silk.

on demand from the international market to generate revenue. Yet it is clear that in this case as well the balance of trade rose during the second half of the eighteenth century, due to the declining imports of finished silk fabrics. The possibility of import substitution by for example cotton and mixed fabrics which can be derived from it evidence that it was hardly so that international competition smothered the eighteenth-century silk sector in the Austrian Netherlands, and this might even have had much to do with the protectionist customs measures towards textile manufacturers.

3.3 *At the Base: The Linen Industry*

The linen industry, the final sector in this overview of 'old' branches in the textile trade, was by far the textile industry's largest sector. Herman Van der Wee has argued that it was overall the most extensive industry in the early modern Southern Netherlands and that it represented the largest export share of all manufactured goods.[75] Yet, though the linen sector was undeniably more important for the economy and produced far more than did any of the other textile branches, it has received much less scholarly attention than a 'modern' product, namely cotton. This likely stems from the out-dated perception that during the eighteenth century the linen sector was waning and that cotton was not only ascendant but would become the emblem of the future and of the Industrial Revolution, as it did in England. Keeping the immense export amounts for linen in mind, we should thus ask the question whether the small-scale proto-industrial linen production has not actually constituted a more important growth potential for the eighteenth-century economy in the Southern Low Countries.

The most important eighteenth-century fabrics containing flax were – besides common linen cloth – tick, lace and cotton-blend fabrics (especially *siamoises* and fustian).[76] Crude flax was an international commodity as well; as noted earlier, it was the third leading textile export. Flax was generally processed by peasants in their homes, as a form of additional income. This is known as proto-industry.[77] However, the finishing (particularly bleaching) of the fabric was done in much larger, 'industrial' enterprises, and tick was woven almost exclusively in cities.[78] Flax was primarily a Flemish and Brabantine

75 Blomme and Van Der Wee, "The Belgian Economy," 5.

76 Hasquin, "Nijverheid," 143.

77 For an introduction to the topic, see: Mendels, *Industrialization*, Ogilvie and Cerman, *European Proto-Industrialization*.

78 In particular the city of Turnhout. Sabbe, *De Belgische Vlasnijverheid*, 42, Vermaut, "De Textielnijverheid," 269–270.

industry, one that was especially important for the region around Ypres.[79] In the Walloon region the broadcloth industry maintained its prominence. As Flemish flax – especially that from Termonde and the Waasland – was among the finest in the world, most historians have assumed that linen cloth became the region's primary export product and that its production for export far surpassed its production for the domestic market.[80] Spain was the foremost market for Flemish linen, with Spanish merchants importing linen in exchange for Spanish wool and transporting the fabrics to Spain's overseas colonies.

The linen proto-industry has attracted much historiographical attention (though not nearly as much as has cotton). However, although historians agree that the sector was of great importance to the region, opinions concerning the success of the linen industry remain divided.[81] What is certain, however, is that production was increasing, according to figures for Ghent, published by Bastin. There was a 50 per cent increase compared to the first half of the eighteenth century, with a peak around 1780.[82] Yet the sector had to cope with growing competition from abroad, particularly from France and England.[83] Moreover, Hilda Coppejans-Desmedt has argued there were no technological improvements taking place and Chris Vandenbroeke has emphasized the transition to the production of coarser – and thus cheaper – linen.[84] This shift, together with growing foreign competition from France and England, led to declining prices for linen and to falling wages; the resultant impoverishment eventually forced peasants into a rural exodus. In short, although the output figures increased, the sector's real income actually declined.[85]

The government did its utmost to support the linen industry, or so it appears from the customs duties. Exports of many kinds of linen fabrics were exempted from duties, whereas imports – depending on the quality of the linen – were

79 Van Werveke, "Beschouwing," xcvi.

80 Vandenbroeke, *Agriculture*, 381.

81 Christiaan Vandenbroeke, "Sociale en Konjuncturele Facetten van de Linnennijverheid in Vlaanderen (Late 14e-Midden 19e Eeuw)," *Handelingen der maatschappij voor geschiedenis en oudheidkunde te Gent* 33 (1979): 122.

82 J. Bastin, "De Gentse Lijnwaadmarkt en Linnenhandel in de XVIIe Eeuw," *Handelingen der maatschappij voor geschiedenis en oudheidkunde te Gent* XXI (1967): 139, Sabbe, *De Belgische Vlasnijverheid*, Vermoesen, *Markttoegang*.

83 Sabbe, *De Belgische Vlasnijverheid*, 21.

84 Coppejans-Desmedt, "De Belgische Textielnijverheid," 27, Vandenbroeke, "Sociale en Konjunkturele Facetten," 126.

85 Sabbe, *De Belgische Vlasnijverheid*, 35, Vandenbroeke, *Agriculture*, 386, Vandenbroeke, "Sociale en Konjunkturele Facetten."

charged from about 15 stivers to 2 guilders per hundred ells (which presumably corresponded to approximately 2.5 per cent of the value). Imports of flax were, on the other hand, free of duties, whereas exports were, as will be seen, entirely forbidden for long periods.[86] Indeed, the government endeavoured to prevent any export of raw materials and to boost exports of products with high labour input (that is, manufactured goods). The trade figures allow for determining whether these efforts led to improvement or if, on the contrary, this aspect of international trade accorded to the often pessimistic view offered by historians.

The export statistics confirm that linen cloth and tick were by far the most stable surplus products in the Southern Low Countries' balance of trade during the second half of the eighteenth century. The major difference between these two types of linen is that tick, as noted, was woven mainly in the cities whereas linen cloth, in its various forms (fine linen, table linen, coarse linen, grey linen, etcetera), was produced in villages in the countryside. Exports of each good exceeded its imports by a large margin throughout the period (Charts 41 to 43). The striking peak in linen imports and exports at the start of the 1780s is attributable to the conflict between France, England and the Republic, a conflict that temporarily increased the scope of the Austrian Netherlands on international markets. Given the huge quantities and amounts in question, the ever more positive trade balance for the two tissues is remarkable, especially because it means that exports of linen and tick in the second half of the eighteenth century constituted close to half of the value of total exports during the period, just as Van der Wee suspected. Moreover, such a finding contradicts historians who argue that the sector – despite remaining one of the Austrian Netherlands' most important – had fallen into decay during the eighteenth century.[87] Apparently, the linen sector was able to maintain its position on the international market (thanks in large part to the Iberian colonies in the Atlantic), and so there was no marked decline.

Converting the trade flows into their monetary values does little to modify the overall picture, primarily because the expensive types of linen accounted for only a very small share of total trade. Yet there is an important difference between Charts 41 and 42. The trade balance in monetary value is less markedly positive than would be expected on the basis of the volumes. The reason for this is that imported linens were generally more expensive than those that

86 NAB, FC, 8874, *Estat ou Tarif des Droits d'entrée et sortie 1680–1792.*

87 Sabbe, *De Belgische Vlasnijverheid*, Vandenbroeke, "Sociale en Konjunkturele Facetten."

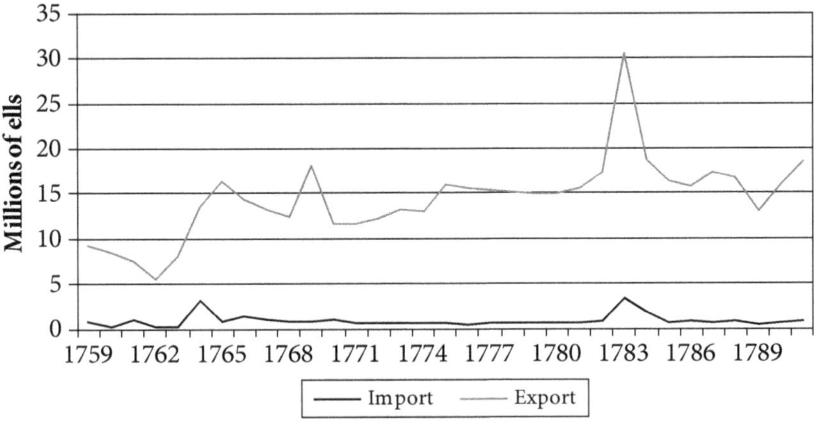

CHART 41 *The trade in linen cloth, 1759–1791*[88]
SOURCE: RELEVÉ GÉNÉRAL, NAB, FC, 5748–5805.

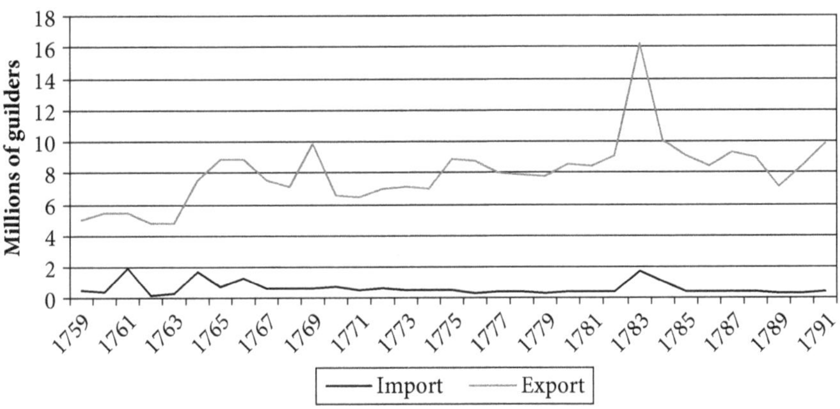

CHART 42 *The trade in linen, converted into monetary value*[89]
SOURCE: RELEVÉ GÉNÉRAL, NAB, FC, 5748–5805.

88 In the source linen fabrics are listed partly in pieces and partly in ells. For the graph the pieces were converted into ells, so that the separate categories could be totalled. It was presumed that a piece equals to 60 ells. Sabbe, *De Belgische vlasnijverheid*, 60.

89 A distinction was made between expensive and inexpensive types of linen. Cheap linen cloth cost about 10 stivers per ell, whereas luxurious types cost on average 2 guilders per ell. Sabbe, *De Belgische Vlasnijverheid*, 34, Vandenbroeke, "Sociale en Konjunkturele Facetten," 149.

CHART 43 *The trade in tick, 1759–1791*
SOURCE: RELEVÉ GÉNÉRAL, NAB, FC, 5748–5805.

were exported.[90] The primary linen exports were white and grey linen; these were merely the fabrics that had undergone relatively little processing, unlike, say, finished tablecloths or the sophisticated *rollet*, which were entered. The linen sector of the Austrian Netherlands thus delivered mostly simple, basic products, in line with Vandenbroeke's above-mentioned expectation.

Crude and combed flax were also important export categories. Although exports of these products underwent strong fluctuations, especially in the case of raw flax, their overall trade balance was always positive. In the customs statistics, we see that crude flax (Chart 44) experienced a brief export boom from 1784 to 1786, followed by a major contraction. The export of combed flax (Chart 45) similarly spiked around 1785, albeit not to its level from before 1765. The contractions are puzzling, particularly because, as we will see below, the customs regime after 1784 had become less strict (allowing these resources to leave the country), just as it had been between 1759 and 1760.[91] Exports could thus have revived just as strongly as before, but it did not. In the case of flax yarn, a raw material primarily for the ribbon and lace industry (Chart 46), the product saw continuously rising exports, even as imports increased as well.[92] The latter is not surprising, given that yarn imports for the local lace industry

90 See Appendix, Table A.6, for the shares of cheap and expensive linen cloth.

91 Peter D'Haeseleer, "Proto-Industrialisering van de Vlasnijverheid in Dertien Gemeenten ten Westen van Aalst (18e – eerste Helft 19e Eeuw)" (Katholieke Universiteit Leuven, 1990), 106.

92 Hilda Coppejans-Desmedt, "De Gentse Vlasindustrie vanaf het Einde van de XVIIIe Eeuw tot de Oprichting van de Grote Mechanische Bedrijven (1838)," *Oostvlaams Verbond van de Kringen voor Geschiedenis* Nieuwe Reeks, 8 (1969): 18.

CHART 44 *The trade in crude flax (semi-logarithmic), 1759–1791*
SOURCE: RELEVÉ GÉNÉRAL, NAB, FC, 5748–5805.

CHART 45 *The trade in combed flax (semi-logarithmic), 1759–1791*
SOURCE: RELEVÉ GÉNÉRAL, NAB, FC, 5748–5805.

were exempt from taxes. On the other hand, domestically produced flax yarn was supposedly of higher quality than its foreign counterpart, which would seem to render it pointless if not counterproductive to import the latter into the region.[93] Explanations for the evolutions in the linen and flax sector will be examined below.

93 L. Truyens, *De Antwerpsche Garentwijndersnatie en haar "Bleyckerye" te Borgerhout* (Brussels: Weissenbruch, 1943), 3.

CHART 46 *The trade in flax yarn, 1759–1791*
SOURCE: RELEVÉ GÉNÉRAL, NAB, FC, 5748–5805.

Although it is not obvious from the voluminous trade flows of flax presented above, the Finance Council regularly opted to curb flax exports, just as seen earlier in the paragraph on the export of unprocessed wool. Probably because of this parallel, responses to the Council's memoranda regularly mistook *lin* (linen) for *laine* (wool).[94] Indeed, both industries were experiencing an almost identical conflict between wool producers and traders on the one hand and textile manufacturers on the other. Both parties had entirely opposing positions on trade duties, and these positions are discernible for the entire period in the sources on the textile trade. The producers of each raw material clearly favoured free exports of raw flax and unprocessed wool and the resulting high prices. The fabric manufacturers, however, preferred that exports be restricted, so that their foreign competitors would face difficulties in procuring resources, and also, or at least according to the manufacturers' arguments, because that would render low production costs. For traders in these materials, who were not simultaneously working as manufacturers or investing in factories, free trade again offered the opportunities with the most benefits. The customs archive unsurprisingly includes numerous examples of traders – of linen and wool, as well of nearly all other fabrics – requesting tariff exemptions and export permissions.[95]

94 NAB, FC, 4869, response to a memorandum from Van Heurck, September 24th 1761.

95 135 of the 1741 collected requests were from merchants requesting lower trade duties (or an exemption). NAB, FC, 4556–4559, 4567–4594, 4600–4606, 4613–4635, 4639–4643, 4688–4689, 4867–4889, 5324–5336.

However, as concerns linen, the export figures show that fabrics manufacturers' worries about foreign competition in fact made little sense and that their arguments were easily debunked. The amount of flax that the Southern Netherlands exported was far from sufficient to produce a linen capacity elsewhere that might constitute a serious threat to domestic production. Even if all of the annually exported raw and combed flax were woven into linens, it would have only yielded an amount equal to barely seven per cent of the overall quantity of linen and tick exported by the Austrian Netherlands.[96] I would argue that the primary motivation of such attempts to prevent flax exports was to keep the prices of the raw material low and thus maximize profit margins for the textile producers.

Although the government, as evidenced in the state archives, sought to establish an optimal equilibrium between the trade priorities of producers and those of fabric manufacturers, and despite the threadbare arguments of the latter, the government nonetheless generally opted to increase export duties on flax or even to prohibit exports of certain types and to certain countries. The exports of retted flax were always the most expensive; those of combed flax – which was, to a small degree, already processed domestically – the cheapest.[97] Due to the increasing costliness of raw materials there were repeated calls for a complete ban on exports of uncombed flax. In 1750, flax exports were indeed temporarily prohibited, but from 1759 to 1766 the Finance Council resolved that the measure entailed excessive disruption of agriculture.[98] In February 1766 a ban on exports was re-instituted, only to be annulled on August 6th of the same year.[99]

A ban on exports of flax yarn to France was also advocated. However, in this case the Finance Council disagreed with the position of the fabrics producers and held that exports had only a minor impact on prices and did not lead to excessive fraud or smuggling.[100] Moreover, yarn spinners were completely dependent on their industry – unlike linen weavers, for whom manufacturing provided additional income – and so the administration preferred not to restrict yarn exports.[101] Merchants remained unconvinced, however, leading Theodore Vanmoorsel to complain that the tariff on crude yarn was excessive

96 Production of one ell of linen required about 0.75 pound of flax. D'Haeseleer, "Proto-Industrialisering," 248.

97 NAB, FC, 8874, tariff book.

98 NAB, FC, 4278 and 4915, note from June 26th 1765. Vandenbroeke, *Agriculture*, 393.

99 NAB, FC, 4916, memorandum, February 8th 1766.

100 NAB, FC, 5330, memorandum signed by De Bredy, bureau de la régie, January 21st 1778.

101 Sabbe, *De Belgische Vlasnijverheid*, 94.

and thus a hindrance to his trade. The customs authorities disagreed with Vanmoorsel's assessment.[102]

In 1784 the administration announced its newest tactic, in a memorandum from the *controleur principal des droits*: henceforth, the government would endeavour to effectively curb smuggling.[103] Even though, according to Etienne Sabbe, the new approach yielded little success, all exports were permitted from that year onwards, provided of course that sufficient export duties had been paid.[104] However, the disappointing flax yield (illustrated by the downward shifts in Charts 44 and 45) prompted policy makers to again change their minds, this time in September 1786.[105] The prohibitions on the export of flax in 1786 not only affected producers and traders, but also led to reprisals from Paris, including an increase in French toll rates on linen from the Southern Netherlands.[106]

Nonetheless, the graphs demonstrate that the government has never significantly enforced the various prohibitions. In fact, flax was abundantly exported throughout the entire period in question, mainly to France and Holland. Yet the restrictions appear to have had some influence, especially the export ban of 1786, which seems to have caused a decrease in flax exports; however, it should be remembered that the other variations cannot be explained by this sort of measure, and so it remains uncertain that the export ban was indeed the cause of the decrease. Moreover, there is, if we hold to this explanation, a somewhat strange development evident in Chart 45: the declines in exports were accompanied by increasing imports. Thus, it was not the case that the export prohibitions rendered the Southern Netherlands more autarkic. In short, the failure of the flax harvest offers a far more viable explanation, as such a setback could well have led to both a decline in exports and a parallel increase in imports.

Another consideration is also relevant. Converting the amount of imported flax to the number of ells that could be produced from it, even at the height of the imports – which, as noted, were barely taxed – yields an amount of only half a million ells; for a time when sixteen million ells of linen and tick

102 NAB, FC, 5324, letter by Theodore Vanmoorsel, April 8th 1761.

103 NAB, FC, 4944, memorandum on flax exports, July 28th 1784. Willy Haagen, "'Uitbuiting-Door-Handel' als Verklaringsfaktor voor de vertraagde Industrialisering van de Linnennijverheid in Vlaanderen," *Handelingen der maatschappij voor geschiedenis en oudheidkunde te Gent* XXXVII (1983): 222.

104 Sabbe, *De Belgische Vlasnijverheid*, 97–98, 108. NAB, FC, 4944, decree liberating flax exports to France, August 19th 1784.

105 NAB, Secret Council, 1162/A, edict by Joseph II, November 29th 1786. Ibid., 97.

106 Ibid., 100–101.

were being exported. This demonstrates that the volumes of imported flax were far from sufficient to produce the numbers of finished fabrics from these parts, and that domestic flax production was thus likely entirely adequate. In other words, the Austrian Netherlands were generally self-sufficient in their production of flax, and flax imports were of little consequence. Import of extra raw materials may have been undertaken in certain regions only for practical reasons (such as location). The customs offices which recorded the largest quantities of flax were St-Philippe, Bruges, Sint-Niklaas, Mons and Luxembourg: as noted, however, even these amounts were generally negligible.[107]

Any assessment of the impact of international trade and trade policy should take into consideration not just the raw materials, but also the entire production chain. Nearly all finished fabrics (linen and tick, as well as cloths, mixed fabrics, lace and silk) were exempted from export duties.[108] As regards linen and tick, the legality of importing raw materials without taxes and then freely exporting whatever fabrics were produced seemed sufficient to spur the industry into flourishing; however, for lace – a product for which the Austrian Netherlands still enjoyed renown – such opportunity was inadequate. It appears that the impact of the customs policy was rather limited or at least ambiguous; the consequences of the trade policy will be examined in a later section. The main conclusion thus far is that, for the linen industry, international trade probably had a positive impact on the region. In fact, the trade in the linen industry's products yielded for the producers a significant source of income. Linen production also accounted for by far the largest surplus in the trade balance, and exhibited a relatively immense RCA.

A crucial question that remains is whether the impressive figures from the customs statistics in fact made sense. As noted, in the second half of the eighteenth century, according to Sabbe, almost the entire linen production was destined for export. Although there are only partial estimates for the magnitude of linen production in the Austrian Netherlands, comparison between collected customs statistics and the production figures from Blomme and Van der Wee present fairly strong correspondence.[109] Blomme has estimated that production for foreign markets was equal to 14,080,000 ells in the period

107 During the sample year 1774, bureaus in each of these places registered about 1500 pounds.

108 NAB, FC, 8874 and 5608, tariff books.

109 There are figures for the region surrounding Alost, for the City of Ghent, and for Brabant and Flanders. Bastin, "De Gentse Lijnwaadmarkt en Linnenhandel in de XVIIe Eeuw," D'Haeseleer, "Proto-Industrialisering," Vandenbroeke, *Agriculture*.

1760–1765.[110] According to the customs statistics for 1765, after conversion, 14,331,582 ells of linen were exported that year. It should be kept in mind that it is unclear exactly how long a piece of linen was. The length of a piece varied depending on the particular type of linen and on local guidelines.[111] Moreover, there are few sources on the matter, and so the figures are not exact, but there is clearly a strong correspondence. However, it is not obvious how sizable the total production of flax (both for domestic needs and for export) was. If we assume that about six pounds of flax was consumed annually per capita (equivalent to eight ells of linen, as it is known that production of one ell of linen required about 0.75 pounds of flax), then 13,637,772 pounds of flax, or 16 million ells of linen, would have been needed to be produced to meet the needs of the inhabitants of the Austrian Netherlands.[112] However, this figure presents an overestimation, in that it ignores the possibility that tissues other than linens were used – indeed, outside Flanders a large amount of wool was also used. A more credible number is Blomme and Van der Wee's estimate (based on figures from Chris Vandenbroeke) of 10,601,864 ells, which would bring the total production of Flanders and Brabant to about 24,700,000 ells.

In short, for all flows of flax observed, one may assume – as do most of these authors – that the production of linen for export was indeed much larger than that for internal use. This is especially the case in light of the major scale of illegal flax and linen exportation; as such exports obviously could not be included in official statistics.[113] However, Sabbe probably overreaches in assuming that the entire production was destined for export. The production and trade figures do not support this, and, according to Bastin, production in fact doubled throughout the eighteenth century.[114] Given that flax and linen exports had not significantly increased during this period, this production increase could not have gone abroad.

Lace, made from flax yarn, is considered to have been one of the traditional success stories of the textile trade in the Southern Netherlands before 1700. Although the eighteenth-century lace industry has generally been neglected

110 Blomme and Van Der Wee, "The Belgian Economy," 5 and 9, Sabbe, *De Belgische Vlasnijverheid*, 34.

111 As mentioned, Sabbe's estimates (in which one piece measured 60 ells) have been used here, but Corluy assumed that the length of one piece was closer to 23 ells. Corluy, "Een Metodologische Poging," 53.

112 Presumably about ten per cent of the used flax was lost during production of linen fabrics. D'Haeseleer, "Proto-Industrialisering," 248, Vandenbroeke, *Agriculture*, 380.

113 Sabbe, *De Belgische Vlasnijverheid*, 108, Christiaan Vandenbroeke, "De Landbouw en Levensmiddelenpolitiek in de Oostenrijkse Nederlanden" (RUG, 1970–1971), 273.

114 Bastin, "De Gentse Lijnwaadmarkt en Linnenhandel in de XVIIe Eeuw," 139.

by historians, it is known that during this period lace from the Austrian Netherlands was exported to the Spanish colonies, the Dutch Republic, France and the Iberian Peninsula.[115] Production of lace for export was thus far more significant than production for the domestic market, despite the product having to compete internationally, especially with British and French lace, the latter of which was becoming increasingly *en vogue*.[116] However, as Jan Van Laerhoven has argued, this particular branch of commerce for the Southern Netherlands did not begin to truly wane until the end of the eighteenth century.[117]

Yet, as concerns the lace trade, the customs statistics corroborate the view of previous historians, namely, that an economic regression took place. It actually transpired even earlier than Van Laerhoven suggests.[118] Even though lace as a commodity was not only exempt from export duties; the yarn needed to produce it was also allowed to be imported free of duties.[119] Thus, although the balance of trade remained favourable during the time period covered in this study, it is clear that foreign demand decreased strongly from 1770 onwards (Chart 47). The primary cause for this was probably the aforementioned competition from British and French lace.[120] In fact, trade policies regularly led to diplomatic tensions between the Southern Low Countries and England and lace was a driving factor behind such events, in particular as the English hindered lace imports from the Austrian Netherlands in an attempt to politically isolate the region.[121] The remarkably low export figures for the beginning of the period elicit a marked degree of wariness as to the accuracy of the pre-1764 customs statistics which has already been noted in the introduction.

With the exception of the lace industry, international trade clearly did not pose a threat to the eighteenth-century linen sector in the Austrian Netherlands. Based purely on the numbers, this sector was faring extremely well during this time and accounted for very large revenue for the eighteenth-century economy. However, it should be remembered that linen was for a large part a rural

115 Degryse, "De Antwerpse Fortuinen," Monique Heeren, *De Kanthandel van de Firma Reyns te Antwerpen in de 18de Eeuw* (KUL, Faculteit van Wijsbegeerte en Letteren, 1966), 95.

116 Heeren, *De Kanthandel*, 166.

117 Jan Van Laerhoven, "De Kanthandel te Antwerpen in de 18de Eeuw: de Firma Van Lidth de Jeude," *Bijdragen tot de Geschiedenis* 54, no. 3–4 (1971).

118 Ibid.

119 NAB, FC, 5606, tariff book, July 1st 1758.

120 NAB, SSW, 2149/1, memoranda on the trade with England, 1780; 4289, *Entrecours du Commerce de ces Pays avec les pays étrangers*. Heeren, *De Kanthandel*, 166.

121 NAB, FC, 4289, *Entrecours du commerce*; NAB, SSW, 1777, note, February 27th 1780.

CHART 47 *The lace trade, 1759–1791*
SOURCE: RELEVÉ GÉNÉRAL, NAB, FC, 5748–5805.

commodity, and so it cannot be credited for spurring the type of classical industrial innovation in urban areas that cotton is often associated with. Yet in the subtle interaction between agricultural innovations, the proto-industry and wider economic development, the linen trade was large enough to possibly play a crucial role.[122] On the other hand, we should not forget that the huge linen exports did not lead to notable improvements in the everyday lives of peasants – the prices paid for their goods were far too insignificant to achieve such returns – but aided in their subsistence.

3.4 *Time for Change: The Cotton Industry*

As mentioned at the beginning of this chapter, the international textile trade in the eighteenth century led to a revolutionary change in the supply of fabrics, via introduction of exotic new tissues made from cotton. In the wider debate over the possible links between international trade and industrialisation, the subject of cotton has elicited controversy, especially in Great Britain. Cotton plays a key role in the literature on international trade, development, industrialisation, globalisation and shifting consumer habits during the eighteenth century. As such, cotton from India is among the most thoroughly examined colonial goods. The fabric was originally introduced in the form of finished tissues; however, in Britain there soon emerged an import substitution industry,

122 The debates on the proto-industry (see the works of among others Mendels, Brenner and de Vries) have indeed often pointed at the capacity for 'modernization' and early types of capitalist organization within traditional sectors.

which many historians consider to have figured at the heart of the British industrialisation process.[123] Entrepreneurs on the mainland endeavoured to develop the same industry; such efforts succeeded fairly quickly in the Austrian Netherlands. However, unlike with Great Britain, the industry in the Austrian Netherlands was not a 'leading sector'; nonetheless, it remains particularly important within the economic historiography of the region.[124]

As regards the textile sector, cotton affords an invaluable measure by which to gauge the extent to which international trade and trade policy supported the industry. Even though the weight of cotton within the export flows was much smaller than that of linen – cotton did represent a large share of imports – the experiences of this typical young industry reveal just as much about the structure and shifts within the economy of the Southern Netherlands. More importantly, this sector presents a convincing case that an internal market could indeed replace international supremacy and catalyse prosperity within this small industry.

The cotton sector in the Austrian Netherlands originally involved only manufactories of mixed fabrics, in which cotton was combined with linen, silk, wool or other yarns. Such fabrics had been produced since the 1720s, but production received an extra boost in 1744, when the government banned imports of French *siamoises*.[125] The eighteenth century also saw widespread spinning of yarns for production of mixed fabrics, thereby necessitating large-scale importation of crude cotton fibre. In Antwerp alone in 1784 about four thousand people (mostly children) were involved in cotton spinning and a thousand people in cotton weaving.[126] The primary resource for this business was crude cotton fibre; cotton printing would not arise until the second half of the eighteenth century. To obtain coloured cotton tissues, manufacturers used not dyed yarns, but dyed or printed white finished fabrics. Consequently, white cotton cloth became a more important resource for the cotton sector in the Austrian Netherlands than was raw cotton and cotton yarn. The fabrics needed to be imported by the various East India companies of other countries.[127] In the Austrian Netherlands, these fabrics came into the possession of the

123 Pomeranz and Topik, *The World*, 215.

124 De Peuter, *Brussel*, 234, Alfons K.L. Thijs, "Aspecten van de Opkomst der Textieldrukkerij als Grootbedrijf te Antwerpen in de Achttiende Eeuw," *Bijdragen en mededelingen betreffende de geschiedenis der Nederlanden* 86, no. 2 (1971), Herman Van Der Wee and Helma Houtman-De Smedt, *De Wereldeconomie in Opbouw 1750–1990* (Leuven: Universitaire Pers Leuven, 1992), 81.

125 A mixed linen-cotton fabric. Thijs, *Van "werkwinkel,"* 149.

126 Ibid., 150.

127 Ibid., 154.

Beerenbroek Company, a printing firm in the village of Dambrugge, near Antwerp.[128] The company had been founded in the mid-eighteenth century and, thanks to holding the relevant patent, held a monopoly over the printing of cotton since 1753. This monopoly lasted until 1778, during which time the company was able to operate unhindered by competition. The patent had been easily obtained, owing to political connections of the company's founders and the government's susceptibility to arguments related to improving the trade balance.[129]

However, none of this could prevent the fact that from 1775 increasing numbers of new printers were being established. The demand for cotton textiles was simply too high and widespread. Start-up capital for cotton printers was generally supplied by young nobility, who, in the decades before, had been enriched by trade.[130] Since the weaving of pure cotton effectively emerged only in the nineteenth century – despite occasional attempts in the second half of the eighteenth century – it was white cotton cloth, and to a lesser extent raw cotton and cotton yarn, that was especially needed as a resource for the cotton and cotton-blend sector in the Austrian Netherlands. The finished products had to compete with cottons from England, France and Holland; the same countries by which the raw materials were imported.[131] It is less clear where cotton fabrics from the Southern Netherlands were exported to, though sources mention France, Spain and the Americas.[132] Printed and mixed-cotton fabrics were also presumably exported to Germany, Liège and the Northern Netherlands.[133]

In short, thanks to evolving consumer preferences the cotton sector flourished and expanded significantly in the eighteenth century.[134] The import of calicoes from 1720 onwards had triggered a revolution in European fashion and throughout the century spurred high demand for light, colourful fabrics. This change in taste is nicely illustrated by the spectacular increase during the

128 According to the industrial census, all of the white cottons for Beerenbroek were coming from the Indies via Holland. Moureaux, *La Statistique*, 267.

129 Thijs, "Schets," 161.

130 Ibid.: 173.

131 NAB, FC, 4557, *Mémoire sur la necessité d'augmenter la filature de coton aux Pays Bas* (s.d.); NAB, FC, 4558, resolution by De Beelen, July 4th 1776. Corluy, "Een Metodologische Poging," 105, 167.

132 NAB, FC, 4642, letter by the Commercial Court of Tournai to the Finance Council, August 18th 1779; NAB, Manuscripts, 850 A; NAB, FC, 4639, piece concerning merchants De Loose from Gent, February 13th 1764.

133 Corluy, "Een Metodologische Poging," 150, Thijs, *Van "werkwinkel,"* 150.

134 Lis and Soly, *Een Groot Bedrijf.*

second half of the century in the numbers of shops selling cotton fabrics.[135] Moreover, cotton and mixed fabrics were not only fashionable; they were also almost as inexpensive as linen: cotton cost eleven to fifteen stivers per ell and plain cotton-linen cost about eleven, while average linen cost ten stivers and flannel almost twenty-one.[136] According to Jan Dhondt, the sector realized huge profits.[137] It is assumed that the growth of the cotton sector – at least in 1812 – was remarkably high compared to that of agriculture and other industries.[138]

Lis and Soly, however, have argued that state support was a crucial factor in the success of the cotton industry.[139] The textile producers in the Southern Netherlands received government support in their efforts to produce the new, evermore popular fabrics. More specifically, according to various authors, customs legislation was used to implement protectionist taxes against foreign competition. One such example was the decree of January 27th 1749, which increased import duties on numerous cheap fabrics, including finished (printed) cotton, linen and wool of lesser thickness, as part of an effort to protect 'Belgian' manufacturers.[140] In 1778 import duties on printed cotton were again increased.[141] Originally, the main goal of these measures was not to improve the export position of the Austrian Netherlands but rather to realise import substitution and thereby boost domestic industry.[142] Many historians believe that the government indeed succeeded in bringing about import substitution and that in this way cotton contributed dynamically to the economic modernization of the Austrian Netherlands.[143] This raises the question of whether these theories are in fact supported by the relevant historical source materials. Was a major share of production intended for foreign markets? Or did the government indeed restrict and hinder imports and endeavour towards import substitution, so as to protect the domestic industry?

---

135 Lemire, *Fashion's Favourite*, Laura Van Aert and Danielle Van Den Heuvel, "Sekse als Sleutel tot Succes? Vrouwen en de Verkoop van Textiel in de Noordelijke en Zuidelijke Nederlanden 1650–1800," *Textielhistorische bijdragen* 47 (2007): 11.

136 Lis and Soly, "Restructuring," Vandenbroeke, "Sociale en Konjunkturele Facetten," 149.

137 Dhondt and Bruwier, "The Industrial Revolution," 351.

138 Blomme and Van Der Wee, "The Belgian Economy," 12.

139 Lis and Soly, "Living," 132.

140 Van Houtte, *Histoire*, 552–553. NAB, FC, 5848, '*Statistique Douanière Autrichienne*,' list of import duties.

141 Lis and Soly, "Living," 134.

142 Lis and Soly, "Restructuring," 109.

143 De Peuter, *Brussel*, 234, Thijs, "Aspecten," Van Der Wee and Houtman-De Smedt, *De Wereldeconomie*, 81.

Various government communications from the second half of the eighteenth century emphasized that international imports and exports hugely impacted the cotton sector. Government representatives and cotton manufacturers alike underscored the sector's dependency on foreign imports and on the foreign markets.[144] As the commercial court of Tournai declared: "One of the largest branches of trade in this country is without a doubt the export of our printed cotton to the French."[145] At the same time, these representatives and manufacturers also bewailed what they considered cutthroat foreign competition on the domestic market for finished cottons.[146]

At first glance, it appears that government policy did in fact directly address these concerns. As the tariff books show, import duties on finished textiles were higher than were export taxes, and exports of finished cotton fabrics were entirely exempted from taxes.[147] Moreover, it was costlier to import printed cotton than white cotton: the former cost one guilder and five stivers per hundred ells (about five percent of the total price); the latter cost just one guilder, or three per cent of total price.[148] However, throughout the eighteenth century, despite regular adjustments to the trade tariffs, local officials continued hammering the point that foreign competition had to be addressed, in particular via implementation of further increased import duties on printed cotton.[149] Moreover, Habsburg policy, with its relatively high import tariffs, was significantly less rigid than that of for example the English, who had instituted a ban on the import of cotton from the Austrian Netherlands.[150] In a remonstrance submitted by the Beerenbroek cotton printer in Antwerp to the Finance Council, the petitioners emphasized that printed cotton had, ever since the Peace of Aix-la-Chapelle, become increasingly popular, one result of which was that the Austrian Netherlands now had to make onerous payments to foreign suppliers.[151] Following the prevailing mercantilist trade ideology, the

---

144 NAB, FC, 4557, *Mémoire sur la necessité d'augmenter la filature de coton aux Pays Bas* (s.d., s.n.); 4641, request by Pierre De Heyder to open a cotton mill, May 27th 1778.

145 "Une des branches du commerce les plus étendues de ce pays consiste sans contredit dans l'exportation de nos cotons imprimés aux français." NAB, FC, 4642, August 18th 1779.

146 NAB, SSW, 2194/2; NAB, FC, 4556–4560.

147 NAB, FC, 8873 and 8874, tariff books.

148 Lis and Soly, "Living," 134.

149 NAB, FC, 4556, 4641 and 4642, *passim*.

150 Koen Paeye, *De Gentse katoennijverheid op de internationale katoenmarkt in de 19e eeuw*, master thesis (Ghent University 2008). Koen Paeye, "De Gentse Katoennijverheid op de Internationale Katoenmarkt in de 19e Eeuw," in *Geschiedenis* (Gent: Universiteit Gent, 2008).

151 NAB, FC, 4640.

petitioners argued that a domestic industry should be developed as quickly as possible.

However, the strength of Viennese trade policy cannot be deduced from its general regulations and statutes. Especially telling are the myriad cases when the administration undertook *ad hoc* measures to improve the position of individual cotton printers against foreign competitors (or, before 1775, of its only cotton printer, Beerenbroek). The archives of the Finance Council offer innumerable details about the lobbying undertaken by owners of cotton printing mills. The various privileges they requested generally concerned complete exemption from import duties on resources and machinery and from export duties on their finished products; sometimes they pleaded for financial support, such as when establishing or expanding a company. The requested exemptions were usually granted, albeit often with conditions attached. In the end, only those white fabrics intended for re-export after finishing were exempted from import duties.[152] This measure reveals some degree of support for exports, even as the files of the Finance Council convey a highly ambiguous image. The administration never enacted universal exemption, and so we can only estimate the share of imported resources that was eventually free from duties. Of course, it is highly plausible that filling the treasury's coffers was of higher priority than protecting the industry, or even that the government simply did not have the political manoeuvrability to fully and openly implement its customs policy without triggering conflicts with nearby countries.[153] Yet was the government indeed stymied in this respect, or did its tactic of implementing countless small measures which were generally unobtrusive to its neighbouring competitors in fact generate greater effects?

To effectively assess the extent to which cotton-related trade policy benefited development of this particular industry in the Southern Netherlands, and to determine whether trade was, in the end, of major importance for the cotton sector, we must look beyond the rhetoric of the day and revisit the customs statistics. Examining figures from the sources reveals trends in the international trade that other sources have not addressed. Comparisons with (partial) production figures will allow for determining how sizable the export figures actually were as compared to production for the home market and the extent to which the region depended on cotton imports. Unlike with the case of the linen industry, however, this entails comparison with a significant amount of

152 NAB, FC, 4558, 4559, 4638, 4639, 4640, 4641, 4642–4644, *Imprimeries de coton 1762–1765, 1774, Imprimeries de toiles de coton à Anvers 1769, toiles de coton etc. 1771–1787, passim.*

153 Lenders, "Ontwikkeling."

material, as cotton has been an exceptionally important topic in the historiography of industries in several countries.

In looking at the traded volumes recorded in the Habsburg customs statistics (Chart 48), it is immediately striking that imports of both white and printed fabrics clearly exceeded exports throughout the period 1759–1791. However, the marked variance between white and printed cotton fabrics renders a much different perspective onto these apparently straightforward figures. In fact, small amounts of white cotton were already being exported – and thus being produced in the region – before the nineteenth century. Nonetheless, the exported amounts of printed cotton were higher and a more marked increase is evident towards the end of the period. In 1788 imports and exports approached the same level, with even a minor surplus for exports. Yet consideration of these figures necessitates a degree of discernment. Whereas the data for exports are likely quite accurate, particularly as there were few if any taxes to be paid and

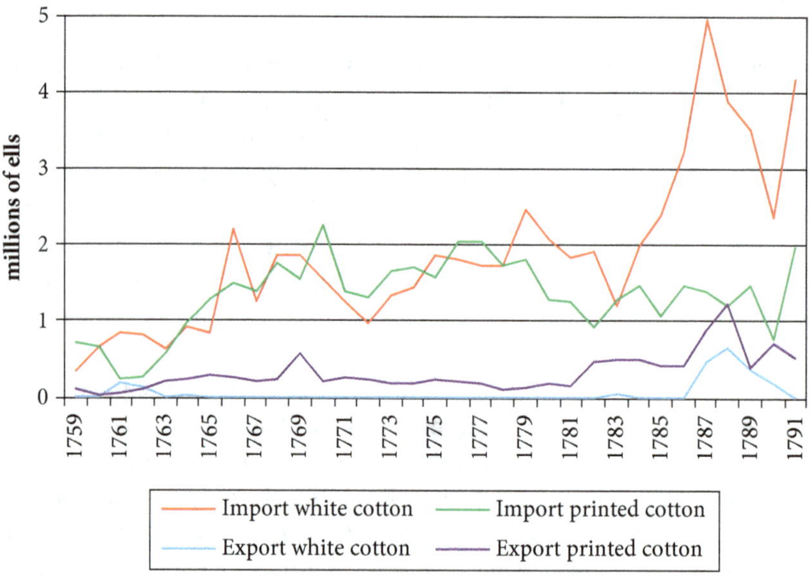

CHART 48 *Import and export of finished cotton fabrics, 1759–1791*[154]
SOURCE: RELEVÉ GÉNÉRAL, NAB, FC, 5748–5805.

154 In the customs statistics, cotton fabrics were partly listed in ells and partly in pieces. For the chart the pieces were converted into ells, so that the separate categories could be added up. In the years 1759 to 1766, white cotton was also divided into "*cotton blanche*" and "*cotton blanche pour Imprimeries.*" These were also added together in the graph. The chart thus contains the total of the categories of white cotton (both in ells and in pieces), printed cotton (ells and pieces) and white cotton for printing.

thus only marginal levels of tax evasion, the actual levels of imports were probably higher than the chart suggests, as for imports there were certainly incentives for circumventing tax obligations. However, it can be assumed that imports of printed cotton stagnated at the close of the 1770s and even declined slightly, and that imports of white cotton continued to increase. In explaining the different progressions of the two curves it is important to remember that white cotton was generally a raw material, given that the local cotton-spinning industry served primarily to supply the mixed fabrics industry. This also means that the difference between imports and exports, and thus the deficit in the trade balance, declines when the figures are converted to monetary values (Chart 49), since white cotton was cheaper than printed fabrics.[155]

Alfons Thijs has established production figures for the Dambrugge-based cotton printer Beerenbroek, who held a monopoly on the printing of cotton from 1753 to 1778. A comparison between these figures and the import figures from the customs statistics says much about the trustworthiness of the latter. Unlike the trade data, the production figures are expressed not in ells, but in pieces. Following Thijs, I have assumed that a piece measured 28 ells.[156] Chart 50 shows that, until 1777, Beerenbroek's annual output of printed cotton was nearly the same amount as what was being imported in white cotton – with just one curious anomaly, in 1766. This correspondence was of course due to the printing company holding a patent over the printing of cotton during

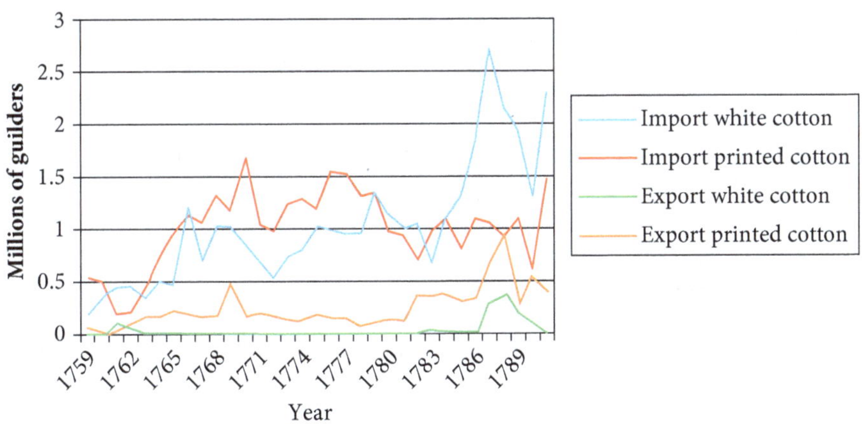

CHART 49 *Import and export of finished cotton fabrics in monetary value, 1759–1791*
SOURCE: RELEVÉ GÉNÉRAL, NAB, FC, 5748–5805.

155 White cotton cost 11 stivers per ell; printed cotton cost 15. Lis and Soly, "Restructuring."

156 Thijs, *Van "werkwinkel,"* 150.

this period, which barred anyone else from buying white cotton.[157] Thijs's figures thus underscore the reliability of the customs statistics in this case. In 1778 Beerenbroek's patent expired, allowing other entrepreneurs to freely establish printing companies. Almost immediately, the share of cotton produced at Dambrugge declined drastically as compared to white cotton imports, dropping well below the one hundred per cent it had enjoyed under the monopoly, and eventually – after some ups and downs – levelling at about 25 per cent.

In examining the production volumes of the Beerenbroek firm in comparison with the quantities of printed cotton exported, the picture becomes more problematic. The export figures from the customs statistics are quite low compared to the quantities produced in Dambrugge (even twenty times less, in 1762). Both the printing house in Dambrugge and those that were launched after 1778 apparently produced primarily for the domestic market and far less

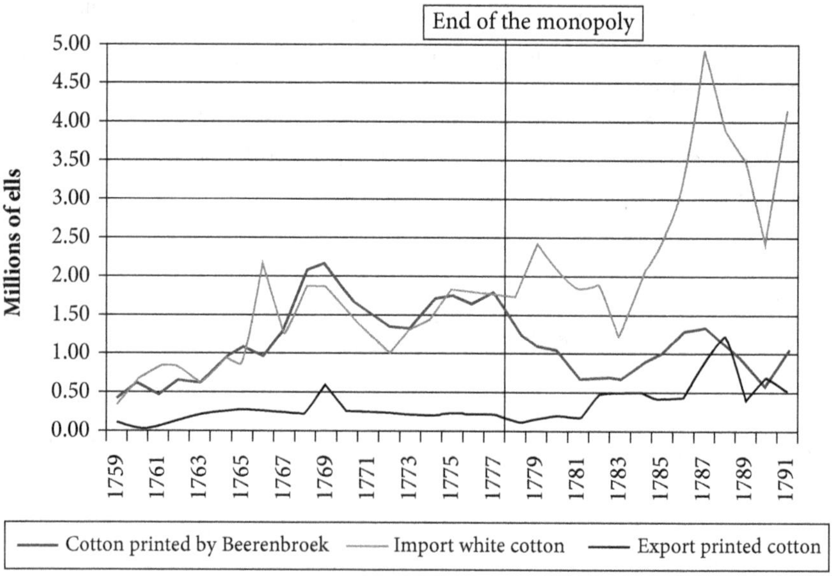

CHART 50 *Cotton production in Dambrugge compared to import and export of cotton fabrics, 1759–1791*[158]

SOURCE: RELEVÉ GÉNÉRAL, NAB, FC, 5748–5805 AND THIJS, 'SCHETS', 185.

157 The deviation is perhaps explained by the fact that violations of the patent were often turned a blind eye on (Lis and Soly, *Een Groot Bedrijf*, 31.); however, considering its size, the deviation is more likely a flaw in the source.

158 I have used the same totals as in Chart 33.

(if at all) for export. However, trade figures reveal another, even more notable evolution. The trend in Chart 48 shows that imports of printed cotton were, before expiry of the patent, on a rising course – just like demand – but from 1778 there is a slight but unmistakable decline! This implies that the vaunted import substitution policy of the Austrian Netherlands gained serious significance only after expiration of the patent that had granted Dambrugge a monopoly over the domestic market. Prior to that, the industrial policy had effectively condemned the Austrian Netherlands to remaining dependent on imports of printed cotton for much longer than necessary. The patent had perhaps helped ensure that the new sector would commence under protective conditions, but it had blocked the sector's further development. As such, it remains questionable whether the monopoly was indeed needed to encourage cotton printing in the Austrian Netherlands or if it was instead primarily the fulfilment of effective lobbying undertaken by influential figures behind the company.

Taking into account all the trade flows for cotton, the Southern Netherlands never saw the balance of the cotton trade become favourable in the eighteenth century, and the exports accounted for only a small share of the country's output. This entails that, in terms of quantities, cotton apparently was chickenfeed for the national economy. This is notable, particularly because, with international debate so often linking cotton to accelerated growth, the risk arises of losing sight of the specific structure of the early modern Belgian economy and overestimating cotton's share in it. It is therefore useful to make comparisons not only with domestic production figures but also with the respective cotton industries of neighbouring countries. For Great Britain, Javier Cuenca Esteban has estimated that cotton accounted for a high percentage of value-added in textile production: 8.6 per cent in 1770 and 25.6 per cent in 1801. Crafts and Harley assume that until 1770 the cotton sector accounted for only 2.6 per cent of industrial production in Britain, but that its share increased rapidly afterwards.[159] As noted previously, cotton accounted for an estimated 15 per cent of total British exports in 1790.[160] In the Dutch Republic the figure was only 3 to 4 per cent, which was still significantly higher than the annual average of one per cent in the Southern Netherlands.[161] Based on trade figures alone, it would appear that 'Belgian' cotton was a relatively minor player in the local

159 Broadberry, Fremdling, and Solar, "Industry," Harley and Crafts, "Cotton Textiles," 141.

160 Davis, "English Foreign Trade, 1700–1774," 302, Van der Wee, "The Western European Woollen Industries, 1500–1750," 461.

161 Smits, Horlings, and Van Zanden, *Dutch gnp*, 50.

economy of the eighteenth century. In short, the remarkable flourishing and exceptional profits that some authors have assumed for the industry are probably exaggerated for the eighteenth century, as at that time the sector still was simply too small to account for such figures.[162]

The customs statistics indeed show that processed cotton was still being imported more than it was exported (also compared to other sectors and regions); yet the differences between white and printed cotton, and certainly the specific evolution of the export industry for printed cotton, strongly suggest that manufacturers exercised some degree of control over the economic changes that were taking place. From the end of the 1770s onwards a modest degree of import substitution was occurring for printed cotton fabrics. However, it would be overreaching to claim that this fledgling industry was a huge dynamic force for the region. The various data confirms that the sector was indeed growing – especially as it was increasingly able to meet domestic demand – but that this was actually primarily due to the expanding domestic market for cotton.[163] Numerous economic historians insist that the "internal forces of growth" in the economy of the Austrian Netherlands were significantly responsible for the calming of the economic climate after 1748.[164] In the relative success story of the cotton sector, the home market indeed emerged as the driving force.

3.5 *Mixed Fabrics*

Thus far, little attention has been directed towards new fabrics that, in terms of absolute volumes, were of minor importance for international trade, but which historians suspect became immensely popular during the eighteenth century. These include new or renewed mixed fabrics, whose compositions were often disputed, since this could vary according to the preferences and technical skills of manufacturers, consumer taste, and the cost of raw materials.

As noted, cotton was initially processed only in factories that produced mixed fabrics, because the region's entrepreneurs had not yet developed the skills to manufacture pure cotton fabrics. Fabrics with cotton and other yarns had been produced since at least the 1720s, but such production did not peak until the second half of the eighteenth century.[165] Fustians had been being

162 Dhondt and Bruwier, "The Industrial Revolution," 351.

163 This does not automatically infer that domestic demand sufficed to cause further growth of the sector during the nineteenth century, but that question exceeds the scope of this volume.

164 Blondé, "Disparities," Dhondt and Bruwier, "The Industrial Revolution," Lis and Soly, "Different Paths."

165 Thijs, *Van "werkwinkel,"* 149.

woven since the sixteenth century, though the term probably did not cover the same overtone.[166] In the eighteenth century, fustians (like siamoises) usually consisted of linen and cotton. Siamoise, however, was much lighter and more modern, in contrast to fustian, which, despite changes in its composition, was a more traditional and presumably also relatively expensive product.[167] Furthermore, dimity, a twilled (partly) cotton fabric, and the sturdy fabric bombazine were also produced domestically. Nanking, a yellow cotton fabric (the name was also occasionally used to refer to calico), could not be manufactured in the Southern Netherlands; the only option was to import it from Asia, by countries where an East India Company maintained operations.[168]

The mixed fabrics industry had, by the mid-eighteenth century, already been functioning for an extended period, and so its composition and economic alignments were far more complex than those of the cotton sector.[169] The industrial census of 1764 offers a snapshot of the various companies processing cotton (crude or yarns) in mixed fabrics that year.[170] The first striking observation from this record is that cotton processing was almost entirely an urban matter, being virtually exclusive to Flanders and Brabant.[171] The companies used varying shares of crude cotton and cotton yarn to produce flannel, bombazine, siamoise, dimit and fustian.[172] These records for 1764 offer data for thirty companies, most of which employed several masters. Of these companies, twenty-two exported nothing, and eight factories were also fully independent of foreign countries for their supply of raw materials. A report from the Chamber of Commerce concerning the experiences of various Antwerp printers notes that many of them operated without benefit of exports.[173] Only nine companies were directly dependant on other countries for raw materials; the rest obtained cotton yarns from Antwerp and were only indirectly dependent on imports of raw cotton. The data concerning the production of these companies is sporadic but does reveal approximately how many people were employed in the mixed fabrics sector: according to the industrial census (which lacks numbers for some companies and likely

166 Ibid., 147.

167 Vermaut, "De Textielnijverheid," 161.

168 After the failure of the Ostend Company, the Austrian Netherlands no longer possessed such a company themselves.

169 Thijs, *Van "werkwinkel,"* 149.

170 Moureaux, *La Statistique*.

171 The two exceptions were a siamoise factory in Mons and a spinning mill in Tournay.

172 Flannel, unfortunately, was recorded in the customs statistics only until 1775.

173 NAB, FC, 4642, October 22nd 1779, Chamber of Commerce in Antwerp, commissioned by the Finance Council.

understates the general situation) there were at least 17,261 workers.[174] For a population of about two million, this is certainly not a negligible figure.[175]

The data on import and export of mixed fabrics bespeak a more complex, and notably less optimistic, scenario for the mixed fabrics industry than that of printed cotton fabrics. The trade figures are also far more revealing of the experiences of the sector than is the preceding static overview, based on the industrial census. Imports of siamoises (see Chart 51) rose sharply almost continuously throughout the period, whereas exports increased only very late, and then only quite moderately. As regards siamoises, it is clear that import substitution in the textile sector did not lead to reduced dependence on imports in absolute terms. For nanking the curve is more erratic, yet here as well one cannot speak of a success story. Imports increased, pointing to the absence of a satisfactory domestic substitute. The relative shifts underlying these absolute volumes are less clear, as little is known about the price fluctuations of the different fabrics.

The pronounced increase in imports of cotton yarns (see Chart 53), alongside the large-scale domestic production of yarns, nonetheless suggests that the local mixed fabrics industry was resilient. Moreover, crude cotton imports also rose slightly. Even though it is clear that the region was not processing enough yarn to prevent further imports of siamoises, nanking and pure cotton

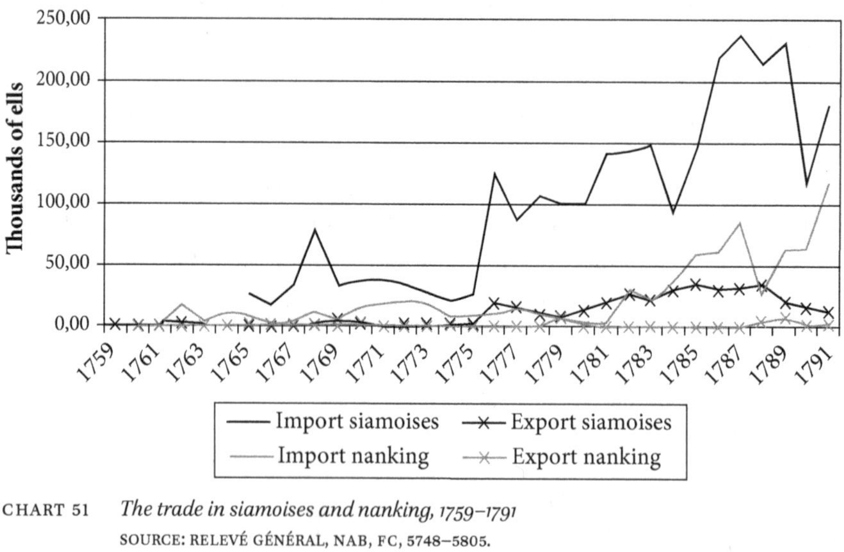

CHART 51 *The trade in siamoises and nanking, 1759–1791*
SOURCE: RELEVÉ GÉNÉRAL, NAB, FC, 5748–5805.

174 Moureaux, *Les Préoccupations*, 394.

175 There were approximately 2.272.962 inhabitants in 1784. Vandenbroeke, *Agriculture*, 380.

fabrics, foreign competition could not have been as fierce as to smother the sector. Such a scenario would have seen resource imports decrease. Estimating the number of ells that could have been produced using imported resources – as was calculated for silk – makes it evident that domestic production must have been many times larger than exports may have led one to suspect.[176] The fact that this sector continued to provide employment to many people is most likely due to flourishing domestic demand for both the imported and domestically produced mixed tissues. Furthermore, the export of semi-cotton fustian, twilled cotton dimit and bombazine all rose strongly after 1776 (see Chart 52). It is known that bombazine was exported in large numbers to Spain.[177] What caused the increase in exports of fustian and dimit after 1784, however, is unknown; and surprising since production of fustian had fallen after 1756.[178] In any case, fustian was an expensive 'old luxury', which appealed to a very different (yet seemingly rather volatile) market than did the cheaper cotton fabrics. This typically urban industry continued to produce a product of very high

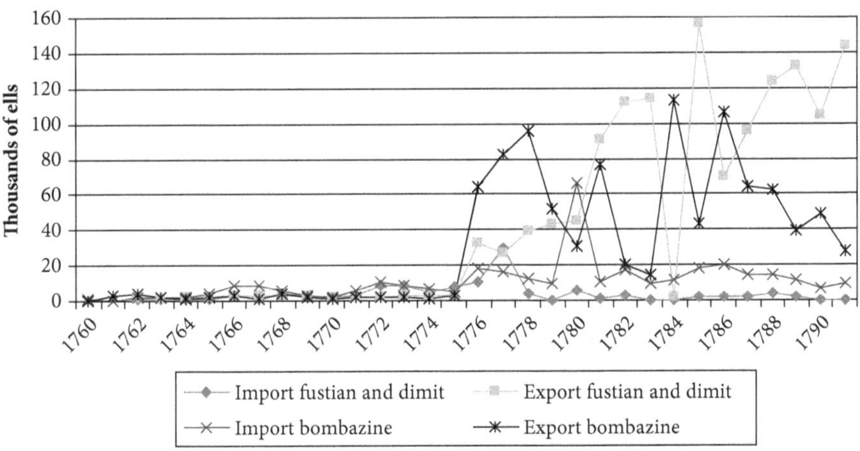

CHART 52 *The trade in fustian, dimit and bombazine, 1760–1791*
SOURCE: RELEVÉ GÉNÉRAL, NAB, FC, 5749–5805.

176 As with silk, it is difficult to estimate how many ells of fabric the imported yarn and raw material could produce. Indeed, for mixed fabrics it is even more difficult, since the share of cotton in these fabrics varied strongly. Assuming that a square ell weighed about 0.171 pounds (or 160 grams per square meter) and an average share of about 50 per cent cotton in the mixed fabrics, the number of exported ells appears to be a fraction of about two per cent (or even less) of the amount that could be made with the imported materials.

177 Moureaux, *La Statistique*, 370.

178 Lefèvre and Lefèvre, *Etude*, 130, Vermaut, "De Textielnijverheid," 161.

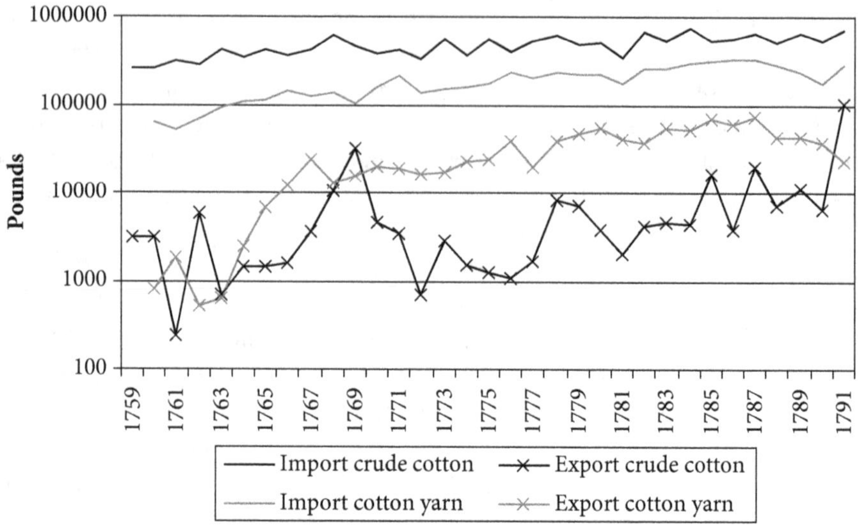

CHART 53 *The trade in crude cotton and cotton yarn, 1759–1791*
SOURCE: RELEVÉ GÉNÉRAL, NAB, FC, 5748–5805.

quality. Meanwhile, import of these three fabrics remained low, except for the peak in bombazine, in 1780.

Thus, though the trade figures hardly suggest that the mixed fabrics industry was withering, its actual production, even at peak levels, was still barely comparable to cotton fabrics. It is likely, based on the industrial census and information from secondary sources, that this assessment also applies to the total production, even though the fabrics were usually somewhat more costly.[179] This would explain why the government had done relatively little to support the mixed fabrics sector. Other than the general exemption (passed in 1749) from export duties issued on all finished fabrics and occasional granting of individual privileges to particular manufacturers of mixed fabrics, the government only once resorted to more drastic measures: namely, in 1744, when it banned imports of French siamoises.[180] That cotton and mixed fabrics were probably gradually replacing traditional woollen fabrics – for example, we saw that both imports and domestic production of serge (in Bruges) had been declining since the mid-eighteenth century – and that the sector has shown to be viable, is thus likely attributable to its own inherent economic and industrial underpinnings.

179 Price data is not available, so we must rely on descriptions from the literature that state that fustian and bombazine were rather expensive. Lis and Soly, *Een Groot Bedrijf*, 165.

180 Thijs, *Van "werkwinkel,"* 149.

4 Explaining the Shifts Within the Textile Sector

4.1 *The Habsburg Trade Policy*

Throughout the histories of the different branches of the textile industry, we have encountered various causes for particular evolutions in the industry's trade flows; these have included evolutions in fashion, increase in the supply of textiles (due to colonial trade), pressure from major stakeholders and developments in trade policy. Certainly this final factor, the so-called *visible hand* of the economy, has been brought to the fore in several ways.[181] As concerns government interference in the different sub-sectors, trade policy often seemed incoherent, inefficient and outdated. The effects it did produce only became evident long after the new policy of 1749 had been implemented. That the policy was indeed composed of countless ad hoc measures has already been signalled by several authors based on this case study.[182] In other words, before addressing the question of how to assess the influence of international trade on the textile sector, I believe it is necessary to draw up the balance for the

TABLE 7 *Policy measures*

Year	Measure	Winners	Losers	Ideological orientation
1749	Liberalising exports of finished fabrics	Textile manufacturers	-	Protectionist[183]
1750	Export ban on crude flax	Textile manufacturers	Agriculture	Protectionist
1756	Increase in the export tariff on crude wool	Textile manufacturers	Agriculture	Protectionist
1759	End of the export ban on crude flax	Agriculture	Textile manufacturers	Liberal[184]

181 The metaphor is borrowed from: Lars Magnusson, *Nation, State and the Industrial Revolution* (London: Routledge, 2009).

182 Lis and Soly, "Restructuring."

183 This measure seems rather liberal (since export is cleared from trade duties), but fits perfectly into a mercantilist point of view, since it is about finished, 'industrial' goods.

184 This is of course an anachronistic label. All measures need to be situated within a mercantilist context, but a few did appear to oppose the common protectionist rules and bestow a somewhat greater freedom on the actors involved. Hence the term 'liberal'.

TABLE 7 *Policy measures (cont.)*

Year	Measure	Winners	Losers	Ideological orientation
1762	Export ban on woollen yarn to Liège	Textile manufacturers	Agriculture and yarn producers	Protectionist
1766	Export ban on crude flax	Textile manufacturers	Agriculture	Protectionist
1766	End of the export ban on crude flax	Agriculture	Textile manufacturers	Liberal
1769	Increase in the import tariff on woollen fabrics	Textile manufacturers	(Foreign producers)	Protectionist
1778	End of the Beerenbroek monopoly	Cotton printers	Serge and baize manufacturers	(Liberal)[185]
1784	Permission to use wool tailings	Broadcloth manufacturers	Wool producers	Liberal
1786	Export ban on crude flax	Textile manufacturers	Agriculture	Protectionist
1787	Export ban on crude wool	Textile manufacturers	Agriculture	Protectionist
Passim	Individual exemptions from trade duties for textile manufacturers	Textile manufacturers	-	Liberal

SOURCE: NAB, FC, BUREAU DE LA RÉGIE DES DROITS D'ENTRÉE ET DE SORTIE, 5848, 4864, 4278, 4915, 4571, 4581, 4916, 4598 AND 4593.

trade policy regarding textiles. It is clear that policy makers swung back and forth between the wishes of resource producers, traders, and entrepreneurs throughout the period, even as they had to take into account international diplomacy. Moreover, as the trade flows for wool, flax and cotton demonstrate, exceptions to the rules were ubiquitous. Nonetheless, when we take a step back, a list of the primary measures undertaken by the government in relation to this sector (Table 7) evidences several fairly coherent lines of policy.

First, it appears that, even though most measures led to a decrease in imports, not all were strictly mercantilist in nature. In particular, one of the main goals of mercantilism – namely, obtaining a positive balance of trade – did

185 This is not really a trade measure, so the categorisation has a somewhat differing content.

not seem to be the central decisive factor for policy makers. Moreover, an area that has typically been labelled as extremely protectionist turns out, upon examination, to present somewhat more liberal tendencies as well. And though that was mostly in the form of ad hoc interventions, the latter were so numerous that in some cases (such as exemption from export bans on resources and on import duties on machinery for cotton printers) they ended up being the norm rather than the exception. Indeed, recent research has shown that while most eighteenth-century rulers did not personally subscribe the new economic theories, they were nonetheless regularly accepted in practice.[186]

Another basic principle of industrial mercantilism – that of taxing exports of manufactured goods less than exports of raw materials and lowering duties on resource imports; thereby spurring industry – díd appear to have been the guiding motive throughout the customs policy. The same overarching concern for industry was evident in the chapter on the salt trade. In the cases of both wool and flax, the government also gave the impression of being concerned primarily with the interests of the nation's industrialists and thus with preventing foreign imports. The same can be said about the privileges accorded to cotton or silk manufacturers. Presumably, the government achieved such aims at least several times, given the decreasing imports of woollen and silk fabrics. Although the government was variously influenced at different times by arguments from resource producers and lobbying from textile manufacturers (and sometimes consumers, as we have also seen with salt), the preceding overview shows that it was usually the manufacturers who were most effective and successful in determining trade regulations.[187] The frequent complaints from resource producers that increasing imports of flax and wool had been avoidable may thus have had a significant degree of truth, but the administration opted to keep resource prices as low as possible. This reinforces the speculation that eighteenth-century 'industrialists' enjoyed effective lobbying channels, through which they could persuade the state to support their positions. The numerous applications found in the archive funds support such conjecture. During this period, textile manufacturing sectors accounted for at least fifty petitions annually (totalling 1741 legible requests), in which manufacturers appealed to the empress or emperor via the Finance Council. Not all the requests were granted, but this hardly prevented entrepreneurs from returning

186 Raoul De Kerf made this finding in the sources of Antwerp silversmiths. Raoul de Kerf, *De juiste prijs in de laatmiddeleeuwse stad: een onderzoek naar middeleeuwse economische ethiek op de ambachtelijke markt en in moralistische lekenliteratuur* (Amsterdam 2010).

187 Sabbe, *De Belgische Vlasnijverheid*, 131.

with additional appeals, since eventually more than two-thirds of the requests were partially or fully adopted (Table 8).

Overall, the adopted policy thus seems to have been fairly coherent, yet this does not entail that it ultimately garnered that many benefits. In the case of

TABLE 8 *Requests per year*

			Ruling				Total
			Granted	Rejected	Unknown	Partially granted	
Year	1758	Count	1	0	0	0	1
		Percentage	100%	0%	0%	0%	100%
	1759	Count	28	4	2	4	38
		Percentage	74%	11%	5%	11%	100%
	1760	Count	16	6	2	4	28
		percentage	57%	21%	7%	14%	100%
	1761	Count	17	5	9	7	38
		Percentage	45%	13%	24%	18%	100%
	1762	Count	33	6	5	7	51
		Percentage	64.7%	11.8%	9.8%	13.7%	100.0%
	1763	Count	17	1	2	3	23
		Percentage	74%	4%	9%	13%	100%
	1764	Count	25	7	6	6	44
		Percentage	57%	16%	14%	14%	100%
	1765	Count	30	10	10	20	70
		Percentage	43%	14%	14%	29%	100%
	1766	Count	28	7	2	12	49
		Percentage	57%	14%	4%	24%	100%
	1767	Count	32	4	9	8	53
		Percentage	60%	8%	17%	15%	100%
	1768	Count	33	14	6	17	70
		Percentage	47%	20%	9%	24%	100%
	1769	Count	31	11	5	10	57
		Percentage	54%	19%	9%	18%	100%
	1770	Count	30	10	6	10	56
		Percentage	54%	18%	11%	18%	100%

		Ruling				Total
		Granted	Rejected	Unknown	Partially granted	
1771	Count	38	6	2	10	56
	Percentage	68%	11%	4%	18%	100%
1772	Count	37	9	5	8	59
	Percentage	63%	15%	8%	14%	100%
1773	Count	26	10	2	4	42
	Percentage	62%	24%	5%	10%	100%
1774	Count	32	6	2	4	44
	Percentage	73%	14%	5%	9%	100%
1775	Count	23	10	0	3	36
	Percentage	64%	28%	0%	8%	100%
1776	Count	42	9	4	5	60
	Percentage	70%	15%	7%	8%	100%
1777	Count	55	8	5	10	78
	Percentage	71%	10%	6%	13%	100%
1778	Count	40	8	2	12	62
	Percentage	65%	13%	3%	19%	100%
1779	Count	53	12	4	6	75
	Percentage	71%	16%	5%	8%	100%
1780	Count	45	15	1	19	80
	Percentage	56%	19%	1%	24%	100%
1781	Count	37	10	12	6	65
	Percentage	57%	15%	18%	9%	100%
1782	Count	22	6	6	5	39
	Percentage	56%	15%	15%	13%	100%
1783	Count	27	5	1	8	41
	Percentage	66%	12%	2%	20%	100%
1784	Count	55	12	5	15	87
	Percentage	63%	14%	6%	17%	100%
1785	Count	75	12	2	11	100
	Percentage	75%	12%	2%	11%	100%
1786	Count	52	23	11	11	97
	Percentage	54%	24%	11%	11%	100%
1787	Count	21	6	8	8	43
	Percentage	49%	14%	19%	19%	100%

TABLE 8 *Requests per year (cont.)*

			Ruling				Total
			Granted	Rejected	Unknown	Partially granted	
	1790	Count	3	1	1	0	5
		Percentage	60%	20%	20%	0%	100%
	1791	Count	55	21	5	13	94
		Percentage	59%	22%	5%	14%	100%
Total		Count	1059	274	142	266	1741
		Percentage	61%	16%	8%	15%	100%

SOURCE: NAB, FC, 4556–4559, 4567–4594, 4600–4606, 4613–4635, 4639–4643, 4688–4689, 4867–4889, 5324–5336.

the textile industries, or at least those which have been discussed here, it has been found that the government's policy did not convincingly alter the prevailing status quo. The starkest example of this was the stagnating wool sector. In other cases – such as the successful linen cloth industry – the customs measures generally seemed unnecessary. The linen trade with Spain and the Spanish Americas was already firmly rooted and would probably have remained stable even without governmental support.[188] However, because linen and tick were, according to policymakers, the largest sources of wealth for the country, government officials sought to boost these sectors even further and to assist them in coping with competition from Holland and England.[189] Furthermore, most of the linen production was exported, and an estimate of the balance of trade, based on nearly all of the most significant categories from the customs statistics, shows that linen indeed accounted for the highest (by far) portion of revenue; as such, it becomes clear that the Southern Netherlands had the most to gain from this sector having a flourishing international trade. Finally, the uniform prohibitive export policy for wool and flax had, at least in the case of flax, limited effect on the trade flows. Apparently, the policy's many exceptions and moderations largely nullified the impact of government intervention. Moreover, the fact that after 1749 any results of the more independent policy were still long in coming is an indication that even instances of successful

188 Duplessis, *Transitions*, 235, Sabbe, *De Belgische Vlasnijverheid*, 94.

189 NAB, FC, 4287, consult of August 27th 1753.

import substitution must be considered in the context of an improving domestic market.

Moreover, a complementary conclusion that emerges from the requests is that the government likely missed an invaluable opportunity due to its limited interest in innovation. Although even the so-called traditional sectors experienced crucial developments during the eighteenth-century, the government sources, in fact, hardly mention issues pertaining to innovation.[190] The single exception occurred in 1776, when the States of Flanders and the Finance Council wished to reimburse a certain Schepers for the transport of a roller for linen and cotton that he had brought from England at his own risk, and to grant him a patent. They explicitly stated that their reason is that they seek to support industrial innovations.[191] However, in all other cases the primary concern was preventing, hindering and substituting imports of finished goods. Yet it is not inconceivable that already during the eighteenth century cotton printing in particular nevertheless witnessed the introduction of an early type of factory model. Although in most cases cotton printing remained purely a handicraft, the companies themselves employed a sizable body of workers, with clear division of tasks.[192] Again, such evolutions in the different sectors were seldom encouraged by the government.

However, it should also be recognised that government policy did actually facilitate certain successes in the textile industry. Absent this policy, the increased demand for printed cotton and other light fabrics could well have triggered a surge in imports, since cheaper versions of these tissues were being imported by Britain and France. Yet such increases did not occur. And though the new trade policy had commenced in 1749, shortly after the Austrian War of Succession, and thus the improvements in terms of imports and exports came very late, the policy was by no means a total failure. In the charts at the beginning of this chapter, imports of 'raw' materials (including white cotton fabrics) increased, relatively, the most. While imports of finished fabrics diminished. For instance, the relative decline of printed cotton imports over the years was in fact a great windfall for the government. Given the difficult international geopolitical situation, the various powerful opponents of the government's

190 Much has been written on the capacity for modernisation present within these sectors, for example in the revisionist debate on guilds (for example Epstein or Lis and Soly) and of course in the literature on the proto-industry (ranging from Mendels to de Vries). de Vries and Van der Woude, *Nederland*, Epstein, "Rodney Hilton, Marxism and the Transition from Feudalism to Capitalism," Lis and Soly, "Restructuring," Mendels, *Industrialization.*

191 NAB, FC, 4558, letters, June 26th 1776 and July 6th 1776.

192 Lis and Soly, "Living," 131, Moureaux, *La Statistique*, Thijs, "Schets," 178.

trade policies (influential entrepreneurs or local governments), and the scale of the domestic market, the different successes in the domestic market were hardly unimportant.

As concerned international trade in cotton, the pursued trade policy clearly strongly impacted the sector and its development. In the wake of myriad ad hoc interventions by the government, a slight degree of import substitution was emerging; this was able to boost cotton printing, albeit only after expiration of the monopoly held by the printing mill in Dambrugge. The pragmatic mercantilist policy, augmented with numerous individual measures, thus indeed brought benefits to some. However, the latter case introduces a point that must be included with the fact that the government's trade policy never led to any fostering of export-driven growth. Even more important is that the industrial policy of the Austrian Netherlands also led to significantly negative effects, as was painfully evident in this sector. In particular, the government's granting of a monopoly impeded and delayed expansion of the cotton sector and thus of possible means for economic growth during the second half of the eighteenth century. This shows, more so than does the revised tariff policy, that cessation of the production monopoly was crucial to the launch of cotton printing after 1779. In short, this aspect of industrial policy actually hampered trade policy. The biggest victim of this delay was of course the consumer, since the combination of hindering cheap imports and monopolising the local market must have lead to artificially high prices.

This overview of the government's trade policy-related measures has shown that trade policy, despite the general reticence if not fear of implementing general measures, was in fact more thought-through than has often been assumed. Just as Hugo Soly suspected, as had Hubert Van Houtte before him, underlying the many individual decisions was a straight-forward objective.[193] Indeed, in the cases of the wool and silk industries, it may well have been precisely inadequately sector-diversified approaches that resulted in these industries missing various opportunities to generate an export industry. Moreover, the architects of the customs policy – including eminent personages like von Cobenzl, de Neny and Delplancq – had to compete with the various, and often conflicting, interests of the Treasury, of other monarchs, and of influential entrepreneurs like Jan Beerenbroek and his associates.

4.2 *Explanations Within the Sector*

The reason why trade in some products – flax, linen and tick – continued to flourish even as trade in others – wool and silk – declined, should not be sought

193 Lis and Soly, "Living," 133, Van Houtte, *Histoire*, 317–318.

primarily in the customs policy, despite its relative efficiency. The ambiguous situation of the textile sector was due mainly to other, intrinsic factors. The general decline of wool and silk is firstly attributable to the rise and success of cheap linen and semi-linen fabrics.[194] Moreover, throughout the eighteenth century, a number of new textiles were introduced to European consumers, which complemented the traditional range. Imports of calicos and nanking, among other new products, led to people increasingly favouring light and colourful fabrics, which were best made from modern materials such as cotton.[195] As noted, this expansion in supply almost immediately triggered a revolution within the textile sector of the Southern Netherlands.

Linen, unlike woollen fabrics, had little to fear from these changing fashions, as it was sold mostly in the Spanish colonies, where demand for newer fabrics was apparently less intense. Given the success of linen and the relative decline of wool and silk, the shift in domestic demand was thus likely the main explanation for general developments in the textile sector.[196] The fact that imports of the lighter woollen fabrics serge and baize collapsed upon opening of the cotton industry makes clear that cotton was likewise preferred over other light fabrics. The evolution of domestic demand was, in other words, of critical importance, and led to imported serge being replaced by locally processed cotton. Of course, we should not overlook the fact that resource imports remained rather stable, what could not have been solely attributable to the production of mixed fabrics. This infers that the traditional fabrics were also still being sold domestically, alongside the newer types.

Of course, shifting demand does not account for every evolution within the sector. Though international trade may introduce new options and greater diversity, domestic supply must still be able to adapt to the developing consumption preferences. Whereas originally it had been foreigners who imported the new fashions (generally from the colonial territories), the early modern industry of the Austrian Netherlands managed in a relatively short time to create a sufficiently high production to supply the same new fabrics. From 1778

194 Vermaut, "De Textielnijverheid," 139–141. The relatively high level of wages in the Southern Netherlands is sometimes cited as a reason for the decline of the textile industry, but here the opinions are divided. See for example: Vandenbroeke, "The Regional Economy," 165. However, wages do not seem decisive, since even in the case of a luxury product such as lace (where price was probably not decisive for consumers) foreign competition was too great.

195 Lis and Soly, *Een Groot Bedrijf*, 17 en 34.

196 Vandenbroeke, "The Regional Economy," 151. The importance of demand for the economy of the Southern Low Countries has been variously detailed in works of Herman Van der Wee and Bruno Blondé.

onwards it was possible to offer a successful domestic cotton substitute for imports. The same mechanism may have played a role in the case of broadcloth, baize, camel cloth, and silk fabrics like velvet. The home market turned out to be unexpectedly powerful in all these cases. In light of the internal shifts in the industry, even the decline of the wool trade appears to have been much less dramatic than it may have seemed at first glance.

Finally, it is possible to identify, via a somewhat indirect approach, other evidence for the strength of the internal market for textiles. The customs sources reveal a small, generally unknown but successful import substitution that occurred in the region; this is discussed in the chapter on colonial commodities. The government strongly encouraged domestic production of foreign dyestuffs (which, according to the customs archives, were primarily intended for use in colouring fabrics), especially that of precious madder.[197] Madder plants were thus exempted from import duties, but exports of crude madder were generally prohibited.[198] The sources show that domestic production of madder subsequently began gradually (re)developing, especially around Antwerp.[199] Other dyestuffs which were processed or finished in small amounts in the region included cochineal, azure blue and litmus.[200] Import levels for most dyestuffs remained stable or even increased, and so overall use of resources presumably grew markedly. This offers further evidence that textile manufacturers were enjoying a boom period. Indeed, within the sources that include requests related to trade in colonial commodities, the most represented groups of petitioners are textile printers (who were often also dyers) and dyestuff producers; their requests also garnered the highest degree of success.[201] Both facts suggest that the government regarded these industries as having high potentials.[202]

197 NAB, FC, 4505, reaction to a request by Joseph Pieters, 1759. The customs archive on dyestuffs is scattered over the numbers 4503–4537.

198 NAB, FC, 4510, Letters by the customs officials concerning *plantes de garance*, January 1st 1767; 4511, letters by the customs officials concerning the export ban for crude madder, July 14th 1768.

199 NAB, FC, 4511, the production appeared to be flourishing around Antwerp.

200 NAB, FC, 4523, a certain Guillaume Leemans from Antwerp produced azure blue, June 22nd 1780, and litmus, December 28th 1780.

201 Thijs, "Schets," 181.

202 The requests aimed at the customs bureau concerning the trade in colonial goods are in: NAB, FC, 4503–4537 and 5256–5267.

5 The Impact of Trade on Different Stakeholders

Definitive statements about the impact of international trade on the textile sector can be developed only in light of what the trade meant for its immediate stakeholders. It is known that the government was torn between various actors and their diverse (often divergent) interests and that it was impossible to forge a trade policy that would satisfy all of these parties at the same time. It was thus surely inevitable that the nation's trade scenario would see both losers and winners, collapses and successes. The sources allow for retracing a significant portion of these groups in eighteenth-century society.

It is hardly surprising that those interest groups, and even specific merchants, who held the most leverage over the authorities were most often favoured by the government. Whoever held or controlled the most resources or most impacted the economy could most effectively devote time and efforts to gaining support from policymakers. Manufacturers were especially competent in influencing trade policy to befit their interests: as Table 9 demonstrates, they were successful in more than two thirds of their applications. Pierre De Heyder, a leading fabrics producer from Lier, saw but one rejection among the 22 requests that are recorded for him.[203] Persons who were entirely dependent on commerce were often hindered by the many taxes the government imposed on the trade flows, and they received only infrequent concessions. Even famous merchants, such as the brothers Romberg and Overman, garnered only variable success with their petitions.[204] This may have been one of the reasons why traders often combined their business with a side profession such as industrial entrepreneur or investor. Such activities had also become increasingly more profitable, and the sources present numerous examples of such merchant-entrepreneurs.[205] One notably prominent name is Antoine Guislain Sergeant, who is mentioned variously as a trader and

203 The rejection was for his request for increased import duty on mixed fabrics from foreign competitors. NAB, FC, 4557, March 14th 1769.

204 The Romberg brothers and Overman appear most often in the requests (91 and 40 times respectively), on a number of 1741 (legible) cases. Moreover, the customs archive contains a series of requests exclusively by them, regarding toll duties: NAB, FC, 5536–5537, *restitution des droits de tonlieu payés par les négociants Romberg et Overman* (1775–1785).

205 Degryse, "De Antwerpse Fortuinen," 93.

manufacturer.[206] He produced, among other things, cotton yarn and siamoises, and saw to selling his goods and entering the necessary raw materials himself. He also imported woollen fabrics into the region.[207] Similarly renowned were the brothers Deloose from Ghent, who were active in several areas. Their main activity was commerce, yet they were also co-directors of several factories.[208] Less known examples include Charles Frison, Cornelius tKint, Josse Clemmen, Charles Devisser, Adrien Metdepenningen, Charles Jerome Barbieri and Paul Joseph De Pestre; the records of the requests offer many additional cases of manufacturers who were active in commerce.[209] After the brothers Romberg and Overman, and Pierre De Heyder, Devisser and Clemmen appear most often in the petitions (28 and 26 times, respectively).

Even more potentially advantageous than combining different economic activities was participating in politics oneself. It was not uncommon for merchants and entrepreneurs to hold a seat in one of the official bodies. Silk merchant Charlier belonged to the customs bureau; his colleagues Nicolas Bacon and Van Heurck sat in the Auditors' Chamber and the Finance Council, respectively. Van Heurck in particular was able to weigh-in strongly on government policy.[210] I found no trace of some-one questioning these men's objectivity, despite being commercially active themselves. It is notable, however, that requests submitted by other official institutions (such as city councils, commercial chambers, the States, etcetera) were less likely to be granted than were requests from individuals (see Table 9). This is related to the fact that institutional requests often sought far more extensive measures than did those of individual entrepreneurs (Table 10). The latter generally wished simply to improve their own positions, which made wide-sweeping or general measures unnecessary.

The various objectives of the applications submitted to the customs office were, as noted in the introduction, remarkably diverse (Table 10). These

206 As a producer in NAB, FC, 4557, 4573 and 4614, as a merchant 4571, 4575 and 5022, and explicitly as both in 4570.

207 NAB, FC, 4571, reaction by Sergeant to a decree from July 12th 1761.

208 NAB, FC, 5249, brothers Deloose co-managed a salt refinery; as traders they are mentioned throughout the different customs series and also in NAB, SSW, 1777 and 2153.

209 NAB, FC, 4572 (yarn and camel cloth factory), 4569 (kersey factory), 4623 (cotton printing mill), 4639 (cotton printing mill).

210 Memoranda written by him can be found for example in NAB, FC, 4283, *Commerce en general*; 4869, September 24th 1761; 5220, January 29th 1755; Manuscripts, 850 A.

TABLE 9 *Nature of the rulings, per professional category*

			Ruling				Total
			Granted	Rejected	Unknown	Partially granted	
Applicant	Manufacturer	Count	468	81	56	98	703
		Percentage	67%	12%	8%	14%	100%
	Merchant	Count	404	126	49	117	696
		Percentage	58%	18%	7%	17%	100%
	Merchant-manufacturer	Count	93	21	19	4	137
		Percentage	68%	15%	14%	3%	100%
	Public institution	Count	18	7	7	6	38
		Percentage	47%	18%	18%	16%	100%
	Producer (raw materials)	Count	0	2	0	0	2
		Percentage	0%	100%	0%	0%	100%
	Unknown	Count	76	37	11	41	165
		Percentage	46%	22%	7%	25%	100%
Total		Count	1059	274	142	266	1741
		Percentage	61%	16%	8%	15%	100%

SOURCE: NAB, FC, 4556–4559, 4567–4594, 4600–4606, 4613–4635, 4639–4643, 4688–4689, 4867–4889, 5324–5336.

included requests for reductions or exemptions from various trade duties, and exceptions to nearly every other government measure. For example, manufacturers and merchants were required to request permission to transport wool or flax within the country: this measure had been instituted in an effort to combat illegal exports of the commodities (as had been done with grain transports), yet ended up imposing much bureaucracy on entrepreneurs. Citizens thus frequently appealed to the government for exceptions to the customs procedures, in hopes that such exemptions would be able to advance their activities. The applications also illustrate that traders in particular often felt that government measures had been unfair or excessive: fines, confiscations and taxes were constantly being challenged by this group.

In general, traders are discussed in sparser detail in the sources than are manufacturers. The traders' arguments are rarely presented in much detail, and so it is difficult to state exactly how international trade or commerce

TABLE 10 *Content of the requests, per applicant category*

		Applicant						
		Manufacturer	Merchant	Merchant Manufacturer	Public institution	Producer	Unknown	Total
Nature of the request	Permit to transport	3	27	0	2	0	5	37
	Permit to import	17	7	2	2	0	7	35
	Permit to export	0	6	0	0	0	1	7
	Supportive measures	45	6	14	2	0	0	67
	Loan or grant	12	0	2	0	0	0	14
	Erection of a factory	37	1	11	2	0	0	51
	Continua-tion of a patent	18	1	3	0	0	0	22
	Monopoly	2	0	0	0	0	0	2
	End of monopoly	0	0	0	2	0	0	2
	Swift handling by customs	11	35	8	0	0	1	55
	Entrepot access	0	22	0	1	0	1	24
	Restitution of duties	20	147	9	5	0	34	215
	Restitution of confiscated goods	35	207	13	5	0	89	349
	Increase of import duties	11	1	2	2	0	0	16
	Increase of transit duties	0	0	0	1	0	0	1
	Increase of export duties	1	0	0	0	0	0	1
	Export ban	3	0	0	0	0	0	3

Diminution of transit duties	0	35	1	2	0	1	39
Diminution of import duties	3	12	2	1	0	0	18
Diminution of export duties	2	1	1	1	1	0	6
Exemption of transit duties	4	6	0	0	1	0	11
Exemption of import duties	11	5	5	0	0	2	23
Exemption of all duties[211]	143	2	18	2	0	0	165
Exemption of tolls	4	8	2	0	0	1	15
Exemption of export duties	1	2	1	0	0	0	4
Permit to re-import semi-processed goods	40	66	10	1	0	7	124
Diminution of duties for a single cargo	27	75	25	0	0	9	136
Flax transport	12	1	0	1	0	1	15
Wool transport	230	7	3	3	0	3	246
Unknown	12	16	5	2	0	3	38
Total	704	696	137	38	2	165	1742

SOURCE: NAB, FC, 4556–4559, 4567–4594, 4600–4606, 4613–4635, 4639–4643, 4688–4689, 4867–4889, 5324–5336.

211 Exemptions from import duties on resources and from export duties on finished goods were generally petitioned for when a textile manufactory was being erected, or shortly afterwards. Such exemptions were one of the most widespread methods to stimulate the industry.

impacted traders or whether their trade was profitable.[212] Yet there are definite indications that there were people in the Southern Netherlands who were acutely interested in pursuing international trade. Many inhabitants of the Austrian Netherlands invested much of their fortunes in the existing trading companies abroad.[213] Trade was a matter of major public and private interest, even though possible actions in this arena often faced boycotts from surrounding nations. The failure of the Ostend Company offers a classic example.[214] Merchants therefore had little choice but to participate in overseas trade via foreign enterprises. The flowering of trade in the nineteenth century certainly indicates that in the previous century there had already been keen interest in trade and that necessary capital for investing was already being collected, though it would not be deployed until much later.

The conflict between producers of raw materials and manufacturers – discussed earlier, in the sections on wool and linen – reveals yet another fault line, this one connected not to the actors as such, but to the region's geographical diversification. Indeed, international trade in textiles did not have a uniform or identical impact throughout the Southern Netherlands. This was because there were crucial differences not only between the regions of Brabant, Flanders and the Walloon departments, but also to some extent between rural and urban areas (even though proto-industrial and urban expansion almost always went hand in hand, according to Van der Wee).[215] First and foremost, the successful linen industry was found largely in the rural areas of Brabant and Flanders. The profits and benefits that this sector was able to reap via the abundant export of linen yielded little if anything for Wallonia. On the other hand, many Flemish cities such as Aalst likely benefited highly from the finishing all kinds of linen fabrics. Inhabitants of other cities (for example Antwerp) complained that they were put at a disadvantage

212 Works on traders and trading companies can fill in this gap, for example: Hilda Coppejans-Desmedt, "Handelaars en Neringdoenden: de 17de en 18de Eeuw," in *Flandria Nostra*, ed. J.L. Broeckx (Antwerp: Standaard-boekhandel, 1957), Roger De Peuter, "Note sur le Grand Commerce à Bruxelles à la Fin de l'Époque Autrichienne," in *Bruxelles au XVIIIe Siècle* (*Etudes sur le XVIIIe Siècle*), ed. R. & Hasquin Mortier, H. (1977), Houtman-De Smedt, "Charles Proli," Jan Parmentier, *Het Gezicht van de Oostendse Handelaar* (Ostend: 2004).

213 Degryse, "De Antwerpse Fortuinen," Christian Koninckx, *The First and Second Chapters of the Swedish East India Company* (*1731–1766*) (Kortrijk: Van Ghemmert publishing, 1980).

214 J. Parmentier, *Oostende & Co: het Verhaal van de Zuid-Nederlandse Oost-Indiëvaart, 1715–1735* (Ghent: 2002).

215 Hasquin, "Nijverheid," 126–127.

by the competition from the countryside.[216] However, Antwerp was probably hindered mostly by other factors – among others the monopoly held by Jan Beerenbroek and the closure of the river Scheldt. Much has been written about the experiences of Antwerp during the eighteenth century. Historians such as Bruno Blondé and Hugo Soly have demonstrated that the city's economy was quite limited in its viability. Antwerp was highly dependent on female and child labour, and the low birth rate indicates that few people lived in conditions stable enough for them to start a family.[217] Yet what about cities elsewhere, such as Ghent, Ostend or even Charleroi? Ghent, as is known, was faring far better than Antwerp.[218] Likewise, Ostend also experienced a relative bloom, thanks in large part to the administration's efforts to transform its port into an attractive juncture for international trade.[219] Unfortunately, little is known for other cities during the second half of the eighteenth century, but since government policy primarily sought to protect the burgeoning urban industries and thus focused mainly on cities and on the previously mentioned shift to cotton and mixed fabrics, I would argue that this inevitably must have had positive effects on urban economies. In Wallonia, on the other hand, the wool sector still employed the largest number of people within the textile sector, and as demand for that product decreased the region had to rely more and more on other income sources, such as steel and coal production.[220]

6 Conclusion

This chapter has confirmed that the textiles available to eighteenth-century consumers in the Austrian Netherlands, as in other Western European regions, still ranged from the traditional to the highly innovative.[221] Most of these

216 Frans Smekens, "Schets van Aard en Beteekenis der Antwerpsche Nijverheid onder het Oostenrijksch Bewind," in *Baekelmans Ter Eere* (1945), 96, Vermoesen, *Markttoegang*.

217 Inge Bertels, Bert De Munck, and Herman (eds.) Van Goethem, *Antwerpen. Biografie van een Stad* (Antwerp: Meulenhoff/Manteau, 2010), 30–31.

218 Degryse, "De Antwerpse Fortuinen," 52.

219 Michael W. Serruys, "The Austrian Netherlands' Transit Policy and the Port of Ostend: Solving the Crisis of the 'Closure of the Scheldt'," in *Crisis and Transition: Maritime Sectors in the North Sea Region 1790–1940*, ed. Lars U. Scholl and David M. Williams, *Deutsche Maritime Studien* (Bremen: 2008).

220 I have found only one example of a factory of "*cotonettes*" and siamoises in the Walloon area. Moureaux, *La Statistique*, 555.

221 Giorgio Riello and Prasannan Parthasarathi, *The Spinning World. A Global History of Cotton Textiles, 1200–1850* (Oxford: Oxford University Press, 2009).

textiles were products of the dynamic domestic textile industry, which, in the eighteenth century, remained the country's most important manufacturing sector. The domestic textile industry continued to hold this standing, despite the deficiency of the Habsburg industrial policy (with its many monopolies) and the fact that it had lost its position as a leading export sector, owing to some of its products no longer being sought after abroad. Other goods emerged from the extensive international supply, not only from Europe but also from the colonies. And it was this international trade and the lure of exotic fabrics (and also, though this exceeds the scope of this chapter, growing wealth amongst ever larger segments of society) that triggered a marked shift in taste.[222] Local demand was thus unmistakably influenced by the introduction of these new types of textiles. At the same time, large-scale economic transformations were occurring, such as the rise of the linen proto-industry and the relative decline of the broadcloth and lace sectors, whose developments can be traced locally over many decades. Yet, though international trade thus undoubtedly vitalised certain textile sectors, and trade in textiles produced various benefits for the Southern Netherlands as a whole (including customs revenue, high profits for some merchants and general diversification of supply for the consumers), many other traders and manufacturers doubtlessly weathered acute difficulties throughout this period.

Nonetheless, the final conclusion concerning the impact of international trade on the textile sector hardly casts the sector in a grim light. This chapter has introduced evidence that international competition exerted more than just negative pressure on the region. Indeed, linen, the major winner in the field of exports, was also the main industrial product. In this sense, international trade contributed to the prosperity of a distinctly important sector. Absent linen, total exports may well have gone the way of certain old-fashioned woollen and silk fabrics. Moreover, the import of textiles had beneficial effects as well, particularly as it led to diversification and a shift in consumption patterns, thereby prompting import substitution. The second half of the eighteenth century was thus not a period of decay, but rather a time of strong internal reorganisation within the sector. Textile producers were able to adapt to new fashions and to offer a substitute product, and thus some were able to weather the surge in international competition.

However, it would be too broad a claim to assert, based solely on this data, that international trade was the driving force behind the economic developments discussed here. To be sure, international trade did pose an exogenous incentive to activate the market. As noted, it spurred diversification and a shift

222 de Vries, *The Industrious Revolution.*

in consumption patterns, and this led to import substitution. As such, although the trade balance remained negative, the government's main objective – achieving import substitution – was likely accomplished, albeit not always in the first place thanks to governmental efforts. (Indeed, such successes were sometimes even realized *despite* government policy, which was a policy of many missed opportunities.) Local demand was thus unmistakably influenced through introduction of these new types of textiles, which triggered a marked shift in taste.[223] Still, for the whole of the textile sector, and especially for the more industrial sectors, such as cotton and mixed fabrics, the main driver behind the changes appears to have been the high demand on the domestic market. International trade alone could not lead to innovation or industrialization, but a strong internal market could, via the process of import substitution. The textile producers were able to adapt to the new fashions and to offer domestic substitutes for out-of-fashion fabrics (such as broadcloth) in the forms of lighter mixed fabrics and newly fashionable cottons. Some fabrics, such as woollen cloth, lost importance (and their leading position on international markets), whereas others, such as cotton and mixed fabrics containing wool, linen and cotton, were able to contribute dynamically to the process of economic modernization.[224] The main driver behind the events over the whole of the textile sector appears to have been demand from the domestic market. Not only for the modern mixed industries, but also for small-scale, high-quality types of production, which held a dynamic of their own.[225] This is a highly significant feature for an internal market to achieve and it implies enormous growth in domestic demand.

The conventional question as to whether exogenous or endogenous factors are more relevant to economic development is in this case not particularly relevant. Both factors were – in the eighteenth century just as much as today – profoundly entwined. Of course, the remarkable resilience of the home market cannot be attributed to the meagre profits generated from international trade (as might be argued for Great Britain, for example), yet we should not dismiss the incentive, presented by trade, to activate this market. Also, we should not overlook several contingent factors that also played a part. Such factors

223 Ibid.

224 De Peuter, *Brussel*, 234, Thijs, "Aspecten," Van Der Wee and Houtman-De Smedt, *De Wereldeconomie*, 81.

225 Lis and Soly, "Restructuring," Herman Van Der Wee, "De Industriële Ontwikkeling in de Nederlanden tijdens de 17de-18de Eeuw. Enkele Kritische Bemerkingen naar Aanleiding van het Debat over de Proto-Industrie en Poging tot Aanvulling van het Synthese-Model," *Academiae Analecta* 46, no. 4 (1984), Vandenbroeke, "The Regional Economy."

included not only wars (the four years of war between England, the Dutch Republic and France pose a striking example), but also failed harvests, epizootics or transport difficulties, all of which disrupted trade flows. Finally, in discussing economic development, it should be noted that even though trade in some goods flourished that this does not necessarily imply significant qualitative impact on economic development. The case of linen offers a case in point: the massive export of linen hardly impacted the large majority of those involved in the industry; as the sector's success derived primarily from the industry maintaining very low wages (and hence low prices). Few individuals were able to reap the fruits of the sector's voluminous sales and the sector would perish dramatically during the nineteenth century.[226] Finally, even in the case of cotton, the windfall profits that some authors have claimed for the sector are likely exaggerated for the eighteenth century, as the sector was then not especially large (the value of the cotton trade was several times smaller than that of common linen).[227] Nonetheless, during the second half of the eighteenth century the Austrian Netherlands generally contended and adapted quite effectively to the pressures and stresses caused by changing consumer preferences. And fabrics such as cotton and mixed fabrics may have dynamically contributed to the process of economic modernization here as well. These developments were a remarkable achievement for what was in fact a rather passive economic agent.

226 Aerts, "De Zuidnederlandse Textielindustrie C. 1600–C. 1850," 21.

227 Dhondt and Bruwier, "The Industrial Revolution," 351.

CHAPTER 8

The Trade in Colonial Commodities

Introducing the Exotic

This chapter is dedicated to those goods which, for most people, come immediately to mind when discussing international trade in the eighteenth century; particularly as such goods play the leading role in international literature on the subject. Exotic commodities such as spices, coffee and tea, cocoa and richly coloured dyestuffs, originating from areas that had only recently been drawn into the European trade network, have always been popular subjects for scholarly attentions. These products had been imported in small quantities since the early seventeenth century, but soon thereafter had to satisfy the widespread desires of the masses. It is not surprising that, almost from the start, historians have wondered how this overseas trade influenced mother countries like Spain, France and Great Britain (and other areas involved in the so-called triangular trade). However, for a region like the Southern Netherlands it was always a far less expedient research topic, although even here colonial commodities play on the minds of researchers.[1] Within the aim of this volume, these goods are vital to include, particularly because they represent a case of commerce that rarely offered any viable domestic substitutes and because consumer demand for colonial products supposedly increased dramatically during the eighteenth century.[2]

It has regularly been argued that colonial trade was the main branch of commerce in the eighteenth century, even for the Austrian Netherlands. However, this assumed standing is likely primarily due to the prestige attached to colonial trade, since the most profitable segments of such trade were owned by foreign companies.[3] Nonetheless, some of the indirect yet positive effects of the trade in colonial goods merit examination. Colonial goods may have functioned as substitutes for traditional foods and raw materials and thereby helped to mitigate ecological constraints posed by traditional agriculture. Moreover, these same commodities created new consumption needs and thus encouraged both individual merchants to increase their revenues and at the

1 J.G. Everaert, "Handel in de Zuidelijke Nederlanden 1650–1795," in *Algemene Geschiedenis der Nederlanden* (1977), 194, Van Houtte, *Histoire*, 291–300, Vandenbroeke, *Agriculture*, 566–585.

2 Anne McCants, "Poor Consumers as Global Consumers: The Diffusion of Tea and Coffee Drinking in the Eighteenth Century," *Economic History Review* 61, no. supplement (2008): 177.

3 Coppejans-Desmedt, "Economische Opbloei," 273.

 | DOI 10.1163/9789004272606_010

same time local industries that offered stand-ins for the imported products. Also, the inhabitants of the Austrian Netherlands did seek to directly control their colonial trade flows in a number of ways. Much has been said about the various failed attempts to establish overseas trade companies here (such as the Ostend Company in the first half of the century, the Company of Trieste (1775–1785) or activities of the Prussian company of Emden), yet it was hardly the case that nobody from the Southern Netherlands was active in colonial commerce.[4] Contraband was, presumably, a common and widespread means by which people participated in colonial trade. Even after abolition of the Ostend Company there remained 'Belgian' factories in colonial regions, despite the trade having been forbidden by neighbouring countries.[5] Another option still open to the Southern Netherlands was financial involvement in foreign trading companies. There are indications that sufficient capital and interest in pursuing colonial trade existed in the Austrian Netherlands, and many local inhabitants indeed invested much of their fortunes in foreign trading companies. By necessity, major entrepreneurial capitals emerged in, among other places, Prussia, Denmark and Sweden.[6] Still, since the Southern Netherlands could not risk overt direct involvement in East Indian or other colonial trades (owing to possible retributions from its neighbouring countries) merchants from the regions – faced with growing needs and demands – had to acquire the bulk of these exotic consumer goods via other European trading partners.

For these other countries the central research question usually concerned whether asymmetrical trade relations between different parts of the world would be profitable for the West. For an area with almost no direct trade with the colonies, the question was entirely different. Why did colonial trade expand in a region where political barriers were certainly not diminishing, unlike in Britain, for example?[7] Did the administration of the Austrian Netherlands endeavour to stop or at least restrict the increasing imports of colonial goods? Did supply indeed grow and prices drop, as they did elsewhere? And what were the consequences of all this for what was in fact a rather passive receiver? The arrival of new commodities onto the European market – including cane sugar from the Caribbean and the Spanish and French Americas, coffee from the

4 References are found in: Houtman-De Smedt, "Charles Proli," 137.

5 In particular Great Britain and the Dutch Republic. Coppejans-Desmedt, "Economische Opbloei," 273, Houtman-De Smedt, "Charles Proli," 136. NAB, FC, 4381, *Compagnie impériale des Indes, 1739–1768*, questions from widow Merat about the payments to her son who is working on a trading post, also many documents on the importance of setting up a trading company for the Austrian Netherlands (s.n., s.d.) 1764.

6 Koninckx, *The First and Second Chapters of the Swedish East India Company (1731–1766)*, 195–197, Michielsen, "Het Kapitalisme," 254, 256.

7 O'Rourke and Williamson, "After Columbus."

Levant, Java from the Americas, tea from China – spurred more wide-ranging effects than simply making certain merchants rich, but what were the specific effects for a region like the Austrian Netherlands? Unlike with cotton (which was of course also a colonial commodity), the goods surveyed in this chapter do not appear to have offered many opportunities for industrial innovation or added value via development of import substitution industries. The commodities examined here (principally coffee, tea, sugar, dyestuffs and cocoa) each had their own particularities, yet all were largely intended for direct human consumption (with the notable exception of dyestuffs). However, as will be seen, their particular influence in the Austrian Netherlands extended beyond what would have been predicted by the old-fashioned mercantilist approach, namely a mere increase in expenses or a deterioration in the balance of trade.

1 The Irresistible Lure of Exotic Produce

The considerable expansion of trade in certain global goods and related changes in consumption patterns are two of the many intriguing facets in the history of the second half of the eighteenth century.[8] These types of developments are also fundamental to the field of commodity chain analysis, which investigates the entire lifecycle of a product. Academic literature often labels colonial goods as having been non-competing goods, as before their arrival there had been no similar goods available. However, as will be seen, such exclusivity was not always the case. Colonial goods did replace certain other products, and manufacturers did occasionally produce import substitutes. Yet the inescapable reality was that colonial goods were new, exotic and difficult to substitute, and so they inevitably triggered various changes. Consequently, it is hardly surprising that, despite the Austrian Netherlands not having any great degree of direct involvement in colonial trade, many people were keenly interested in taking part in it. The central question, however, is whether value could be added after such goods had entered the country's borders.

The component segment of these new goods within total imports was already immense midway through the eighteenth century. For the sample of goods for which I have calculated the value of the balance of trade, my estimations suggest that up to 45 per cent of the value of imports came (via neighbouring countries) from areas in Asia, the Americas and even Africa (Chart 54). A sizable part

8 Berg, "In Pursuit," Clunas, "Modernity," Engerman and O'Brien, "The Industrial Revolution," Kenneth Pomeranz, *The Great Divergence: China, Europe and the Making of the Modern World Economy* (Princeton: 2000), J. Walvin, *Fruits of Empire: Exotic Produce and British Taste, 1660–1800* (Basingtoke: 1997).

of this (ten to twenty per cent) consisted of textile fibres and fabrics, which usually underwent further processing in domestic industries. The remaining portion was generally food and beverages (mainly coffee, tea and sugar). Surprisingly however, the share of colonial goods within imports did not increase markedly. This share was relatively high in the years 1778–1782, but no linear trend is evident, especially when textiles are omitted (Chart 55). In absolute value the imports of colonial goods increased, yet not as quickly as did imports in general (Chart 56). The share of colonial goods within international trade was thus unmistakably large, though it was not the fastest increasing sector. There were, however, certain commodities whose import levels indeed rose immensely, as will be seen.

Contrary to what conventional historiographical discourse surrounding this type of commodities would suggest, colonial trade was probably not especially profitable for most, save perhaps the importing merchants. For the Austrian Netherlands this is fairly obvious, since such goods, once having been imported, were rarely re-exported; excluding printed cotton, re-exported goods accounted for no more than one or two per cent of total exports. However, this also holds true for the main European trading countries. Even for Britain, the profits from colonial trade (again excluding re-exports of cotton) before the nineteenth century accounted for no more than one per cent of GNP, according to Patrick O'Brien.[9]

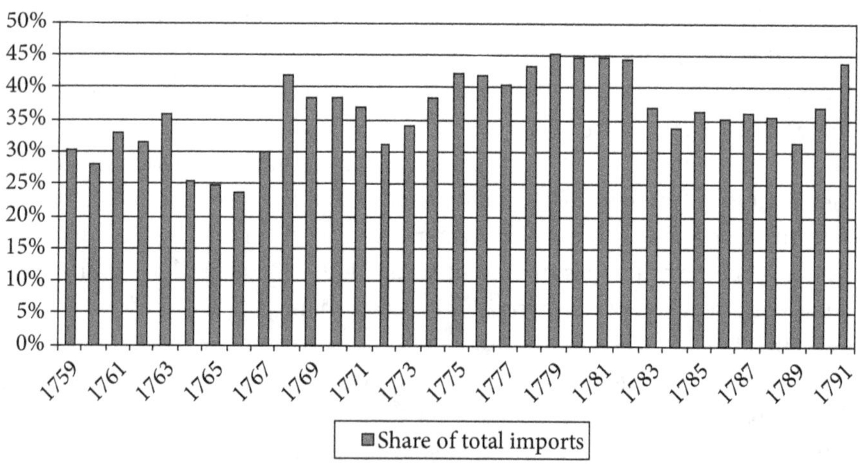

CHART 54 *Share of colonial goods in total import value (with cotton and silk)*[10]
SOURCE: RÉLÉVÉ GENERAL, NAB, FC, 5748–5805.[11]

9 Cited in: McCants, "Poor Consumers," 173.

10 The goods included are: rice, candy sugar, cinnamon, cloves, nutmeg, saffron, pepper, indigo, cochineal, gallnuts, madder, chocolate, tea, coffee, white powdered sugar, white cotton, printed cotton, siamoises and crude silk. Crude silk was not entirely a colonial commodity, as much of it was from Italy. Unfortunately, it is not known how large this amount was.

11 For the list of sources on the prices, see Appendix A.2.

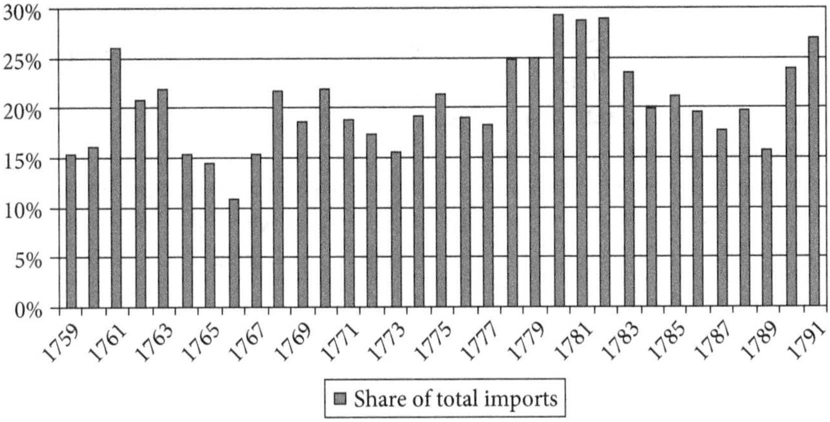

CHART 55 *Share of colonial goods in import value (excluding cotton and silk)*[12]
SOURCE: RÉLÉVÉ GENERAL, NAB, FC, 5748–5805.

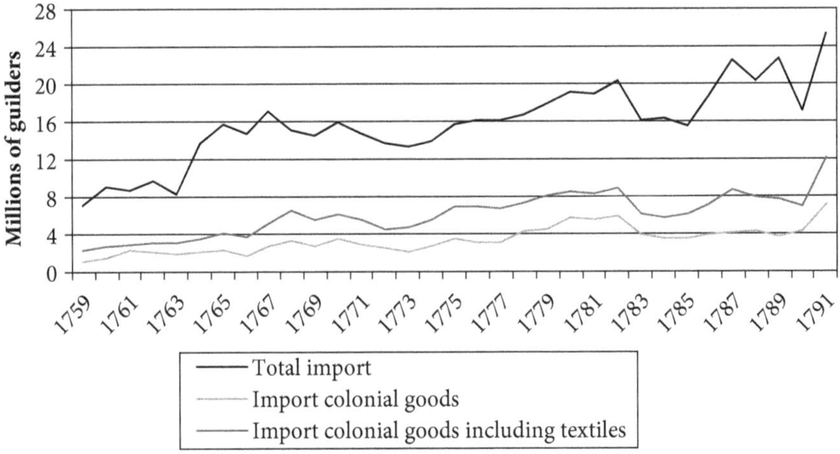

CHART 56 *Imports in monetary value, 1759–1791*
SOURCE: RÉLÉVÉ GENERAL, NAB, FC, 5748–5805.

Yet, as will be seen traders and manufacturers still endeavoured to benefit from the high demand for and gradually increasing popularity of the new commodities.

Important to note is that the Austrian Netherlands also maintained highly significant, albeit indirect, exports to the colonies, as noted in the chapter on textiles. Linen cloth from the region remained the main exported commodity

12 The goods included are: rice, candy sugar, cinnamon, cloves, nutmeg, saffron, pepper, indigo, cochineal, gallnuts, madder, chocolate, tea, coffee and white powdered sugar.

of the time and was generally exported via Spain to the Iberian colonies. This traffic is often overlooked, since the Austrian Netherlands did not possess colonies of their own. Linen generally garnered low prices, however, and so its exports were not extremely profitable; nonetheless, the huge volumes of this trade should not be overlooked.

Cotton and silk have been discussed extensively in previous chapters, so what are the other goods to be examined here and where did they originate? Sugar is the most documented good among colonial foodstuffs and constituted the largest volume among traded colonial wares. It was probably the most important colonial commodity (at least among foodstuffs), particularly because it had countless applications and facilitated development of a new branch of manufacturing: namely, sugar refining. This explains why the archives include a separate series of documents for sugar, while sources on coffee, tea, spices, drugs and even dyestuffs are all mixed together. Sugar was also an important complement to coffee and tea, whose consumptions rose correspondingly. As one government memorandum noted, "Rock candy sugar is much consumed, in relation to the use of tea, which seems to have become necessary."[13] The customs statistics distinguish four kinds of sugar: sugarloaves and rock candy (large sugar crystals) were intended for immediate consumption; so-called powdered sugar (white or brown) needed further refining.[14] Brown powdered sugar required a high degree of further processing and will thus sometimes be referred to as crude sugar (since no actual crude sugar – known as molasses – was imported) and white sugar will be referred to as semi-refined. According to Corluy most crude and semi-refined sugar consumed in the Southern Netherlands originated from English colonies in the West Indies; the sugar refineries in Antwerp, however, apparently employed trading companies from France, Holland and only to a minor extent England, to obtain sugar from locations throughout all of the West Indies.[15] Dusart, a refiner from Mons, for example imported his resources from Nantes,

13 "Le sucre candys est d'une grande consomption, par rapport à l'usage du thé qui paroit être devenu nécessaire." NAB, FC, 5256, June 16th 1734: "memoire sur le sucre candys".

14 Vandenbroeke, *Agriculture*, 572. A sugarloaf (a pressed, cone-shaped piece of sugar) was the form in which refined sugar was produced and sold until the late 19th century, when granulated and cube sugars were introduced. "The Useful Arts and Manufactures of Great Britain" (London 1846).

15 Corluy, "Een Metodologische Poging," 97, Helma Houtman-De Smedt, "Korte Historische Schets van de Suikerraffinaderij" Cels, Aerts en Compagnie "(1760–1806) en van haar Latere Evolutie (1806–1951)," *Bijdragen tot de Geschiedenis* LXIII (1980): 299, Houtman-De Smedt, "Charles Proli," 118–119.

France.[16] Nonetheless, for Great Britain the second half of the eighteenth century still was "the zenith of sugar's imperial role," and it was not until the following century that British sugar producers would lose ground.[17] Finally, the industrial records of 1764 note a sugar refinery in Ghent that imported crude sugar from "*l'Inde par Ostende*".[18] The records do not identify the refinery's intermediary (or if there was one). This may offer a minor example of direct colonial trade with India, but it is unlikely. Besides importing crude or partly refined sugar, the Southern Low Countries also imported the finished sorts of sugar, albeit in much smaller quantities. It is known that France and Holland manufactured and exported finished candy sugar at the time.[19] According to some sources, Dutch candy sugar was highly coveted in the region, thanks to its outstanding quality as compared to sugar from Antwerp.[20]

Information about other colonial commodities remains scanty. Cochineal and indigo (two types of dyestuff used for textile – principally cotton – dyeing) originated from the Spanish and Portuguese colonies, and were thus traded mostly by Spain.[21] Some dye houses stated that their pigments were from Holland, France and even the Southern Netherlands themselves: Antwerp, to be precise.[22] And though Moureaux believed that many colonial products entered this region from France, most trade records in fact usually highlight the importance of the two great competitors of the age: namely, the Dutch Republic and Great Britain.[23] Coffee was indeed supplied by France, as well as by these aforementioned empires, though the latter two clearly took the lead as concerned tea, spices and other dyestuffs.[24] For cocoa the "*Dictionnaire de Commerce*" stated again that Holland was its neighbour's biggest supplier.[25]

The products that increased most in terms of import volume and value – and thus those products for which demand appeared to explode, since import

16 Moureaux, *La Statistique*, 562.

17 Mintz, *Sweetness*, 156.

18 "From the Indies through Ostend". Moureaux, *La Statistique*, 325.

19 Immanuel Wallerstein, *Mercantilism and the Consolidation of the European World-Economy, 1600–1750*, 3 vols., vol. II, *The Modern World-System* (New York: Academic Press, 1980), 102.

20 NAB, FC, 5256, June 16th 1734, *Memoire sur le sucre candys*, s.n.; 5265, memorandum on the quality and price of candy sugar, October 1st 1791.

21 Corluy, "Een Metodologische Poging," 51.

22 Holland is recorded in: Moureaux, *La Statistique*, 135, 142, 343, 364, 1175. Indigo from France and cochineal from Antwerp in: Moureaux, *La Statistique*, 632.

23 Moureaux, "Le Commerce."

24 Corluy, "Een Metodologische Poging," 95, 101, 102, 120.

25 NAB, FC, 8580, Dictionnaire de commerce, composed by Delplancq, 1776.

is a reliable proxy for consumption of non-domestically produced goods – were powdered ('crude') sugar, coffee, cocoa and cocoa husks (Charts 57 to 59). (The husks were used in preparation of a type of spicy beverage.[26]) Even in terms of monetary value (Chart 60) these imports rose consistently; the prices

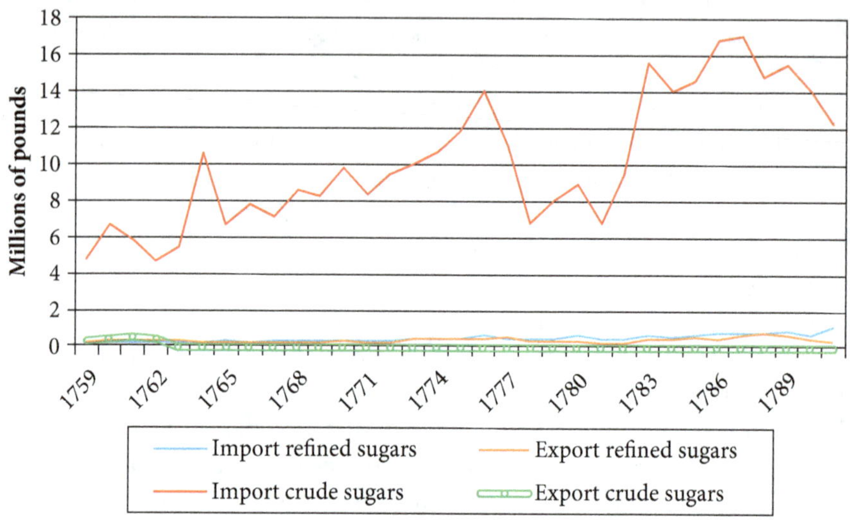

CHART 57 *The sugar trade, 1759–1791*
SOURCE: RELEVÉ GÉNÉRAL, NAB, FC, 5748–5805.

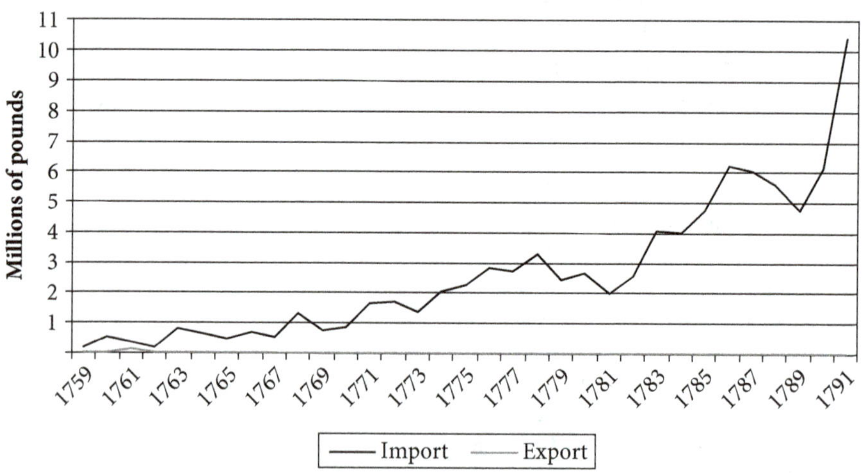

CHART 58 *The coffee trade, 1759–1791*
SOURCE: RELEVÉ GÉNÉRAL, NAB, FC, 5748–5805.

26 Vandenbroeke, *Agriculture*, 568.

do not appear to have shown any steeply declining trends as they had elsewhere throughout Europe at the beginning of the century and later during the nineteenth century (Chart 67).[27] Yet, despite increasing demand, prices also did not rise, probably because supply was easily able to stay abreast. The increasing demand for coffee and cocoa is easily explainable by the fact that the taste for each was very particular. As soon as consumers had enjoyed a nip they needed to buy them again to acquire the same taste sensation.[28] It is thus not surprising that "Since [...] coffee is in fashion we notice that consumption increases every day in Flanders."[29] Sugar emerged in tandem with these newly discovered pleasures and also triggered much innovation in cooking. Coffee consumption (along with that of tea, chocolate and sugar) percolated through all layers of Western European society rather rapidly. This is substantiated by the inclusion of certain coffee-related household goods in probate inventories.[30] Unfortunately, the Southern Netherlands's trade in coffee grinders does

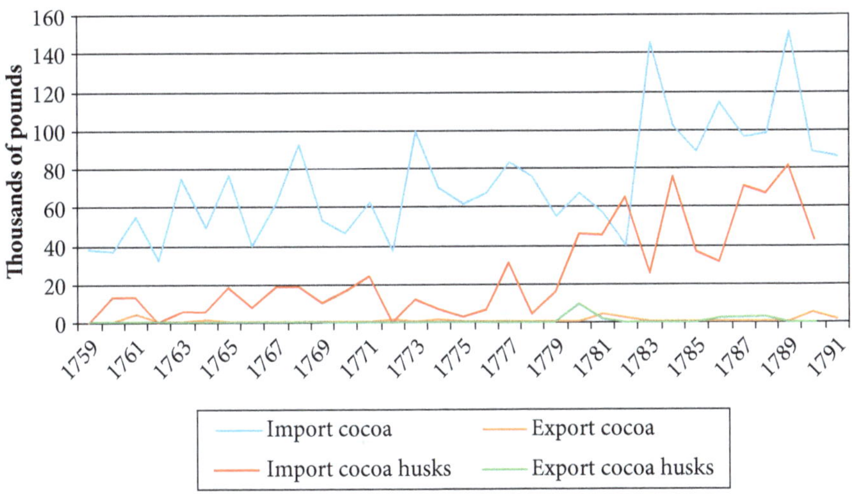

CHART 59 *The cocoa trade, 1759–1791*
SOURCE: RÉLÉVÉ GENERAL, NAB, FC, 5748–5805.

27 Prices were found in: McCants, "Poor Consumers," 174, 177, Posthumus, *Nederlandsche Prijsgeschiedenis*, 58,182.

28 McCants, "Poor Consumers," 198–199.

29 "depuis que [...] le caffé est la mode on remarque que dans la province de Flandre la consommation augmente tous les jours." NAB, FC, 4503, Mémoire concis concernant la consommation du thé et du caffé, 1741, s.n.

30 Bruno Blondé and Hilde Greefs, "Werk aan de Winkel. De Antwerpse Meerseniers: Aspecten van de Kleinhandel en het Verbruik in de 17de en 18de Eeuw," *Bijdragen tot de*

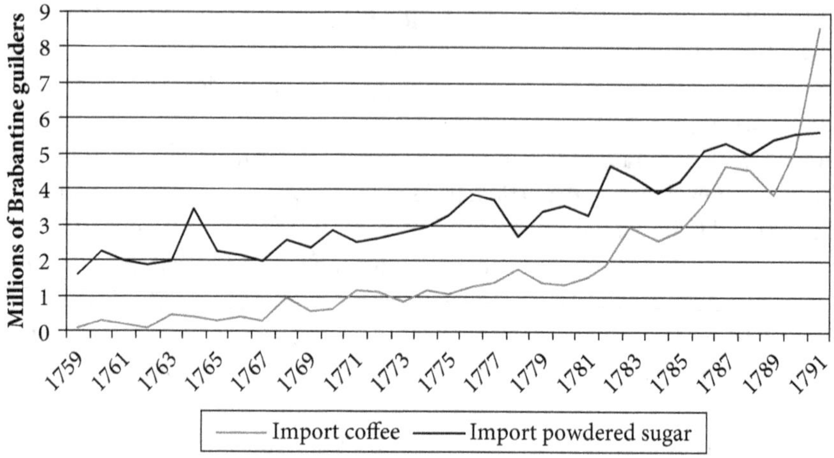

CHART 60 *The coffee and sugar trade, in monetary value*[31]
SOURCE: RÉLÉVÉ GENERAL, NAB, FC, 5748–5805, N.W. POSTHUMUS, NEDERLANDSCHE PRIJSGESCHIEDENIS, P. 58 AND 182.[32]

CHART 61 *The trade in coffee grinders, 1759–1791*
SOURCE: RÉLÉVÉ GENERAL, NAB, FC, 5748–5805.

Geschiedenis 84 (2001): 216–218, McCants, "Poor Consumers," 187, Wouter Ryckbosch, *A Consumer Revolution under Strain? Consumption, Wealth and Status in Eighteenth-Century Aalst (Southern Netherlands)*, *Dissertation* (Antwerp: 2012), Ilja Van Damme, "Antwerpse Klanten en Kleinhandelaars tussen Continuïteit en Vernieuwing, ca. 1648–ca. 1748" (Universiteit Antwerpen, 2006), 382, Vermoesen, *Markttoegang*, 319–326.

31 The figures for sugar are overstated, as I have used prices for white powdered sugar – which was more expensive – for both kinds of semi-refined sugars.

32 Posthumus's prices were converted into Brabantine guilders (1.1 times Amsterdam guilder).

not evidence any equally rising trends (Chart 61). We cannot draw conclusions from this, however, for coffee grinders were also manufactured domestically, and so imports would not have represented the entire supply. Besides coffee grinders the customs statistics also do not mention utensils or tableware linked to any specific colonial commodity, other than sugar moulds and millstones for sugar refining in the year 1761.

Interestingly, the trade in other colonial goods did not appear to advance markedly: tea imports, in fact, even declined slightly (Chart 62); indigo

CHART 62 *The tea trade, 1759–1791*

SOURCE: RÉLÉVÉ GENERAL, NAB, FC, 5748–5805.

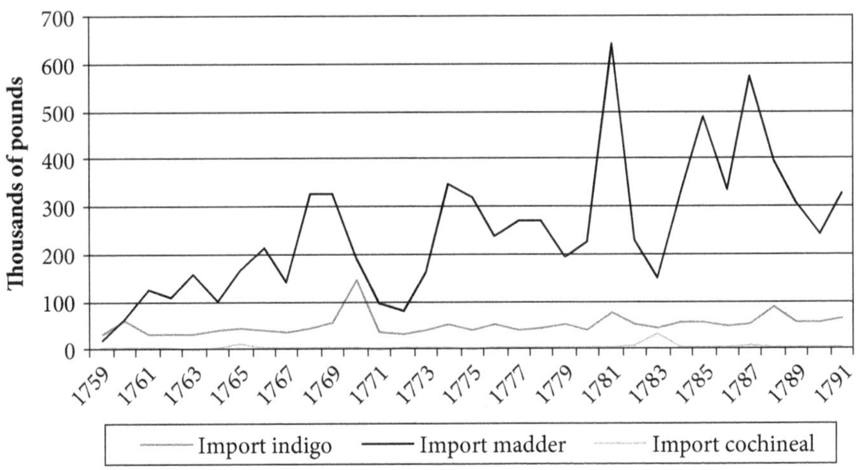

CHART 63 *The import of dyestuffs, 1759–1791*

SOURCE: RÉLÉVÉ GENERAL, NAB, FC, 5748–5805.

progressed slowly but fairly consistently; madder and, to a smaller extent, cochineal showed high degrees of volatility (Chart 63), as did rice; and spices generally oscillated at around the same level (Chart 64). In each of these cases, the images of remarkable growth do not hold. Unfortunately, the sources do not span a period of adequate duration that would allow for pinpointing whether an increase had already occurred or would follow later. Tea, for example, had likely already experienced its great leap at the beginning of the century, and so while imports had indeed stopped rising they nonetheless remained quite high.[33] During the first half of the eighteenth century tea had already been shipped to Ostend in immense amounts by the Ostend Company (1722–1731), but the company's abolition may have cost the product some of its popularity.[34] The available data suggest that during this thirty-year period coffee was surpassing tea in the region, unlike in Great Britain, for example, where tea remained preponderant.[35]

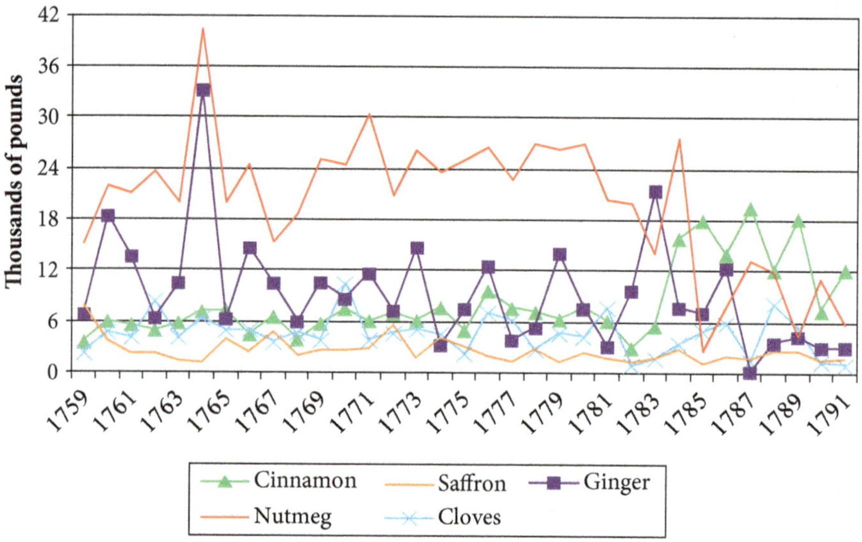

CHART 64 *The import of spices, 1759–1791*[36]
SOURCE: RÉLÉVÉ GENERAL, NAB, FC, 5748–5805.

33 Blondé and Greefs, "Werk," 219.

34 Parmentier, *Oostende*.

35 Mintz, *Sweetness*, 108, Raymond Van Uytven, *Geschiedenis van de Dorst. Twintig Eeuwen Drinken in de Lage Landen* (Leuven: Davidsfonds, 2007), 147.

36 Notwithstanding modest imports, the sources on import tariffs for spices suggest that these were not especially high and therefore did not act as a deterrent. NAB, FC, 4506, communication by De Beelen, April 20th 1761, states that some believe that spices were free of import duties; 4532, decree by the FC, March 31st 1787, s.n., import tariff on cinnamon is 3 pennies per pound.

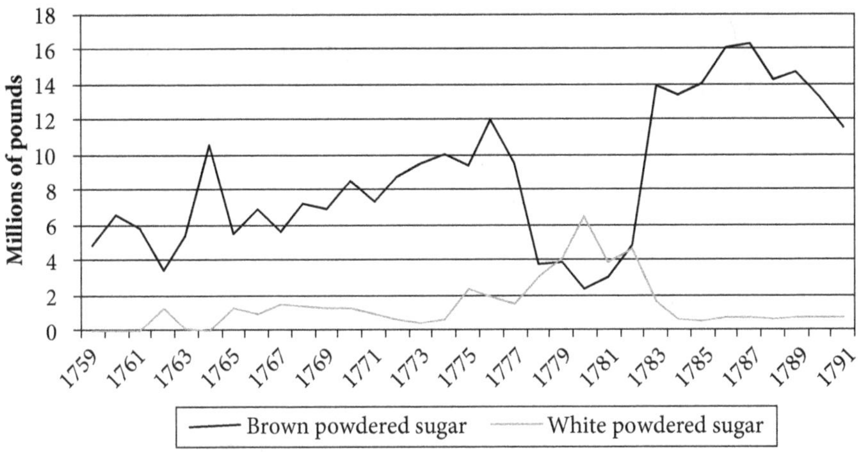

CHART 65 *Imports of semi-refined sugar, 1759–1791*
SOURCE: RÉLÉVÉ GENERAL, NAB, FC, 5748–5805.

The tea and spice trade in the region do not evidence any true revolution in consumption, though it had cleared the way for consumption of exotic products, but coffee and sugar do so *a fortiori.*

2 Incorporating the New

Colonial imports clearly constituted a major share of overall imports and were generally increasing, albeit not always as steeply as expected. Thus, it is not surprising that many people endeavoured to reap maximal benefits from this trade, not in the least by trafficking the popular commodities as contraband. As discussed in the chapter on the salt trade, the high demand for foreign supply often led traders to resort to illegal methods. Tea and coffee in particular were often imported fraudulently, despite the government's efforts to counter the illicit trade.[37] Some customs officials even advised lowering import tariffs, but the *bureau de la régie* preferred reinforcing the economic trade barriers.[38]

37 NAB, FC, 4508, memorandum by de Cazier, Cobenzl and De Keerle, March 11th 1765: there is significant fraud of tea and coffee in the departments of Turnhout and Antwerp, therefore the number of offices through which they may enter is limited; 4509: various letters regarding fraud; 4518: letter to the bureau of Chimay, August 5th 1775, de Müller writes that coffee is often smuggled in small quantities; 4532, letter to the *brigadiers ambulans* of Namur, February 24th 1787 on armed coffee smuggle, signed by Weiss.

38 NAB, FC, 4520, memoir on coffee smuggle in Charleroi, by Didier, December 15th 1777; 4522, memoir on coffee smuggle in Luxemburg, November 29th 1779, Paradis and Delplancq believe it is best to lower the local import tariffs for coffee, but not for tea.

At the end of the century there were apparent signs of improvement, with councillor Vandevelde sending a letter to all customs offices to inquire whether the rumours about fraud diminishing were true.[39] Unfortunately, such hopes were quelled by a subsequent memorandum warning of large gangs of traffickers on the route from Nivelles to Liège.[40] Sugar was also subject to contraband, from at least 1733 to 1794.[41] This did not always happen on a large scale, but even small offences met with strong repercussions.[42]

However, the arrival of new exotic goods entailed a number of far more profound consequences than just increased smuggling. Instead of simply purchasing and consuming goods provided by countries more active in importing colonial products, the Austrian Netherlands soon found ways to incorporate (or 'internalize') some of the products into the domestic economy. Besides the highly significant shifts in everyday consumption patterns, there were other, albeit less far-reaching, impacts on the early modern industry. As will be seen, colonial trades led to various concrete changes that were generally quite beneficial, even giving rise to a few profitable economic developments, including new branches of industry and retail.[43]

A well-known example of such industrial development in the Southern Low Countries is sugar refining. It is commonly held that sugar refining flourished in the eighteenth century, and this development is substantiated in the sources. As seen in Chart 57, refined sugar comprised only a small share of total sugar imports. Moreover, crude or semi-refined sugar imports were clearly rising, and there was even a moderate increase in refined-sugar exports.[44] Also, among the semi-refined sugars the major share was that of brown powdered

39 NAB, FC, 4533, letter by Vandevelde, March 28th 1791.

40 NAB, FC, 4534, *Memoire concernant la fraude de caffé dans le Hainaut*, s.n. (later than June 4th 1791).

41 NAB, FC, 5256, letter by sugar refiner F. De Wael concerning fraudulent imports of refined sugar, August 22nd 1733; 5260, communication to the city of Antwerp regarding candy sugar smuggling, October 8th 1760; 5267, cases of contraband, 1793–1794.

42 5260, a request by Hendrickx (October 13th 1756) contained false statements and this clearly shocked the customs bureau: "nous avons l'honneur de dire que nous sommes surpris de voir que le dit Hendrickx ose si impunement en imposer à un corps aussi respectable que celuy de vos seigneuries illustrissimes ou il scait que lé vérité doit être le fondement des représentations." ("We have the honour of saying that we are surprised to see that this Hendrickx dares to impose himself with such impunity on a body so respectable as that of your illustrious lordships while he knows that the truth must be the basis of representations.")

43 For the latter, see also: Blondé and Greefs, "Werk."

44 The rise in exports had already been noticed by: Degryse, "De Antwerpse Fortuinen," 112.

sugar, the least refined of the two types (Chart 65). There is a peculiar exception during the years 1779–1782, when white powdered sugar suddenly surpassed brown sugar. This may have stemmed from the four year's war, which significantly impacted many trade flows, albeit usually resulting in heightened rather than diminished commercial and industrial activity. In any case the data prove that a prosperous and expanding sugar refining sector must have been present. And, indeed, while Antwerp had a long tradition in sugar refining, an industry which was recovering after the hardships of the early eighteenth century, new refineries were now appearing in such places as Brussels, Ypres and Ghent.[45] Ghent, in particular, saw local sugar refining become an important industry.[46] The emergence of numerous new refineries during the second half of the century resulted not only from the fact that the sugar refining industry was doing well (thanks especially to rising demand for sugar); the costs of establishing such factories were fairly modest, and so opening a sugar refining business posed relatively low risks.[47]

A central reason why the Southern Netherlands were able to benefit from their inhabitants' desire for sugar was likely the support the sector received

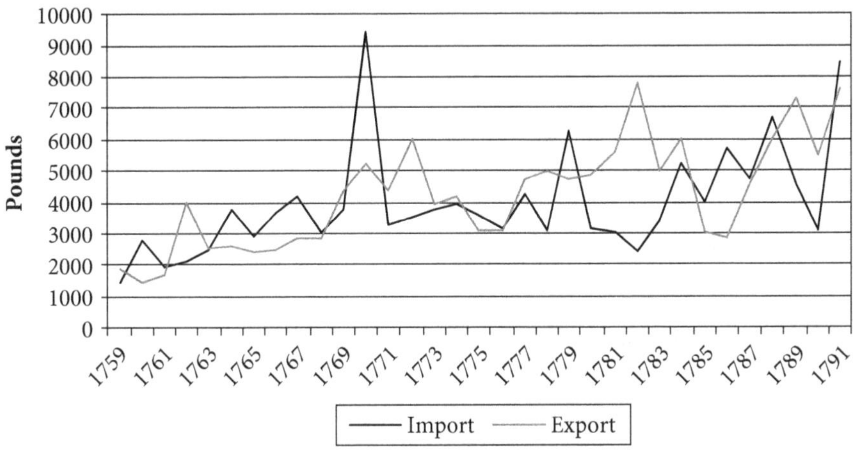

CHART 66 *The chocolate trade, 1759–1791*
SOURCE: RÉLÉVÉ GENERAL, NAB, 5748–5805.

45 Lebrun et al., *Essai*, 81, Moureaux, *La Statistique*, 69–70, 267, 407, Alfons K.L. Thijs, "De Geschiedenis van de Suikernijverheid te Antwerpen (16de-19de Eeuw): een Terreinverkenning," *Bijdragen tot de Geschiedenis* LXII (1979), Vandenbroeke, *Agriculture*, 573.

46 Coppejans-Desmedt, *Bijdrage*, 188, Van Moorhem, "Sociaal Economisch Survey," 53.

47 Coppejans-Desmedt, *Bijdrage*, 189, Duplessis, *Transitions*, 236, Israel, *The Dutch Republic*, 1089, Van Moorhem, "Sociaal Economisch Survey," 37.

from the government. The administration, as always, approved several individual tariff exemptions to support certain manufacturers, and in the case of sugar, there was also a much more general tariff policy.[48] The earliest tariff books record that import rights on sugar were significantly higher than export rights. In 1756 the government went even further, fully liberating exports of sugar that had been refined in its provinces, on condition that these exports' provenance had been officially determined.[49] Furthermore, the import rights were differentiated based on the extent to which the imported product had been processed abroad. Fully refined sugar (in loaves or candy) was extremely costly to import, with duties amounting to, respectively, eight and a half and four and a half guilders per hundred pounds (close to ten per cent of their value).[50] In the same spirit, the rights on brown powdered sugar were slightly less than those on white powdered sugar.[51] As an extra stimulus for entrepreneurs, sugar refiners could obtain additional discount on the tariffs if they could prove that their imports were intended as a resource for their factories and that the sugar had not been refined elsewhere in Europe.[52] The customs administration also apparently turned a blind eye to certain customs offences not detrimental to the government. For example, the Habsburg administration was aware that three Bruges-based sugar refineries were exporting sugar

48 NAB, FC, 5258, deed for the refinery of Denis Ryckaert and Antoine Joseph Latteur in Brussels, September 10th 1749, granting them 'the same privileges and exemptions as the Antwerp refineries'; 5260, Pierre Joseph De Quesne receives an exemption for exporting sugar from the Basteyns refinery, March 6th 1760; 5262, Exemption for Albert Goddyn, September 16th 1765 and for Jacques de Kersmaecker, March 20th 1766.

49 NAB, FC, 5260, communication to all customs offices, March 20th 1756: signed by Baron De Lador; 5606, tariff book, handwritten note "Dispositions de 20 mars 1756, 6 novembre 1760 et 15 juin 1761, sucre raffinée de ces pays libre de sortie, tonlieu et de convoy"; 5264, Memorandum and letters by Van Heurck proving that he was among the fiercest advocates of free sugar exports.

50 NAB, FC, 5606: In 1670 and 1680 "sucre candis et en pain le cent pesant 8 [guilders]- 10 [stivers] entrée," handwritten remark: "Regulative du 27 janvier 1749, sucre en pain le cent pesant 4-12-0 entrée".

51

NAB, FC, 5606	entrée	sortie
sucre en poudre blanc	1-10-0	0-15-0
sucre en poudre brun	1-4-0	0-15-0

52 NAB, FC, 5606, handwritten remark: «*Ordonnance de 26 juin 1762: Sucre en poudre blancs ou bruns qui entreront pour le compte des raffineurs de ces pays pour l'usage de leurs raffineries ne payeront, parmi quelques formalités, 6 sols*»; 5262, The ordinance of March 2nd 1765 had hightened import tariffs on powdered sugar (that had been partially refined in Europe) to 2 guilders, 8 stivers per hundred pounds, but the 6 stivers for manufacturers is preserved; 5263, copy of the ordinance of March 2nd 1765.

fraudulently (due to high import duties levied by France) but did not take action.[53] Certainly in the case of sugar the government appeared to be fully cognizant of the importance of substituting the sugar imports with domestic sugar. The sector indeed seems to have managed to satisfy almost all domestic demand for sugar, particularly as crude sugar imports were many times higher than were imports of refined sugar.

The sources also reveal a second, generally unknown import substitution triumph that occurred in the region. As noted in the chapter on textiles, there appears to have been gradual development of a renewed domestic madder production. Madder, the base material for production of a red-coloured pigment, had already been produced much earlier in the region but had declined drastically during the seventeenth century, possibly because of the recurring political tensions in the region. In the second half of the eighteenth century the government again strongly encouraged domestic production of foreign dyestuffs, having realised "That madder was one of the most precious commodities and a trade branch which alone has so long supported Zeeland and caused it to blossom, consequently deserving (…) to be encouraged."[54] The government thus exempted madder plants from import duties and partially barred exports of crude madder.[55] The sources suggest that the renewed madder production was indeed successful, especially around Antwerp.[56] Among others, Joseph Pieters – who appears to have pursued nearly every possibly profitable line of business – submitted a request for building a drying oven for madder.[57] In consequence of these developments, exports of madder increased. Other dyestuffs that were processed or finished in small amounts in the region included cochineal, azure blue and litmus.[58] Most dyestuffs were exempted from import duties, excluding finished litmus and azure blue.[59] In general, this successful domestic production explains why imports of most exotic colours

53 Moureaux, *La Statistique*, 366–367.

54 "que la garance est une des denrées la plus précieuse et une branche de commerce qui seule a si longtemps soutenu et fait fleurir la Zeelande qui mérite par conséquence […] d'être favoriser." NAB, FC, 4505, reaction on a request by Joseph Pieters, 1759, s.d.

55 NAB, FC, 4510, Letters by the customs officials on 'plantes de garance', January 1st 1767; 4511, letters by the customs officials on the export ban for crude madder, July 14th 1768.

56 NAB, FC, 4511: the production appeared to be flourishing around Antwerp.

57 NAB, FC, 4514, request, November 1st 1771.

58 NAB, FC, 4523: a certain Guillaume Leemans from Antwerp produces azure blue, June 22nd 1780, and litmus, December 28th 1780.

59 NAB, FC, 4509, litmus is not free from import duties, communication by de Beelen, March 5th 1766; 4524, half-processed azure is free of duties, but finished sorts were not, communication to the bureau of Bruges, April 9th 1781.

were rather stable (excepting madder, whose imports were still increasing (see Chart 63)) even as imports of white cotton, the other resource for textile printers, were rising sharply.

That domestic production of dyestuffs was persistently encouraged and consequently flourished, alongside stable or increasing import flows of both dyestuffs and unfinished cotton fabrics, is further proof that yet another manufacturing sector was faring quite well. As the chapters on cotton and mixed fabrics have suggested, textile printers were indeed flourishing. As noted, all dyestuffs save litmus (and in 1781 also finished azure) had been exempted from import duties in 1766, so as to support their importation.[60] Curiously, even after this general exemption textile dyers and printers continued sending requests to the Finance Council seeking exemption of import duties. These were granted in all 52 cases requesting tariff exemptions (save for two cases, whose rulings are unknown), but it is odd that the practice remained so common and appeared to have even been mandatory.[61] Perhaps the procedure was used as a means of leverage to ensure the printers' loyalty and monitor the sector. Of all applicants within the series on colonial commodities, textile dyers were the best represented manufacturers, followed closely by dyestuff producers (Table 11). As these were the two groups who most often saw their demands granted, it is likely that the government regarded their respective industries as having the highest potentials.

An interesting remark in the context of these new branches is the possibility that textile printers, for example, were able to escape the traditional guild structures from the age more easily than most manufacturers simply because many of their techniques were new. The sources on dyestuffs include a deed for a certain Pierre Antoine Desfontaines from Tournai stating that "He can work as a textile dyer without being subject to any guild."[62] This would have been quite a liberal disposition in 1760, years before Joseph II's more overt campaign against the craft guilds.

Another originally colonial commodity long associated with the Belgian area, even becoming one of its prime gastronomic specialties, is, of course, chocolate. It thus merits examining whether production of this delicacy also dates back to the second half of the eighteenth century. Were chocolate production and sales already ascendant in the Austrian Netherlands? Although the commodity had already been available in Europe for some time, it should

60 NAB, FC, 5606 and 8874, tariff books, "teintureries" handwritten remark on March 5th 1766.

61 The exception is in NAB, FC, 4505, request by André Fisquet, June 16th 1760.

62 "il pourra exercer sa profession de teinturier sans etre assujeti à aucun corps de métier." NAB, FC, 4505, December 22nd 1760.

TABLE 11 *Occupation of the applicants*

			Ruling				Total
			Approved	Partially approved	Rejected	Unknown	
Occupation of applicant	Dyestuff producer	Count	46	4	3	4	57
		% within applicant	80.7%	7.0%	5.3%	7.0%	100.0%
	Manufacturer (non-specified)	Count	5	0	2	1	8
		% within applicant	62.5%	0.0%	25.0%	12.5%	100.0%
	Merchant	Count	267	53	48	20	388
		% within applicant	68.8%	13.7%	12.4%	5.2%	100.0%
	Public institution	Count	1	0	0	1	2
		% within applicant	50.0%	0.0%	0.0%	50.0%	100.0%
	Sugar refiner	Count	13	2	6	0	21
		% within applicant	61.9%	9.5%	28.6%	0.0%	100.0%
	Textile printer	Count	55	0	3	8	66
		% within applicant	83.3%	0.0%	4.5%	12.1%	100.0%
	Unknown	Count	4	1	0	1	6
		% within applicant	66.7%	16.7%	0.0%	16.7%	100.0%
Total		Count	391	60	62	35	548
		% within applicant	71.4%	10.9%	11.3%	6.4%	100.0%

SOURCE: NAB, FC, 4504–4534 AND 5260–5265.

be remembered that the history of chocolate differed markedly from that of the mass consumption goods coffee and tea. Chocolate, which was usually consumed as a thick liquid, would remain a luxury item until around 1900.[63] But even given these circumstances there was a noticeable albeit irregular

63 Blondé and Greefs, "Werk," 218–219, Mintz, *Sweetness*, 111,114, Van Uytven, *Geschiedenis*, 131.

increase in cocoa imports (Chart 59) and even a slight increase in the exports of finished chocolate (Chart 66). This suggests that domestic chocolate manufacturing was growing to some extent, although most of the cocoa was still prepared as a beverage. Unfortunately, the customs sources reveal little about chocolate production and mention only a few cocoa merchants. The industrial records of 1764 note only one chocolate factory, in Herve. This site supposedly produced about 600 pounds that year, but other than this there are no further details about the factory.[64] Though there were surely other chocolate producers (or producers who prepared small amounts of it, as a side-line to other activities) the scarcity of data is not particularly odd, especially as the traded volumes of cocoa, and certainly of chocolate, remained fairly small as compared to other commodities noted in this chapter. Cocoa was thus a far less influential branch of manufacturing than were the previously discussed branches.

The success of various new products also benefited the eighteenth-century retail sector. Changes in this sector reflected the trends discussed so far, including the rising demand for coffee, sugar and chocolate. As discussed in the previous chapter, the numbers of shops selling new textiles containing cotton fibres were increasing; other authors have attested that grocers were also adding other new commodities to their assortments.[65] Hot beverages such as coffee and tea became especially important for the retail business. There is particularly strong evidence for this development for the city of Antwerp – where, in

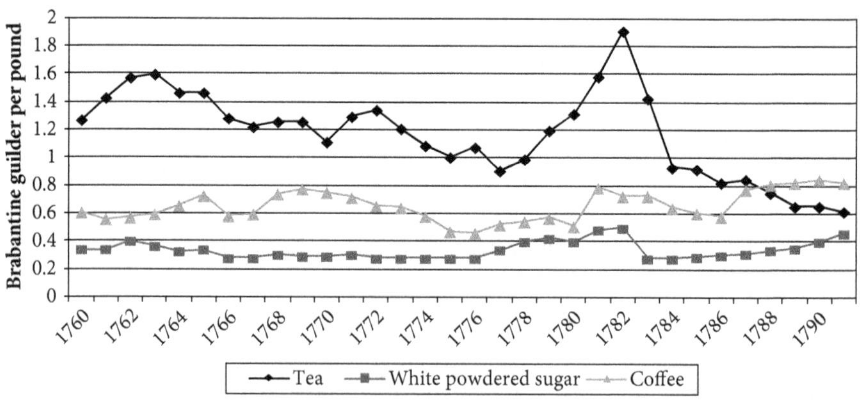

CHART 67 *Prices of coffee, tea and powdered sugar, 1760–1791*
SOURE: N.W. POSTHUMUS, NEDERLANDSCHE PRIJSGESCHIEDENIS, P. 58, 182 AND 190.

64 Moureaux, *La Statistique*, 1151.

65 Van Aert and Van Den Heuvel, "Sekse," 11, Van Damme, "Antwerpse Klanten," 383.

1792, at least 76 shops were selling coffee, tea and sometimes chocolate – and for Maastricht, but similar evolutions were taking place throughout the rest of Western Europe as well.[66] This would have entailed that another group was also enjoying the success of colonial commodities: namely, the wholesalers. Although the sources from the *bureau de la régie* do not offer a complete list of all eighteenth-century traders in the Austrian Netherlands, they show that importing colonial commodities was undertaken by a diverse group of merchants.[67] Among the 388 requests from traders, 152 names appear only once; 36 appear twice. Most of these names are not familiar from other historical sources, and so it is likely that the merchants owned small businesses. A few of the merchants are recognizable, however, since they were also active in other sectors, often as manufacturers or industrial financiers. Examples include Pierre De Heyder, the widow de Nettine, Jan Beerenbroek and Charles Devisser, each of whom appeared to have occasionally traded in coffee, tea or sugar. Among the merchants who petitioned several times, we find various well-known traders, including Nicolas Bacon, the infamous Joseph Pieters, and Antwerpeners Basteyns and Aerts. The most active trading company in this sector again appeared to be that of the brothers Romberg, whose seventeen requests were all accepted, save one.[68] The products most often traded by the petitioners were coffee (129 of the 388 cases) and tea (109), and combinations thereof (26 requests). Sugar and dyestuffs are also mentioned (respectively, 30 and 34 times), but cocoa, exotic drugs and spices are rarely noted. This is reflected by the small amounts recorded in the customs statistics for these products.

In the long term few of the colonial products would see actual domestic substitutes, examples of which are difficult to identify for the eighteenth century. The first known reference to chicory in the sources dates from 1792.[69] Around this time the administration had begun to realise that the vegetable might offer a suitable replacement for coffee, though it was not until the

---

66 Blondé and Greefs, "Werk," 226, A. Schuurman, J. de Vries, and A. Van der Woude, *Aards Geluk. De Nederlanders en hun Spullen van 1550 tot 1850* (Amsterdam: 1997), Erwin Steegen, *Kleinhandel en Stedelijke Ontwikkeling: het Kramersambacht te Maastricht in de Vroegmoderne Tijd* (Hilversum: 2006), 267.

67 The Finance Council archives include a list of Ghent traders, but this appears to be an exception. NAB, FC, 4283: list of the important merchants by the principal official of Ghent, October 20th 1771.

68 The ruling in the case of this exception is unknown: NAB, FC, 4519, request on the restitution of duties on madder, May 20th 1776.

69 NAB, FC, 4535, memorandum from 1792 mentioning chicory, s.d.

French period that it would be introduced to a wider public.[70] Other than chicory, it was usually the case that colonial commodities replaced other foodstuffs, rather than vice versa. Indeed, in 1741 the administration voiced concern that coffee and tea would ruin the sales of beer.[71] Beer consumption had diminished due to coffee and tea imports, but, except in the early years of the second half of the eighteenth century, this did not appear to have been a major concern, save for the fact that the tax on beer consumption, which was yielding increasingly less revenue, needed to be replaced by other income sources.[72]

For this investigation, however, it is more relevant and interesting to know how much added value the above-mentioned emergent sectors actually represented within the country's economy. While we lack some specific data on this topic, in most cases the potential for creating added value probably remained quite limited. In the end, colonial imports certainly did not appear to pose any significant threat to the Austrian Netherlands' economy, primarily because imports were not increasing more rapidly than were general imports, and various import substitutions were indeed occurring. Colonial goods were, in many cases, redirected for use in other industries, in particular sugar refining and cotton printing, so the Austrian Netherlands were clearly more than passive receivers of popular new goods. Moreover, the region even benefited directly from the existence of colonial markets by selling domestically produced linens that were intended to be shipped to the colonies. But in the end, for this region, colonial trade remained fairly minor, and thus this trade as such cannot be regarded as having been an engine for economic growth. It is possible, however, that the region sought to benefit from the ever-growing trade flows through the transit of colonial commodities, but this is a topic for the following chapter.

Thus far we have examined an extensive range of aspects regarding colonial trade. It certainly represented a huge share of the incoming trade flows during the period, even though this share was increasing relatively slowly. A possible central reason why not all colonial goods were able to penetrate the market as had coffee, was overly high prices. However, this factor is contradicted by the price data from the Amsterdam stock market, one of the important origins of colonial commodities for the Southern Netherlands. This data shows that the price of coffee was somewhat higher at the end of this 33-years period, while

70 Eric Vanhaute, "'Eens Gedronken, Steeds Geschonken'. Over Suikerij en Peekoffie als Surrogaat voor Exotische Drank," in *Orbis in Orbem. Liber Amicorum John Everaert*, ed. Jan Parmentier and Sander Spanoghe (Ghent: Academia Press, 2001).

71 NAB, FC, 4503, *Mémoire concis concernant la consommation du thé et du caffé*, 1741, s.n.

72 Van Uytven, *Geschiedenis*, 172, Vandenbroeke, *Agriculture*, 568.

the price for sugar – a product for which demand was also increasing – remained more or less the same; also, the price of tea was generally decreasing, save for a peak during the period when the Dutch Republic was at war with other large European states. Thus, there is apparently no clear coherence between shifts in prices and in demand.

3 Market Capacity or Smart Policy?

The government's position within the previously noted evolutions has thus far only been discussed sporadically. However, as in other sectors, the rulers played a highly active role via the development and implementation of the country's international trade policy. The question of how an administration still influenced by mercantilist thinking reacted to ever-rising imports of finished consumption goods (coffee, in the first place) is quite interesting. We have seen that the government certainly did not adopt an idle or aloof position in respect to the various incorporation processes mentioned earlier. However, not all of the colonial goods were from the outset recorded in the tariff books. Coffee and tea were initially not included, as they were hardly known around 1670–1680. The Barrier Treaty of 1699 mentions coffee and tea, but stipulates that the Southern Netherlands could not tax them for more than five per cent of their value, since the products afforded highly lucrative trade for the commercial superpowers of the time.[73] The same was probably true for many other colonial commodities. As noted, fiscal gains became possible only after 1749. Since 1751 entry rights on coffee and tea amounted to around ten per cent of their value.[74] However, these goods had by then become well known and highly sought after, and thus fraudulent trading became unavoidable. It was difficult to uphold high tariffs, especially for coffee, because such restrictions spurred further smuggling and illegal importing.[75] Chocolate had been known much longer, and had even been processed in the Austrian Netherlands since the second half of the seventeenth century; and so both cocoa and chocolate had

73 Vandenbroeke, *Agriculture*, 567.

74 3 pennies per pound according to NAB, FC, 8580, tariff book; 4522, decree of October 23rd 1751 fixing the import tariff on tea on 3 pennies per pound; 5606, tariff book of 1670, handwritten remark from July 9th 1759, "Caffé et thé Sortie libre".

75 According to the dictionary of trade this was not so much a problem for tea. In case of coffee, however, raising tariffs to 4 pennies per pound was untenable because of fraud. NAB, FC, 8580; 5606, tariff book of 1670, handwritten remark, June 12th 1766, "Caffé […] entrée 0-1-6" (one and a half penny).

been included in the tariffs of 1670 and 1680.[76] Yet again the duties remained quite low until 1764.[77] All of this entailed that instituting and managing an active tariff policy was fraught with myriad obstacles.

On top of this, there was much internal dissension concerning the desirability of taxes on colonial goods in the first place. The memoranda on international trade from 1754 contain a note from an anonymous merchant, who wrote to Vienna: "I already told you that our tariffs are too high for our merchants to be able to re-export."[78] The merchant also states that the government wished to levy high taxes on transit in order to generate high incomes, but that traders feared that such measures would cripple their competitiveness. He also claims that many taxes had already increased. Surprisingly, councillor Van Heurck agreed with the anonymous author that many goods could be imported (mainly from Holland) without harming domestic production. Such goods, as identified by Van Heurck, included spices, dyestuffs, tea, coffee, cocoa, crude silk, rice, sugar and grain, among others. According to Van Heurck, import taxes on these goods should be lowered.[79] He was hardly the only policymaker to hold this view. Customs officials Tomboy and Libeau pleaded for free imports of cocoa in 1782.[80] And, as discussed earlier, some members of the administration also pleaded for lower tariffs on tea and coffee.[81] Moreover, though the *bureau de la régie* officially preferred to maintain tariffs, it appears that, as concerned colonial commodities, disagreements between the government and traders or manufacturers were often settled in favour of the latter two – in 71.4 per cent of the cases, as compared to 61 per cent of the requests concerning textiles, 63.9 per cent for coal and 47.5 for salt. Perhaps the government had realized that import substitution was impossible and that consumption

76 Blondé and Greefs, "Werk," 217–218, Vandenbroeke, *Agriculture*, 568. NAB, FC, 8873–8874, tariff books of 1670 and 1680.

77 NAB, FC, 4507, communication by counselor De Beelen, August 18th, 1764. The tariff was almost tripled.

78 "je vous ai déjà dit, que nos droits sont trop forts pour que nos marchands puissent faire le commerce de réexportation." NAB, Manuscripts, 850 A: memorandum on trade in the eighteenth century (446 pages), s.n. to unknown receiver in Vienna, s.d. (probably 1754), page 20.

79 NAB, Manuscripts, 850 A: memoranda on trade in the eighteenth century (446 pages), Van Heurck, s.d. (probably 1754), page 292.

80 NAB, FC, 4526, memorandum concerning duties on cocoa, bureau de la régie, June 8th 1782, signed by Tomboy and Libeau.

81 NAB, FC, 4506, communication signed by De Beelen, June 23rd 1761, tariffs on tea are lowered by one sixth; 4522, memorandum on coffee smuggle in Luxemburg, November 29th 1779, Paradis and Delplancq believe it best to lower the local import tariffs for coffee, but not for tea.

would remain high regardless. What is certain, however, is that this approach resulted in the government forgoing what was likely a huge source of tax revenue, and that decisions about these matters were considered with great caution.

All in all, attempts to immobilize imports were thus rare. The primary reason for this appears to have been that – besides coffee, which simply would be smuggled when tariffs became high, and tea – a sizable proportion of the imports consisted of resources (such as crude sugar and dyestuffs) that were useful in domestic industries. As we have seen, the government often tried to support these industries, albeit not always with equal success, through measures such as individual benefits and exemptions (in the case of textile dying) and a far more general tariff policy (in the case of sugar).[82] In the case of both of these sectors government policy and strong demand probably went hand in hand in spurring their activities. Even chocolate production, a less important branch of industry, received support, in this case by the government's levying lower import rights on cocoa than on chocolate, and even lower rights in the case of "*cacao à faire chocolat*".[83] A notable finding from the sources is that local governments (i.e. city councils) intervened less than in previous sectors. In fact, not even half a per cent of the requests were submitted by public institutions.[84] This was likely because these commodities were still considered more as luxury items, unlike with coal or salt, and because the sectors involved were still small and provided little employment Likewise, in this case it was clear that trade policy was already firmly committed to aiding entrepreneurs.

82 NAB, FC, 5258, deed for the refinery of Denis Ryckaert and Antoine Joseph Latteur in Brussels, September 10th 1749, granting them 'the same privileges and exemptions as the Antwerp refineries'; 5260, Pierre Joseph De Quesne receives an exemption for exporting sugar from the Basteyns refinery, March 6th 1760; 5262, Exemption for Albert Goddyn, September 16th 1765 and for Jacques de Kersmaecker, March 20th 1766; 5260, communication to all customs offices, March 20th 1756: signed by Baron De Lador; 5606, tariff book, handwritten note «*Dispositions de 20 mars 1756, 6 novembre 1760 et 15 juin 1761, sucre raffinée de ces pays libre de sortie, tonlieu et de convoi*».

83 NAB, FC, 8580, *Dictionaire de commerce* (composed by Delplancq, 1776) states that import rights on cacao were lower than on chocolate; 5606: cocoa to make chocolate, per 100 pounds: 2 guilders on entry; idem, handwritten remark, June 11th 1764: cacao du cent pesant (100 pounds): 6 guilders on entry; 4507, communication by De Beelen, August 18th 1764: the import tariff on chocolate amounts to 3 pennies per pound (or 15 guilders per 100).

84 See Table 11.

4 Conclusion

This chapter leaves little doubt that colonial trade, just as it did throughout the world, had a significant impact on the early modern economy of the Southern Low Countries. Here as well as elsewhere, it gave rise to new consumer cultures.[85] A remarkable initial observation, however, is that though colonial imports indeed increased in this region in the second half of the century, they did so at a lower rate than did overall imports. Thus, the idea that colonial commodities entered the market as a sort of sudden tidal wave should be nuanced. In particular, given the fact that these colonial goods were not notably hindered by trade policy that may be an indication that not all of them were yet as sought after as were sugar and coffee. Of course, this does not weaken the evidence for the consumption revolution that was presumably sparked by the latter two products.

Yet what is even more interesting, particularly within the scope of this work, is that when these exotic commodities entered into the economy of the Austrian Netherlands, they instigated processes which clearly went beyond sales and consumption. Just as cotton fabrics and silk fibres served as resources for textile manufacturing, so too was sugar used in the expanding sugar refining business; likewise, indigo and other dyestuffs assisted in modernizing the textile (dying) sector. Moreover, besides this 'incorporation of the new', manufacturers even succeeded, albeit cautiously, in providing certain domestic substitutes for dyestuffs, and would later also develop alternatives for coffee and cane sugar. This chapter thus reinforces arguments for the intrinsic strength of the home market and its emerging industries. Moreover, as will be discussed in Part IV, colonial wares also provided great opportunities within the Habsburg transit policy.

However, one should not overestimate the role of these new industries linked to colonial trade. Unlike Great Britain, the Austrian Netherlands never succeeded in raising a similar re-export industry. Thus, for the Austrian Netherlands, colonial trade did not serve as an engine of widespread economic growth or give rise to any new 'leading sectors'. In short, the importance of colonial trade did not approach that of the coal or textile sectors, and probably not even that of salt. Nonetheless, trade in colonial goods clearly changed the face of the Austrian Netherlands, just as it had in the rest of the Early Modern European society.

85 Berg, "In Pursuit," 88.

CHAPTER 9

The Coal Trade

A Motor for Development?

1 "The Basis, as Always, was Coal"[1]

In studying the economic history of the eighteenth-century Austrian Netherlands examining the trade in textiles was rather predictable and also logical. Despite the troubles this sector was facing, it remained highly influential and important throughout the region. And, more importantly, we have seen that certain products of that sector indeed played a dynamic role within the eighteenth-century economy of this region. However, new textiles such as cotton are not the only products that have always been linked to innovation and development in international historiography. Another industry that has been specifically linked with the Industrial Revolution is coal. In the Austrian Netherlands as well, the coal sector provides an exciting case study, especially because during the second half of the eighteenth century the commodity not only became intertwined with myriad other manufacturing activities in Western Europe but also developed into a hugely important sector in its own. Understanding the coal trade facilitates valuable new insights into trade in general and allows for a further broadened view on the economic transformations during the eighteenth century and the possible motors behind it.

As said, historiography has always linked the story of coal to the history of industrialisation.[2] Great Britain, in the second half of the eighteenth century, was the first country to witness the nascent signs of the process that historians now label the Industrial Revolution. Myriad economic, social, technological and environmental conditions were necessary to generate this specific development; it will suffice to note that Britain possessed several capacities and characteristics necessary to support such development. The British Isles not only controlled an empire that provided the country with direct supplies of resources such as cotton and sugar; it also possessed various high quality resources – coal of course, but also English wool for example – on its own

1 Sidney Pollard, *Peaceful Conquest. The Industrialization of Europe 1760–1970* (Oxford: Oxford University Press, 1982), 87.

2 Bayly, *The Birth*, Church and Wrigley, *The Industrial Revolutions*, Hobsbawm, *Industry*, Pollard, *Peaceful Conquest*.

 | DOI 10.1163/9789004272606_011

domestic soil.[3] The area which would later become known as Belgium was rich in one such area: namely, its natural abundance of coal. It has been frequently observed that a significant incidence of mineral fuels was a principal condition for a region's industrial success. The situation was no different in the case of the Southern Low Countries: "To a large extent, the success of early industrialising Belgium was based on the coal deposits in the Sambre-Meuse region."[4]

The major reason why such substantial influence has been attributed to coal is that the resource had – just as other forms of fossil fuel would do later – unfettered various restraints that restricted the energy supply. When the process of mining coal had been adequately refined, the resultant industry was able to deliver an essentially unlimited supply of fuel for domestic and industrial use. Such provision was impossible to obtain via wood, peat and other traditional energy sources.[5] Moreover, coal was exceptionally well suited for steam engines, which provided more continuous and consistent power than did water-, animal- or human-driven forces.[6] Such developments suggest that absent coal the industrial revolution would have been almost entirely infeasible.[7] A common view among economists and historians is that, as economist Jeremy Rifkin has noted, "Our entire civilisation has been built on the fossil remains of the Jura."[8] And indeed: initially, the high costs of transportation led to industrialisation occurring mostly in the immediate vicinities of coal deposits.[9] During the eighteenth century coal replaced wood as a heat source in an ever growing number of industries. As coal production and application techniques reached higher levels of sophistication – a high point being the use of cokes for melting iron – this number continued rising steadily.[10]

Contemporary sources from the eighteenth-century Southern Low Countries evidence that coal use also emerged in a growing number of industries – including

3 O'Brien, "Mercantilism," 476–478, Van Houtte, *Histoire*, 265.

4 Broadberry, Fremdling, and Solar, "Industry," 12.

5 Coal has a calorific value of 27 MJ/kg, wood can provide 9 to 14 MJ/kg and peat 15 MJ/kg. H.Y. Afeefy, J.F. Liebman, and S.E. Stein, "Neutral Thermochemical Data," in *Nist Chemistry Webbook, Nist Standard Reference Database Number 69*, ed. P.J. Linstrom and W.G. Mallard (Gaithersburg: National Institute of Standards and Technology, 2011), Michael D. Bordo, Alan M. Taylor, and Jeffrey G. Williamson, *Globalization in Historical Perspective* (Chicago: Chicago University Press, 2005), 30. http://webbook.nist.gov, retrieved June 22nd, 2011.

6 E.A. Wrigley, *Poverty, Progress, and Population* (Cambridge: Cambridge University Press, 2004), 82.

7 Hasquin, "Nijverheid," 158.

8 Jeremy Rifkin, *The Hydrogen Economy* (New York: Penguin, 2002), 64.

9 Pollard, *Peaceful Conquest*, xiv–xv.

10 O'Brien, "Mercantilism," 478.

in the textile industry and in salt refineries, gin distilleries, and glassworks, and for production of metal wares such as nails and weaponry – until eventually almost every industrial sector relied on the resource.[11] Not surprisingly, demand for coal subsequently soared, thereby rendering coal mining one of the sectors that, according to Jan Dhondt, generated "exceptionally high profits" for the Austrian Netherlands.[12] Various studies have ranked the coal production of the Southern Low Countries as one of the enabling factors for the nineteenth-century process of modernisation.[13] Moreover, contemporary sources identify coal as the principal commercial commodity of the Hainaut region. Many people and industries throughout Western Europe depended on coal as a prime source of revenue.[14] This is because coal, unlike other 'industrial' sectors, such as the printing of cotton textiles, was characterized by a dual nature: on the one hand it was a raw material for countless industries; on the other it was a significant industry in itself, one that furnished and sold products to households and firms, at home and abroad. In short, the importance of coal for the late eighteenth-century economy and for the start of the industrial revolution is generally held to be incontrovertible. The Habsburg government and its administration held a similar view at the time, as will be illustrated shortly.

However, to date, an important aspect has been absent from the highly technologically determined narrative of the influence of coal. We know hardly anything about the eighteenth-century trade flows or about the various actors involved in the international coal trade. Yet familiarity with both the organization of these agents (merchants, producers, consumers and the government) and the flows of the actual goods is essential for understanding the eighteenth-century economy of the Southern Netherlands. By integrating these economic and social facets into a history of the international coal trade it becomes possible to shed new light on the history of an immensely important era. Information about import and export flows of coal can help in identifying the extent to which the Austrian Netherlands were self-sufficient in their resource supply. Moreover, these trade flows offer a clue about the degree of coal consumption in the Southern Netherlands and thus about the progress of industry during the eighteenth century; this allows for testing existing ideas about Early

11 NAB, FC, 5031, 5067 and 9113: these documents contain various requests from manufacturers who used coal for fuel, see below for details. Pollard, *Peaceful Conquest*, 88.

12 Dhondt and Bruwier, "The Industrial Revolution," 351.

13 Broadberry, Fremdling, and Solar, "Industry," Dhondt and Bruwier, "The Industrial Revolution," Hasquin, "Nijverheid," 158, Lebrun et al., *Essai*.

14 NAB, FC, 5021, "mémoire pour le retablissement du commerce des charbons de terre qui se tire dans le pays et comté de hainaut...," s.n., 1753.

Modern industrialisation. Finally, an analysis of the international coal trade facilitates answering a crucial question: namely, did the fact that the Southern Netherlands were gifted with a large stock of coal allow for the country's people to improve themselves financially? In other words: was coal also exported from this region? All of these elements can be summarized into one question: namely, how did the international coal trade influence the eighteenth-century Austrian Netherlands?

Addressing such questions concerning trade flows is far from impossible, for the necessary data on import and export are of course available. However, for answering the question about the importance of international trade for the coal sector, the study of import and export flows is only a first step. It remains necessary to confront the numbers with (partial) production figures and, especially, with information from agents involved in the coal trade. In this way it becomes possible to answer numerous questions concerning evolutions in the eighteenth-century coal sector and consequently about Early Modern industry in general.

2 The Coal Sector: In Britain's Shadow?

Most of the existing scholarship about coal in the Austrian Netherlands dates from several decades ago. Nonetheless, the literature still offers valuable insights, for example by Cécile Douxchamps-Lefèvre, who ventured into the question of international trade.[15] What becomes especially clear in those works is that coal use (within households and by manufacturers) underwent markedly strong growth throughout the eighteenth century.[16] Coal was, as noted in the introduction, the major source of energy not only in Britain but elsewhere, including in the Low Countries.[17] Yet coal mining and use was hardly new. Indeed, documentary evidence for coal mining in the Borinage area dates to the thirteenth century.[18] However, a great deal of technological improvement was necessary before coal became widely accepted as an energy source. Other obstacles were present as well, such as in 1759 when the city of Ghent banned use of coal for textile bleachers. As late as 1778 various city officials still believed that using coal would stain the

15 Cécile Douxchamps-Lefèvre, "Le Commerce du Charbon dans les Pays-Bas Autrichiens à la Fin du XVIIIe Siècle," *Belgisch Tijdschrift voor Filologie en Geschiedenis* 46 (1968).

16 Joseph Ruwet, *Avant les Révolutions: le XVIIIe Siècle, Etudes d'Histoire Wallonne* (Brussels: Fondation Charles Plisnier, 1967), 23.

17 Hasquin, "Nijverheid," 136.

18 Jean Vercleyen, *Histoire du Charbon* (Brussels: Labor, 1965), 65–74.

fabrics being manufactured.[19] Many other people also believed that coal fumes and smells were harmful and thus sought ways to purify the process. In the case of the Austrian Netherlands we know of such attempts undertaken by a certain François de Somer from Ghent.[20] During the second half of the eighteenth century coal mining and processing achieved a reputation of viable trustworthiness, spurring entrepreneurs to begin inundating the government with applications to mine the coal veins.[21] However, with the new mining techniques and machinery rendering investment costs much higher, coal mines increasingly began to take the form of capitalist enterprises – for example, with shareholders, rather than merchants, providing the capital.[22]

The main early modern coal producers – and thus the Southern Low Countries' principal competitors in the industry – were Britain and the Prince-Bishopric of Liège.[23] France, which exported mainly to the Tournai region, was also a competitor, as were various smaller producers such as the Saar basin.[24] Hainaut and Namur were the primary suppliers within the Austrian Netherlands; they were able to market much of their production to the foreign markets of France and Holland, yet also targeted the domestic market.[25] In the latter case the trade flows generally went from the southern Walloon area to the northern provinces of Flanders and Brabant.[26] However, Flemish manufacturers and

---

19 NAB, CP, 1162/B, printed decree from 1759 by the government of Ghent; letter from 1761 by the bleachers from Ghent; letter from 1778 by the city officials from Bruges.

20 NAB, FC, 5031, François De Somer from Gent claimed to have discovered such a process and asked for a twenty years patent. He did not receive a patent, but the government granted him some benefits, such as the exemption from import duties for his resources (March 3rd 1779).

21 NAB, FC, 4999, *passim*: requests for the mining of coal veins. The technological improvements in this sector have been extensively documented, see for example: Roger Burt, "The Extractive Industries," in *The Cambridge Economic History of Modern Britain*, ed. Roderick Floud and Paul Johnson (Cambridge: Cambridge University Press, 2004), 436.

22 Coppejans-Desmedt, "Handelaars," 482.

23 Lebrun et al., *Essai*, 81, Eugène Schneider, *Le Charbon. Son Histoire – Son Destin* (Paris: Librairie Plon, 1945), 104, Louis Trenard, "Le Charbon avant l'Ère Industrielle," in *Charbon et Sciences Humaines*, ed. Louis Trenard (Den Haag: Mouton, 1963).

24 NAB, FC 5026, letter by the customs bureau to the bureau of Tournai concerning French imports, September 17th 1764. Hasquin, "Nijverheid," 137. Apparently, coal was being imported from Holland, but its exact origins were unknown: NAB, FC, 5026, permission by the customs bureau to the city officials of Antwerp to import thirty quarters of coal from Holland at the old tariff, August 2nd 1764.

25 Dardel, *Navires*, 192. NAB, FC, 5030, memoir from the customs bureau concerning exports to Holland, 1774; 5031, letter from the widow Maes, Ghent, October 13th 1779.

26 Lebrun et al., *Essai*, 343.

consumers assumed that English coal was of finer quality than domestic produce, and so preferred to acquire supplies overseas.[27] Moreover, the English benefitted from numerous well-equipped harbours and mines that were located near the sea, both of which kept transport costs low.[28] The Walloon producers, however, were forced to transport their coal via roads and rivers; moreover, even for domestic trade they were obliged to pass through the town of Condé-sur-l'Escaut, which had fallen to the French after the Peace of Nijmegen. The requisite route from Hainaut to Tournai entailed high transit fees to France.[29] Besides such logistical and financial complications, numerous interior barriers also hampered coal transport in the Low Countries. Local privileges and tolls, even at the end of the pre-industrial era, remained major impediments to trade.[30] One major consequence of these conditions was that coal from different regions could potentially differ significantly in quality and price. The historical debates and discussions about the coal industry have not neglected to mention these various elements that were crucial to development of the industry. However, such elements have not been investigated to a sufficient degree. Consequentially, much of the historical tale underlying the coal trade remains unexposed and unexamined.

3 International Trade: *Source de prospérité* or Paralysing Influence?[31]

As with the previous sectors, the Habsburg trade statistics offer significant assistance in determining the impact of coal on the eighteenth-century balance of trade. Coal, although it was not traded to the same scale as textiles, ranks among the ten most traded commodities of the period. The share of coal among overall imports to the Southern Netherlands varied between one and four percent (Chart 68). This figure peaked between the years 1769 and 1773, when coal imports were at their highest. The share of overall exports was even

27 Hasquin, "Nijverheid," 128, 137.

28 Lucienne Van Meerbeeck, "La Crise Charbonnière et le Problème des Transports en Belgique au XVIIIe Siècle," in *Premier Congrès International de Géographie Historique* (Brussels: 1931), 293.

29 NAB, FC, 5021, the *marchands chaufourniers* (including Derasse) complain about the high transit tariffs when passing Condé, 1753.

30 Bruno Blondé and Raymond Van Uytven, "Langs Land- en Waterwegen in de Zuidelijke Nederlanden. Lopend Onderzoek naar het Preïndustriële Transport," *Bijdragen tot de Geschiedenis* 82, no. 2 (1999): 138.

31 Briavoinne, *De L'industrie*, 83, Lebrun et al., *Essai*, 343.

higher, but it also experienced more extreme fluctuations: for example, from one percent in 1764 to eight percent in 1781. The average annual contribution of coal to the total value of exports during the 33-year period was just below four percent. Coal was thus hardly an insignificant commodity in the balance of trade and consequently received considerable attention from the customs administration.[32] Average annual coal exports from the Austrian Netherlands amounted to ten percent of average English exports during the same years (excluding 1781, when exports from the Austrian Netherlands peaked).[33] In comparing the evolution of the coal trade with that of the total import and export figures (Charts 69 and 70), it is clear that the fluctuations in the coal share generally match those in the coal trade. Thus, we must not look for the explanation for these shifts in the overall trade flows, but in the coal sector itself.

As mentioned before, the different opinions on the influence of the coal trade go back to the eighteenth century itself. Coal was not so different from many other sectors in this period (for example wool and flax) in the sense that

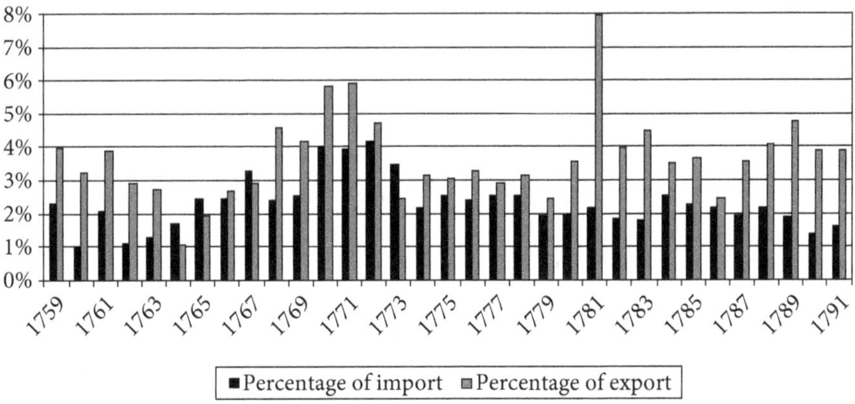

CHART 68 *Share of coal imports and exports in total import and export (in value), 1759–1791*[34]
SOURCE: RELEVÉ GÉNÉRAL, NAB, FC, 5748–5805 AND 5025.

32 The fund of the Finance Council contains sixteen boxes on the coal trade. NAB, FC, 5019–5035, "Douanes: houille ou charbon de terre."

33 Data from the customs statistics compared to figures provided by David Ormrod, *The Rise of Commercial Empires. England and the Netherlands in the Age of Mercantilism, 1650–1770*, vol. 10, *Cambridge Studies in Modern Economic History* (Cambridge: 2003), 254.

34 For trade totals, I have used the estimates from the chapter on the balance of trade. The prices are based on NAB, FC, 5025, letter by the city council of Ostend, March 2nd 1763 and Verlinden and Craeybeckx, *Documents pour l'Histoire des Prix et des Salaires en Flandres et en Brabant*, Vol II, 799. See below for details on prices.

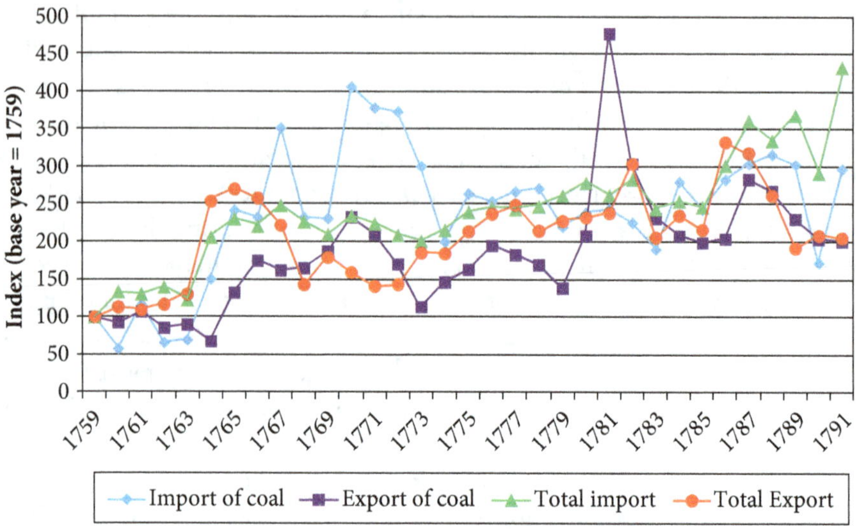

CHART 69 *Index of the coal trade and total international trade, 1759–1761*
SOURCE: RELEVÉ GÉNÉRAL, NAB, FC, 5748–5805 AND 5025.

the sector was troubled by the same conflict between producers (or in this case specifically: mine-owners) on the one hand and manufacturers that made use of the resource on the other.[35] The government was torn between the wishes of both factions. One of the consequences was that the height of trade duties fluctuated regularly to please manufacturers and traders at times, and the Walloon coal miners at others. The administration used high import duties to encourage coal exploitation, but these could just as well result in malpractices by the mine owners, because such a protectionist measure furnished them with a monopoly position compared to foreign competitors. In other words it allowed them to demand excessively high prices for their product. Anyhow, duties were probably almost never that steep that they could severely hinder imports, even though certain imports – for example from England – were possibly forbidden during some years.[36] In any case, the customs administration had travelled a long way. The tariff of 1680 that was signed under international political pressure and that was still mostly valid in the second

35 Hasquin, "Nijverheid," 126–128.

36 I believe this was the case since explicit approval to import English coal needed to be granted. NAB, FC, 5023, permission to sell English coal in Ostend during two months, signed by Baron de Lador, June 21st 1758; this coal could not be transported and sold to Bruges afterwards, idem, de Lador, August 2nd 1758; 5029, a number of Antwerp merchants is granted permission to import English coal, April 23rd and June 27th 1770; 5034, brewers from Bruges ask permission, no response, December 16th 1776.

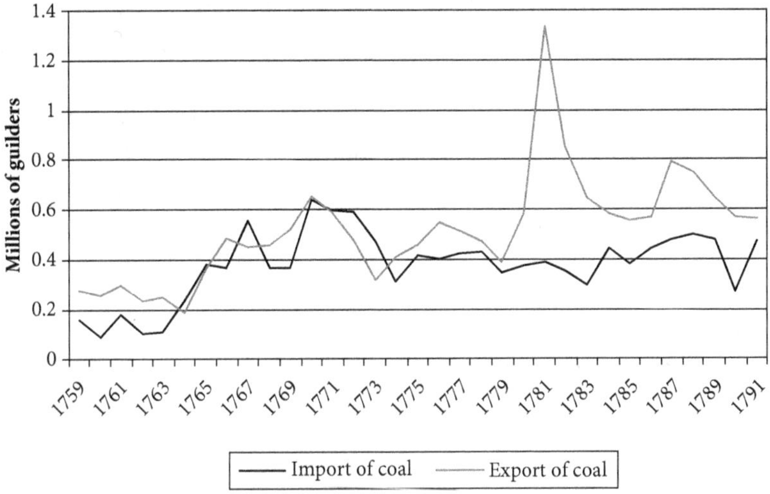

CHART 70 *The coal trade in value, total international trade in value, 1759–1791*
SOURCE: RELEVÉ GÉNÉRAL, NAB, FC, 5748–5805 AND 5025.

half of the eighteenth century, had been particularly advantageous for the English coal suppliers.[37] So apparently the customs officials again needed to consider conflicting foreign demands on top of the domestic bickering. All of these difficulties show through the source material and have affected the writings about coal.

37 NAB, FC, 8874, «*ESTAT OU TARIF des DROITS d'entrée et sortie sur les marchandises, manufactures et denrées*», 1680.

Now what are the conflicting opinions in historiography so far? Since eighteenth-century manufacturers claimed English coal was of higher quality than the domestic kind, it is believed to have been given preference most of the time. The Flemish in particular preferred Newcastle coal over that from Hainaut according to Hervé Hasquin.[38] Most authors therefore agree that foreign competition posed a serious threat. However, they also assume that from 1761 onwards things started to look brighter for several reasons: the improvement of road networks, the new independent customs policy and the increase in demand, both from population growth and from the growing use of coal.[39] These factors are believed to have caused a decline in coal imports from Britain after 1773. Duplessis among others supposes that coal from Charleroi could replace the previously dominant import from England.[40] Moreover, coal from Charleroi succeeded to break through even in the Dutch Republic during the four years' war in 1779–1782. This should have given a strong boost to exports.[41] Lebrun goes even further and emphasizes that "The economic prosperity of the Borinage region depended almost entirely on the mining and trading of coal."[42] Douxchamps-Lefèvre tempers this enthusiasm a little by pointing out that the Austrian Netherlands at the end of the eighteenth century still depended heavily on imports. This did not lead to crisis however, since at the same time export was also high. These contradictory trends were simply the outcome of the location of the coal deposits and the physical barriers resulting from it.[43]

So much for the positive assessments of the developments in the coal trade. The negative comments can in fact all be brought back to the fierce competition from England and Liège, and the fact that the customs policy did not tackle it properly. Briavoinne warned that despite the emergence of numerous mines and coal furnaces in his country, the British coal industry crippled the growth of the sector.

> Despite the abundance of coal mines, iron ore, blast furnaces and forges in the country, the English coal and Swedish iron entered the domestic market and crippled the growth of these industries.[44]

38 Hasquin, "Nijverheid," 128, 137.

39 Douxchamps-Lefèvre, "Le Commerce," 421, Hasquin, "Nijverheid," 137.

40 Duplessis, *Transitions*, 236.

41 Hasquin, "Nijverheid," 138.

42 "la prospérité économique du Borinage est fondée presque exclusivement sur l'extraction et le commerce du charbon" Lebrun et al., *Essai*, 343.

43 Douxchamps-Lefèvre, "Le Commerce," 416.

44 "Malgré les nombreuses houillères, le minerai de fer, les hauts-fourneaux et les forges du pays, la houille anglaise et le fer de Suède arrivaient sur le marché intérieur et paralysaient l'essor de ces branches de production." Briavoinne, *De L'industrie*, 83.

Hilda Coppejans-Desmedt and Lucienne Van Meerbeeck also criticize the lack of measures that were taken to assist the coal and metal industries.[45] Indeed, government policy failed miserably in the case of this commodity.[46] Most other literature on the competition with Great Britain also focuses on the customs policy. The large imports from the Isle would not have simply been due to the large consumption of local production within Hainaut itself, but also to the customs policy that was pursued.[47] Moreover, Van Meerbeeck identifies a number of other problems besides the low tariffs, that – according to her – were symptoms of crisis. Especially in terms of transportation, she detects many obstacles. The most important one being that while the British mines were located conveniently near the shore, Wallonia depended on a single transport route via the Haine and the Scheldt to Flanders, that forced its traders to pass through the French town of Condé.[48] The importance of a decent transportation infrastructure has also been stressed in international literature on industrial development.[49]

The sources that the *bureau de la régie* has collected are mostly in line with the latter, pessimistic view, but they treat a much wider range of subjects than just foreign competition. Moreover, they touch upon a much larger variety of topics than the customs archive on textiles did, especially on all kinds of internal difficulties which affected international trade. We unsurprisingly stumble on countless signs of disagreements within these documents that naturally result from the varying interests and motives of those involved, but on one topic they nonetheless all seemed to agree, i.e. the transportation issue. Foreign coal could be transported cheaper because it faced lower duties than the excessive rights which France demanded at Condé.[50] Yet, France should not be the only one blamed for the cost difference. It was also a consequence of numerous domestic obstacles and tolls of which the *droit de marlotage* that Hainaut itself collected and the so-called *lastbreuk* (the obligation for traders to reload

45 Coppejans-Desmedt, "Aspecten," 74.

46 Van Meerbeeck, "La Crise," 289, 302.

47 Van Meerbeeck, *Etude*, 161.

48 Van Meerbeeck, "La Crise," 296.

49 Balassa, "The Process," 4.

50 NAB, FC, 5021, the *marchands chaufournier* (coal mining merchants) complain about high transit on the passage via Condé, 1753; 5029, a brewer from Eeklo complains about some difficulties which occurred when transporting through Condé, such as a flood, March 5th 1770.

their cargo in Ghent) are most illustrious.[51] On those two topics, however, the different parties no longer agreed. Traders petitioned the government to deal with the aforementioned obstacles and the central government did not understand herself why Hainaut held on to the *marlotage* while this clearly harmed exports.[52] Officials from that province argued in their defence that the *marlotage* was small change in comparison with the rights the French demanded at Condé and the burden of the *lastbreuk*, and they clenched to their two centuries-old right.[53] Other suggestions were thus made to deal with the transport costs and obstacles. To revive the trade in coal a 1753 memorandum had already stipulated that a channel to Tournai should be dug so that Condé could be avoided. Another possibility according to the anonymous author was to dissuade France from the exorbitant rights by threatening it with higher duties on French coal imports.[54] In other words: a customs war was afoot.

Surprisingly, little was said about export duties, except for some rare pleas to the customs bureau pro moderation, or even abolition of duties. The suppliants, merchants Joseph Renson, the widow Buivort and the well-known Nicolas Bacon, hoped that such measures would increase the export of local coal, but the bureau questioned whether it would not bear too great a financial loss if the product would be exempted from export taxes.[55] Nonetheless, export from some customs offices around Ostend was presumably liberated as of 1760.[56] Besides this no general action seems to have been undertaken,

51 NAB, FC, 5025, letter by the city of Ostend, March 2nd 1763. Blondé and Van Uytven, "Langs Land- en Waterwegen," 138.

52 NAB, FC, 5025, letter by De Grysperre, September 13th 1763.

53 The *marlotage* was 32 guilders per boat (compared to 168 guilders of passage rights at Condé). NAB, FC, 5022, letter from the Count and States of Hainaut, August 1st 1760; 5025, letter from the deputies of Hainaut, signed by De Maleingreau, May 31st 1763.

54 NAB, FC, 5021, "*memoire pour le retablissement du commerce des charbons de terre* (…)," 1753. The same question is repeated in 1786: FC, 5033, memoir by attorney Criquillion on measures in favour of the Walloon coal producers, April 22nd 1786.

55 NAB, FC, 5022, letter, s.n. and reply by the *bureau de la régie*, July 17th 1760; 5022, authorization from the bureau to Madame Simon Buivort and Joseph Renson to export coal at a lower tariff, August 27th 1760; 5023, Memoir by Nicolas Bacon to de Müllendorf about the coal exports of the English to Holland. He suggests to cancel export duties in order to increase exports, October 10th 1759.

56 NAB, FC, 5022, the Finance Council announces that coal exports from the offices of Ostend, St-Philippe, Newport and Zelzate are exempt from taxes, March 8th 1760; 8874, handwritten remark in the tariff book, March 8th 1760.

but in rare cases exporting merchants were allowed to pay lower duties on their cargo.[57]

Another measure that was rarely contested was granting exemptions from the rights on resource imports for coal producers, such as the free importation of timber from Liège, iron or machine parts.[58] Not surprising since all other industries needed coal, so the coal industry had an impact on the price and welfare of many goods. On top of this the sources indicate that coal producers saw their requests being met more frequently than manufacturers or merchants did. Yet there were a few calls claiming that the different forms of aid did not lead to lower coal prices and that in fact only the coal producers themselves were better off. The city officials of Ostend were clearly ill-tempered when accusing these miners of being "*mauvais patriots*" making use of an "*injuste monopole.*"[59] A thorough analysis of the different requests that were directed to the government by producers, consumers, merchants or public institutions will follow below, since they show some fascinating trends in commercial policies.

The largest disagreement was the one on the height of import tariffs. Import restriction is the topic that deals directly with foreign competition, and on this point, consumers and producers were diametrically opposed. Coal producers asked year after year for an increase in the import tariff on foreign coal, what according to them was needed to avoid the bankruptcy of Hainaut.[60] In 1761 the import tariff on English coal was indeed raised from six stivers per quarter (of 300 pounds) to 30 stivers in Ghent, Ostend, Antwerp, Newport, St-Philippe and Bruges.[61] However, since this equals a tax increase from about twenty

57 NAB, FC, 5022, Madame Simon Buivort and Joseph Renson, August 27th 1760; 5025, Augustin Zoude, July 11th 1763; 5032, J.S. Toebast, October 19th 1782.

58 Exemptions for resources: NAB, FC, 5029, June 25th 1771, Huart and Castiau; 5030, April 23rd 1772, Germain Jenault; 5031, July 27th 1778, Bastin; November 10th 1779, coal miners of Lodelinsart; 5032, February 12th 1783, De Wolf. Exemptions for machines or machine parts: NAB, FC, 5030, May 24th 1773, Nicolas François Debehault; April 23rd 1774, coal miners of Blaton; 5031, June 25th 1778, André Puissant; 5033, May 21st 1784, Limal; November 13th 1784, Pierre Joseph Danderesse; September 13th 1786, Turmigny.

59 NAB, FC, 5024, complaints from the city of Ostend about the high price of coal from Hainaut, September 13th 1762.

60 NAB, FC, 5022, letter by coal mine owners from Hainaut containing different requests to heighten the tariffs on foreign coal, December 17th 1760; 5027, requests from producers in Namur, August 8th 1768; 5030, requests from Charleroi, August 2nd 1773; 5033, requests from Mons, June 7th 1784.

61 NAB, FC, 5022, printed decree signed by de Cazier, de Keerle and Müllendorf, December 27th 1761.

percent of the price to a staggering 100 percent – in other words a mere doubling of the price – the decree resulted in a tidal wave of criticism from these cities. The elevated duties forced users in Flanders and Brabant, who previously preferred to buy cheaper English coal, to turn to expensive coal from Hainaut. The latter coal cost 63 to 64 stivers (*sols*) per 500 pounds in 1763, while English coal cost only 43 to 44 stivers for the same amount. Or at least it did without the import duty. In 1767 the aldermen of Antwerp mentioned a similar price of 15.25 stivers per *waeg* (144 pounds) for premium British coal and 18.5 stivers for the best coal on the Brussels market. Considering that Antwerp imported 60,000 quarters (*rasières*) yearly, this equals a total difference in expenditure of 20,000 florins.[62] The large price difference was not their only argument to lower taxes. Importers from the Flemish and Brabantine towns argued first of all that British coal was in fact very useful for the Austrian Netherlands because it was mainly used to produce all kinds of export goods that the English coal traders bought and imported fraudulently in their own country under the guise of the coal commerce. Secondly, they pointed out the danger of a further price increase due to higher duties or an import ban. This would be extremely dangerous "because coal made up the principal heating source for the people of Antwerp."[63] The threat was not merely hypothetical, since for example brewers from Bruges already complained about the excessive height of coal prices in Mons. According to them, the only way to persuade the coal producers to lower their price was by lowering import duties.[64] A brewer from Eeklo stated that coal was "the commodity most necessary to my profession."[65] Most entrepreneurs therefore agreed – as long as the aforementioned obstacles for coal from Hainaut had not been lifted – that the duties on English coal should be returned to their old level.

Despite all this criticism new requests to increase the tariffs or even install a ban on both English and Liège coal also continued to be raised throughout the second half of the eighteenth century. Producers from the Charleroi area complained that their countless investments did not boost their sale of coal, due to the import of coal from abroad, especially from Liège. According to the *maîtres*

62 NAB, FC, 5025, letter by the city of Ostend asking to lower import duties on English coal as long as the *marlotage* and other internal barriers existed, March 2nd 1763; 5027, letter by the mayor and aldermen of Antwerp requesting permission to import English coal at a lower tariff, November 10th 1767.

63 "comme la houille fait le principal chauffage du peuple à Anvers." NAB, FC, 5027, letter by the mayor and aldermen of Antwerp, November 10th 1767.

64 NAB, Conseil du Gouvernement Général, 821, September 10th 1787.

65 "la denrée la plus necessaire à l'exercice de sa profession." NAB, FC, 5029, petition to the customs bureau by J.S. Toebast, March 5th 1770.

charbonniers from Mons – a city where a quarter of the inhabitants was claimed to have been active in the coal industry – there was great misery, because the English competition on foreign markets was fierce. The decrease in foreign demand led, in their view, to the expensiveness of coal in the mother country, since production costs could not be compensated. Their solution was to increase the trade duties on British coal once more.[66] It never came that far. On the contrary, throughout the years, dozens of exceptions to the high fees were allowed. Firstly, individual manufacturers from different cities in the northern regions could import English coal at a reduced rate. Afterwards, the entire city needs of Antwerp, Malines, Ostend and Bruges could even be purchased at this lower rate.[67] Their pleas even led to a general decline in the import taxes in a number of customs bureaus on the Flemish border from 1789 onwards.[68] This despite deeply disappointed reactions from Charleroi, where the producers argued that it belonged to the responsibility of a good government to first and foremost support the trade in domestically produced coal.[69]

Unfortunately, 1786 is the last preserved year in the series of the customs office on coal. It would of course have been very interesting to unearth the visions in the troubled years that would follow. Secondly these sources focus primarily on the trade policy while it would be more useful to discover what impact trade and international competition truly had. The supposed effects of the government measures mentioned in the sources have not been tested so far. One could only rely on the judgments made by those involved, who of course all had their own agendas when addressing themselves to the Finance Council. So we are left with our questions about the influence of trade. Did increased import duties bring about positive effects for domestic coal producers? Did the sector indeed make progress after 1761 and do we see a decline in imports especially after 1773? Or did the tariffs only render coal too expensive, just as consumers feared? Did the Southern Netherlands manage to be self-sufficient in terms of energy supply and was this even desirable? Was there some growth in the export? Did transportation improvements in the second half of the eighteenth century have a positive impact on the trade in coal? The questions are far from original, but without real trade data answers could be

66 NAB, FC, 5030, letter by coal producers from Charleroi, August 2nd 1773; 5033, letter by *maîtres charbonniers de Mons*, June 7th 1784.

67 For all requests: see Appendix, Table A.8.

68 Namely the offices of Newport, Ostend, Bruges, Zelzate and Lillo. NAB, FC, 8874, handwritten remark in the tariff book, June 13th 1789.

69 NAB, FC, 5027, response to a letter from November 10th 1767.

nothing more than speculation, since the sources are – as always – coloured by the competing desires of those who wrote them.

4 The Coal Flows

We cannot resolve all of these questions directly, but international trade figures can certainly give us an important indication of the answers. Although some of the aforementioned historians are without a doubt familiar with the Austrian customs statistics – Douxchamps-Lefèvre has even discussed them in great detail – they have not referred to the actual amounts of imports and exports.[70] As a result, we still do not know how the trade flows evolved. So once more the customs statistics can turn out to be a true goldmine for present-day historians.

In the customs registers coal is divided into three separate categories, according to their quality and their designated use. Regular coal (*charbon de terre* or *charbon de cochet*) was used in most industries that were mentioned in the introduction, while small coal (*menu charbon* or *charbon de forge*) delivered a much more intense heat that was needed to feed the heavy industries like the metallurgic industry.[71] The third kind (*terre houille*) was less pure and thus a lot cheaper. It was mainly used in households for heating. What is strange is that the price of small coal was not higher than that of regular coal. Verlinden and Scholliers' data even suggests that it was less expensive.[72] A possible explanation is that the Austrian Netherlands produced far more *charbon de forge* than regular coal (even ten times more in the coal mines of which Moureaux published the accounts).[73] The price difference might therefore have been merely a matter of supply and demand, and not of the intrinsic qualities of the coal. However, Ormrod attested that the price ratio was similar in Britain, so a more suitable explanation may lie in the different technical properties of the two types.[74] The intense heat of small coal possibly made it

70 Douxchamps-Lefèvre, "La Statistique."

71 Unfortunately, it is very difficult to estimate the exact calorific value of the different kinds of coal in the past. But *terre houille* could probably be compared to brown coal (lignite), that delivers about half the calorific value of hard coal (15 MJ/kg instead of 27 MJ/kg), what accounts for its lower price. The sources suggest furthermore that regular coal had a lower heating value than small coal.

72 Verlinden and Scholliers, *Dokumenten*, Deel II, 797–799.

73 Philippe Moureaux, *Les Comptes d'une Société Charbonnière à la Fin de l'Ancien Régime* (Brussels: Koninklijke commissie voor Geschiedenis, 1969).

74 Ormrod, *The Rise*, 250.

less suited for most common applications, so that it did not compete directly with regular coal and there was no intercommunion in the price setting.

When we examine the trade flows of the first coal category, i.e. the ordinary coal that was used in most eighteenth-century industries (Chart 71), we immediately notice that the import of coal increased throughout the period that the customs statistics cover. This increase was clearly not avoided by the tariff of 1761. Exports on the other hand followed a very whimsical course. The war between England, France and the Dutch Republic in 1779–1783 explains one of the short-term peaks in the output, but for the other highs and lows interpretations are not up for grabs. The sources are mostly silent about exports, since this was not a very large concern for the administration. Its main aim was to avoid import so that the market would be eager for domestically produced coal. Consequently we know very little about possible changes in export tariffs, except that export from some customs offices was presumably liberated as of 1760.[75] In the other departments nine pennies (*deniers*) had to be paid for regular coal and six for small coal, which was probably no more than two percent of the value.[76] Furthermore, the remarkably low figures before 1764 most likely have to be attributed to the fact that there were still many flaws and irregularities in the source during the first years of its implementation. The reason for the unexplained fluctuations must thus possibly be sought in the countries that purchased Belgian coal.

In the case of the rise in imports however, we do not need to look very far for an explanation. On one hand, the countless exemptions from the import tariffs for cities and entrepreneurs in Brabant and Flanders make it rather unsurprising that imports experienced little nuisance during the last third of the century.[77] On the other hand the demand for coal from industry did not cease to increase, so supply just had to follow the flow. A rise in demand is thus the most obvious explanation for the evolution of both trade flows (imports and exports). It meant that the domestic market grew, so that – even when production also expanded – exports were probably not vital for the prosperity of the mining sector. All in all, imports grew steadily while exports did not truly decrease. Accordingly the balance of trade remained favourable for regular coal throughout the entire period. However, it is possible that in reality imports grew even stronger, since a proportion of the English coal that was granted access at a lower tariff rate may have been left out the statistics.

---

75 The offices of Ostend, St-Philippe, Newport and Zelzate. NAB, FC, 8874, handwritten remark in the tariff book, March, 8th 1760.

76 NAB, FC, 8874.

77 See Appendix, Table A.8.

CHART 71 *The trade in regular coal, 1759–1791*[78]
SOURCE: RELEVÉ GÉNÉRAL, NAB, FC, 5748–5805.

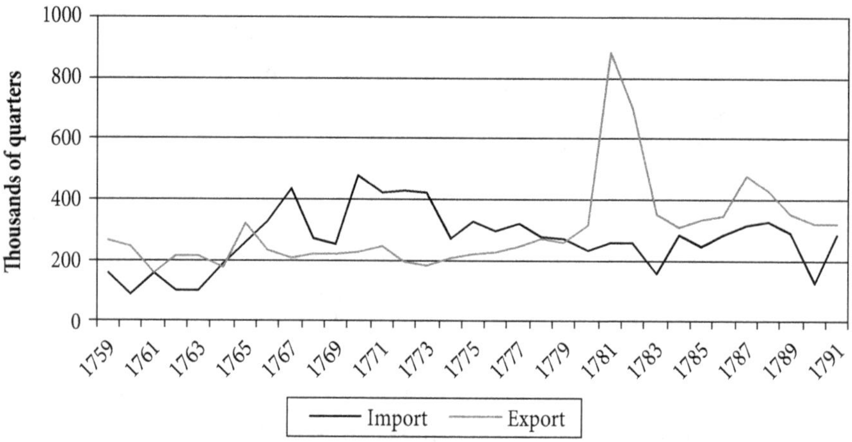

CHART 72 *The trade in small coal, 1759–1791*[79]
SOURCE: RELEVÉ GÉNÉRAL, NAB, FC, 5748–5805.

78 In the customs statistics regular coal was partly noted in "*charretées*" (cartloads) and partly in "*Pesées.*" 1 *pesée* equals 144 pounds (NAB, FC, 5030, note on exports, August 2nd 1779). The weight of a *charretée* is unfortunately uncertain, but we have assumed it equals the weight of 5 quarters (1 quarter = 300 pounds, NAB, FC, 5022, letter by J.J. De la Tombeke, Tirlemont, November 30th 1760), in order to be able to count the total volume. Horace Doursther, *Dictionnaire Universel des Poids et des Mesures Anciens et Modernes, Contenant des Tables des Monnaies de tous les Pays* (Amsterdam: 1965), 91.

79 This chart also shows the calculated total of small coal, that was originally registered in quarters and in cartloads, see above: footnote Chart 4.

Chart 72 shows the trade in so-called 'small coal' or *menu charbon*. This commodity was apparently traded in much larger quantities than regular coal and the trade flows tell a completely different story. Although it is not a shocking turnaround, we do see a decline in imports starting from 1773, just as Hervé Hasquin suspected. It is strange that the same did not happen to regular coal, while the import duties on that type were initially higher – in other words, more restrictive – than for small coal. For regular coal import duties amounted to one and a half stiver per *pesée* or *waeg*, and export duties to three quarters of a stiver (nine pennies). For small coal, duties were only one stiver for import and half a stiver for export.[80] As has been said previously, English coal probably had to pay six stivers for import. In 1761 the duties on small coal were raised to 30 stivers (or one and a half guilder), but so were the duties on regular coal.[81] The most important question is therefore why the shift occurred only in 1773 and not before. And why solely in the case of small coal? Hasquin has mentioned road improvements and the new customs policy as possible explanations, but the latter was already established in 1749, so 1773 seems rather late to see the results of the modifications.[82] Moreover, the sources also did not lead us to suspect that infrastructure had improved all that much by 1773.

Anyway, the decrease in imports remains very modest. The reason that precisely the small coal imports were declining was presumably that the coal basins around Charleroi mainly produced this *menu charbon*, and that it was also the kind that the region needed most itself.[83] So as the number of coal pits in the area gradually increased, the need for foreign small coal in Wallonia faded gradually. It is important to note that the coal which entered the southern part of the Austrian Netherlands in all probability did not come from England, but from Liège and France. At the same time, even though manufactures in Flanders and Brabant firstly used regular coal – which imports were on a steady rise – they also used small coal. The sources show that cities in Flanders and Brabant (such as Antwerp, Malines, Ostend and Newport) were allowed to import many thousands of quarters of English coal, so we know this amount could not have consisted entirely of regular coal (since those import

80 According to the tariff of 1680 for the entire Austrian Netherlands: NAB, FC, 8874, «*Estat ou Tarif des Droits d'entrée et sortie sur les marchandises, manufactures et denrées*».

81 NAB, FC, 8874, handwritten remark in the tariff book, September 17th 1761.

82 Hasquin, "Nijverheid," 128.

83 The production of small coal was about ten times larger than that of regular coal, according to the partial figures by Moureaux. Moureaux, *Les Comptes*, 43.

figures – as we have seen in Chart 71 – are far too low to account for all English imports).[84] Small coal may have been less suited for small industries, but it was also cheaper, which explains their demand for it.

Is it possible to estimate the proportions of coal imported from England to test the hypothesis that domestic small coal did not only replace Walloon imports from Liège and France, but also imports from England? To a certain degree it is. Even though the customs statistics did not explicitly state the origin or destination of the goods included, we can deduce these by looking at the departments where goods entered or left the region. As said in the introduction the customs bureau where a commodity was recorded was not always the one nearest to the point of entry. And of course many goods did not originate from border regions at all. But since we already have a rather clear picture of the major coal suppliers based on historiography, we can make some rather safe assumptions in this case. The results in Chart 73 show that the modest import decrease from 1773 onwards indeed can be attributed primarily to a

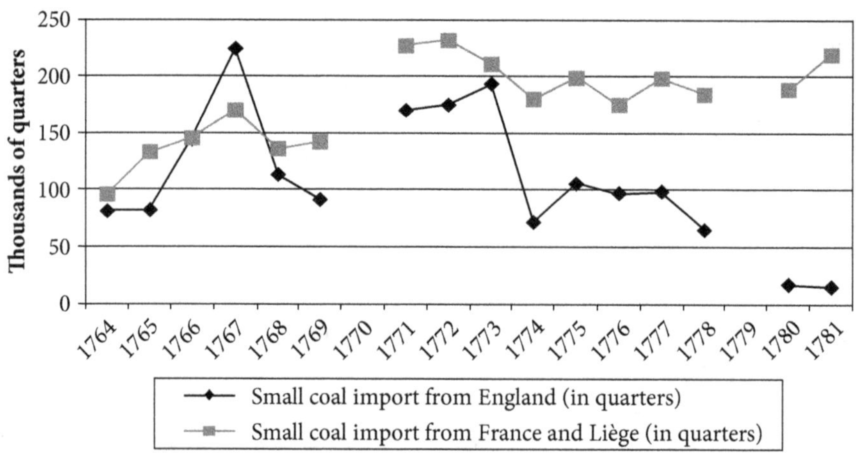

CHART 73 *The import of small coal according to origin, 1764–1781*[85]
SOURCE: RELEVÉ GÉNÉRAL, NAB, FC, 5756–5791.

84 NAB, FC, 5025, Newport and Bruges together can import 100,000 quarters, September 13th 1763; 5027, Antwerp imports 60,000 quarters annually, November 10th 1767; 5028: Ostend may import 13,333 quarters, October 23rd 1769; Antwerp can import 40,000 quarter, Malines 10,000, December 4th 1769; 5029, Lier can import 6000 quarters, January 13th 1770.

85 Subtotals for the 21 departments are only available for the years 1764–1769, 1771–1778 and 1780–1781. To calculate imports from England amounts were added from: Turnhout, Antwerp, St-Philippe, Ghent, Bruges, Ostend, Newport, Ypres and Sint-Niklaas. For French/Liège imports I used Tournai, Mons, Chimay and Charleroi.

decline in English coal imports. Other imports remained more or less stable, but – and the opposite would have been most surprising – import figures to the prime coal producing departments, Mons and Charleroi, also decreased.

Small coal exports also remained even for the largest part of these thirty-three years, but the four years' war again led to a sudden upsurge in exports, just as it did in the case of regular coal. In 1779 merchants in the Austrian Netherlands were already aware of the growing diplomatic difficulties between France and England and they realized that these would cause problems for the European supply of coal, which was mainly conducted through the Dutch Republic. Merchants such as the widow Maes from Ghent tried to relieve the distress by beginning to transport coal from Anzin in France to Holland herself (hence at the same time avoiding that the Prince-Bishopric of Liège would reap the fruits of this temporary trading opportunity).[86] Unfortunately traders failed to truly consolidate the positive trend and exports almost immediately relapsed to just a little above the previous level. Nonetheless, from 1780 onwards the balance of trade was also advantageous in the case of small coal.

The cheaper household coal (*terre houille*) experienced a brief rise in exports at the beginning of the four years' war as well and even stuck to a slightly higher level afterwards, but all in all the traded amounts were much smaller than in the two previous classes (Chart 74). Imports fell slightly around 1771, but rose

CHART 74 *The trade in terre houille, 1759–1791*[87]

SOURCE: RELEVÉ GÉNÉRAL, NAB, FC, 5748–5805.

86 NAB, FC, 5031, request by Maes for lower duties on the trade from Anzin to Holland (not granted), October 13th 1779.

87 This chart also shows the calculated total of *terre houille*, that was originally registered in quarters and in cartloads.

again in the following years. Moreover, fluctuations continued to occur during the rest of the period. In any case, from 1769 onwards, the balance of trade again was positive. Unfortunately the tariff books do not declare the duties on household coal, so we do not know whether the government took any steps to support this sector. However, it is most plausible that this import tax was lower than the previous ones, since a letter from the customs bureau mentioned that merchants sometimes disguised coal coming from France as *terre houille* to pay lower duties.[88] Given the limited amount of household coal imports, this scheme only seemed to have been successful in rare cases.

In sum, the achievements seen in the three categories are not wildly impressive, but contemporaries and earlier historians that gave a very bleak assessment of the situation of the Southern Low Countries' coal industry are certainly proven wrong here. This becomes even clearer when we add the three separate types of coal together in one graph (Chart 75). In total, exports did increase slightly during the second half of the eighteenth century, reaching a sharp – but temporary – climax in 1781. Imports were at their high point in 1770, but lessened somewhat during the last part of the century, despite an unremitting rise in demand. The Austrian Netherlands thus became increasingly autarkic and managed at the same time to play a more important role in international trade. The older historiography was thus probably largely fooled by the conflict of interests that took place in the eighteenth century itself, when it was in the interest of the coal producers to suggest that their situation was pressing

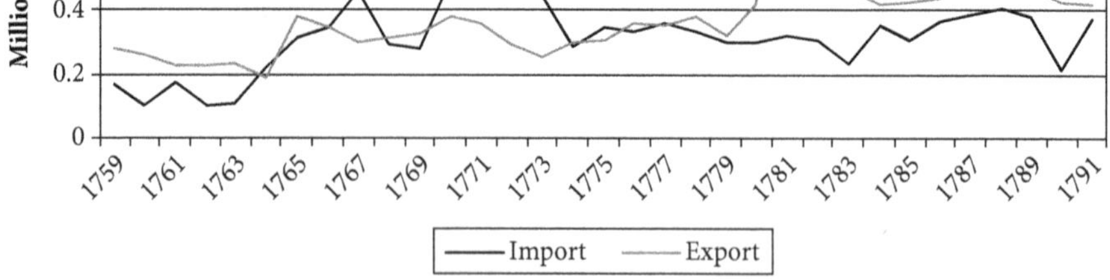

CHART 75 *Sum of all coal flows, 1759–1791*
SOURCE: RELEVÉ GÉNÉRAL, NATIONAL ARCHIVES BRUSSELS, COUNCIL OF FINANCE, 5748–5805.

88 NAB, FC, 5026, Letter to the customs officials of Tournai, September 17th 1764.

(so that the degree of protection would be increased) while the consumers made it seem like the quality of indigenous coal was disproportionate to the price, as an excuse to obtain their supplies elsewhere. In reality the situation seems far less dour than the sources suggested.

When we calculate the total trade flows in monetary value (Chart 76) these conclusions still hold. The balance of trade becomes even slightly more favourable since imported coal (or at least the share of it that was supplied by Great Britain, being almost all *charbon de terre* and also a substantial part of the small coal) was cheaper than domestic coal. We are not entirely certain about the exact proportion of coal originating from England and the price that should be used for foreign coal, so the absolute amounts of imports and exports in value should be taken with a pinch of salt. Based on the above-mentioned trade flows per department (which we have from 1764 to 1781) it appears that usually between around one third of small coal imports came from England, so this share was probably relatively inexpensive.[89] Anyhow, even in case of some

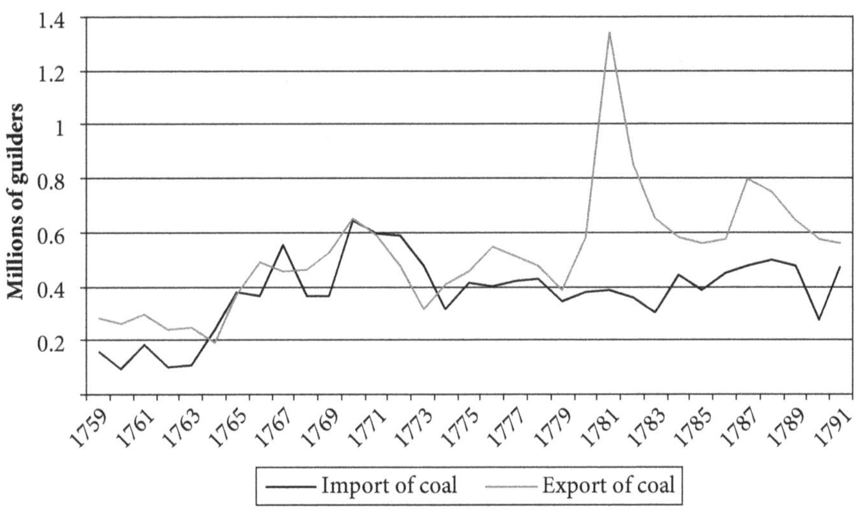

CHART 76 *Sum of all coal flows in monetary value, 1759–1791*[90]
SOURCE: RELEVÉ GÉNÉRAL, NATIONAL ARCHIVES BRUSSELS, COUNCIL OF FINANCE, 5748–5805 AND 5025.

89 The average percentage for the period 1764–1781 is 35. It shows a declining trend. See Appendix, Table A.9, for the exact figures.

90 For regular coal I have used the prices given by the city of Antwerp (since they mainly used this type), NAB, FC, 5025, March 2nd 1763. For small coal I have used the prices given by Verlinden: Verlinden and Craeybeckx, *Documents pour l'Histoire des Prix et des Salaires en Flandres et en Brabant*, Vol II, 799. *Terre houille* was not included due to a lack of price data and the relatively small quantity traded.

deviation from these figures, it is clear that the Austrian Netherlands' coal sector was already quite strong. If it was not for the many internal barriers to trade, the sector might have truly lived up to its potential. On the other hand, while attaining a positive balance was one of the administration's overarching aims, present-day historians should question whether this was truly beneficial for the country as a whole.

As always, it is very revealing to oppose the trade figures – without neglecting their flaws – to production estimates. The latter are unfortunately very scarce and not specified in terms of coal types. Production figures from the year 1796 give an estimated output of 540,000 tons of coal in the Austrian Netherlands.[91] The partial production estimates for earlier years, given by Ph. Moureaux, suggest that there had been a strong production increase between 1768 and 1790.[92] When we convert the figures from the customs statistics into tons, we arrive at about 52,000 tons (375,950 quarters) imported and 59,000 tons (420,341 quarters) exported in 1791, which is respectively a bit below and above ten percent of the total production. Firstly, this means that the Austrian Netherlands had indeed become highly autarkic in their energy supply by the end of the eighteenth century. Secondly, it is safe to say that the size of exports was certainly not negligible. As we have seen it represented on average two to four percent of the overall trade balance. Probably even more, since the customs statistics only provide minimal estimates. Nonetheless, by international standards the exported quantity is still modest. By comparison, in the same year the British exported 632,000 tons of coal, more than ten times as much for a population of about triple size.[93] The Habsburg tolls and export taxes probably remained too high to achieve a real increase in exports, since fiscal considerations were given priority over the promotion of exports. On the other hand, these figures provide strong ammunition that – just like in the case of cotton and mixed fabrics – domestic demand was the prime force behind the coal industry. If it had not been for the four years' war exports would have been even smaller. It was therefore logical that the government focused mainly on domestic sales, i.e. import substitution of English coal, and it appears to have been rather successful in this respect.

91 Hasquin, "Nijverheid," 137.

92 Moureaux, *Les Comptes*, 43–45.

93 B.R. Mitchell and Phyllis Deane, *Abstract of British Historical Statistics* (Cambridge: Cambridge University Press, 1971), 120. Unfortunately we do not have data on the entire British output for this year.

5 Effects of the Coal Trade on the Habsburg Economy

In short, the coal sector succeeded in keeping imports down, while slightly expanding her foreign market. Does this also mean that the eighteenth-century industry was doing well? And did this evolution have any positive effects on the rest of the eighteenth-century economy? Hard to say. The Habsburg government at least was probably quite pleased. The Austrian Netherlands did not manage to become entirely self-sufficient, but when we compared imports to the estimated domestic production above we see that a volume equal to less than ten percent of this amount was imported. However, in the case of imports it makes more sense to look at the different types of coal separately. As said earlier, import of small coal was slightly decreasing, presumably because large industries such as the metallurgical sector were located mostly in Wallonia, close to the domestic coal deposits. Nevertheless, small coal still made up three quarters of the import total at the end of the century even though regular coal had encountered a rather steep rise. The growth in the import of regular coal can probably be attributed to a rise in demand from Flemish and Brabantine manufacturers, what we already suspected when looking at the sources.[94] It therefore implies that these companies were doing quite well and hence had greater resource requirements. Moreover the trade flows certainly suggest that the coal sector itself was also flourishing, even though exports represented only a small part of total production. Jan Dhondt was thus probably right to state that it was a very profitable business.[95]

However, before one should think that the story is an overall success, there is also a downside to record. Instead of just facilitating domestic trade, rulers chose to make English coal more expensive. Perhaps they did so because this was the easiest option, and the one that procured money instead of entailing costs, what would have been the case when digging a new channel for instance. However, for the whole of the economy this was presumably not the best idea, since it helped the Borinage to advance, but led to increased production costs for industries in the rest of the Southern Netherlands, and to higher expenses for ordinary consumers. Looked at from this angle, unrestricted imports and thus a less favourable balance of trade would have actually been more profitable. What is interesting is that there is a noteworthy analogy with the salt trade. Salt – especially crude salt – was also a resource for a great number of industries, so that mercantilists would generally agree that importing it is a

94 NAB, FC, 5031, 5067 and 9113. Pollard, *Peaceful Conquest.*

95 Dhondt and Bruwier, "The Industrial Revolution," 351.

good thing. Nonetheless duties on salt were also heightened, as we have seen earlier.[96]

On the other hand, the very large number of aforementioned exemptions to the taxes (and the ones we have seen in the case of the salt trade) indicate that entrepreneurs did not have to complain all that much. On the contrary, Table 12 shows that when manufacturers – located mainly in Flanders and Brabant – petitioned the government regarding the coal supply to their enterprises, they got what they asked for in seventy per cent of the cases. Yet, the Walloon coal producers and the public institutions (which were mostly city governments

TABLE 12 *The share of granted applications per actor category*

			Ruling				Total
			Approved	Rejected	Unknown	Partially approved	
Occupation of the applicant	Institution	Count	18	0	4	0	22
		% within applicant	81.8	0	18.2	0	100
	Manufacturer	Count	19	5	4	0	28
		% within applicant	67.9	17.9	14.3	0	100
	Merchant	Count	15	6	3	5	29
		% within applicant	51.7	20.7	10.3	17.2	100
	Coal producer	Count	36	4	6	0	46
		% within applicant	78.3	8.7	13.0	0	100
	Unknown	Count	4	7	3	5	19
		% within applicant	21.1	36.8	15.8	26.3	100
Total		Count	92	22	20	10	144
		% within applicant	63.9	15.3	13.9	6.9	100

SOURCE: NAB, FC, 5022–5034.

96 NAB, FC, 5224, October 6th 1764.

from the north) who filed requests to the central government were even more successful. Around 80 per cent of their petitions was approved. On the other hand, it was true that the increased import duties which had been demanded by the coal miners did not seem to have any immediate consequences for the trade flows: there was only a small decrease in coal imports during the period I have studied. So the coal producers were – from their point of view – certainly correct when keeping up their complaints. Then again, foreign competition was probably never detrimental, since imports were small compared to domestic production. At the same time the many successful requests on the part of eighteenth-century manufacturers suggest that it was rather unlikely that the trade duties could have made coal prices escalate – like the latter grumbled – since there were so many exceptions to them. The prices merely remained relatively high since few measures were taken to get rid of internal trade barriers.[97]

The precise effects of international trade thus varied according to which actor was considered. What is remarkable is that in the case of coal the difference is marked by a very clear geographical divide, much more than it did for textiles where the difference ran also along the boundaries between urban and rural environments. For conclusions regarding the coal sector we can discriminate between the southern Walloon area and the Northern provinces of Brabant and Flanders. This however does not imply that the history of coal was mainly dominated by geographical factors, such as Douxchamps-Lefèvre argued, since that would do great injustice to the efforts of the actors involved.[98] The heart of the matter is simply that the coal producers were purely located in the south, while a lot of consumers were located in the north, easily reachable by foreign suppliers but with high transport costs in case of internal trade.[99] Unfortunately we know only little about the owners or investors in eighteenth-century coal mines, except for some enterprises that have been studied separately, because in the sources used here they usually addressed themselves to the administration in groups of anonymous members, represented by a lawyer.[100] Anyhow, for the producers and the region in which they

97 The figures of Verlinden confirm that prices did not inflate much during the second half of the eighteenth century. Verlinden and Craeybeckx, *Documents*, 797–799.

98 Douxchamps-Lefèvre, "Le Commerce," 393.

99 The danger of a mercantilist vision – and of many other economic models – is exactly that is hides the fact that foreign import is sometimes easier or cheaper. K. Berrill, "International Trade and the Rate of Economic Growth," *The Economic History Review, New Series* 12 (1960): 352.

100 Marcel Gillet, "Charbonnages Belges et Charbonnages du Nord de la France Aux XVIIIe et XIXe Siècles," in *Mélanges Offerts À G. Jacquemyns* (Brussels: 1968), Jacques Liébin, *Bois-du-Luc: Un Charbonnage Hainuyer du 17e au 21e Siècle* (Mons: 2004), Moureaux, *Les Comptes*.

were located the higher tariffs and various supportive measures (such as tax-free imports of machines) were propitious, but possibly rather superfluous since demand soared unflinchingly.[101] For the smaller manufacturing industries in Flanders and Brabant the tariff measures were undesirable, but far from detrimental as they were granted all kinds of exceptions and other privileges (Table 13).

TABLE 13 *Content of the requests*

		Occupation of the applicant					Tota
		Institution	Manufacturer	Merchant	Coal producer	Unknown	
Nature of the request	Infrastructure	1	0	0	1	0	2
	Moderation of import duty on English coal	14	15	2	0	2	32
	Moderation of import duty	2	6	4	3	0	15
	Supportive measures	2	1	1	13	0	19
	Restoration of confiscated goods	0	0	3	1	10	14
	Restitution of duties	0	1	11	0	5	17
	Increase of import duty	0	0	0	5	0	5
	Exemption from all duties	1	4	0	2	0	7
	Moderation of transit duty	2	1	4	8	1	16

101 Unfortunately we do not have data on coal consumption to quantify the increase in demand. This remains an unexplored territory in the research on coal. It is possible that accounts from individual towns provide some clues on the overall trend in consumption, but an absolute figure is much harder to come by.

	Occupation of the applicant					Total
	Institution	Manufacturer	Merchant	Coal producer	Unknown	
Moderation of duties	0	0	0	2	0	2
Exemption from export duties	0	0	1	1	0	2
Exemption from import duties on resources and machinery	0	0	1	10	0	11
Unknown	0	0	0	0	1	1
otal	22	28	29	46	19	144

SOURCE: NAB, FC, 5022–5034.

This still leaves one group standing in the cold: the traders. In earlier days they had often provided the necessary capital for the development of mines, in return for coal provisions, but now they were left to their own devices.[102] Their requests concerned exemptions or reductions of taxes, but since these were mostly aimed at increasing their own profit margins, the government usually saw little point in granting them. Much more than the other parties involved in the coal trade, merchants met resistance. Table 12 suggests that only half of their wishes were granted, but in the cases where we do not know the petitioner's occupation, the content and formulation indicates that these were probably also merchants. That implies that in more than half of their appeals traders were (partially) denied their requests. Even influential traders such as Nicolas Bacon – who acted as an advisor for the Auditor's Office (the *Chambre des comptes*) – only saw parts of their wishes conceded.[103] The number of requests that was granted fluctuated

102 The reason for this switch is food for further research. Coppejans-Desmedt, "Handelaars," 482.

103 NAB, FC, 5023, a request to lower export taxes was not answered, October 10th 1759; 5022, request to lower *entrepot* (a bonded warehouse) taxes was partially granted, March 8th 1760; 5022, only some of the supportive measures Bacon asked for were granted, July 24th 1760.

over time, but without any clear trend. Only in the last seven years (1780–1786) the success ratio was slightly higher, especially for merchants.[104] All in all the pursued policy was a very moderate one.

6 Parallels between the Salt and the Coal Sector

We have encountered considerable resemblances between the respective histories of the salt and the coal sectors in the Southern Netherlands. Trade in these commodities was characterized by a basic duality, in that each was both a resource for industry and a retail commodity. Similarly, coal mining and salt refining were active industries in their own rights (interestingly, with some degree of overlap, as salt refining also required the product of coal mining). Various parallels have thus arisen in the history of each commodity, even as marked differences in availability and in degree of novelty had significant and varying consequences in the respective accounts.

First, in both cases the relevant historical sources evidence the hazards of price increases that stemmed from higher import duties. Such developments were extremely detrimental, since both commodities were indispensable to consumers from all levels of society. Price increases could trigger extensive deprivation and misery, especially among the lower classes. Second, both trades were hindered by various internal obstacles. For example, as regards salt, the merchants Pieters and Mertens submitted complaints about the seemingly countless transhipments and stoppages for counting which they encountered when transporting salt through Brabant and which caused protracted delays.[105] The city of Leuven concurred with their charges; however, as was common, these and similar complaints clashed against the authority of tradition, such that little could be done to address the merchants' complaints.[106] Cities like Malines were highly resistant towards surrendering ancient rights, such as the right of *dechargage* and *mesurage*.[107] Consequentially, as in the coal industry, no general measures were taken to eliminate these and other such obstacles. A report by councillors de Cazier and de Keerle indicates a

104 Table A.8 (Appendix) shows the share of granted applications per period.

105 NAB, FC, 5218, complaint from Joseph Pieters concerning transport difficulties, July 28th 1753; 5226, Letter by merchant Mertens, complaint about delays due to measuring, March 6th 1765.

106 NAB, FC, 5218, note from the city of Leuven added to Pieters' complaint, July 28th 1753.

107 NAB, FC, 5218, letter from the city of Malines, August 1753; 5223, bundle on Pieters' complaints that mentions Malines' right of entrepot for salt, fish and oats, August 25th 1762.

third – and essential – trade element which these commodities shared.[108] The authors emphasize the vital importance resource imports held for the salt industry. According to them, importing resources was never harmful and should never be hindered – quite the contrary, in fact! In this particular study de Cazier and de Keerle discuss measures which can be undertaken towards easing importation of *sel de Roche* from England to refinement centres in the Southern Netherlands.

In the coal industry, however, the government went much further in its efforts to facilitate production. Both industries received frequent tax exemptions and moderations; the salt refiners, however, could not expect or rely on many other accommodations, whereas coal producers could. In regards to the salt industry, the government's policies thus seem less considered and less extensive. Before 1749 there had of course been no possibility of any real policy; likewise, in the years following the Treaty of Aix-la-Chapelle the administration still seemed excessively concerned with observing old decrees (hence the many notes concerning fraud, for example). Another concern appeared to be safeguarding tax revenues, which is hardly surprising, given the enormous government debts Maria Theresa had inherited. The salt sector was also quite likely a victim of the necessity (and the habit) of regarding salt as a fiscal means.[109] As de Müllendorf noted to Kaunitz in a briefing: "Salt has always been viewed as a commodity that can be taxed considerably, and is even fit to become a financial means."[110] However, we have seen that even in the 1750s policy makers had already recognized the necessity of supporting domestic industries. Why they had not yet done more to boost the private salt refiners and had let the sector become yet another case of import substitution (with refined salt imports clearly lagging instead of remaining at generally the same, albeit very moderate, level) was probably twofold. First, the low import levels of refined salt demonstrate that the 'Belgian' salt sector was already viable. Second, the fact that salt companies were quite small (usually consisting of no more than a few people) and often operated under near-crippling financial duress rendered them far less influential than the coal mining companies. The latter companies were, as this chapter has shown, relatively sizable economic actors, with considerable purchasing power and therefore far greater political influence.

108 NAB, FC, 5224, report on English rock salt, December 17th 1763.

109 Adshead, *Salt*, Kurlansky, *Salt*, 225–228, Mollat, *le Rôle*, Multhauf, *Neptune's Gift*.

110 "Le sel a toujours été envisagé comme une denrée susceptible d'un impôt considérable, et propre à devenir un moien de finances" NAB, FC, 5248, memoir by de Müllendorf addressed to Kaunitz, end of December, 1764.

7 Conclusion

The study of the international trade flows of coal has again revealed a number of new insights in the fortune of the coal sector, and even of the whole of the eighteenth-century economy. We can now give a more substantiated answer to the question regarding the influence of the international coal trade on the eighteenth-century Austrian Netherlands. The balance of trade was clearly favourable for regular coal and for *terre houille*, and from 1780 onwards it was also advantageous in the case of small coal, the category with the largest volume traded. In other words: in a purely quantitative point of view the coal sector was doing well. The government indeed put a lot of energy in preventing imports, instead of other trade measures. This did not render the Southern Netherlands fully autarkic in guaranteeing their own energy supply – in spite of the large domestic coal production – but they probably came pretty close. Also, they almost certainly could have been able to manage this, if it were not for the many obstacles between the location of the coal basins and the consumers (a lack of transport infrastructure and many local taxes such as the *marlotage* and *lastbreuk*). These made importing coal from England a lot more effortless for the Northern parts of the area. The immense impact of transport costs all through the eighteenth century will become even clearer in the chapter on transit trade. Clearing such internal obstacles might even have led to an even greater domestic trade or to a permanent increase in exports instead of a brief one. However, one reason that the government did not go all the way to bring about self-sufficiency could have been that coal was a resource for many industries, so there was no reason (certainly not in an industrial mercantilist's view) to oppose the import of a cheaper variety.

What is more important however is that we could deduct an increase in demand from the trade figures that suggests a rather rosy picture of the rest of the Low Countries' industry. Export all in all played a marginal role, so it was the domestic economy that required an ever growing amount of coal. This surely arouses suspicion that manufactories were developing, both in terms of innovation and of size. The history of this commodity once again suggests that the Southern Netherlands were capable of realizing a certain degree of import substitution, following from a growing home market. Also, it is interesting to see that coal exports did encounter a strong boost during the four years' war, just as most historians would expect. So in this case the Southern Netherlands were indeed able to fill in the gap due to Britain's occupation with military activities.

Lastly, the commercial policy that we could reconstruct based on the sources on coal, turned out to be very nuanced. The government seemed even more puzzled than in previous cases and did never fully take sides, probably because of the dual nature of the commodity itself (both an industrial commodity and a resource). Its choices were in any case not shaped by mercantilist motives, but came about after a complex interplay of forces between all actors involved. It was a constant compromise between the aspirations of resource producers, the manufacturing industry and the fiscal interests of regional and central governments themselves. In the end, they seem to have tried to accommodate both the wishes of large coal producers and other industries, but not so much those of regular consumers.

As I had hoped, coal brought in a new piece of the puzzle that is the history of international trade. Surprisingly, in the case of coal the largest threat did not come from foreign competitors – such as the sources suggest – but rather from domestic obstacles and transport costs. Nonetheless, a certain degree of import substitution took place at a time of strongly growing demand, which could thus indeed function as a motor for development.

CHAPTER 10

To Trade or Not to Trade?

The Grain Trade

The Austrian Netherlands, despite the relative success of various domestic manufacturing sectors (such as salt and cotton) and of the country's coal mining industry, remained primarily an agrarian region during the eighteenth century. As was the case with most of Europe at the time, the nation's agricultural sector employed what was by far the largest segment of the population and accounted for approximately half of gross domestic product.[1] Thus, although grain may seem an odd choice for studying international trade flows in the Austrian Netherlands – since studies on the historical grain trade usually focussed on the high exports from the Baltic, Prussia or other important rural regions – we now have the necessary data to determine how grain – the prime agricultural output – was faring in the Southern Low Countries. This allows for assessing whether the apparently thriving domestic economy was indeed backed by a successful primary sector.

Of course, unlike for the Baltic and similar regions, for urbanised Western Europe, including the Southern Netherlands, it might easily be assumed that striving for autarky in foodstuffs had always been the regular course of action.[2] Yet it quickly becomes apparent that this approach did not hinder international trade in grains. After all, the trading of grain (for the purpose of meeting general consumption needs) had been occurring throughout the world for most of human civilisation. Ancient Egypt, Greece and Rome are all known to have participated in cross-local grain trades; in fact, this underscores the impression that certain regions have always produced more grain than they needed, while others produced less.[3] Therefore, "world trade provided opportunities beyond the limits of domestic markets and agricultural productivity."[4] In the eighteenth century, Amsterdam remained the prime staple market for the international grain trade, though the Dutch Republic itself did not produce significant amounts of grains. The details of how Amsterdam attained this

1 Aerts, "Economische Interventie," 115.

2 Milja van Tielhof, *The 'Mother of All Trades': The Baltic Grain Trade in Amsterdam from the Late 16th to the Early 19th Century*, vol. 3, *The Northern World* (Leiden: Brill, 2002).

3 R.L. Beukenkamp, *De Wereldgraanhandel* (Wageningen: H. Veenman & Zonen, 1945), 7–9.

4 Derek H. Aldcroft and Anthony Sutcliffe, *Europe in the International Economy 1500 to 2000* (Cheltenham: Edward Elgar, 1999), 33.

 | DOI 10.1163/9789004272606_012

position of "European granary" will not be outlined here; it merits noting, however, that the Baltic grain trade with Amsterdam was so important as to have been frequently labelled the *moedernegotie* ('mother of trades').[5] Numerous studies have examined this trade, yet literature on the international grain trade of the eighteenth century rarely mentions other regions, despite the fact that such areas – England and France, for example, as well as the Austrian Netherlands – were also exporting notable amounts.[6]

There are at least two reasons why this region affords an excellent case study. First, though the balance of trade has shown that the Austrian Netherlands were not an important export region in general, there was another product, besides linen, which the region was able to frequently export in enormous amounts: namely, grain. Of course, for bulk trades such as grains, large volumes did not necessarily imply high incomes (as opposed to so-called 'rich' trades in spices or exotic commodities); nonetheless, estimations for the balance of trade make clear that it is prudent not to dismiss this trade.[7] In fact, within Western Europe, the Austrian Netherlands were nearly the only remaining international supplier of grain.[8] Second, and more importantly, grain offers an indispensable case study in general, as it was the essential base of the economy.[9] Grain prices affected the entire economy, since domestic demand for grain was largely income inelastic; thus, because the trade could affect these prices, there was, in the case of grain a highly concrete link between international trade and the local economy. Feeding the population has always been the prime goal of agriculture, and so it is likely that the importance of grain was an important obstacle to participating in international trade. Though the enormous export levels suggest otherwise, we will see that during some years there were in fact huge drops in export volumes. This makes for a multi-layered, tumultuous history, wherein exports allowed some people to realize tremendous gains but led others to face terrible losses.

Moreover, there are myriad elements that influenced grain production and trade which we will need to take into account, including population growth, weather conditions, productivity, transport possibilities, and prices. Also, numerous sub-questions should be addressed when studying the effects of

---

5 Beukenkamp, *De Wereldgraanhandel*, 35–39, van Tielhof, *The 'Mother of All Trades'*.

6 Ormrod, *The Rise*, 208.

7 van Tielhof, *The 'Mother of All Trades'*, 2.

8 Vandenbroeke, *Agriculture*, 189.

9 Wigbolt Tijms, *Groninger Graanprijzen. De Prijzen van Agrarische Producten tussen 1546 en 1990*, vol. 31, *Historia Agriculturae* (Groningen/Wageningen: Nederlands Agronomisch Historisch Instituut, 2000), 14.

international commerce on grains. Did the Austrian Netherlands indeed become self-supporting during the eighteenth century, as suggested by Chris Vandenbroeke?[10] Did this allow for grain to become one of the region's prime export commodities, with a stable export surplus on the balance of trade?[11] Or were only a few regions (such as Brabant, perhaps) becoming export-oriented? If autarky was indeed the main goal, what political choices were made to counter exports? We know that from 1749 onwards economic policy in general had become much more thought-through, not least as regards the grain supply.[12] Influential councillors like Paradis and Delplancq pleaded for severe scrutiny of the grain flows and they opted for a different form of protectionism than had previously been adopted.[13] Rather than opting to explicitly favour or hinder exports, based on which measure would render the highest profits, constant adjustments were made to the rates of tariffs and even to the granting of permission to export. It was a dynamic and engaged policy which – rhetorically, at least – strongly opposed the emerging ideas of physiocrats who sought to liberate the grain trade. Yet, as we will see, grain exports nonetheless often remained high, and so the central question to address is how the Austrian Netherlands achieved this.

1 Grains in the Eighteenth-Century Austrian Netherlands

As grain has not always been the most popular topic amongst economic historians, it is worthwhile to set out a few facts about the use of grain in the eighteenth-century Southern Netherlands. Grain remained by far the primary source of nourishment for the inhabitants of the region. The earlier observation about grain prices affecting the entire economy was in fact a fairly drastic understatement: indeed, any rise in grain prices could easily entail malnutrition and death for thousands, whereas low prices implied poverty and hardship for peasants. Grain thus affected every part of society. In addition to more commonly known grains, such as wheat and rye, which are used for baking bread, other types, such as spelt and meslin (a mixture of wheat and rye) also merit mentioning. Of these, wheat was usually sold at the highest prices; but grain prices will be examined in greater detail later on. Buckwheat was

---

10 Vandenbroeke, *Agriculture*, 81, C. Vandenbroeke, "Landbouw in de Zuidelijke Nederlanden 1650–1815," in *Algemene Geschiedenis der Nederlanden* (Haarlem: 1980), 80.

11 Verhulst, *Landbouwproduktiviteit*, I.

12 Vandenbroeke, *Agriculture*, 159.

13 Ibid., 174.

unsuitable for bread baking, but was also grown as a foodstuff (for example, to be processed in pancakes or porridge) in regions with poorer soils such as the Campine Area. In the rest of the country it was cultivated mainly as forage, complementing the use of oats (for instance in the Waasland polders).[14] Another highly important use for grain was, of course, brewing beer. Here, barley – in its germinated form, known as malt – was the prime resource. Finally, grains also had industrial uses; these were less extensive, but included paper production, book binding and leather tanning (which required rye flour).[15] However, the only practice that is mentioned with any degree of regularity within the grain-related sources is the use of wheat in production of (clothing) starch. In particular, from 1782 onwards the archive contains occasional applications for establishing a new *amidonerie*, or starch factory.[16]

It is widely assumed that agriculture had begun to flourish in Flanders and Brabant in the seventeenth and eighteenth centuries, thereby becoming 'the Garden of Europe'.[17] During the Austrian period the output of arable produce was growing even more strongly than it ever had previously (albeit, according to some, not as fast as population growth) possibly rendering the Austrian Netherlands agriculturally self-sufficient.[18] Much of this was related to the widespread diffusion of small farms – at least in inland Flanders – whose land productivity was higher than that in England and the Dutch Republic.[19] Coastal Flanders, on the other hand, was characterized by large, commercial farms

---

14 Ibid., 108.

15 Sheila Pelizzon, "Grain Flour, 1590–1790," *Review* 23, no. 1 (2000): 87.

16 NAB, FC, 4792–4809, *passim*.

17 For the nineteenth century this scenario has been shown to have been a myth, as productivity was far outstripped by massive population growth. Bruno Blondé, *Een Economie met verschillende Snelheden: Ongelijkheden in de Opbouw en de Ontwikkeling van het Brabantse Stedelijke Netwerk (Ca. 1750–Ca. 1790), Verhandelingen van de Koninklijke Vlaamse Academie van België voor Wetenschappen en Kunsten* (Brussels: 1995), 245, Verhulst and Vandenbroeke, *Landbouwproduktiviteit*, i–ii.

18 An overview of grain yields during the eighteenth century can be found in: Guy Dejongh and Erik Thoen, "Arable Productivity in Flanders and the Former Territory of Belgium in a Long-Term Perspective (from the Middle Ages to the End of the Ancien Régime)," in *Land Productivity and Agro-Systems in the North Sea Area (Middel Ages-20th Century): Elements for Comparison. In Comparative Rural History of the North Sea Area; CORN Publication Series 2*, ed. Erik Thoen and Bas Van Bavel (1999). Existing estimates for production and consumption are overall not very detailed, but this deficiency will be rectified by: *Rural Economy and Society in the North Sea Area: Land Use and Productivity* (eds. Erik Thoen and Tim Soens), Turnhout, Brepols, forthcoming.

19 Guy Dejongh, *Tussen Immobiliteit en Revolutie. De Economische Ontwikkeling van de Belgische Landbouw in een Eeuw van Transitie, 1750–1850* (Leuven: 1999), 232.

that focused mainly on cattle breeding. Grain yields were presumably comparable in coastal and inland Flanders (in contrast to regions with poor, sandy soils; in particular the Campine Area) due to respectively large-scale agricultural enterprises on the fertile polder soils and intensive farming methods (both in terms of labour and fertilizer) elsewhere.[20] The primary sector – whose main activity remained grain production – was immensely important for the Austrian Netherlands: an estimated 80 per cent of the population was active in the sector and it offered a share in added value of about 50 per cent.[21] Such developments, along with the ever-present concerns about food security, explain why grain was by far the most widely and thoroughly discussed traded commodity within the source materials on international trade and customs issues of the eighteenth-century Southern Low Countries.[22]

2 Changing Policies: Fickleness or Decisiveness?

Summarizing what this plethora of sources presents is nearly impossible, particularly because grain-related trade policy was constantly evolving and, as a consequence, stakeholders were relentlessly trying to influence it. Nonetheless, we can determine some of the policy's major aspects via the recurring themes within the administration's legacy. The sources' general discourse clearly emphasizes the importance of domestic food security. Every department was required to send annual reports concerning the success of the grain harvest and the level of grain prices.[23] This information was processed immediately,

20 Erik Thoen, "'Social Agrosystems' as an Economic Concept to Explain Regional Differences. An Essay Taking the Former County of Flanders as an Example (Middle Ages-19th Century)," in *Landholding and Land Transfer in the North Sea Area (Late Midle Ages-19th Century), CORN Publication Series 5*, ed. Bas van Bavel and Peter Hoppenbrouwers (Turnhout: Brepols, 2004).

21 Dejongh, *Tussen Immobiliteit*, 13, Vandenbroeke, "Landbouw in de Zuidelijke Nederlanden 1650–1815," 73–74.

22 The files specifically on the trade in grains are in NAB, FC, 4704–4817 and there are also interesting files on grain prices in the following numbers.

23 Nearly every filing box of the customs archive on grains ("douanes: Grains foin paille pois feves") includes originals or copies of the letters with reports that were sent to the *bureau de la régie* in Brussels. For the years studied here, the numbers are: NAB, FC, 4719–4809. But there are files spanning the period 1749–1794 (4704–4817). Information about the methods used to collect grain prices are found in a 1759 memorandum from the Finance Council, NAB, FC, 4828. And in: Erik Buyst, Stefan Dercon, and Bjorn Van Campenhout, *Road Expansion and Market Integration in the Austrian Low Countries During the Second*

such that when a shortage was anticipated or when grain prices exceeded a certain level the Finance Council could opt to install a (partial) export ban.[24] The idea that swift action was imperative had been present from the beginning of the new customs organization in 1749 and, especially in the case of grain, had entered into policymakers' thinking, as high grain prices were believed to be extremely dangerous.[25] Often, export bans were complemented by various measures intended to hinder domestic transports over longer distances, because officials feared that such transports could easily facilitate fraudulent exports.[26] The duchy of Limburg played a leading role in such cases, for its geographical particularities made it an easier target for smugglers.[27] Owners of mills that were situated near the border were also in a special position, since they sometimes milled grain for peasants from the other side of the border and were significantly affected by the restrictions in exports or transport.[28]

Half of the 18th Century (Leuven: Center for Economic Studies, 2000), 5, Verlinden and Scholliers, *Dokumenten*, Vol. 4, 1–166.

24 An overview of the changing measures can be found in: Vandenbroeke, *Agriculture*, 174–181. And in the Appendix, Table A.10.

25 NAB, FC, 4704, note to the Finance Council, s.n., 1749.

26 NAB, FC, 4710: "Reflexions de la part des députés des Flandres sur le placcart emané le 18 jan 1757," s.d. this letter agrees with the export ban, but calls the obstacles to internal transport harmfull; 4739, magistrates from Louvain (Van Couwenhoven) ask to limit grain sales to a few official markets, 1769; 4751, ban on grain transports within the department of Chimay, June 10th 1771; 4754, prohibition to sell grain outside official markets, November 7th 1771; 4780, letter that mitigates the rules on grain transport to areas close to the border, September 25th 1776, s.n.; 4782, dispositions facilitating internal transports, February 27th 1777. Another reason to limit grain sales to official markets might have been to guard its quality, but this is never stated within the sources.

27 NAB, FC, 4730, note from the customs bureau, s.n., transport from Luxemburg to Limburg is prohibited, April 18th 1768; 4741, decree by De Keerle, de Cazier, de Witt prohibiting grain exports from Limburg, May 12th 1770; 4750, decree prohibiting bakers from Hodimont to get grain from other regions, may 25th 1771; 4759, Note by Perin (commissioned by Delplancq) on the relatively high level of fraud in Limburg, which necessitates extra measures, January 13th 1772; 4767, letter by the city council of Herve (signed Mertens) complaining about the scarceness and expensiveness of grain on official markets in Limburg (Aubel), they ask to allow transports from other regions to provide free grain to Limburg bakers, since they fear for public insurrections, August 7th 1773; 4768, different pieces on permitted transports to Limburg 1771–1772, by clerk Ernst van Dalhem; 4775, permission to transport flour to Limbourg, with the condition of preventing its further export, signed by Ternois, April 6th 1775.

28 NAB, FC, 4740, file on mill-owners from borderlands, 1770; 4776, letters granting mill-owners that were previously allowed to procure inland grain to continue this practice despite the prohibition of may 1st 1773; within the rest of the series on the grain trade, we can find

It should be noted that the Austrian Netherlands were hardly alone in this regard and that neighbouring countries also frequently opted to restrict grain exports or even prohibit them during periods of price increases or failing harvests.[29] In this regard, the Habsburg grain trade policy was fairly commonplace.

However, despite the policy's apparently consistent and singular objective, grain continued being exported throughout the period 1759–1791. The grain trade, just like the other commodities examined in this study, was afforded countless exemptions to the rules (in this case, to the recurring export bans). Sometimes, more general exemptions were decreed for certain regions, for specific types of grains, for trade through the port of Ostend and for over-land trade.[30] However, transport was of critical importance for bulk products such as grains – and, as detailed earlier, also for coal, as evidenced by numerous complaints regarding transport obstacles – so allowing over-land exports solely could come pretty close to prohibiting export on the whole. This is confirmed by a preliminary estimation of the share of land trade, based on the year 1774.[31] Besides these more general measures, there were also many individual permits permitting merchants to export grain shipments during periods of export prohibition (285 recorded cases, see Table 14); these permits were

---

frequent individual permissions for mill-owners to transport grain, or to mill foreign grain and export the flour, see Table 1.

29 NAB, FC, 4724, the Finance Council asks to investigate the effects of the English export ban, February 19th 1762; 4729, letter to the customs bureau on the French export ban, November 24th 1767; 4743, printed French ban, "arrest du conseil d'état du roi," July 14th 1770.

30 NAB, FC, 4719, letters from the customs bureau allowing exports from Namur, March 1st 1759; 4781, decree allowing grain export by land, December 23rd 1776; 4797, letter about liberating grain trade and entrepot in Ostend, August 13th 1783; 479, communication from the customs bureau allowing trade via land, November 29th 1784; 4800, communication allowing flour exports from Bruges, Ostend and Newport, June 15th 1785; 4809, regulations for the port of Ostend, noting that grains traded in Ostend are exempt from duties, June 11th 1781. The general decrees concerning prohibition of grain exports are also often limited to a selection of departments.

31 In calculating the share of exports presumably leaving the country by sea during 1774 (the year for which departmental data has been gathered), it becomes clear that this share likely constituted it at least two thirds of total exports. In this year export was allowed for most grains, up until September. 71 per cent of exports were recorded in Ostend, Newport, Antwerp and Brussels. Brussels is included because much of the Ostend trade was presumably registered there, since the companies based their administration in Brussels. Of course, it remains difficult to assess whether this was indeed overseas or fluvial trade, so the statement about prohibition of shipping exports remains hypothetical.

TABLE 14 *Overview of the requests sent to the Finance Council*

			Applicant category							Total
			Army	Consumer	Merchant	Mill owner	Producer	Public institution	Unknown	
Request	Diminution of duties	Count	0	2	5	1	0	0	0	8
		% within request	0%	25%	63%	13%	0%	0%	0%	100%
	Exemption of duties	Count	0	17	10	19	1	0	0	47
		% within request	0%	36%	21%	40%	2%	0%	0%	100%
	Exportban	Count	0	2	1	0	0	5	0	8
		% within request	0%	25%	13%	0%	0%	63%	0%	100%
	Permission to export	Count	12	32	285	5	7	14	6	361
		% within request	3%	9%	79%	1%	2%	4%	2%	100%
	Permission to reexport	Count	0	1	4	7	0	0	0	12
		% within request	0%	8%	33%	58%	0%	0%	0%	100%
	Permission to reimport	Count	0	5	3	13	0	0	0	21
		% within request	0%	24%	14%	62%	0%	0%	0%	100%
	Permission to transit	Count	1	1	32	0	0	0	0	34
		% within request	3%	3%	94%	0%	0%	0%	0%	100%
	Permission to transport	Count	12	92	41	61	2	9	1	218
		% within request	5%	42%	19%	28%	1%	4%	1%	100%
	Restitution of confis-cated goods or duties	Count	0	3	90	8	0	1	1	103
		% within request	0%	3%	87%	8%	0%	1%	1%	100%
	Supportive measures	Count	0	1	4	10	0	1	0	16
		% within request	0%	1%	25%	63%	0%	1%	0%	100%

TABLE 14 *Overview of the requests sent to the Finance Council (cont.)*

			Applicant category							Total
			Army	Consumer	Merchant	Mill owner	Producer	Public institution	Unknown	
	Unknown	Count	0	5	7	6	0	0	2	20
		% within request	0%	25%	35%	30%	0%	0%	10%	100%
Total		Count	25	161	482	130	10	30	10	848
		% within request	3%	19%	57%	15%	1%	4%	1%	100%

SOURCE: NAB, FC, 4718–4809.

often granted with the explicit condition (and demand) that the merchants not raise their prices.[32] Thus, even in years that saw a general ban on exports, there always remained some degree of legal export. This is curious, for clearly the government was concerned about domestic grain supply and its prices. Occasionally, government authorities divulged the reasons for allowing these exports (for example because the grain had already been promised to a certain buyer or because the transport ship in question was already waiting in the harbour); more often, however, no justifications were forthcoming, leaving local traders and later historians to wonder about the government's actual intentions.[33] A strong argument that may account for some of these unexplained permissions to export is as follows:

> In spite of the different permissions granted to merchants […] the grain price has not risen on the markets: this is sufficient proof of the abundance of grain and the necessity of sending it abroad.[34]

32 The practice of asking merchants for a *soumission* (a promise not to raise prices) was most current at the beginning of the studied period. For example in NAB, FC, 4714, "soumissions jusqu'au 15 d'avril 1758"; 4715, June-August 1758; 4718, December 1758.

33 NAB, FC, 4798, "Liste de toutes les permissions, qui, depuis la défense de la sortie du froment, ont été accordées pour des parties de cette espèce de grain," s.n., s.d. In this list the reason that is given is that the ships were on the break of leaving. The same is noted in: NAB, FC, 4726, permission for Bernard Pharazijn and J.B. Lyssens, November 18th 1765; idem, permission for Henry Van Schelle, November 14th 1765.

34 "Malgré ces différentes permissions accordées à différens négocians […] le prix des grains n'a point haussé dans les differens marchés : cette preuve seule suffirait pour constater

Overall, requests from merchants that were granted permission to export are significantly more numerous than those that were rejected (63.4 per cent versus 26.3, see Table 15). As such, it is interesting to identify the merchants who succeeded in persuading the government not to restrict the grain supply to only the domestic market and how these merchants made their case. Those who received favourable rulings included not only well-known and

TABLE 15 *Share of requests granted*

			Ruling				Total
			Granted	Rejected	Partially granted	Unknown	
Request	Diminution of duties	Count	4	4	0	0	8
		% within request	50.0%	50.0%	0.0%	0.0%	100.0%
	Exemption of duties	Count	35	11	0	1	47
		% within request	74.5%	23.4%	0.0%	2.1%	100.0%
	Export ban	Count	1	2	0	5	8
		% within request	12.5%	25.0%	0.0%	62.5%	100.0%
	Permission to export	Count	229	95	15	22	361
		% within request	63.4%	26.3%	4.2%	6.1%	100.0%
	Permission to reexport	Count	11	0	1	0	12
		% within request	91.7%	0.0%	8.3%	0.0%	100.0%
	Permission to reimport	Count	13	2	5	1	21
		% within request	61.9%	9.5%	23.8%	4.8%	100.0%
	Permission to transit	Count	19	10	2	3	34
		% within request	55.9%	29.4%	5.9%	8.8%	100.0%

l'abondance des grains et la necessité d'en envoyer à l'etrange." NAB, FC, 4713, bundle of *permissions* with justification, signed by Marquis de Herzelles, De Cordeys, Bellanger, March 8th 1758. In another bundle dating from March 15th the same authors even say that the prices have decreased.

TABLE 15 *Share of requests granted (cont.)*

			Ruling				Total
			Granted	Rejected	Partially granted	Unknown	
	Permission to transport	Count	139	55	13	11	218
		% within request	63.8%	25.2%	6.0%	5.0%	100.0%
	Restitution of confiscated goods or duties	Count	53	24	23	3	103
		% within request	51.5%	23.3%	22.3%	2.9%	100.0%
	Supportive measures	Count	3	12	0	1	16
		% within request	18.8%	75.0%	0.0%	6.3%	100.0%
	Unknown	Count	4	10	0	6	20
		% within request	20.0%	50.0%	0.0%	30.0%	100.0%
Total		Count	511	225	59	53	848
		request within	60.3%	26.5%	7.0%	6.3%	100.0%

SOURCE: NAB, FC, 4718–4809.

influential merchants such as Jean and Pierre Deloose or Frans Solvyns, but also many people who were apparently active only in the field of the grain commerce. Frequently recurring names include Barthelemi Corthout, from Leuven; Bernard Pharazijn and Hennesy, from Antwerp; Henry Van Schelle and J. Saelden, from Brussels; and Leemans, from Malines. This supports Hubert van Houtte's hypothesis that grain commerce was largely the domain of numerous medium-size entrepreneurial families.[35] Moreover, the cases in which a permission to export was not granted were apparently those in which foreigners sought to export; examples include the abbeys of Stavelot (Liège) and Trier, though even these petitioners sometimes received permission. When foreigners are excluded from the data, exemptions to the export

35 Van Houtte, *Histoire.*

bans are even more common. This suggests that traders did not necessarily need to rely upon a powerful lobby or to hold a seat in one of the government's various institutions, as a standard request for exemption usually sufficed.

The fact that some measure of grain exports was always permitted implies that, besides traders, grain producers also profited from the opportunities to expand their sales across the border. Interestingly, the producers themselves are rarely explicitly mentioned in the customs sources. In only one protocol is it stated that exports might encourage agriculture, and there are only ten requests from grain producers (see Table 14).[36] What is certain is that the latter were large, well-resourced farmers, who were capable of marketing their grains themselves (in contrast to peasants who did not have the necessary material or capital). Some authors provide information about such farmers who had their own produce brought to the market by skippers and optionally hired brokers to sell it (which is seen as a characteristic of a highly market oriented agriculture, usually linked to large polder farmers), but I have not found explicit examples within my own sources.[37] However, other avowed supporters of grain exports were found in letters by the States of Flanders and Brabant, and in the person of the chancellor of court and state in 1782, who believed it was more likely that grain, rather than becoming too expensive, would in fact become too cheap.[38] At least one anonymous pamphlet suggested that a premium be awarded for exporting grain, which could be suspended in case of shortage.[39] Another pamphlet, from 1783, goes so far as to state that those pleading for prohibitions were simply basing their arguments on lies. The pamphlet, which

---

36 NAB, FC, 4780, *Extrait de protocole du conseiller des finances Baudier du Samedi 13 juillet 1776.*

37 Pieter De Graef, "Polderpioniers in de 'Nieuwe Dyckagie van Calloo'. Marktgerichtheid en Risicobereidheid van de eerste Generatie Landbouwers in Kallopolder, ca. 1665–ca. 1710" (University of Antwerp, 2010–2011), Jean-Marc Moriceau, *Les Fermiers de l'Île-de-France. L'Ascension d'un Patronat Agricole (XVe-XVIIIe Siècle)* (Paris: Fayard, 1994), 462–465, Piet van Cruyningen, *Behoudend maar Buigzaam. Boeren in West-Zeeuws-Vlaanderen, 1650–1850* (Wageningen: 2000), 207–211.

38 NAB, FC, 4709, letter by States of Flanders arguing that the ban inflicted too many disadvantages, Ghent, February 10th 1757; 4791, letter by the States of Brabant asking to end the export ban, since prices were low, s.n.; 4793, letter by States of Flanders saying that the circumstances are well enough to allow exports, September 3rd 1782; 4794, "Copie d'un P.S. de son altesse le chancelier de cour et d'etat à son altesse le Prince de Starhemberg, en date du 16 novembre 1782."

39 NAB, FC, 4709, "*reflexions sur la sortie des grains,*" 1757.

also excoriates the French *Police de grains*, appears to have been written by someone who also produced considerable amounts of grain.[40] Emperor Joseph II also strongly favoured liberating grain exports.[41] In 1786 he circulated an edict which declared all grain and flour trade to free of restrictions on import, export and storage. According to the edict, this was the most effective way to ensure a constant and affordable grain supply, and to prevent monopolization.[42] This measure revealed the emperor to be a true physiocrat, but many of his local administrators thought the edict excessive.

For their primary argument, the local opponents of free grain exports without exception exploited the threats of price increases, or, in other words, the *cherté des vivres*. Many of the written requests seeking an export ban were submitted by city councils, in the interest of protecting their populations (the consumers); councils also feared civil unrest, though no examples of such events were recorded during the period.[43] Nonetheless, for the years during which grain exports were allowed, substantial portions of the archived sources are dedicated to complaints about grain prices. The most vehement backer of export restrictions was, as noted, the administration within the Southern Netherlands, in particular chancellor Kaunitz. Efforts towards restricting exports had dominated the work of the new customs bureau from the beginning. And so strongly did customs officials believe in this cause that it was even explicitly decreed that grain smugglers could be executed.[44] However, unlike with the salt trade, the archived sources pertaining to grain include no examples of arrests that escalated into violence.[45]

A final comment should be noted, about a group of consumers that has not been encountered elsewhere in the discussed sources on trade: namely, the

40 NAB, FC, 4797, untitled, *Il est rare que les hommes saisissent la verité…*, s.n., s.d., probably 1783. The author speaks about the "fruits de mon champ" and was thus probably a producer.

41 Vandenbroeke, *Agriculture*, 181.

42 NAB, FC, 4803, printed edict by Joseph II, December 11th 1786.

43 NAB, FC, 4725, request for an export ban by Ostend, August 3rd 1765; 4726, request for an export ban by Brussels, November 16th 1765; 4739, letter by the city council of Ypres stating that since exports had been permitted foreign merchants had been robbing their grain, thereby spurring huge price increases, September 28th 1769; NAB, FC, 4771, letter by the city of Ostend complaining about the scarcity of grains, August 8th 1774; 4787, request for an export ban by Antwerp, December 23rd 1780.

44 NAB, FC, 4710, printed edition of the "Placcard Défendant la sortie de toutes sortes de Grains, Du 18 Janvier 1757." This placard followed the prohibition of grain, flour and bread exports that had been decreed the previous September 28th but which was not being respected.

45 NAB, FC, 5226, Doctor's report on the death of a salt smuggler, March 23rd 1765.

army. Garrisons were usually stationed near the border, often in areas that were not allowed to receive grain transports. Thus, when such garrisons needed new supplies they were required to petition the Finance Council. However, this appears to have been no more than a formality, as these requests were nearly always granted (there was only one exception in 26 cases).[46] Interestingly, this arrangement also permitted an apparently counterproductive measure. The army was supposed to eschew any import of foreign grain for its own use and entrepreneurs contracted to provision grain to the military were in theory obliged to buy the necessary grain only from domestic producers. Nonetheless, when grain prices became too high these entrepreneurs could request to import certain amounts; these requests were rarely refused, despite the contracts explicitly noting the importance of stimulating the local economy and bolstering tax revenues.[47]

Having discussed the various stakeholders directly affected by international trade in grains and their interests in relation to it, we should now address the reality of the trade flows. Thus far, it can be concluded that, though there were clearly recurring motives within the grain policy – a policy which, in general, was designed to ensure a stable supply of grain – the policy remained coloured by the countless (and often successful) efforts to influence the policymakers. The following section will analyse whether the customs statistics offer evidence that this policy affected grain flows and prices. And – more importantly – the share of grains that the Austrian Netherlands exported (and imported), regardless of the government's official positions, will shed light on the development of the eighteenth-century primary sector.

3 The International Grain Trade: Capricious Flows

As discussed elsewhere in this volume, grain exports played a leading role in international trade, though this role was less uniform or consistent than that of linen. Whereas export flows of linen were generally unwavering, those for grains shifted markedly from year to year (see Chart 77). In the beginning (1759–1766) exports were fairly stable (and quite high); from 1767 onwards, however, they fluctuated greatly. Some years even saw the balance of trade become slightly negative, owing to exports falling to trifling levels. In general

---

46 See Appendix, Table A.11.

47 Contracts with the entrepreneurs and other sources on the eighteenth-century military can be found in Thomas Goossens, *The grip of the state? Government control over provision of the army in the Austrian Netherlands (1725–1744)*, *Conference paper* (2011).

there was a formidable surplus of exports over imports, even despite frequent export bans, with exports averaging 3.63 times higher than imports. In terms of monetary value, grain exports sometimes amounted to over half a million guilders. This figure accords with the image of the highly productive Flemish husbandry, though in other years grain exports were only modest.[48] On the other hand, imports were similarly modest throughout the entire period for which there is trade data, despite imports generally being exempted from duties.[49] Moreover, the fluctuations in imports show a correspondence to those in exports – this becomes clearer in the figures for separate types of grain – despite expectations that imports would be high when exports were very low, and vice versa. This may be partially attributable to the Austrian Netherlands maintaining nearly sufficient grain production and to the fact that shortages (due to harvest failures) were seldom limited to a single country.[50]

Because transport costs were a critical factor for a relatively low priced bulk product such as grain, one would expect that interest in improving transport infrastructure (for example canals and paved roads) would have influenced the grain trade. However, nothing within the sources hints at such developments. According to Buyst and others, the absence of any clear impact of infrastructural improvements stems from the fact that tolls on paved roads kept fixed transaction costs high (as was the case with coal transports), thereby discouraging bulk trades.[51] The spectacular improvements in transport achieved during the second half of the eighteenth century would thus become truly tangible only during the nineteenth century. This is discussed further in the chapter on transit.

In examining the grain flows in detail (Chart 78), it becomes clear that oscillations in the grain exports reflected the export bans instituted by the local government. Thus, though the authorities never opted to completely bar exports, their measures exerted a marked influence. Wheat exports dropped following the export bans of 1767, 1770, 1775, 1780 and 1789; the export ban of

48 Verhulst and Vandenbroeke, *Landbouwproduktiviteit*, i.

49 NAB, FC, 4730, communication on the liberation of oats imports, February 27th 1768; 5606, the import of wheat, rye, spelt and barley are exempt from duties, April 18th 1768; 4754, communication on the liberation of all grain imports, November 5th 1771.

50 On the sufficiency of the grain production, see: Dejongh, *Tussen Immobiliteit*, 250, Vandenbroeke, "Landbouw in de Zuidelijke Nederlanden 1650–1815," 81–82.

51 Bruno Blondé, "Feeding Cities: Transportation Costs, Paved Roads and Town-Countryside Relationships in Eighteenth-Century Brabant," in *Food Supply, Demand and Trade: Aspects of the Economic Relationship between Town and Countryside*, ed. Erik Thoen and Piet Van Cruyningen (Turnhout: Brepols, 2012), Blondé and Van Uytven, "Langs Land- en Waterwegen," Buyst, Dercon, and Van Campenhout, *Road Expansion*, 28.

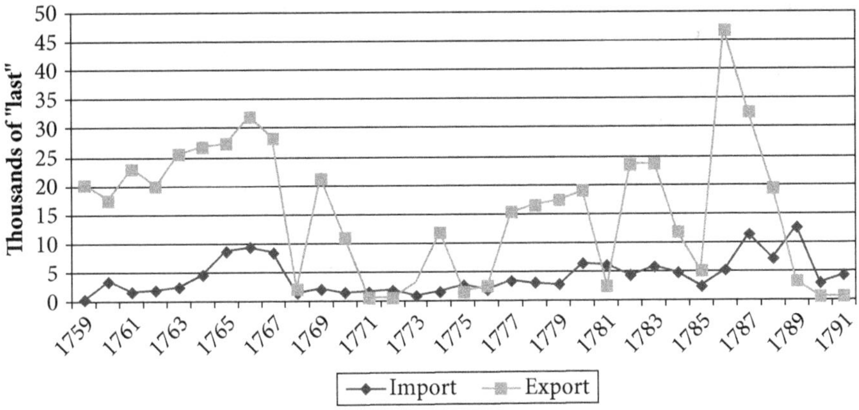

CHART 77 *Total grain trade, 1759–1791*[52]
SOURCE: RÉLÉVÉ GENERAL, NATIONAL ARCHIVES BRUSSELS, FINANCE COUNCIL, 5748–5805.

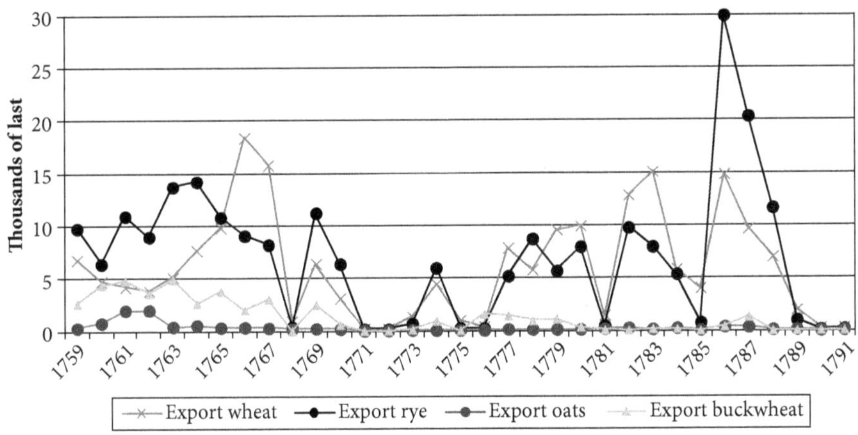

CHART 78 *Export of wheat, rye, oats and buckwheat, 1759–1791 (1767: ban on wheat, rye and buckwheat; 1770: wheat, rye and buckwheat; 1774: ban on all types of grains; 1777: buckwheat; 1780: wheat, rye and buckwheat; 1782: ban on all types; 1784: idem; 1789: idem)*
SOURCE: RÉLÉVÉ GENERAL, NATIONAL ARCHIVES BRUSSELS, FINANCE COUNCIL, 5748–5805.

52 The included grains are: wheat, rye, regular barley, spelt, oats and buckwheat. There is some variety in the exact weight and volume of a *last* for different types of grains. For barley, one *last* equals approximately 3200–3400 pounds; for wheat 4600–4800 pounds, or close to 3000 litres; and for rye 4000–4200 pounds. Posthumus, *Nederlandsche Prijsgeschiedenis*, LV, Verlinden and Scholliers, *Dokumenten*, Vol. 4, xvii.

1784 had a smaller impact, though it too led to a plunge. The same can be said for rye: each decree had immediate effect on the subsequent period's volume of exports (except in 1783). This offers yet another strong case for the customs statistics' representativeness of the movements in foreign trade. As concerned oats, buckwheat and barley, there appeared to have been other factors that influenced trade flows, as these flows appeared to have been less affected by policy measures. For buckwheat the figures were simply decreasing throughout the thirty-year period, suggesting that this grain was losing appeal. The less clear-cut image for these grains may of course result from the fact that their exported amounts were far smaller than those of wheat and rye and were thus more sensitive to occasional small-scale changes in the activities of merchants and producers.

In 1774 – the year for which departmental customs data was collected – almost all grain exports were recorded in the customs bureaus of Brussels and Antwerp (both in Brabant) or Ostend (in Flanders): 73 per cent of wheat exports and 79.5 per cent of rye exports. Other departments play a marginal role in the customs statistics. Of course, although this suggests that Brabant and Flanders were the prime grain exporting regions of the period it is not verifiable that they in fact were, for exports were not required to be recorded at the point of their initial departure.

The next question is whether the grain flows were reflected in the grain prices. Jan Materné has detailed the international grain prices set by the Amsterdam stock market and sent to Brussels.[53] Posthumus' renowned work included prices with the same background.[54] Of course, not all these prices were specifically for grains from the Austrian Netherlands. Yearly prices on the Amsterdam market are available only for Brabantine buckwheat; some are available for Brabantine wheat as well. In the case of rye I have used an average of available prices for grain types that were grown in proximity of this region (see Chart 79). The few figures on Brabantine wheat are apparently almost identical to the average price based on Koningsberger, Frisian, Zealand and Polish wheat; thus the average prices for rye are likely strong evidence of price movements in the Austrian Netherlands as well.[55]

All of the international market prices were highest in the years 1770–1773 and 1789–1790. These coincide with years in which the Austrian Netherlands (and, sometimes, neighbouring countries) instituted export bans. Such bans arose in large part thanks to the administration's meticulously tracking of

53 Materné, *De Prijzenadministratie*.

54 Posthumus, *Nederlandsche Prijsgeschiedenis*, 1–31.

55 The rye price is composed of Koningsberger, Prussian and brown rye prices.

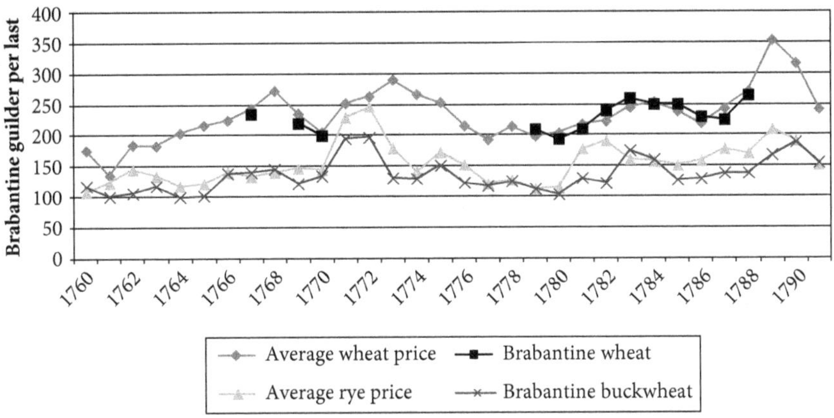

CHART 79 *Grain prices on the Amsterdam stock market, 1760–1791*
SOURCE: POSTHUMUS, 1943, 1–31 AND MATERNÉ, 1994, 143–188 AND 341–388.

changes in prices. Export trends show that many traders adhered to the bans and that exports of domestic grain subsequently decreased; nonetheless, the bans did not seem to be particularly effective in combating high prices. Prices slowly became more modest again (leading to cessation of the export ban), albeit not as markedly as the quickly evolving trade flows would suggest. This is hardly surprising, however, because the prices of grains from neighbouring countries evolved similarly, due to supra-national events and because the total amounts of grain traded in Europe were many times greater than those exported by the Austrian Netherlands. The regime's grain-related trade policies should not be expected to have impacted the overall European market. Nonetheless, given the importance of grain in the eighteenth-century diet, even small changes in prices had immediate impact, and so the administration hoped at least to affect local prices. The administration was highly concerned about grain prices and frequently requested information from city officials about rates. This information was compiled by the Finance Council and has been published by Chris Vandenbroeke.[56] Chart 80 shows the evolution of average grain prices on twenty local markets in the Austrian Netherlands. Here we see that prices were moderating in the years following the export bans of 1774, 1782, 1784 and 1789. Nonetheless, the possibility that an export ban was not the best way to deal with grain shortages or high prices cannot be excluded;

56 Christiaan Vandenbroeke, "Het Prijsonderzoek van de Regering voor de Steden van de Oostenrijkse Nederlanden voor Graangewassen, Vlas en Garen (1765–1794)," in *Dokumenten voor de Geschiedenis van Prijzen en Lonen in Vlaanderen en Brabant (XIIIe-XIXe Eeuw)*, ed. C. Verlinden (Bruges: De Tempel, 1973).

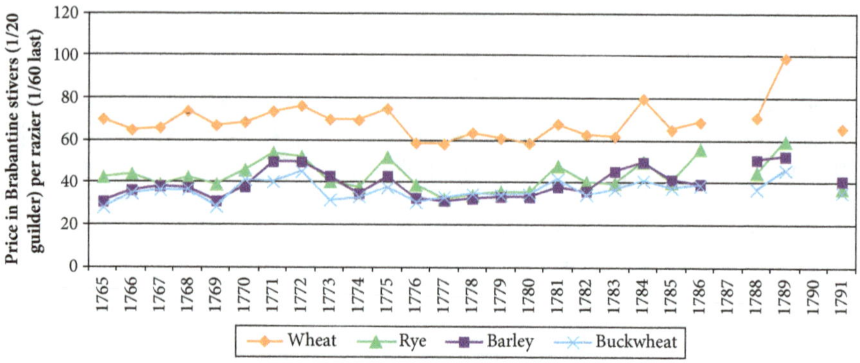

CHART 80 *Grain prices on the local market, 1765–1791*
SOURCE: VANDENBROEKE, 1973, 7–117.

it was certainly one of the easiest ways within the administration's reach, however, and was seemingly rather effective. Finding means to boost productivity would likely have been better, but such measures were much more complicated and difficult to achieve and were simply impossible in case of short-term crisis. Whether liberating the grain trade would have led to constant (or even increasingly) high exports remains unanswered. It is possible that in some years the exports would have automatically adapted to lower yields, yet free export could also have stimulated productivity increase. Within the given context, however, this is merely conjectural.

Flanders and Brabant are considered to have been among the leaders in terms of agricultural productivity, even during the second half of the eighteenth century, when the region witnessed huge population increase and concomitant surges in demand for the previously-mentioned industrial applications of grain.[57] Guy Dejongh was thus not overly optimistic in his work on Belgian agriculture. Productivity growth had accelerated, but probably not apace with the need for grains.[58] This would explain why, though for many years the sources note reasonably good harvests and the memoranda sent to the Finance Council were often optimistic about the state of production, many

57 Bas Van Bavel and Erik Thoen, *Land Productivity and Agro-Systems in the North Sea Area, Middle Ages – 20th Century. CORN Publication Series* 2, ed. CORN, vol. 2 (Turnhout: Brepols, 1999), Adriaan Verhulst, *Précis d'Histoire Rurale de la Belgique* (Brussels: Editions de l'université de Bruxelles, 1990), 155–158. *Rural Economy and Society in the North Sea Area: Land Use and Productivity* (eds. Erik Thoen and Tim Soens), Turnhout, Brepols, forthcoming.

58 Dejongh, *Tussen Immobiliteit*, 237.

people directly involved in the trade continued requesting that exports be barred.[59] Not surprisingly, the issue aroused constant vigilance.

Yet the fact remains that export levels were high. Comparing grain exports to total production in the Austrian Netherlands shows that exports amounted on average to about twenty per cent of domestic production.[60] English grain exports during the 1760s, in contrast, probably accounted for just eight per cent of domestic production.[61] Moreover, in eighteenth-century Western Europe, being able to export was a remarkable achievement in itself. Comparing the Habsburg statistics to the estimates for Baltic grain exports – regarded by the Dutch as the foundation of the economy – and to English exports, which had actually begun surpassing the former by the beginning of the eighteenth century, the figures were not particularly low: with an average of 15,655 lasts, compared to 36,548 and 65,740 last respectively (and the latter two include malt as well).[62] Grain from the Austrian Netherlands was sought after in Tuscany, its flour in America, and of course the exported grain also went to Amsterdam, from where it was shipped to numerous unspecified destinations.[63] The story that emerges from the data on international trade thus supports Christiaan Vandenbroeke's more optimistic view about agriculture, rather than the very cautious one of Dejongh.

4 Conclusion

The central finding of this chapter is that throughout the second half of the eighteenth century – a period of significant population growth – there continued to be exports of grains from this region. These exports were often quite

59 NAB, FC, 4733, «*Mémoire* [...] *sur l'état de production de cette année*», despite abundant rainfall, harvests were good, September 7th 1768; 4742, «Mémoire sur le commerce des grains du 18 juillet 1770», reasonable harvests, but export should remain forbidden, s.n.; 4770, communications on the grain yield April 1774; 4780–4781, communications on the grain yield, April 1776; 4787, memorandum by Botte, stating that the grain harvest was good, but that, because the harvests of potatoes and vegetables were poor, more flour was needed, October 9th 1780; 4790, communications on the grain yield, April 1781; 4808, communications on the wheat and rye yield, 1791.

60 Vandenbroeke, "Landbouw in de Zuidelijke Nederlanden 1650–1815," 84.

61 What probably also had much to do with the early British focus on exporting industrial goods. Ormrod, *The Rise*, 207.

62 van Tielhof, *The 'Mother of All Trades'*, 4 and 36.

63 NAB, FC, 4794, letter by Comte de Piccolomini from Tuscany, October 5th 1782, and *Copie d'un P.S. de son altesse le chancelier de cour et d'etat à son altesse le Prince de Starhemberg, en date du 16 novembre 1782.*

considerable, even in an international perspective. Thus, we can conclude that the primary sector in the Austrian Netherlands was faring quite well. This has previously been argued, usually quite convincingly, by renowned scholars such as Chris Vandenbroeke and Bruno Blondé, and we now have the necessary figures to substantiate the story. The growing demand from a flourishing home market was clearly backed by a thriving agricultural economy – at least in terms of productivity (for the ever shrinking peasant farms of the eighteenth century, grain production alone was probably not sufficient to earn a decent living).

Surprisingly, grain turns out to be the sector where trade policy most impacted actual trade flows. For textiles, coal and colonial commodities, evolutions often occurred despite, rather than as a result of, official trade policy. Here, export bans in particular were actually quite influential, though the sources nonetheless recorded widespread fraud and frequent adjustments and exceptions. The story remains somewhat schizophrenic, in a sense, because those who likely most favoured exports (the grain producers) are largely unmentioned in the sources, whereas those who were most opposed authored the majority of the surviving accounts. But this data demonstrates that there was sufficient domestic grain supply and that international trade in general thus constituted an opportunity rather than a threat for a sector that clearly remains one of the pillars of the Austrian Netherlands' economy.

PART 4

The Development of Transit Trade as the Trade Policy's Litmus Test

CHAPTER 11

Transit Trade

Ever since the closure of the Scheldt in 1585, policy makers within the Southern Netherlands have tried to regain a firmer grip on the Western European trade flows. Without its major port, Antwerp, the Southern Netherlands had lost a great part of the international passage of ships, much to the benefit of foreign cities like Amsterdam, London or Le Havre. The fact that the region also could not rely on a colonial hinterland to directly supply it with certain new commodities added to this downfall. Unsurprisingly, the new trade and customs policy that had been developed after 1749 focussed strongly on the possible transit and transport functions of the well-situated Austrian Netherlands. Transited goods are goods which were not consumed or processed on domestic territory, but that travelled immediately to neighbouring areas.[1] This sets them apart from so-called re-exported goods for which value had been added during their passage through the region.[2] Still, the two terms were sometimes confused by administrators and traders, even though duties on re-exported goods – which had been processed by domestic manufacturers – were generally lower than those on transit.[3] Possibly, the confusion derives from the fact that in both cases the region could reap the fruits of local toll excises, transit or *entrepot* (warehouse) taxes; and of valuable shipping and trade services.[4] Also, transit trade was a profitable business in its own for the local middlemen that were active in it. The brothers Romberg and Overman are renowned examples of merchants who played this field. Hubert Van Houtte wrote in 1920 that contrary to 'regular commerce' (i.e. imports and exports): "Transit trade is almost always profitable."[5]

1 The *relevés* of 1759 and 1760 do not include this category yet, only imports and exports.

2 NAB, FC, 4586, note on the different taxes for transited and re-exported cotton; 4601, in a letter from the customs bureau to the brothers Romberg a clear divide is made between transit and re-export, March 28th 1768.

3 NAB, Manuscripts, 850 A, bundle of memoirs regarding trade during the eighteenth century, folio 20, s.n., s.d. The author talks of levying high taxes on transit to provide a steady income, but also states "que nos droits sont trop forts pour que nos marchands puissent faire le commerce de reexportation" (that our taxes are too high for our merchants to re-export). He probably mixed the terms up here, since re-export of domestically manufactured goods was often exempt of taxes (see chapter on the textile trade).

4 Coppejans-Desmedt, *Bijdrage*, 188, Van Houtte, *Histoire*, 357.

5 "le commerce du transit est presque toujours lucratif'." Van Houtte, *Histoire*, 357.

 | DOI 10.1163/9789004272606_013

The eighteenth-century sources show that the Habsburg government devoted meticulous care to the development of this transport and transit policy. I have retrieved clear indications about the importance that the rulers attached to transforming the Austrian Netherlands into a genuine transit hub or a crossroad within Western Europe and its international trade network.[6] Their attempts focussed on two fields. Firstly, large investments were made in developing new transport infrastructure, such as paved roads and canals to connect different regions. The port of Ostend was assigned a leading role within the transport network and had to complement Austria's Italian ports, such as Trieste.[7] The second aspect of the transit policy was through the tariffs. In order to boost activity in the region, different taxes were presumably levied on transit than on imports and exports. Unfortunately these were not noted in the tariff books and are also difficult to trace within other sources, as is explained in the introduction. For the products included in the previous chapters, transit duties often appear to have amounted to only 0.5 percent of a commodity's worth, but it is difficult to satisfactorily ascertain their heights.[8]

The historiographical evaluations of the transit policy have become ever more divided in recent years. Initially, historians closely followed the government's discourse. Nineteenth-century author Briavoinne and even economic historian Hubert Van Houtte were quite convinced that the transit policy had turned out to be a success. According to them, the administration particularly seized upon the heated tension between Britain, France and the Republic

6 Some important pieces regarding transit can be found in: NAB, SSW, 2194/2, printed tariffs on transit (transit from the Dutch Republic, Liège and Germany to French Flanders, May 21st 1778; overseas transit, May, 18th 1778; transit from Holland to Liège and Germany, August 29th 1778; transit from France to the Dutch Republic, Liège and Germany, May 23rd 1778; transit from French Flanders, May 20th 1778); NAB, FC, 4279, memoirs of Nicolas Bacon regarding transit, 1753–1754; 4290, memoir regarding transit; 5863, note by de Müllendorf on attracting transit trade (making use of the conflict between England and France), September 1779; 8576, notes from Delplancq on transit and other trade topics; NAB, Manuscripts, 2452, correspondence between de Neny and Kaunitz on transit and other topics, 1751–1753.

7 NAB, SSW, 2153 and 2194/2; NAB, Manuscripts, 850 C; NAB, FC, 4279, 4281, 4284 and 4304; NAB, CAPV, 499; OS, FHKA, NHK, Kommerz Litorale, 1007.

8 NAB, FC, 4525, communication to Romberg stating that the transit duty on indigo and cochineal equals 0.5% of the traded value on May 23rd 1778; 4529, chocolate is included in a list of goods (not specified, May 18th 1778) for which the transit duty is 0.5%, signed by Weiss, October 2nd 1784; 4558, decree by De Beelen, cotton fabrics are charged with a transit duty of 0.5%, July 4th 1776; 4629, muslin and others fabrics are charged with 0.5 % percent when transited to France, letter by Overman, April 11th 1785.

(1779–1782) to tighten its grasp on the transit trade in the region.[9] Especially the trade between Britain and the Republic was presumably diverted to the neutral Southern Low Countries in the years 1780–1784, as both nations hoped to lower their opponent's trade revenues. Hilda Coppejans-desmedt is optimistic as well as regards the government's accomplishments, despite their problems in combating domestic tolls and barriers.[10] Michael Serruys calls the transit policy with its combination of tariffs and infrastructural improvements – and albeit its shortcomings – the first structural solution for the closure of the Scheldt.[11] Even Greta Devos, who is very sceptical about measuring the volume of trade flows moving through Ostend, appears rather positive about the effects of the new measures.[12] And indeed, road infrastructure had certainly improved tremendously throughout the second half of the eighteenth century, and has therefore even been regarded by some as having been one of the driving forces behind economic development in the Southern Netherlands.[13]

However, both the effects of the advance in transport opportunities and of the transit policy in general have recently been questioned, at least when it comes to the second half of the eighteenth century.[14] Bruno Blondé has pointed out the very short service life of the heightened eighteenth-century transit trade and the increased activity in the port of Ostend.[15] And other renowned economic historians such as Erik Buyst and Raymond Van Uytven have casted their doubts as well on this so-called transit boom. Even the efforts of the Austrian government to encourage transit between their own hereditary lands and the Southern Netherlands knew little success, says Helma De Smedt.[16] One of the reasons for failure that these authors mention are the persistently high domestic tolls and internal taxes, which allegedly even increased in the years 1785–1786.[17]

9 Briavoinne, *De l'Industrie*, 88, Van Houtte, *Histoire*, 357. Briavoinne even broadens the "window of opportunity" created by the struggle between the maritime powers to the years 1777–1783.

10 Coppejans-Desmedt, "Economische Opbloei," 278.

11 Serruys, "The Austrian Netherlands," 168.

12 Devos, "Oostenrijkse Douanestatistiek," 346.

13 Dejongh, *Tussen Immobiliteit*, 286, Dejongh and Segers, "Een Kleine Natie," 171.

14 Blondé and Van Uytven, "Langs Land- en Waterwegen," Buyst, Dercon, and Van Campenhout, *Road Expansion*, 28.

15 Blondé, *Een Economie*, 241.

16 Houtman-De Smedt, "Charles Proli," 126.

17 Bruno Blondé, *Een Economie met Verschillende Snelheden: Ongelijkheden in de Opbouw en de Ontwikkeling van het Brabantse Stedelijke Netwerk (Ca. 1750–Ca. 1790), Verhandelingen*

To assess the results of the customs administration's actions and uncover the true developments of transit trade, I will first of all return to the estimated trend in the value of total transit trade. Afterwards I will compare it to domestic demand to make statements about the significance of the flows. The main question is whether the Austrian Netherlands were able to increase the volume and/or value of transited goods flowing across their territory, but secondly I also hope to find the underlying explanations for the trends in the transit trade. Afterwards I will see whether the general image is reflected by some of the case studies included in this book. We will see that there are a number of parallel developments, but also striking differences springing from the many ad hoc-measures and the specificity of the goods. A leading role within this chapter is played by the port of Ostend, because the Habsburg rulers aspired to turn precisely that spot into the beating heart of Western Europe's transit hub. The customs statistics will provide the evidence for the success or failure of their efforts.

I have used the same 272 goods for which international wholesale prices are available as in the chapter on the balance of trade, to estimate the evolution of the value of total transit trade. The absolute value of the flows in Chart 81 is thus not exact, but the trend makes a good claim on representativeness. The value of transit trade increased modestly until 1778, followed by a short transit boom in the years 1779–1783. This sudden and short-lived stronger growth can probably not be put on the account of the government's actions – which had commenced much earlier and were rather constant throughout the period – but was likely due to an external factor: the aforementioned four year's of war between France, the Republic and Great-Britain that temporarily weakened these big competitors. On the other hand, government efforts may still have been a necessary but not entirely sufficient condition. After the war, the value of transit stabilized at a relatively high level (five times higher than it had been 30 years before), even surpassing the value of exports in a number of years. Compared to the value of imports (Chart 82) we see that transit increased from around a third of import value in the first years to more than two thirds at the end of the period. That implies that the region did manage to become relatively active in the international transport scene, although – as we will see – it was not the case in every sector.

---

van de Koninklijke Vlaamse Academie van België voor Wetenschappen en Kunsten (Brussel: 1999), 242, L. Van Buyten, "Bronnen voor de Geschiedenis van de Transitohandel en de Transitowegen in de Oostenrijkse Nederlanden. De Doorvoerhandel op Lorreinen," in *Histoire Économique de la Belgique. Traitement des Sources et État des Questions. Actes du Colloque de Bruxelles (Ie-IVe Sections)* (Brussels: Historica Lovaniensia, 6, 1972).

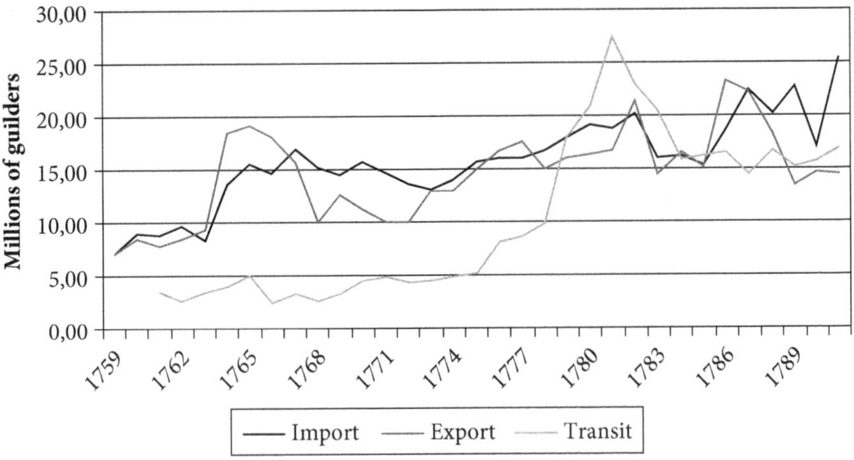

CHART 81 *Import, export and transit, 1759–1791*
SOURCE: RÉLÉVÉ GENERAL, NAB, FC, 5748–5805.

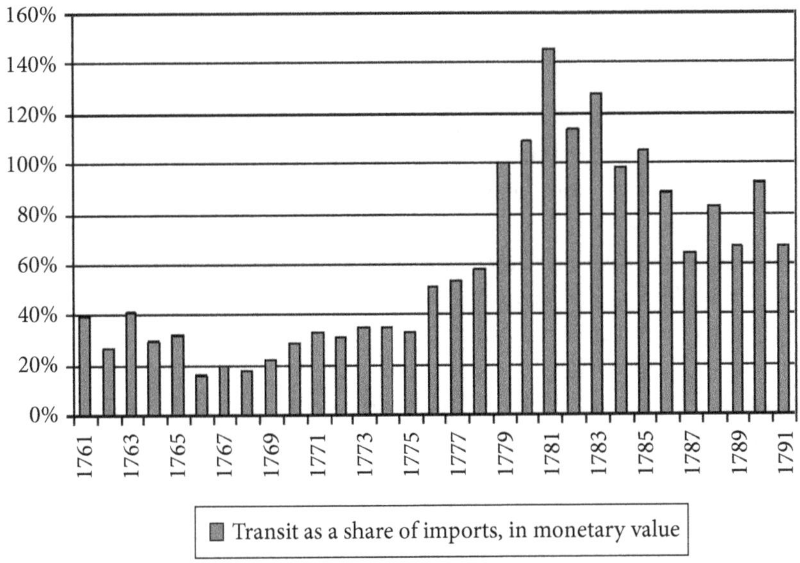

CHART 82 *Transit as a share of imports, in monetary value, 1761–1791*
SOURCE: RÉLÉVÉ GENERAL, NAB, FC, 5750–5805.

In the sources on the salt trade for example, the movement of the transit flow appears much more fortuitous than the estimated total (Chart 83). Strangely, there is absolutely no sign of the assumed transit boom during the four year's war. The transit of salt was increasing, but very irregularly and less markedly than in the previous graphs. The reason is not up for grabs since remarkably

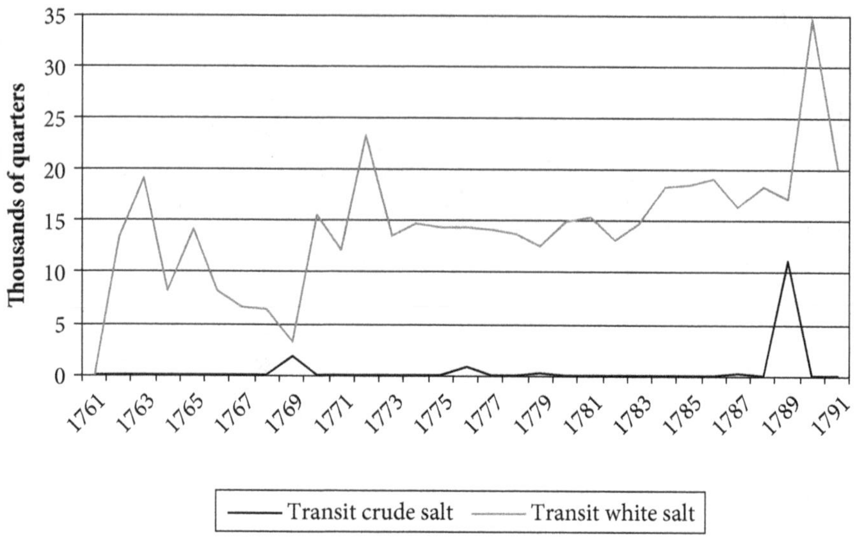

CHART 83 *The transit of white and grey salt, 1761–1791*
SOURCE: RÉLÉVÉ GENERAL, NAB, FC, 5750–5805.

little has been said about the transit of international commodities via the Austrian Netherlands. The few times it is mentioned authors only mention shipments of refined or white salt, what is surprising since the share of white salt within the import and export flows was negligible.[18] The data on transit from the customs statistics confirms that white salt was transited much more intensively than grey salt, possibly because local demand for grey salt was large enough to gulp down all passing shipments of crude salt.

When we look at the transit flows for coal – another increasingly important resource for Western Europe – the chart is even more capricious than that of salt (Chart 84). Yet the most striking aspect of this specific transit trade is that the figures are remarkably low compared to export or import (for the three types: regular coal, small coal and *terre houille*). Cécile Douxchamps-Lefèvre has discussed the transit routes of coal and assumed that there was a very intense movement of foreign coal via the two big fluvial axes, the Meuse and the Sambre, but on the basis of the data from the customs statistics it is quite unbelievable that a great deal was undertaken to cause these routes to gain popularity.[19] Possibly the internal barriers which have been discussed extensively in the chapter on the coal trade have aided

18 NAB, FC, 5241, several pieces on the transit of refined salt, 1786; 5246, letter "*concernant le sel entrant en le Luxembourg*" deals with the transit of salt from Lorraine.

19 Douxchamps-Lefèvre, "Le Commerce," 418–419.

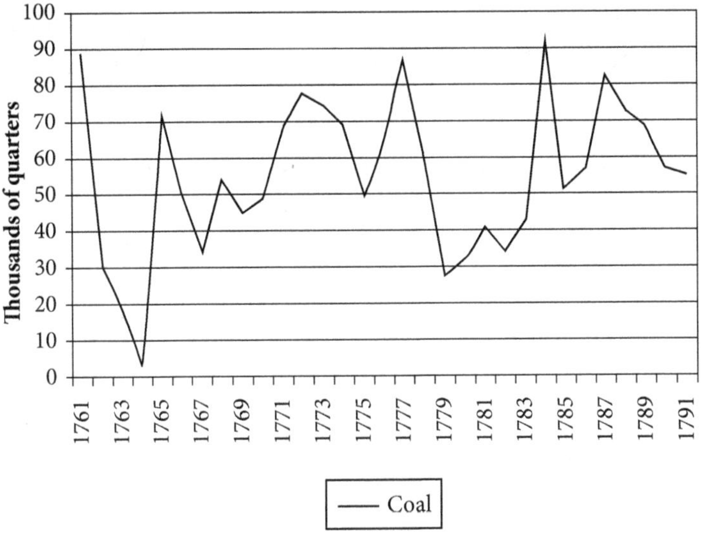

CHART 84 *The transit of coal (total), 1761–1791*
SOURCE: RÉLÉVÉ GENERAL, NAB, FC, 5750–5805.

in crippling the growth potential of the coal transit. Indeed, we have seen that for bulk trades such as coal, salt or grain, the infrastructural improvements did not have many effects. Buyst and others believe that the tolls on paved roads kept fixed transaction costs on precisely these products high, since the toll depended on the number of horses.[20] That meant that the growing road network was especially beneficial to merchants of small, high-value commodities.[21]

So how about the more luxurious trades, like for example tea, spices or cocoa? In the case of the colonial commodities the evolution of the transit trade is especially revealing in numerous ways. Firstly, attempting to become a transit hub for these commodities was more or less the only possible way to

20 Blondé and Van Uytven, "Langs Land- en Waterwegen," Buyst, Dercon, and Van Campenhout, *Road Expansion*, 28. Grain was actually never included in the decrees concerning transit policy, since the government feared that increased grain transports would lead to bigger contraband.

21 Another possible explanation why a fall in transport cost is not always accompanied by an increase in transit (or sales) for certain goods, is the fact that when the supply of a product could not grow current users would bid higher prices, thereby nullifying the effects of the lower costs. For details on this mechanism see: Liam Brunt, "Where There's Muck, There's Brass: The Market for Manure in the Industrial Revolution," *Economic History Review* 60, no. 2 (2007): 358–359.

benefit from the ever rising demand for colonial goods throughout Europe, seen as the Austrian Netherlands were not providing these themselves. And secondly, since the import volume of these goods is an excellent proxy for domestic consumption, they enable us to compare the transited volume with the height of consumption; thereby telling us something about the importance of the volumes that were transited via the Austrian Netherlands to the rest of Europe. Lastly, as said, they are precisely an example of a so-called 'rich trade', so they complement the story told in the paragraphs on bulk goods such as salt and coal.

Indeed, the transit of the strongest growers in terms of demand (coffee and sugar) was swiftly increasing as well, and this almost throughout the entire period covered by the statistics. In the case of sugar we again see this transit boom slowing down after 1782 in the case of sugar. In the other cases however (tea, spices and cocoa) there is either only a minor increase in transit or a brief peak at the height of the international struggle in Europe (Chart 85 and 86). Still, when we add all of the colonial transit flows together (Chart 87) there clearly was growth in this sector, albeit somewhat slower than the growth in imports. When we compare the amount of transited commodities with the consumption of these goods in this small region (in other words, with their import volume, Chart 88) we see that the amount of goods transited through this region mostly remained well below 50 per cent of imports. That means

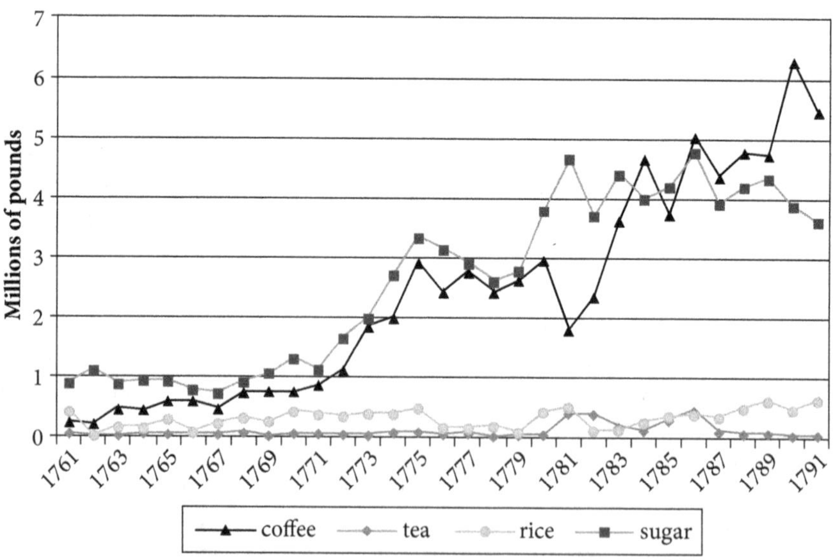

CHART 85 *The transit of coffee, tea, rice and sugar, 1761–1791*
SOURCE: RÉLÉVÉ GENERAL, NAB, FC, 5750–5805.

that our colonial transit trade was at no point capable of fully supplying the bigger regions abroad. One could thus say that the Austrian Netherlands did not fully made use of their transit potential and did not play the role of an 'interloper', like some other small countries – such as Denmark – did at the time.[22] And this despite the excellent transport-infrastructure and the willingness of merchants to take part in transit trade.[23] However, for a small region the heights of the transited amounts were actually rather surprising, and they were still improving.

The charts on the transit flows of textiles especially highlight improvements of the transit trade around 1780, so precisely at the height of the afore-mentioned international struggle. In the cases of for example textile resources (crude flax, wool, silk and cotton, Chart 89) and also broadcloth, cotton or mixed fabrics, transit only increased markedly around 1780. This explains complaints such as that from Count von Kaunitz in the year 1775:

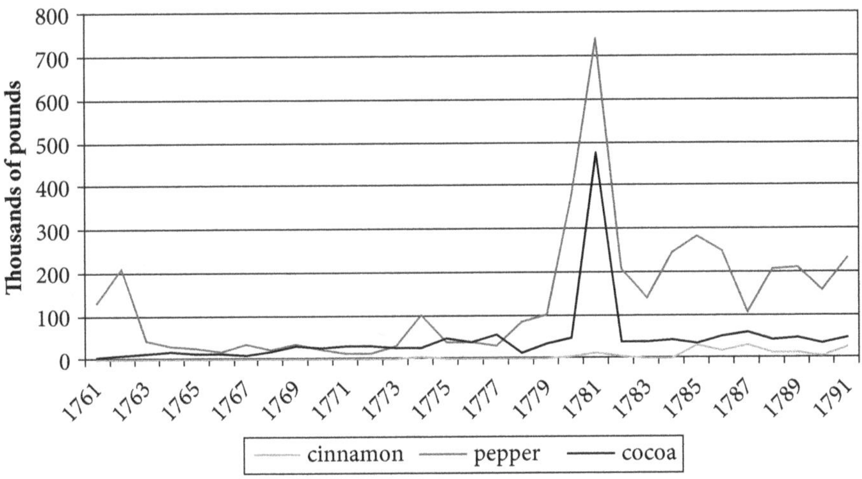

CHART 86 *The transit of cinnamon, pepper and cocoa, 1761–1791*
SOURCE: RÉLÉVÉ GENERAL, NAB, FC, 5750–5805.

22 Jan de Vries, Markus Denzel, and Philipp Rossner, *Small is Beautiful?: Interlopers and Smaller Trading Nations in the Pre-Industrial Period* (Stuttgart: Franz Steiner Verlag, 2011), Klas Rönnbäck, "Who Stood to Gain from Colonialism? A Case Study of Early Modern European Colonialism in the Caribbean," in *World Economic History Congress* (Utrecht: 2009).

23 Houtman-De Smedt, "Charles Proli," 126.

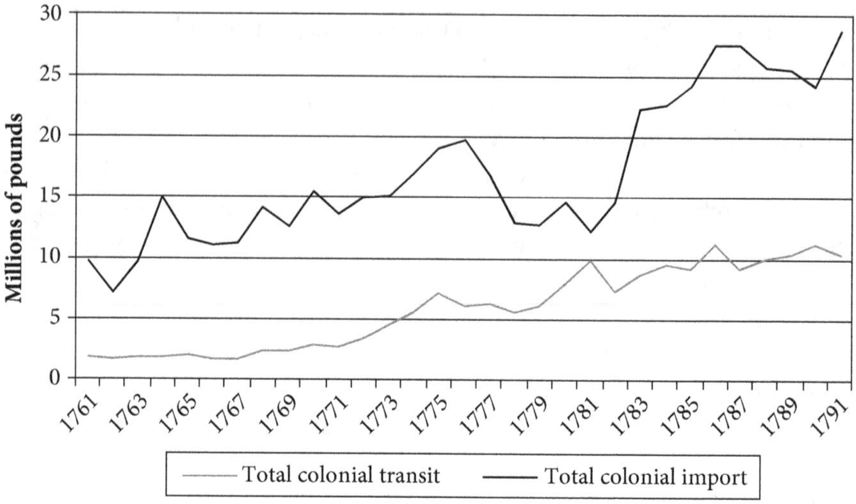

CHART 87 *Total colonial imports and transit, 1761–1791*[24]

SOURCE: RÉLÉVÉ GENERAL, NAB, FC, 5750–5805.

CHART 88 *Transit-import ratio, 1761–1791*

SOURCE: RÉLÉVÉ GENERAL, NAB, FC, 5750–5805.

24 This chart contains the sum of the data on sixteen colonial commodities: coffee, tea, cocoa, indigo, madder, rice, sugar (sum of all types), chocolate, cinnamon, pepper, saffron, nutmeg, ginger, cloves, vanilla and cochineal.

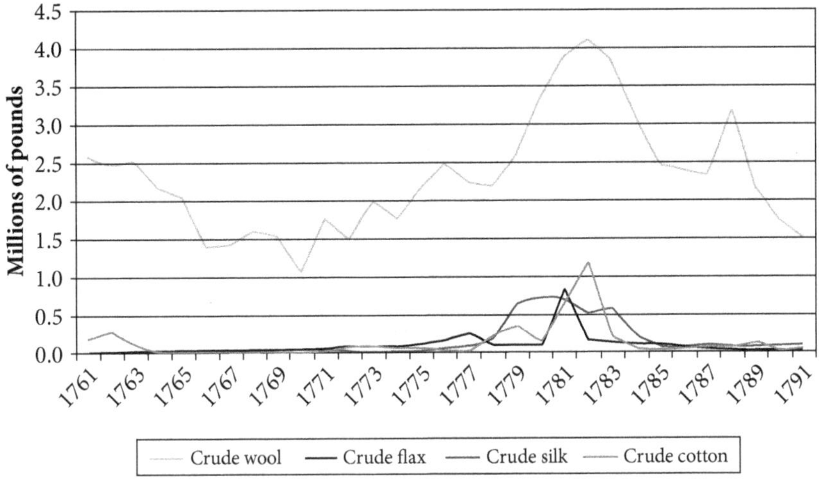

CHART 89 *The transit of raw materials for the textile sector, 1761–1791*
SOURCE: RÉLÉVÉ GENERAL, NAB, FC, 5750–5805.

> 'The committee notes among others that the Finance Council still has no solution in the tariff project that should take place within the bilateral trade.'[25]

Moreover, in most cases a relapse in the transited volume occurs soon after that year, reducing transit to its pre-war level. The peak that accordingly shows on the graphs is particularly sharp in the case of crude cotton. Only for siamoises and cotton fabrics (Chart 90) transit did remain higher than before the boom, probably because these were particularly popular tissues, so that transit was presumably driven up all over Europe.

Before drawing a more general conclusion on the transit trade we should have a look at the particular evolutions taking place in Ostend, since the port played an important role within the Habsburg trade policy. Many steps were taken by the administration to foster the growth of the port of Ostend. For example, in the sources on the trade in exotic produce it was one of the returning motives, since colonial goods usually formed a relatively steady or growing commerce (both import and transit trade). The most popular approach was diversifying transit duties according to their locus of entry. For instance the transit of tea and dyestuffs was taxed less when entering via Ostend.[26] In the

25 'Le committé (du commerce réciproque A.C.) observe entre autres que (les membres du conseil des finances A.C.) n'ayant pas encore de resolution sur le projet de tarif qui doit avoir lieu dans le commerce reciproque.' OS, FHKA, NHK, 1008 (February 12th 1775).

26 NAB, FC, 4509, communication of July 9th 1766, dyestuffs entering via Ostend are exempt of toll duties, s.n.; 4516, communication to all customs offices by de Beelen, September

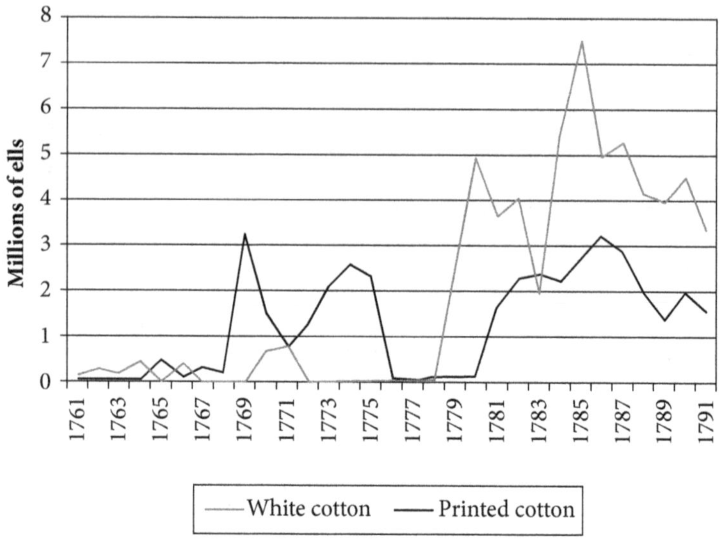

CHART 90 *The transit of cotton fabrics, 1761–1791*
SOURCE: RÉLÉVÉ GENERAL, NAB, FC, 5750–5805.

case of coffee and sometimes grains, transit was even forbidden except when it went through the new main port.[27] Wool, a product which was considered to have been of vital importance for the Ostend harbour and for some influential merchants, such as the brothers Deloose, provides another example of lower transit duties for merchants passing through the port.[28] In 1781 a more general step was taken to boost transit by declaring Ostend a free port, in the hope of

13th 1773, import duties on tea entering in Ostend are lowered by half; 4517, letter to Romberg exempting indigo that entered via Ostend from transit duties and entrepot duties; 4532, memoir for the offices in Herve suggesting to install an export duty on dyestuffs except the one that entered through Ostend, March 29th 1787.

27 NAB, FC, 4510, letter regarding a decree on the coffee transit, January 7th 1767. The volume of grains in transit relative to their overall traded amounts was even smaller than coal, but of course, the grain commerce was exceptional, since transit of the different types of grains was often forbidden because of the constant fear for illegal grain exports. NAB, FC, 4797, letter about liberating grain trade and entrepot in Ostend, August 13th 1783; 4800, communication allowing flour exports from Bruges, Ostend and Newport, June 15th 1785; 4809, regulations for the port of Ostend, grains traded in Ostend are exempt from duties, June 11th 1781.

28 NAB, FC, 4872, letter by de Grysperre regarding the transit of crude wool, December 12th 1761; idem, "*Laines 1763*," merchants request the same diminution (by half) of transit duties as the port of Ostend has received earlier (Deloose and others), July 7th 1763.

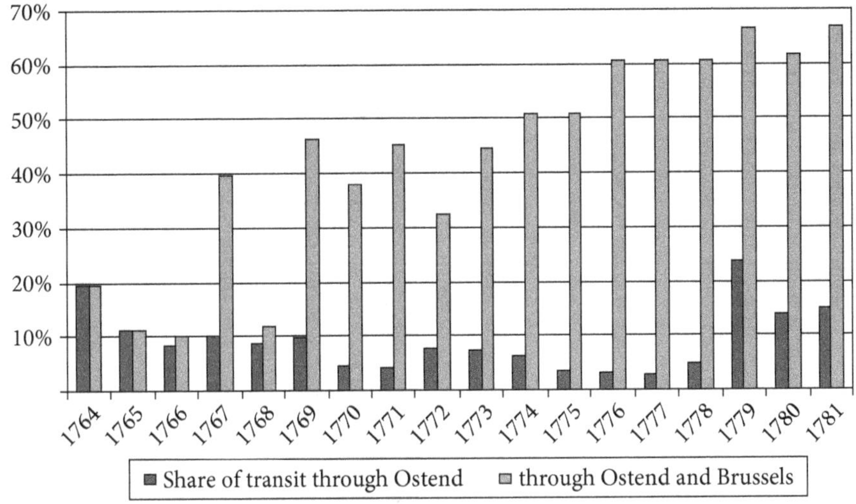

CHART 91 *The share of colonial transit passing through Ostend and Brussels, 1764–1781*
SOURCE: RÉLÉVÉ GENERAL, NAB, FC, 5756–5791.

further enhancing the attractiveness of the harbour.[29] We can use the detailed information on trade per department to see whether Ostend transit indeed managed to flourish.

Since I only have detailed figures for the different departments for a selection of goods, I have chosen to look at the evolution of Ostend's share for those products whose transit was supposedly fiercely encouraged by the government; in particular coffee, tea, semi-refined sugar (brown and white), indigo and Spanish wool. Chart 91 shows the share of the volume of these six products recorded at customs bureaus in Ostend, within their total transited amount. However, since many merchants gained the privilege to register their goods in Louvain or Brussels, and because of the increasing practice of exempting traders from all sorts of administrative red tape at Ostend, it is difficult to measure the true amount of transit going through the port.[30] In 1781 Ostend was even freed entirely from trade duties and formalities.[31] Also, many companies active there had their official seat in Brussels, for example the Rombergs. This is why I also included the transit through the Brussels' customs department (that

29 Coppejans-Desmedt, "Economische Opbloei," 276.

30 Devos, "Oostenrijkse Douanestatistiek," 337. A new example mentioned in the customs' archive is that merchants were no longer obliged to use an official warehouse, but could store their goods at home, *chez lui dans un magasin convenable à double clefs* (NAB, FC, 4518).

31 Ibid., 339.

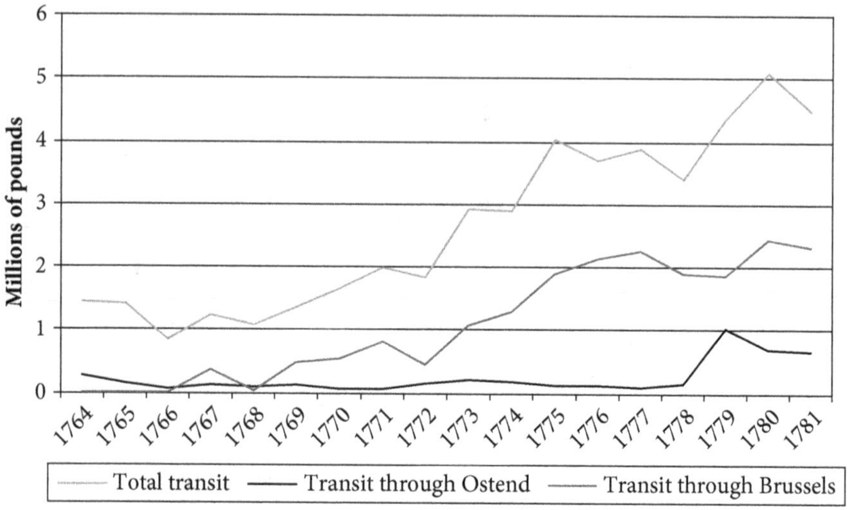

CHART 92 *The height of colonial transit through Ostend and Brussels, 1764–1781*
SOURCE: RÉLÉVÉ GENERAL, NAB, FC, 5756–5791.

included Louvain) in the graph. The results certainly place some question marks to the efficiency of the Ostend policy, since transit through Ostend and Brussels actually increased at a lower pace than overall transit (Chart 92). Also, we do not see a clear increase in the share in 1781, the year Ostend became a free port, but unfortunately we lack the data to tell what happened in the years following America's independence and whether it did augment Ostend's importance later on. Still, since the practice of granting a license to register trade in Brussels was usually given to Ostend merchants, we see that the Ostend transit trade was certainly growing.

In the end, the image we got from the results of the Habsburg transit and transport policy is much nuanced. The success story brought forward by some historians who saw it as one of the engines driving economic development in the region has rightfully been questioned. And the government itself apparently overestimated the reach of its new customs policy. There were certainly improvements in the transit sector, but often they appear only very late and turn out rather modest, especially compared to the attention given to transit in the sources. Products for which transit grew most during this period were those whose popularity boomed in eighteenth-century Europe, namely coffee, sugar, cotton and mixed fabrics. Other relative improvements in the transit trade were only really felt from about 1780 onwards, and this increase was not merely due to the efforts of the government, but likely also to the four year's war. Moreover, Henri Delplancq himself acknowledged that the Austrian

Netherlands made insufficient use of their neutrality during that war.[32] That explains why after the war, transit fell back again. Even in Ostend, the city at which most of the government's actions were aimed, transit did not flourish as much as some authors have expected. Moreover, for a product such as coal we could even call the transit policy a failure.

The question that remains to us is what the reason was for the limited impact of the transit policy on certain products. It is clear that the transport infrastructure expanded immensely during this period, as well as the port infrastructure in Ostend.[33] So in this field progress was unmistakably made. Also, as we saw in the beginning of this chapter, the administration made many alterations to the height of customs duties, albeit – as always – never on a general level. What the government did appear to do as a general measure – at least after 1778 – was the levying of lower transit duties for commodities travelling via the port of Ostend.[34] Some merchants still wrote that the transit tariffs remained too high to establish a flourishing transit trade and their memoirs stated that the government actually wished to further increase these allegedly high taxes on transit in order to gain high incomes, what would plummet merchants' competitiveness.[35] But of course these complaints fit logically in a lobbying discourse designed to get the administration to lower all kinds of transaction costs. The true reason for the modest improvement is probably the one that was already given by Blondé, Van Uytven and Buyst; namely that transit was still much hindered by internal barriers such as tolls and high transportation costs.[36] This is corroborated by the fact that according to the customs statistics bulk trades (namely coal and salt), which had to pay the highest barrier duties, experienced the smallest impact of the transit policy, while relative luxury goods such as coffee actually did very well. Chart 93 shows that while coal never surpassed the level of transit of 1761, the volume of transited colonial goods grew five times larger. Policy makers seem to have underestimated

---

32 OS, FHKA, NHK, Kommerz Litorale, 1010, folio 588, memoir (July 9th 1779).

33 Blondé, *Een Economie*, Serruys, "The Austrian Netherlands."

34 Devos, "Oostenrijkse Douanestatistiek," 341.

35 NAB, SSW, 2194/2, September 22nd 1784; NAB, Manuscripts, 850 A, letter by an unknown trader at Vienna, s.d., supposedly 1754, p. 20, NAB, FC, 4601, the brothers Romberg wish to transit silk and other fabrics through the Southern Netherlands, but argue that transit duties should be lowered first, March 28th 1768; 4629, comparable request by the brothers Overman, April, 11th 1785; 4871, "Extrait de protocolle du conseiller Baudier du 10 aout 1763" mentions a trader from Ghent, Carpentier, who demands lower transit duties on wool, otherwise he will move his activities to Amsterdam (request granted).

36 Blondé and Van Uytven, "Langs Land- en Waterwegen," Buyst, Dercon, and Van Campenhout, *Road Expansion*.

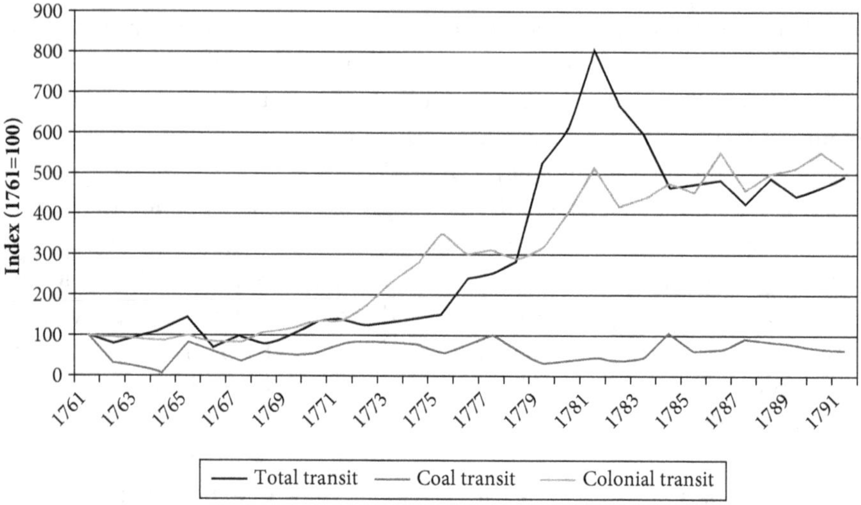

CHART 93 *Comparison of the trends in transit, 1761–1791*
SOURCE: RÉLÉVÉ GENERAL, NAB, FC, 5750–5805.

the weight of these tolls or were simply no match for the local institutions levying them. Therefore, transit trade remains only a modest success story that was strongly boosted by the diplomatic circumstances of the era. It should thus not come as a surprise that we will have to wait until the nineteenth century to witness the birth of a thriving services industry in the Southern Netherlands.

Conclusion

The trade evolutions, which can be read from the Habsburg customs statistics, combined with the sources from the different stakeholders in international trade, have certainly opened several new perspectives on the relation between international trade and economic development. First, in investigating the Southern Netherlands' economy from the perspective of international trade, more clarity has been brought to the discussions about both the changing structure of the eighteenth-century economy in the region, and its condition. At the same time this approach has spotlighted various aspects linked to international trade which remained hidden in existing macroeconomic studies: the foremost among these aspects being the varying effects of the active role played by a new customs administration, the efforts of various individual actors (consumers, resource producers, manufacturers, merchants) to maximize their welfare (often through influencing the government by means of trade-related arguments), the changes in product supply brought about by international flows of goods and the huge importance of imports for a national economy. This has shown that the most revealing answers are brought about not through determining whether international trade was profitable or detrimental, but rather through adopting a wide outlook on the myriad economic changes with which international trade is entwined.

Much had already been said about the new Habsburg customs policy launched in 1749. The numerous examples of this policy discussed throughout the previous chapters underpin the hypotheses of Lis and Soly, De Smedt, Thijs, Vandenbroeke, and others, that this policy was an active instrument designed to support trade and industry, and that it was indeed highly coherent when one looks beyond the ad hoc initiatives. Not only did the administration operate from overarching economic reasoning (with, surprisingly, a strong focus on supporting manufacturers in finding import substitutes rather than on boosting exports), it was also constantly monitoring economic developments in order to adjust trade policy when necessary. The latter is of course most visible in the case of grains, since dearness of grains might lead to widespread uproar. One can thus not deny the relatively great importance of central government intervention during the second half of the eighteenth century in all of the sectors discussed, because of the myriad measures that were taken throughout the second half of the eighteenth century, affecting all of the parties involved. The revived importance of the state in the debate on international trade (influenced by O'Brien, North, Robinson and Acemoglu) is thus

 | DOI 10.1163/9789004272606_014

very much deserved. The government can be labelled a 'key factor' in the eighteenth-century economy whose activities were felt throughout all levels of society.[1]

However, this certainly does not mean that all of the measures taken were effective or always had a strong and far-reaching impact, and it certainly does not imply that they were all beneficial on a large scale. In tracking the actual results of the trade policy for the different sectors, no homogeneous overarching narrative can be developed. Indeed, we have seen that in a number of cases the impact and efficiency of the policy has been inflated (for example the Ostend policy), that effects of one measure were different for each affected product according to different contextual factors (the wool and flax exports for instance) and that a number of government decisions were in fact counter effective: in the cases of the cotton monopoly and the royal salt refinery they actually impeded the growth of the sector as a whole. Moreover, while – besides the latter two examples – most of the ways in which individual companies were supported (such as via tax exemptions and monopolies) were certainly beneficial to the respective applicants and industries, yet at the same time could lead to artificially higher prices for consumers and hindered imports of foreign goods of potentially higher quality (such as certain fabrics, coal and refined salt).

There are various reasons why the government's interventions did not always have the desired results. First, the central government did not succeed in dealing with local or regional obstacles to trade. Local governments retained the right to levy tolls and other kinds of taxes on trade, transport and storage. This was especially hampering for bulk trades such as coal, salt and to a minor extent grains. Secondly, the administration remained bound by the restrictions imposed by surrounding nations (even though she often secretly circumvented these, as we saw in the case of duties on the salt import). Also, more importantly, the administration tried to take into account the wishes of different stakeholders. While manufacturers usually were aided most and the industrial policy thus sporadically went against vested interests of corporations and merchants, exemptions on import duties for foreign goods were also often granted to consumers and traders alike (Table 16). The government thus often toned down its own policy. Lastly, in many cases, circumstances might have had more to do with the success or failure of certain sectors, than policy had. I will come

1 An idea that can be traced back to: Alexander Gerschenkron, *Economic Backwardness in Historical Perspective* (Cambridge: 1962). However, Gerschenkron only referred to the role of the state in economies that caught up with industrialized nations in the nineteenth century and later. He never refers to the eighteenth century.

TABLE 16 *Overview of all petitions*

			Ruling				Total
			Granted	Rejected	Partially granted	Unknown	
Occupation of the applicant	Army	Count	23	1	0	1	25
		Percentage	92%	4%	0%	4%	100%
	Consumer	Count	89	51	12	9	161
		Percentage	55.3%	31.7%	7.5%	5.6%	100%
	Institution	Count	59	14	14	13	100
		Percentage	59%	14%	14%	13%	100%
	Manufacturer	Count	626	118	90	110	944
		Percentage	66.3%	12.5%	9.5%	11.7%	100%
	Merchant	Count	1031	347	111	216	1705
		Percentage	60.5%	20.4%	6.5%	12.7%	100%
	Merchant/ manufacturer	Count	97	22	21	4	144
		Percentage	67.4%	15.3%	14.6%	2.8%	100%
	Mill-owner	Count	85	26	9	10	130
		Percentage	65.4%	20%	6.9%	7.7%	100%
	Producer[2]	Count	42	10	6	0	58
		Percentage	72.4%	17.2%	10.3%	0%	100%
	Unknown	Count	93	48	17	50	208
		Percentage	44.7%	23.1%	8.2%	24%	100%
Total		Count	2145	637	280	413	3475
		Percentage	61.7%	18.3%	8.1%	11.9%	100%

SOURCE: NAB, FC, 4505–4517, 4520, 4522–4534, 4556–4559, 4567–4594, 4600–4606, 4613–4635, 4639–4643, 4688–4689, 4719–4809, 4867–4889, 5022–5034, 5221–5243, 5260–5265, 5325–5336.

back to the different reasons for growth or decline besides policy below, but it is clear that for example high demand has done more to boost the transit of certain goods than the general customs measures could.

On the other hand, the suggestion that trade policy was still not effective because the government often chose to levy high taxes only because of the income this would generate for the treasury does not hold.[3] Of course,

2 This includes producers of raw materials: coal, flax and wool.

3 Briavoinne, *De L'industrie*, 83.

merchants ceaselessly called for lower taxes. As their success rate in doing so was high, it would be rather stupid not to try again. For manufacturers of finished goods, as said, the number of granted exemptions was even higher. So while the empress and emperor in Vienna were possibly much occupied with benefiting their empire and its treasury, the high level of autonomy afforded to the Southern Netherlands' administrators allowed them to guard the interests of the region and do their utmost to protect its burgeoning industry.[4] Since establishing a factory was actually rather inexpensive during the eighteenth century (for instance, it cost less than building a ship), this government policy was likely more important than acquiring investment capital.[5] For future research it might thus prove most valuable to compare the relative success of protectionist policy in the Southern Low Countries with attempts by other 'infant industries' all over the world. On the other hand, the entrepreneurs and merchants who held the highest 'leverage' over the authorities (such as owners of big enterprises like coal mines) were – not surprisingly – relatively the most successful in influencing the customs policy. While the government did modify its approach somewhat during the period examined in this study, such as by reconsidering granted monopolies, continuing most exemptions for manufactories and specific import bans on foreign manufactured goods (such as textile fabrics) might have been the main reason why trade policy did not lead to a general increase of public welfare during the eighteenth century.[6]

The underlying motive within the heads of the designers of the trade policy has always been that international trade could constitute both a severe threat to the nation and a potentially huge motor for its economic development and growth. That was also the overarching question within the international debate on international trade sketched in the introduction to this volume, but it is now clear that this is a very narrow view on the effects of international commerce. First of all, it is clear that compared to today, the trade deficit per head (even compared to wages) was very modest. This is no surprise because we have seen that for many bulk products (salt, coal and grains) the region was nearly autarkic. Even for a region lacking colonies or large foreign trade companies, international trade did not threaten to smother domestic producers. At the same time, the different chapters have shown that international trade in itself was also not the motor for economic development in the Austrian

4 Coppejans-Desmedt, "Aspecten," 72.

5 Coppejans-Desmedt, *Bijdrage*, 189, Duplessis, *Transitions*, 236, Hasquin, "Nijverheid," 159, Israel, *The Dutch Republic*, 1089, Van Moorhem, "Sociaal Economisch Survey," 37.

6 G. Van Dievoet, *Patrice de Neny (1716–1784) et le Gouvernement des Pays-Bas Autrichiens*, *Standen en Landen* (Kortrijk: UGA, 1987), 76.

Netherlands (cases of export-driven growth (i.e. sectors spurred by an increase in foreign demand) are scarce). The macroeconomic contradiction thus makes no sense, since both imports and exports have nonetheless brought about major changes in the face of the Southern Netherlands' economy during the second half of the eighteenth century, both in direct and indirect ways.

Imports in the first place were of the utmost importance for economic growth, not least as they supplied the region with the necessary resources for innumerable kinds of production processes. The Southern Netherlands imported ever growing amounts of resources for industry such as unrefined salt and sugar, dyestuffs, white cotton, wool and flax (but also some products that have not been included in this study, such as peat). These rising resource imports do not only point to the success of the sectors that used them, but also show that these sectors often depended to a very high degree on the international resource market. Imports moreover provided greater diversity in available consumer goods and thereby led to strongly changing consumption patterns. This thus changed the very face of the eighteenth-century economy and culture. The huge popularity of a number of new goods, such as fashionable fabrics including cotton and siamoises, and foodstuffs such as coffee, sugar and (later on) chocolate, moreover gave an impulse to the domestic industry to develop local substitutes for these products. The development of new sectors – notable examples are cotton printing and sugar refining – was the direct consequence of this trade. Their success can not only be read from increasing resource imports, but also from declining or stagnating imports of numerous competing finished products.

Of course, some of the region's sectors also did benefit directly from foreign demand, or, in other words, from exports. Especially for the primary sector in the Austrian Netherlands, the importance of exports is undeniable. Agriculture (grains) and the production of industrial resources (coal and flax), two sectors that evidenced a very high potential for growth, each exported a relatively large part of their production and thus owed their success at least partially to international trade. Moreover, exports remained hugely important for one type of manufacturing studied here: the linen industry. Both the linen cloth produced by the proto-industry and the tick manufactured in cities such as Turnhout were exported in immense amounts. It is safe to say that these sectors would have fared much poorer without foreign demand. This thus however again leads us to the broader issue of the origin of this export success and its relationship to improving living standards. The huge export of especially rural produce (in the chapter on the balance of trade we have seen that other goods with a very high exported value were coleseed, hops and seed oil) was mostly due to a huge labour surplus and hence very low wages for producers.

That means that for most of the people involved, this trade did not lead to increased welfare. On the other hand, export did grant an indispensable addition to subsistence-level peasant incomes.

In the end, the above-mentioned changes in both imports and exports clearly point to a relatively flourishing economy and large intrinsic economic strength in this region. First, the imports of growing amounts of consumption goods (not only colonial ones such as coffee and tea, but also French wine for instance) infer modestly growing (albeit not necessarily generalised, as the many examples of the relatively low wages of the region show) welfare of eighteenth-century inhabitants of the Austrian Netherlands. Indeed, the growth of international trade in the region (about five per cent per annum) was definitely much higher than the estimated growth rate of world intercontinental trade (1.26 per cent per annum throughout the eighteenth century).[7] Secondly, the study of the international trade flows has presented strong indications about the different levers of early modern economic development in the region, namely the linen proto-industry, agriculture and the production of coal (and it is possible some other sectors not included in this research, for instance luxury goods such as decorations, also enjoyed improved export positions).

Yet above all, the study of international trade has underscored the tremendous capacity of the Austrian Netherlands' home market as an economic motor. Indeed, the domestic market played a strategic role in boosting the nation's industry.[8] The declining or stable imports of foreign manufactured goods (in particular textiles, white salt and refined sugar) alongside increased imports of resources for the production of such goods, strongly suggest an increase and potential for growth in domestic demand, and – equally important – the capability of the internal market to meet it. Not only in the modern cotton sector, but also in the widespread production of salt, fustian, flannel and chemicals such as bleach, can we find indications of homespun growth. Most of these undertakings were still 'traditional' and small-scale (just like the linen industry) but the research nonetheless reveals them to have been quite dynamic, just as economic historians such as Vandenbroeke, Lis and Soly and Van der Wee suspected.[9] They were not the typical sectors linked to growth in the nineteenth century, but clearly merit renewed scholarly attention. In the end, international trade contributes to a picture of the eighteenth-century Southern Netherlands as an increasingly vibrant economy, with a remarkable capacity for growth within the domestic market.

---

7 Ronald Findlay and Kevin H. O'Rourke, "Commodity Market Integration, 1500–2000," *NBER working paper series* 8579 (2001): 14.

8 Blondé, *Een Economie*, de Vries, *The Industrious Revolution*.

9 D'Haeseleer, "Proto-Industrialisering," 10–11.

Appendices

A.1 The Habsburg Customs Statistics

The digitized database is available online: http://dx.doi.org/10.1163/9789004272606. Readers who want to use the database are required to contact the author for permission (a.coenen@uu.nl).

SOURCE: NAB, FC, 5748–5805

A.2 Products Included in the Balance of Trade

Product	Available years	Source
Rice	1760–1791	Nicolaas W. Posthumus, Nederlandsche prijsgeschiedenis (Leiden 1943) 40–41
Buckwheat	1760–1791	Posthumus, p. 46
Wheat	1792	Luk Corluy, Een metodologische poging tot uitwerking van een ekonomisch model van de buitenlandse handel voor het departement Gent in de Oostenrijkse Nederlanden tijdens de tweede helft van de XVIIIe eeuw, onuitgegeven doctoraatsverhandeling (KUL 1972) 108; FC 4828; Ao 1266
Rye	1794	Posthumus, p. 24, FC 4828
Spelt	1794	FC 4828
Barley	1794	FC 4828
Oats	1794	FC 4828, Ao 1266
Coleseed	1760–1791	Posthumus, p. 50–51
Rapeseed	1794	FC 4828
fish oil	1791	FC 4953
Seed oil	1770	FC 4305
Cows	1754–1794	Ao 1266
Hops	1791	FC 4953 and 4828
Eggs	1754–1794	Ao 1266
Irish butter	1760–1791	Posthumus, p. 69
Butter	1760–1791	Posthumus, p. 70–71
Dutch soft cheese	1761	Ao 1266
Stockfish	1760–1791	Posthumus, p. 92

 | DOI 10.1163/9789004272606_015

Products Included in the Balance of Trade (*cont.*)

Product	Available years	Source
Figs	1760–1791	Posthumus, p. 102
Almonds	1760–1791	Posthumus, 107
Raisins	1760–1791	Posthumus, 111
Sugar candy	1760–1791	Posthumus, p. 70–71
Cinnamon	1760–1791	Posthumus, 149
Cloves	1760–1791	Posthumus, 156
Nutmeg	1759–1780	Posthumus, 161
Saffron	1760–1791	Posthumus, 165
Pepper	1760–1791	Posthumus, p. 74 and Corluy, p. 201
Snuff	1760–1776	Posthumus, p. 208
Starch	1760–1791	Posthumus, p. 224
Russia leather	1760–1791	Posthumus, p. 362
Iron wire	1760–1791	Posthumus, p. 399
Copper wire	1760–1780	Posthumus, p. 404
White lead (dyestuff)	1760–1791	Posthumus, p. 427
English copperas	1760–1780	Posthumus, p. 195
Indigo	1760–1791	Posthumus, p. 417
Cochineal	1760–1791	Posthumus, p. 420
Nut gall	1760–1791	Posthumus, p. 454
Madder	1760–1791	Posthumus, p. 414
Gunpowder	1760–1791	Posthumus, p. 473
Soda	1760–1791	Posthumus, p. 468
Borax	1772–1780	Posthumus, p. 466
Mercury	1760–1791	Posthumus, p. 480
Lead (in bricks)	1792	Corluy, p. 216
Yellow wax	1792	Corluy, p. 300
French wine	1760–1791	Posthumus, p. 226–227
Brandy	1792	Corluy, p. 362
White cotton fabrics	1785	SSW 2153
Printed cotton fabrics	1785	SSW 2153
Velveteen (cotton)	1785–1786	SSW 2153
Mending	1791	FC 4953
Flax (tow)	1791	FC 4953
Flax (combed)	1769–1789	FC 4951–4953
Flax (crude)	1769–1789	FC 4951–4953
Flax yarn	1769–1789	FC 4951

Product	Available years	Source
Woollen blankets	1759–1768	FC 5748–5805
Spanish wool	1770–1791	Posthumus, p. 267
Woollen fabrics	1785	SSW 2153
Linen cloth	1765	Sabbe, p. 34, Lis and Soly, 1990 and Vandenbroeke, 1979
White linen cloth	1785	SSW 2153
Canvas (sail cloth)	1721	G. Willemsen, 'Contribution à l'histoire de l'industrie linière en Flandre', Annales de la société d'histoire et d'archéologie de Gand 7:2 (1907) 223–340, 238
Baize	1762	FC 4571
White soap	1760–1791	Posthumus, p. 485
Potash	1792	Corluy, p. 284
Frisade	1762	FC 4571
Camel cloth	1765	FC 4597
Barracan	1751	FC 4564
Serge	1753	FC 4564
Flannel	unknown	Lis en Soly, 1990
Muslin	1785–1786	SSW 2153
Queues et pennes	1772	FC 4598
Nails	1787	FC 5067
Coal (imported), *pesée*	1765	FC 5027
Coal (exported), *pesée*	1765	FC 5027
Regular coal, cartload	1759–1791	Verlinden, C. and J. Craeybeckx, Documents pour l'histoire des prix et des salaires en Flandres et en Brabant (Brussels, 1959–1973), II, pp. 797–8
Small coal, quarter	1759–1782	Verlinden, C. and J. Craeybeckx, Documents pour l'histoire des prix et des salaires en Flandres et en Brabant (Brussels, 1959–1973), II, p. 799
Siamoise		Lis en Soly, 1990
Worked tin	1778.00	Verlinden, p. 846
Tallow candles	1759–1768, 1771	Verlinden, p. 823
Fresh meat	1751	FC 5320 and 4564
Olive oil	1759–1783	Verlinden, p. 746

Products Included in the Balance of Trade (*cont.*)

Product	Available years	Source
Chocolate	1788	Verlinden, p. 776
Tea	1758, 1788–1791	Verlinden, p. 775
Coffee	1760	Posthumus, p. 181–182
White powdered sugar	1778–1784	Verlinden, p. 763
Wine vinegar	1788–1789	Verlinden, p. 780
Beer vinegar	1788–1790	Verlinden, p. 781
Salted herring	1759–1791	Posthumus, p. 44
Fresh salmon	1761–1783	Verlinden, p. 741
Peas	1759–1767; 1768–1791	Verlinden, p. 683
Beans	1759–1767	Verlinden, p. 686
White salt	1759–1791	Verlinden, p. 829–832
Peat	1759–1764	Verlinden, p. 789
Crude silk	1759–1791	Posthumus, p. 123–127
Sulphur	1759–1791	Posthumus, p. 469–470
Tartar	1759–1791	Posthumus, p. 199
Plaster	1759–1791	Posthumus
Wild shrubs	1759–1791	FC 5748–5805
Hop shoots and vine	1759–1791	FC 5748–5805
Slate (framed and in books)	1759–1791	FC 5748–5805
Various weaponry	1759–1791	FC 5748–5805
Brooms and brushes	1759–1791	FC 5748–5805
Wood (different sorts)	1759–1791	FC 5748–5805
Woodwork (big and small)	1759–1791	FC 5748–5805
Firewood	1759–1791	FC 5748–5805
Mixed hosiery	1759–1791	FC 5748–5805
Knitted garments	1759–1791	FC 5748–5805
Ashes of straw etc	1759–1791	FC 5748–5805
Wax in figures	1759–1791	FC 5748–5805
Horse hair (worked)	1759–1791	FC 5748–5805
Crystal (worked)	1759–1791	FC 5748–5805
Gilded leather	1759–1791	FC 5748–5805

Product	Available years	Source
Gilded copperware	1759–1791	FC 5748–5805
Lace (silk)	1759–1791	FC 5748–5805
Lace (linen)	1759–1791	FC 5748–5805
Broadcloth (residuals)	1759–1791	FC 5748–5805
Balm and elixirs	1759–1791	FC 5748–5805
Syrup of zebrinus (medicinal)	1759–1791	FC 5748–5805
Spirits	1759–1791	FC 5748–5805
Mineral water	1759–1791	FC 5748–5805
Medicinal water	1759–1791	FC 5748–5805
Cologne and scented waters	1759–1791	FC 5748–5805
Chinese ink	1759–1791	FC 5748–5805
Printing ink	1759–1791	FC 5748–5805
Silk (waste)	1759–1791	FC 5748–5805
Taffeta (washed)	1759–1791	FC 5748–5805
Tin-plate	1759–1791	FC 5748–5805
Hard fruits	1759–1791	FC 5748–5805
Manure (pigeons etc)	1759–1791	FC 5748–5805
Bran flour	1759–1791	FC 5748–5805
Bread	1759–1791	FC 5748–5805
Timepieces	1759–1791	FC 5748–5805
Beer dregs	1759–1791	FC 5748–5805
Scientific instruments	1759–1791	FC 5748–5805
Mathematical instruments	1759–1791	FC 5748–5805
Optical instruments	1759–1791	FC 5748–5805
Medicinal instruments	1759–1791	FC 5748–5805
Reed and straw	1759–1791	FC 5748–5805
Truffles	1759–1791	FC 5748–5805
Cork stopper	1759–1791	FC 5748–5805
Wicker-work in hazel	1759–1791	FC 5748–5805
Wicker-work in hazel (*mandriers*)	1759–1791	FC 5748–5805
Knick-knackery	1759–1791	FC 5748–5805
Trifles	1759–1791	FC 5748–5805

Products Included in the Balance of Trade (*cont.*)

Product	Available years	Source
Artificial flowers	1759–1791	FC 5748–5805
Furniture	1759–1791	FC 5748–5805
Mustard	1759–1791	FC 5748–5805
Mats (for packing)	1759–1791	FC 5748–5805
Garments and linens	1759–1791	FC 5748–5805
Small linens	1759–1791	FC 5748–5805
Embroidery and linens	1759–1791	FC 5748–5805
Garments for women	1759–1791	FC 5748–5805
Embellishments	1759–1791	FC 5748–5805
Flax yarn	1759–1791	FC 5748–5805
Coconuts	1759–1791	FC 5748–5805
Church decorations	1759–1791	FC 5748–5805
Tools for artisans	1759–1791	FC 5748–5805
Saddler's ware	1759–1791	FC 5748–5805
Porcelain	1759–1791	FC 5748–5805
Plaster statues	1759–1791	FC 5748–5805
Wax figures	1759–1791	FC 5748–5805
Mixed trimmings	1759–1791	FC 5748–5805
Pastry	1759–1791	FC 5748–5805
Marble (à jouer)	1759–1791	FC 5748–5805
Stones (in statues)	1759–1791	FC 5748–5805
Demolition material	1759–1791	FC 5748–5805
Soap and pomade	1759–1792	FC 5748–5805
Sand	1759–1793	FC 5748–5805
Mixed seeds	1759–1794	FC 5748–5805
Syrup and fruit juices	1759–1795	FC 5748–5805
Chimney soot	1759–1796	FC 5748–5805
Tapestry	1759–1797	FC 5748–5805
Quilted cotton	1759–1798	FC 5748–5805
Cloth for sifting	1759–1799	FC 5748–5805
Cloth for furniture	1759–1800	FC 5748–5805
Worked linen	1759–1801	FC 5748–5805
Varnish	1759–1802	FC 5748–5805
Window glass (in squares)	1759–1803	FC 5748–5805

Product	Available years	Source
Glasses for dessert	1759–1804	FC 5748–5805
Flowers (bulbs and plants)	1759–1805	FC 5748–5805
Gold and silver (piastres)	1759–1806	FC 5748–5805
Silver coinage	1759–1807	FC 5748–5805
Silver filings	1759–1808	FC 5748–5805
Fagots	1759–1809	FC 5748–5805
Drums	1759–1810	FC 5748–5805
Old sails	1759–1811	FC 5748–5805
Firework	1759–1812	FC 5748–5805
Wood waste	1759–1813	FC 5748–5805
Wood for seals	1759–1814	FC 5748–5805
Wood for planks	1759–1815	FC 5748–5805
Small brooms	1759–1816	FC 5748–5805
Broom sticks	1759–1817	FC 5748–5805
Oars	1759–1818	FC 5748–5805
Wooden mills	1759–1819	FC 5748–5805
White wood for clogs	1759–1820	FC 5748–5805
Wooden heels	1759–1821	FC 5748–5805
Ladders	1759–1822	FC 5748–5805
Wood for musical instruments	1759–1823	FC 5748–5805
Old wood	1759–1824	FC 5748–5805
Leather mittens	1759–1825	FC 5748–5805
Mixed ashes	1759–1826	FC 5748–5805
New hats	1759–1827	FC 5748–5805
Old hats	1759–1828	FC 5748–5805
Slaked lime	1759–1829	FC 5748–5805
Horse blankets	1759–1830	FC 5748–5805
Copper engravings	1759–1831	FC 5748–5805
Lace (fake gold and silver)	1759–1832	FC 5748–5805
Broadcloth for mittens and socks	1759–1833	FC 5748–5805
Volatile salt	1759–1834	FC 5748–5805
China root	1759–1835	FC 5748–5805
White mallow	1759–1836	FC 5748–5805

Products Included in the Balance of Trade (*cont.*)

Product	Available years	Source
Lavender oil	1759–1837	FC 5748–5805
Medicinal herbs	1759–1838	FC 5748–5805
Calluna vulgaris	1759–1839	FC 5748–5805
Worked iron	1759–1840	FC 5748–5805
Yarn from goat wool	1759–1841	FC 5748–5805
Waffles	1759–1842	FC 5748–5805
Goatskin gloves	1759–1843	FC 5748–5805
Inner liners for hats and wigs	1759–1844	FC 5748–5805
Oil dregs	1759–1845	FC 5748–5805
Cabbages	1759–1846	FC 5748–5805
Asparagus and hops shoots	1759–1847	FC 5748–5805
Butter milk	1759–1848	FC 5748–5805
Cucumbers	1759–1849	FC 5748–5805
Paper drawings	1759–1850	FC 5748–5805
Worked metal	1759–1851	FC 5748–5805
Bronze ware	1759–1852	FC 5748–5805
Bracelets	1759–1853	FC 5748–5805
Decorated almanacs	1759–1854	FC 5748–5805
Briefcases	1759–1855	FC 5748–5805
Fire screens	1759–1856	FC 5748–5805
Sword ties etc	1759–1857	FC 5748–5805
Belts	1759–1858	FC 5748–5805
jeux de camagnolle	1759–1859	FC 5748–5805
Cardboard boxes	1759–1860	FC 5748–5805
Paper bags and bonnets	1759–1861	FC 5748–5805
Silver knives	1759–1862	FC 5748–5805
Honey waffles	1759–1863	FC 5748–5805
Ox strings	1759–1864	FC 5748–5805
Silk neckties	1759–1865	FC 5748–5805
Beauty spots (taffeta)	1759–1866	FC 5748–5805
Embroidery	1759–1867	FC 5748–5805
Post caps	1759–1868	FC 5748–5805
Headdresses	1759–1869	FC 5748–5805

Product	Available years	Source
Children's bonnets	1759–1870	FC 5748–5805
Silk bonnets	1759–1871	FC 5748–5805
Priest's bonnets	1759–1872	FC 5748–5805
Fur collars	1759–1873	FC 5748–5805
Embellishments for coaches	1759–1874	FC 5748–5805
Earthen statues	1759–1875	FC 5748–5805
Straw (cut)	1759–1876	FC 5748–5805
Straw for roofing	1759–1877	FC 5748–5805
Paper (glued)	1759–1878	FC 5748–5805
Whisks	1759–1879	FC 5748–5805
Tubs of blue stone	1759–1880	FC 5748–5805
Stones (polished for fireplaces and statues)	1759–1881	FC 5748–5805
Goat pâté	1759–1882	FC 5748–5805
Rasps	1759–1883	FC 5748–5805
Flywheels	1759–1884	FC 5748–5805
Indian reed	1759–1885	FC 5748–5805
Old shoes	1759–1886	FC 5748–5805
Sandals	1759–1887	FC 5748–5805
Sugar (fruits à devises)	1759–1888	FC 5748–5805
Tobacco plants	1759–1889	FC 5748–5805
Regular soil	1759–1890	FC 5748–5805
Muslin	1759–1891	FC 5748–5805
White linen cloth	1759–1892	FC 5748–5805
Lint	1759–1893	FC 5748–5805
Glasses (Bohemia)	1759–1894	FC 5748–5805
Optical glass	1759–1895	FC 5748–5805
Boar sows	1759–1896	FC 5748–5805
Distilled liqueurs	1759–1897	FC 5748–5805

SOURCE: PER PRODUCT LISTED IN THE THIRD COLOMN OF TABLE.

A.3 Local Production Figures for Refined Salt

City	Number of refineries	Total number of workers	Salt production per year (in quarters)	Production for export
Brussels	2	6	3.000	None
Nivelles	2	2	320	None
Antwerp	2 (Basteyns and Pieters)	26	19.187	None
Ghent	1 (10 Masters)	28	20.000	None
Termonde	1	2	Unknown	None
Bruges	7	14	4.200	A small amount to Holland
Ostend	3	11	6.320	None
Newport	3	3	800	None
Ypres	4	12	Unknown	None
Diksmuide	2	2	Unknown	None
Courtrai	1	3	1.000	None
Oudenarde	3	6	7.000	None
Menen	1	12	1.000	None
Tournai	7	7	Unknown	None
Mons	13	13	1.200	A small amount to Liège
Ath	9	9	7.200	A small amount to Liège
Charleroi	3 (Dubreux, Yernaux and Thibeau)	10	2.760	Some export (not specified)
Namur	1	1	Unknown	A small amount to Liège
Total	**65**	**167**	**73.987**	**Unknown**

SOURCE: PH. MOUREAUX, LA STATISTIQUE INDUSTRIELLE DANS LES PAYS-BAS AUTRICHIENS À L'ÉPOQUE DE MARIE-THÉRÈSE. DOCUMENTS ET CARTES (BRUSSEL 1974–1981).

A.4 Moderation of Import Duties on Grey Salt

ource NAB, FC)	Year	Date	Claimant	City	Ruling	Occupation of the claimant
221	1759	July 23rd	Pierre François Carpentier	Bruges	Granted	Merchant
221	1760	June 26th	Henry Gaucheret	Brussels	Unknown	Salt producer
225	1764	October 22nd	city officials	Brussels	Granted	Public institution
225	1764	October 27th	States of Brabant[1]	Brabant	Rejected	Public institution
225	1764	October 27th	city officials	Leuven	Granted	Public institution
225	1764	October 29th	city officials	Antwerp	Granted	Public institution
226	1764	December 4th	States of Flanders[2]	Ghent	Rejected	Public institution
228	1765	May 24th	States of Brabant[3]	Brabant	Granted	Public institution
229	1765	July 26th	States of Namur[4]	Namur	Granted	Public institution
237	1773	August 11th	Germances	Ninove	Granted	Salt producer
235	1779	August 19th	Lemerel[5]	Brussels	Granted	Manufacturer
235	1779	August 30th	Vierendeels	Ghent	Granted	Manufacturer
238	1780	November 27th	Lemerel	Brussels	Granted	Manufacturer
239	1782	July 29th	Lemerel	Brussels	Granted	Manufacturer
240	1783	August 23rd	Lemerel	Brussels	Granted	Manufacturer
241	1786	March 6th	Defoux	Brussels	Granted	Salt producer

SOURCE: NAB, FC, 5221–5241.

1 Denial to the request by the States of Brabant to revoke the duty elevation of October 6th 1764. The request itself is also in NAB, FC, 5225 (October 16th 1764).

2 In this case there is no standard request; instead, a very bulky communication by the deputies of the States of Flanders (in Ghent) concerning elevation of the salt duties suggests another general lowering of the duties.

3 Denial to the request by the States of Brabant to revoke the elevation of October 6th 1764. The request itself is also in NAB, FC, 5228 (October 14th 1765).

4 Denial to a request by the deputies of the "three members of the State and County of Namur" to revoke the elevation of October 6th 1764. The request itself is also included: NAB, FC, 5229, March 27th 1765.

5 Lemerel owned an ammonium salt factory and refined his own salt.

A.5 Extract From Departmental Figures, 1764–1781

Year	Export white salt (in quarters)	Export from Charleroi	Percentage of total export	Import crude salt (in quarters)	Imports to Ghent and Ostend	Percentage of total import
1764	1932.71	685.33	35	32722.75	26477.00	81
1765	510.25	337.88	66	26642.86	26179.50	98
1766	927.63	773.75	83	87517.81	85839.25	98
1767	745.13	568.00	76	53699.17	52434.17	98
1768	779.96	609.50	78	38517.75	37438.00	97
1769	1032.58	699.00	68	56144.38	55490.75	99
1770	1438.04	1022.50	71	40949.77	40700.75	99
1771	1837.02	1288.25	70	54669.63	54134.94	99
1772	2697.82	1762.75	65	67034.25	66995.63	100
1773	2288.25	1898.13	83	54199.13	54082.38	100
1774	2995.40	2361.50	79	59316.88	59314.00	100
1775	3139.46	2233.50	71	54869.06	54426.31	99
1776	2854.83	1957.00	69	61497.71	61371.25	100
1777	2279.83	1782.50	78	53347.38	53345.25	100
1778	560.42	180.17	32	56401.92	55714.54	99
1779	1744.63	1563.00	90	57877.25	54978.50	95
1780	324.25	2.00	1	59241.75	54367.50	92
1781	2548.00	2181.00	86	65936.75	55940.00	85

SOURCE: RELEVÉ GÉNÉRAL, NAB, FC, 5756–5791.

A.6 Composition of the Linen Trade, According to Value (1759–1791)

Expensive varieties, in ells[6]		Inexpensive varieties, in ells[7]		Shares of the total number of ells			
Import	Export	Import	Export	Expensive import	Expensive export	Cheap import	Cheap export
64,653	230,999	758,882	9,090,848	7.9	2.5	92.1	97.5
137,873	780,348	182,479	7,729,411	43.0	9.2	57.0	90.8
897,370	1,069,318	245,243	6,539,749	78.8	14.1	21.5	86.0
69,069	1,308,276	198,203	4,257,016	26.8	23.5	77.0	76.5
102,322	510,246	132,898	7,653,851	43.9	6.3	57.0	93.8
105,450	444,472	3,047,360	13,358,682	3.4	3.3	97.2	98.2
180,112	422,426	710,116	15,924,787	22.3	2.6	87.8	97.5
319,983	1,151,457	1,199,376	13,180,125	21.6	8.0	81.1	92.1
114,738	577,330	876,031	12,748,651	11.7	4.3	89.5	95.8
172,137	570,267	660,456	11,838,995	22.4	4.6	86.1	95.4
148,863	526,532	677,505	17,609,702	18.3	2.9	83.1	97.2
125,953	463,110	989,380	11,189,973	11.5	4.0	90.3	96.1
113,362	427,026	483,146	11,175,562	19.1	3.7	81.3	96.4
210,361	564,283	477,378	11,817,456	35.7	4.6	81.0	96.0
162,918	297,717	461,430	12,954,961	26.5	2.3	75.1	98.1
131,846	337,811	483,204	12,723,856	21.8	2.6	80.0	97.7
121,424	568,924	541,178	15,507,966	18.5	3.6	82.5	96.9
5076	639,644	560,739	14,989,430	0.9	4.1	99.1	95.9
17,833	225,030	713,807	15,160,801	2.4	1.5	97.6	98.5
18,570	184,500	705,492	15,053,371	2.6	1.2	97.4	98.8
9774	167,750	589,521	14,874,632	1.6	1.1	98.4	98.9
17,996	658,366	643,132	14,366,875	2.7	4.4	97.3	95.6
12,668	371,861	722,470	15,300,224	1.7	2.4	98.3	97.6
6435	280,322	802,356	17,029,094	0.8	1.6	99.2	98.4

6 The expensive varieties include: Cambrai, rollet and batiste, chintz, linen for tablecloth and napkins, Silesian linen, "Boldavid," "douel," glazed linen, "talette" and the white and coloured linen which is explicitly labelled a expensive in the statistics themselves. Pieces have been converted into number of ells.

7 The cheap varieties include: white linen, grey linen, cheap coloured linen, linen for handkerchiefs, towels and mattresses, "drol," slate blue and striped. Pieces have been converted into numbers of ells.

Composition of the Linen Trade, According to Value (1759–1791) (cont.)

Expensive varieties, in ells		Inexpensive varieties, in ells		Shares of the total number of ells			
Import	Export	Import	Export	Expensive import	Expensive export	Cheap import	Cheap export
13,949	596,163	3,468,573	29,930,592	0.4	2.0	99.6	98.0
100,755	419,272	1,765,936	18,390,642	5.4	2.2	94.6	97.8
4831	559,327	733,252	15,805,300	0.7	3.4	99.3	96.6
8439	396,777	828,819	15,321,246	1.0	2.5	99.0	97.5
13,858	419,397	680,113	16,876,058	2.0	2.4	98.0	97.6
32,604	438,535	752,763	16,232,980	4.2	2.6	95.8	97.4
22,378	405,314	530,287	12,582,332	4.0	3.1	96.0	96.9
7767	288,415	609,321	15,764,222	1.3	1.8	98.7	98.2
25,279	394,146	809,760	18,126,817	3.0	2.1	97.0	97.9

SOURCE: NAB, FC, 5748–5805.

A.7 Small Coal Imports According to Origin, 1764–1781

Year	Small coal import from England (in quarters)	Small coal import from France and Liège (in quarters)	Total small coal imports (in quarters)	Share of English imports
1764	81045.85	93673.83	189075.10	42.90%
1765	104547.70	128178.67	256697.08	40.70%
1766	162061.50	138723.00	324666.50	49.90%
1767	247024.50	165284.00	433018.25	57.00%
1768	113304.00	128237.50	268983.75	42.10%
1769	93333.75	140381.00	252947.88	36.90%
1770	–	–	–	–
1771	171789.30	213014.50	420364.30	40.90%
1772	176633.00	216617.25	425797.50	41.50%
1773	199687.30	202712.00	424019.42	47.10%

Year	Small coal import from England (in quarters)	Small coal import from France and Liège (in quarters)	Total small coal imports (in quarters)	Share of English imports
1774	74546.00	170239.17	270822.00	27.50%
1775	109095.00	191833.75	327006.50	33.40%
1776	97558.75	166102.83	294257.75	33.20%
1777	98997.25	193588.50	321040.58	30.80%
1778	65827.13	187514.83	275809.38	23.90%
1779	–	–	–	–
1780	17962.50	192844.30	232652.75	7.70%
1781	15551.00	203403.00	258937.00	6.00%

SOURCE: RELEVÉ GÉNÉRAL, NATIONAL ARCHIVES BRUSSELS, COUNCIL OF FINANCE, 5756–5791.

A.8 Applications to Import English Coal at the Old Tariff (Before December 17th 1761)

Date	Applicant	City	Decision
1762, August 5th	City officials	Antwerp	Granted
1763, March 2nd	City officials	Ostend	Granted
1763, July 25th	Manufacturers	Lier	Unknown
1763, August 16th	Salt and sugar refiners	Antwerp	Granted
1764, March 29th	François Danys	Unknown	Rejected
1764, April 22nd	Brewers	Antwerp	Granted
1764, May 11th	Deheyder and co.	Lier	Granted
1764, August 2nd	City officials	Antwerp	Granted
1764, September 17th	City officials	Malines	Granted
1768, July 17th	Textile printers	Antwerp	Granted
1768, August 8th	City officials	Antwerp	Granted
1768, August 27th	Deheyder and co.	Lier	Granted
1769, October 23rd	City officials	Ostend	Granted
1769, December 4th	City officials	Antwerp and Malines	Granted
1770, January 3rd	City officials	Lier	Granted
1770, March 5th	J.S. Toebast	Eeklo	Rejected

Applications to Import English Coal at the Old Tariff (Before December 17th 1761) (cont.)

Date	Applicant	City	Decision
1770, March 12th	Deheyder and co.	Antwerp	Granted
1770, August 16th	Warnot	Antwerp	Unknown
1770, October 24th	City officials	Malines	Granted
1771, February 16th	City officials	Bruges, Ostend, Newport	Granted
1771, March 1st	La motte en co	Antwerp	Granted
1771, June 22nd	City officials	Malines	Unknown
1772, July 8th	Various manufacturers	Antwerp	Granted
1773, April 12th	Various manufacturers	Antwerp	Granted
1777, March 1st	Jean Basteyns	Antwerp	Granted
1781, August 6th	City officials	Antwerp	Granted
1783, July 26th	d'Hooge	Ghent	Granted
1783, August 6th	City officials	Antwerp	Granted
1784, May 12th	City officials	Antwerp	Granted

SOURCE: NAB, FC, 5024–5033.

A.9 The Share of Granted Applications per Actor Category, Subdivided in Three Periods

			Ruling				Total
	1759–1769		Approved	Rejected	Unknown	Partially approved	
Occupation of the applicant	Institution	Count	9	0	1	0	10
		% within applicant	90	0	10	0	100
	Manufacturer	Count	12	1	2	0	15
		% within applicant	80	7	13	0	100
	Merchant	Count	5	0	2	3	10
		% within applicant	50	0	20	30	100
	Coal producer	Count	5	1	2	0	8
		% within applicant	63	13	25	0	100

	1770–1779		Ruling				Total
			Approved	Rejected	Unknown	Partially approved	
	Unknown	Count	1	3	2	1	7
		% within applicant	14	43	29	14	100
Total		Count	32	5	9	4	50
		% within applicant	64	10	18	8	100

	1770–1779		Ruling				Total
			Approved	Rejected	Unknown	Partially approved	
Occupation of the applicant	Institution	Count	4	0	2	0	6
		% within applicant	67	0	33	0	100
	Manufacturer	Count	5	3	2	0	10
		% within applicant	50	30	20	0	100
	Merchant	Count	5	5	1	1	12
		% within applicant	42	42	8	8	100
	Coal Producer	Count	18	3	1	0	22
		% within applicant	82	14	5	0	100
	Unknown	Count	2	4	1	3	10
		% within applicant	20	40	10	30	100
Total		Count	34	15	7	4	60
		% within applicant	57	25	12	7	100

The Share of Granted Applications per Actor Category, Subdivided in Three Periods (cont.)

			Ruling				Total
	1780–1786		Approved	Rejected	Unknown	Partially approved	
Occupation of the applicant	Institution	Count	5	0	1	0	6
		% within applicant	83	0	17	0	100
	Manufacturer	Count	2	1	0	0	3
		% within applicant	67	33	0	0	100
	Merchant	Count	5	1	0	1	7
		% within applicant	71	14	0	14	100
	Coal producer	Count	13	0	3	0	16
		% within applicant	81	0	19	0	100
	Unknown	Count	1	0	0	1	2
		% within applicant	50	0	0	50	100
Total		Count	26	2	4	2	34
		% within applicant	76	6	12	6	100

SOURCE: NAB, FC, 5022–5034.

A.10 Decrees Allowing or Prohibiting Grain Exports[8]

Archive number	Date	Content of the decree
4708	September 28th 1756	Export ban on all types except buckwheat
4708	October 23rd 1756	Export ban on buckwheat
4720	May 2nd 1759	Permission to export all types of grain
4726	November 6th 1765	Export ban on oats and buckwheat
4726	November 28th 1765	Export ban on rye
5606	July 9th 1766	Permission to export rye (12 guilders per last)
4727	September 1766	Permission to export buckwheat (6 guilders per last)
5606	June 4th 1767	Export ban on wheat and rye
4728	January 31st 1767	Export ban on barley (*orge et soucrion*)
4728	May 27th 1767	Export ban on wheat
4728	June 4th 1767	Export ban on rye
5606	November 12th 1767	Export ban on buckwheat
5606	April 18th 1768	Export ban on spelt
4736	February 27th 1769	Permission to export buckwheat
4738	August 26th 1769	Permission to export all types of grain
4740	April 23rd 1770	Export ban on wheat, rye and barley
4742	May 28th 1770	Export ban on spelt
4743	August 4th 1770	Export ban on buckwheat
4746	November 6th 1770	Export ban on *soucrion*
4778	April 18th 1774	Permission to export buckwheat (6 guilders per last)
4770	July 9th 1774	Permission to export wheat and rye
4771	September 3rd 1774	Export ban on all types of grain
4783	August 2nd 1777	Restrictions on export
4783	November 3rd 1777	Export ban on buckwheat
4784	August 14th 1778	Permission to export rye
4784	September 2nd 1778	Permission to export barley (*orge*)
8874	September 14th 1780	Export ban on buckwheat
8874	November 15th 1780	Export ban on rye
4787	December 30th 1780	Export ban on wheat
4788	January 15th 1781	Export ban on spelt
8874	January 3rd 1782	Permission to export wheat

8 For details on the content of most of these decrees, Vandenbroeke, *Agriculture*, 174–196.

Decrees Allowing or Prohibiting Grain Exports (*cont.*)

Archive number	Date	Content of the decree
4795	December 31st 1782	Export ban on all types of grain
8874	May 10th 1783	Permission to export wheat
8874	June 30th 1783	Permission to export rye
4797	July 21st 1783	Permission to export grains from Luxemburg
4797	September 10th 1783	Permission to export grains from Marche and St Vith
4797 and 4799	October 4th 1784	Permission to export buckwheat
4799	October 25th 1784	Export ban on all types of grain
4801 and 8874	November 26th 1786	Permission to export all types of grain
4805	April 4th 1789	Export ban on all types of grain

SOURCE: NAB, FC, 4708–8874.

A.11 Requests by Military Parties

Source number	Date	Applicant	Request	Ruling
4728	June 30th 1767	Colonel du Regiment de Brouw	Permission to transport	Granted
4728	July 4th 1767	Commandant de fort de Lillo	Permission to transport	Granted
4731	May 13th 1768	Commandant de fort de Lillo	Permission to transport	Granted
4750	May 2nd 1771	Garrison Sas van Gent	Permission to transport	Granted
4751	Jun 20th 1771	Garrison at Baden Durlach	Permission to transport	Granted
4753	August 21st 1771	Garrison Sas van Gent	Permission to transport	Granted
4756	October 9th 1771	Garrison la Philippine	Permission to transport	Granted
4756	October 30th 1771	Garrison at Hulst	Permission to export	Granted

Source number	Date	Applicant	Request	Ruling
4754	December 4th 1771	Garrison at Bergen-op-Zoom	Permission to export	Granted
4758	January 22nd 1772	Garrison la Philippine	Permission to export	Rejected
4760	February 3rd 1772	Garrison Sas van Gent	Permission to transport	Granted
4763	November 9th 1772	Garrison at Axel	Permission to export	Granted
4766	May 12th 1773	Garrison at Scheldt	Permission to transport	Granted
4767	August 4th 1773	Garrison at Ysendijck	Permission to export	Granted
4769	March 17th 1774	Garrison at Ysendijck	Permission to export	Granted
4771	September 22nd 1774	Garrison Sas van Gent	Permission to export	Granted
4772	October 22nd 1774	Garrison Sas van Gent	Permission to export	Granted
4773	December 5th 1774	Garrison Sas van Gent	Permission to export	Granted
4785	August 4th 1779	Garrison at Hulst	Permission to export	Granted
4789	April 4th 1781	Regiment of Esterhazy	Permission to transit	Granted
4791	February 9th 1782	Garrison at Axel	Permission to export	Granted
4804	February 3rd 1791	Garrison Sas van Gent	Permission to export	Granted
4807	July 12th 1791	Garrison at Hulst	Permission to transport	Granted
4809	November 16th 1791	Garrison at Ysendijck	Permission to transport	Granted
4807	July 22nd 1791	Garrison at Ysendijck	Permission to transport	Unknown

SOURCE: NAB, FC, 4728–4809.

Bibliography

I Primary Sources

Austria

Österreichisches Staatsarchiv

Finanz- und Hofkammerarchiv, Neues Hofkammerarchiv, Kommerz Litorale, Akten (inventory: Hofkammerarchiv Austria, *Inventar des wiener hofkammerarchivs* (Vienna 1951).)

- Numbers 1003–1010: "Kommerz der österreichischen Niederlande mit den Erbländern."

Belgium

National Archives Brussels

1 *Finance Council* (*Inventory Number I 103*)

Customs statistics: «*Relevé Général des Marchandises, Manufactures et Denrées Entrées, Sorties et Transitées Par les Vingt et un Départemens des Païs-Bas Autrichiens*».

- Number 5748: Relevé Général 1759.
- Numbers 5749, 8912 and 8914: Relevé Général 1760.
- Numbers 5750 and 5751: Relevé Général 1761.
- Numbers 5752 and 5753: Relevé Général 1762.
- Numbers 5754 and 5755: Relevé Général 1763.
- Numbers 5756 and 5757: Relevé Général 1764.
- Numbers 5758 and 5759: Relevé Général 1765.
- Numbers 5760 and 5761: Relevé Général 1766.
- Numbers 5762 and 5763: Relevé Général 1767.
- Numbers 5764 and 5765: Relevé Général 1768.
- Numbers 5766 and 5767: Relevé Général 1769.
- Numbers 5768 and 5769: Relevé Général 1770.
- Numbers 5770 and 5771: Relevé Général 1771.
- Numbers 5772 and 5773: Relevé Général 1772.
- Numbers 5774 and 5775: Relevé Général 1773.
- Numbers 5776 and 5777: Relevé Général 1774.
- Numbers 5778 and 5779: Relevé Général 1775.
- Numbers 5780 and 5781: Relevé Général 1776.
- Numbers 5782 and 5783: Relevé Général 1777.
- Numbers 5784 and 5785: Relevé Général 1778.

- Numbers 5786 and 5787: Relevé Général 1779.
- Numbers 5788 and 5789: Relevé Général 1780.
- Numbers 5790 and 5791: Relevé Général 1781.
- Numbers 5792 and 5793: Relevé Général 1782.
- Number 5794: Relevé Général 1783.
- Numbers 5795 and 5796: Relevé Général 1784.
- Numbers 5797 and 5798: Relevé Général 1785.
- Numbers 5799 and 5801: Relevé Général 1786.
- Numbers 5800 and 8917: Relevé Général 1787.
- Number 5802 (and NAB, Manuscripts, number 2780): Relevé Général 1788.
- Number 5803: Relevé Général 1789.
- Number 5804: Relevé Général 1790.
- Number 5805: Relevé Général 1791.

Tariff books: «*Estat Ou Tarif des Droits d'entrée et sortie sur les marchandises, manufactures et denrées*»

- Number 8873: tariff book from 1670, with corrections until 1792.
- Number 8874: tariff book from 1680, with corrections until 1792.
- Number 5606: reprint of the 1670 tariff book (1760).
- Number 5607: «*Receuil général des Marchandises, Manufactures, denrées et matières reprises et non reprises aux tarifs des années 1670, 1680 et 1683 et qui paient les droits d'entrée et sortie suivant les dits tarifs et ordonnances dérogatoires. N°5*».
- Number 5608: Copy of the 1680 tariff book.
- Number 5591: Remarks on the customs duties, until 1669.
- Number 8792: Remarks on the customs duties, until 1680.

Other sources regarding tariffs

- Number 4270: «*Protocole du Conseil des Domaines et finances de Sa MAjesté L'Imp.ce Douairiere et Reine Apostolique Concernant les affaires Courantes des Droits D'Entrée et de Sortie commencant le 3 Novembre 1768 et finissant le 18 juillet 1771.*»
- Number 4271: «*Protocole des droits d'entrée et de sortie, commencant le 24 juillet 1771 et finissant*»
- Numbers 5671–5672: «*Recueil des ordonnances et dispositions émanées relativement aux droits d'entrée, sortie & autres, pendant l'année 1768*»
- Number 5729: «*Ordonnances et dispositions qui opèrent dans la province de Limbourg. L'entrée et la sortie*»

- Numbers 4278, 4279, 4281, 4283, 4284, 4287, 4289, 4290, 4298 and 4304: various letters and memoirs on «*Commerce en général*».

Product-related customs sources

- Numbers 5403–4537: Douanes: Epiceries, thé, caffé, chocolat, drogues et teintures.
- Numbers 4556–4560: Douanes: Etoffes de laine, d'or, de soie et toiles de coton généralité.
- Numbers 4563–4596: Douane: Etoffes de laines de toutes espèces.
- Numbers 4597–4598: Draps faits de queue et penne.
- Numbers 4599–4607: Douanes: Etoffes d'or, d'argent, de soie, velours de soie et soie crue et filée.
- Numbers 4608–4609: Douanes: Education des vers à soie et plantation des muriers.
- Numbers 4610–4637: Douanes: toiles de tous genres.
- Numbers 4638–4644: Douanes: imprimeries de toiles de coton.
- Numbers 4683–4687: Douanes: Fouleries.
- Numbers 4688–4689: Douanes: Gazes et crêpes de soie, de fil, marli, treilli, etc.
- Numbers 4704–4809: Douanes: Céréales.
- Numbers 4856–4890: Douanes: Laines.
- Numbers 4892–4899: Douanes: draperies de Limbourg.
- Numbers 4999, 5019–5034: Douanes: charbons.
- Numbers 5215–5249: Douanes: sel et raffineries.
- Numbers 5256–5267: Douanes: sucre et raffineries.
- Numbers 5319–5339: Douanes: toiles.

Sources on prices

- Number 4828: Monthly prices from different markets for grains, seeds, oil, linen, yarn and hops.
- Numbers 4818–4838: grain prices, «Régitre des prix des grains à Amsterdam».
- Numbers 4950–4953: flax prices.

Sources on customs organisation and staff

- Numbers 5853–5854, 5863, 6399, 8576.

Dictionnaire de Commerce (by Henri Delplancq)

- Number 8580

2 *National Archives Brussels, Secretariat of State and War (Inventory Number T 100)*

- Number 1777: Notes by Henri Delplancq.
- Numbers 2149 and 2153: Memoirs on international trade.

3 *National Archives Brussels, Manuscripts (Inventory Number I 115)*

- Numbers 850 and 2452: Memoirs on trade.

4 *National Archives Brussels, Auditor's Office (Inventory Number I 001)*

- Number 1266: Grain prices.

5 *National Archives Brussels, Chancellerie Autrichienne Des Pays-Bas à Vienne (Inventory Number T 129)*

- Number 499: Notes regarding the Port of Ostend.

6 *National Archives Brussels, Conseil du Gouvernement Général (Inventory Number I 071)*

- Number 821: Notes regarding coal consumption.

II Secondary Sources

Acemoglu, D., Johnson, S. and Robinson, J. 'The Rise of Europe: Atlantic Trade, Institutional Change and Economic Growth', *American Economic Review* 95, no. 3 (2005), pp. 546–579.

Acemoglu, D. and Robinson, J., *Why Nations Fail. The Origins of Power, Pros-perity and Poverty* (London, 2012).

Adshead, S.A.M., *Salt and Civilization* (Basingstoke, 1992).

Aerts, E. 'De Zuidnederlandse Textielindustrie C.1600–C.1850', *Alumni Leuven* 13, no. 1 (1982), pp. 18–21.

——. 'Economische Interventie van de Centrale Staat in de Spaanse en Oostenrijkse Nederlanden (1555–1795)', in S. Dubois and J. Yante eds., *Gouvernance et Administration dans les Provinces Belgiques du XVIe au XVIIIe Siècle*, (Brussels, 2009), pp. 107–142.

Afeefy, H.Y., Liebman, J.F. and Stein, S.E. 'Neutral Thermochemical Data', in P.J. Linstrom and W.G. Mallard eds., *Nist Chemistry Webbook, Nist Standard Reference Database Number 69*, (Gaithersburg, 2011).

Aldcroft, D.H. and Sutcliffe, A., *Europe in the International Economy 1500 to 2000* (Cheltenham, 1999).

Allen, R. "The Great Divergence in European Wages and Prices from the Middle Ages to the First World War," in: *Explorations in Economic History* 38 (2001) 411–447.

——, Wages, Prices & Living Standards: The World-Historical Perspective', http://www.economics.ox.ac.uk/members/robert.allen/WagesPrices.htm (2009).

——, "Why the Industrial Revolution was British: Commerce, Induced Invention, and the Scientific Revolution," in: *The Economic History Review* 64, 2 (2011) 357–384.

André-Félix, A., *Les Débuts de l'Industrie Chimique dans les Pays-Bas Autrichiens* (Brussels, 1971).

Bairoch, P., *Economics and World History: Myths and Paradoxes* (New York, 1993).

Balassa, B. 'The Process of Industrial Development and Alternative Development Strategies', *Essays in International Finance* 141 (1980).

Bastin, J. 'De Gentse Lijnwaadmarkt en Linnenhandel in de XVIIe Eeuw', *Handelingen der maatschappij voor geschiedenis en oudheidkunde te Gent* XXI (1967), pp. 131–162.

Bayly, C.A., *The Birth of the Modern World, 1780–1914* (Oxford, 2004).

Berg, M. 'In Pursuit of Luxury: Global History and British Consumer Goods in the Eighteenth Century', *Past & Present* 182 (2004), pp. 85–142.

Berg, M. and Hudson, P. 'Rehabilitating the Industrial Revolution', *Economic History Review* 45, no. 1 (1992), pp. 25–40.

Bernard, B., *Patrice-François de Neny (1716–1784). Portrait d'un Homme d'État.* Edited by R. Mortier and H. Hasquin. Vol. 21, *Etudes sur le XIIIe Siècle* (Brussels, 1993).

Berrill, K. 'International Trade and the Rate of Economic Growth', *The Economic History Review, New Series* 12 (1960), pp. 351–359.

Bertels, I., De Munck, B. and Van Goethem, H.E., *Antwerpen. Biografie van een Stad* (Antwerp, 2010).

Beukenkamp, R.L., *De Wereldgraanhandel* (Wageningen, 1945).

Bigwood, G., *Les Impôts Généraux dans les Pays-Bas Autrichiens. Etude Historique de Législation Financière* (Leuven, 1900).

Blomme, J. and Van Der Wee, H. 'The Belgian Economy in a Long-Term Historical Perspective: Economic Development in Flanders and Brabant, 1500–1812', in, *Workshop on Quantitative Economic History*, (Leuven, 1993).

Blondé, B. 'Transport and the Economic Development of Brabant in the 18th Century', in, *Economic Growth and Structural Change. Comparative Approaches over the Long Run on the Basis of Reconstructed National Accounts. Workshop on Quantitative Economic History*, (Leuven, 1993).

——, *Een Economie met verschillende Snelheden: Ongelijkheden in de Opbouw en de Ontwikkeling van het Brabantse Stedelijke Netwerk (Ca. 1750–Ca. 1790)*, *Verhandelingen van de Koninklijke Vlaamse Academie van België voor Wetenschappen en Kunsten* (Brussels, 1995).

——. 'Disparities in the Development of the Brabantine urban Network: urban Centrality, Town-Countryside Relationships, and Transportation Development, 1750–1790', in C. Núnez ed., *Proceedings Twelfth International Economic History Congress*, (Madrid, 1998).

——. 'Feeding Cities: Transportation Costs, Paved Roads and Town-Countryside Relationships in Eighteenth-Century Brabant', in E. Thoen and P. Van Cruyningen eds., *Food Supply, Demand and Trade: Aspects of the Economic Relationship between Town and Countryside*, (Turnhout, 2012), pp. 123–141.

Blondé, B. and Greefs, H. 'Werk aan de Winkel. De Antwerpse Meerseniers: Aspecten van de Kleinhandel en het Verbruik in de 17de en 18de Eeuw', *Bijdragen tot de Geschiedenis* 84 (2001), pp. 207–229.

Blondé, B. and Van Uytven, R. 'Langs Land- en Waterwegen in de Zuidelijke Nederlanden. Lopend Onderzoek naar het Preïndustriële Transport', *Bijdragen tot de Geschiedenis* 82, no. 2 (1999), pp. 135–158.

Bordo, M.D., Taylor, A.M. and Williamson, J.G., *Globalization in Historical Perspective* (Chicago, 2005).

Briavoinne, N., *De l'Industrie en Belgique. Sa Situation Actuelle. Causes de Décadence et de Prosperité* (Brussels, 1839).

——, *Mémoire sur l'État de la Population, des Fabriques, de Manufactures et du Commerce dans les Provinces des Pays-Bas, Depuis Albert et Isabelle jusqu'è la Fin du Siècle Dernier* (Brussels, 1841).

Broadberry, S. and Campbell, B. 'GDP Per Capita in Europe, 1300–1850', *World Economic History Congress* (2009).

Broadberry, S., Fremdling, R. and Solar, P. 'Industry, 1700–1870', in S. Broadberry and K.H. O'Rourke eds., *Unifying the European Experience: An Economic History of Modern Europe*, (2008).

Brouwers, D., *La Fabrique des Queues et Pennes dans le Duché de Limbourg en 1766.*

Brulez, W. 'De Zoutinvoer in de Nederlanden in de 16de Eeuw', *Tijdschrift voor Geschiedenis* 68, no. 2 (1955), pp. 181–192.

——. 'De Handelsbalans der Nederlanden in het Midden van de 16de Eeuw', *Bijdragen voor de Geschiedenis der Nederlanden* XXI (1967), pp. 278–310.

Brunt, L. 'Where There's Muck, There's Brass: The Market for Manure in the Industrial Revolution', *Economic History Review* 60, no. 2 (2007), pp. 333–372.

Burt, R. 'The Extractive Industries', in R. Floud and P. Johnson eds., *The Cambridge Economic History of Modern Britain*, (Cambridge, 2004), pp. 417–450.

Buyst, E., Dercon, S. and Van Campenhout, B., *Road Expansion and Market Integration in the Austrian Low Countries during the Second Half of the 18th Century* (Leuven, 2000).

Chanda, N., *Bound Together, how Traders, Preachers, Adventurers, and Warriors shaped Globalization* (New Haven, 2007).

Charles, L., Coenen, A. and Daudin, G. 'Comparing Early Trade Statistics: The Case of the Austrian Netherlands and France from 1759 to 1791', *EHES Conference (Dublin)* (2011).

Charles, L. and Daudin, G. 'Le Bureau de la Balance du Commerce au XVIIIe Siècle', *Revue d'Histoire moderne et contemporaine* (accepted for publication).

Chartres, J.A. 'Introduction', in R.A. Church and E.A. Wrigley eds., *The Industrial Revolutions. Volume 1* (Oxford, 1994).

Church, R.A. and Wrigley, E.A., *The Industrial Revolutions*. 11 vols (Oxford, 1994).

Clark, G.N., *A Farewell to Alms: A Brief Economic History of the World* (Princeton, 2007).

Clunas, C. 'Modernity Global and Local: Consumption and the Rise of the West', *American Historical Review* 104 (1999), pp. 1497–1511.

Coenen, A. 'Katoen en Economische Groei. De Katoenhandel in de Oostenrijkse Nederlanden tussen Politieke Ambities en Economische Realiteit 1759–1791', *Tijdschrift voor sociale en economische geschiedenis* 8, no. 2 (2011), pp. 32–60.

Coleman, D.C. 'Mercantilism Revisited', *The Historical Journal* 23, no. 4 (1980), pp. 773–791.

Coornaert, E., *Un Centre Industriel d'autrefois: la Draperie-Sayetterie d'Hondschoote (14e–18e Siècles)* (Paris, 1930).

Coppejans-Desmedt, H., *Bijdrage tot de Studie van de Gegoede Burgerij te Gent in de XVIIIe Eeuw* (Brussels, 1952).

——. 'Economische Opbloei in de Zuidelijke Nederlanden', in, *Algemene Geschiedenis der Nederlanden*, (Utrecht, 1955), pp. 261–286.

——. 'Handelaars en Neringdoenden: de 17de en 18de Eeuw', in J.L. Broeckx ed., *Flandria Nostra*, (Antwerp, 1957), pp. 465–512.

——. 'Pogingen tot Opbeuring van de Gentse Wolnijverheid bij de Aanvang van de XIXe Eeuw', *Handelingen der maatschappij voor geschiedenis en oudheidkunde te Gent* XXI (1967).

——. 'De Gentse Vlasindustrie vanaf het Einde van de XVIIIe Eeuw tot de Oprichting van de Grote Mechanische Bedrijven (1838)', *Oostvlaams Verbond van de Kringen voor Geschiedenis Nieuwe Reeks*, 8 (1969), pp. 1–24.

——. 'De Belgische Textielnijverheid op Nieuwe Wegen door een Nieuwe Mentaliteit. Schets van een Historisch Ontwikkelingsproces', in, *Vijfde Nationaal Kongres voor Industriële Archeologie: Textiel*, (Ghent, 1977), pp. 25–51.

——. 'Aspecten van de Industriële Politiek in de Oostenrijkse Nederlanden', in H. Houtman-De Smedt ed., *Overheid en Economie. Economische Aspecten van de Overheidspolitiek in en met Betrekking tot de Oostenrijkse Nederlanden*, (Antwerp, 1989).

Coppens, H. 'De Financiën van de Centrale Regering van de Zuidelijke Nederlanden aan het Einde van het Spaanse en onder Oostenrijks Bewind (Ca. 1680–1788)', *Verhandelingen van de Koninklijke Academie voor Wetenschappen, Letteren en Schone Kunsten van België, Klasse der Letteren. Brussel* 54, no. 142 (1992).

——. 'Bureau voor het Beheer van de Douanerechten (1737–1794)', in E. Aerts ed., *De Centrale Overheidsinstellingen van de Habsburgse Nederlanden (1482–1795)*, (Brussels, 1995), pp. 523–530.

Corluy, L. 'Een Metodologische Poging tot Uitwerking van een Ekonomisch Model van de Buitenlandse Handel voor het Departement Gent in de Oostenrijkse Nederlanden tijdens de Tweede Helft van de XVIIIe Eeuw', (KUL, 1972).

Crafts, N.F.R., *British Economic Growth During the Industrial Revolution* (Oxford, 1985).

——. 'Exogenous or Endogenous Growth? The Industrial Revolution Reconsidered', *Journal of Economic History* 55 (1995), pp. 745–772.

Crouzet, F., *Britain, France and International Commerce*, (1996).

D'Haeseleer, P. 'Proto-Industrialisering van de Vlasnijverheid in Dertien Gemeenten ten Westen van Aalst (18e – eerste Helft 19e Eeuw)', (Katholieke Universiteit Leuven, 1990).

Dardel, P., *Navires et Marchandises dans les Ports de Rouen et du Havre au XVIIIe Siècle* (Paris, 1963).

Daudin, G., *Commerce et Prospérité. La France au XVIIIe Siècle* (Paris, 2005).

Davis, R. 'English Foreign Trade, 1700–1774', *Economic History Review* 15 (1962), pp. 285–303.

——, *English Overseas Trade 1500–1700* (London, 1973).

——, *The Industrial Revolution and British Overseas Trade* (Leicester, 1979).

De Graef, P. 'Polderpioniers in de "Nieuwe Dyckagie van Calloo." Marktgerichtheid en Risicobereidheid van de eerste Generatie Landbouwers in Kallopolder, Ca. 1665–Ca. 1710', (University of Antwerp, 2010–2011).

De Herdt, R. 'Het Uitroeien van de Runderpest in Vlaanderen (1769–1785). Regeringsmaatregelen en Oppositie ertegen', *Tijdschrift voor industriële cultuur* 23, no. 3 (2003), pp. 73–89.

De Peuter, R. 'Note sur le Grand Commerce à Bruxelles à la Fin de l'Époque Autrichienne', in R.H. Mortier, H. ed., *Bruxelles au XVIIIe Siècle (Etudes sur le XVIIIe Siècle)*, (1977), pp. 27–32.

——, *Brussel in de Achttiende Eeuw* (Brussels, 1999).

de Vries, J., *The Industrious Revolution. Consumer Behaviour and the Household Economy, 1650 to the Present* (Cambridge, 2008).

de Vries, J., Denzel, M. and Rossner, P., *Small Is Beautiful?: Interlopers and Smaller Trading Nations in the Pre-Industrial Period* (Stuttgart, 2011).

de Vries, J. and Van der Woude, A., *Nederland 1500–1815. De eerste Ronde van Moderne Economische Groei* (Amsterdam, 1995).

Deceulaer, H. 'Between Medieval Continuities and Early Modern Change: Proto-Industrialization and Consumption in the Southern Low Countries (1300–1800)', *Textile History* (2006), pp. 123–148.

Dechesne, L., *Industrie Drapière de la Vesdre avant 1800* (Liège, 1926).

Degryse, K. 'De Antwerpse Fortuinen: Kapitaalsaccumulatie, - Investering en - Rendement te Antwerpen in de 18de Eeuw', *Bijdragen tot de Geschiedenis* 2005, no. 1–4 (2005).

Dejongh, G., *Tussen Immobiliteit en Revolutie. De Economische Ontwikkeling van de Belgische Landbouw in een Eeuw van Transitie, 1750–1850* (Leuven, 1999).

Dejongh, G. and Segers, Y. 'Een Kleine Natie in Mutatie. De Economische Ontwikkeling van de Zuidelijke Nederlanden/België in de Eeuw 1750–1850', *Tijdschrift voor Geschiedenis* 114 (2001), pp. 171–194.

Dejongh, G. and Thoen, E. 'Arable Productivity in Flanders and the Former Territory of Belgium in a Long-Term Perspective (from the Middle Ages to the End of the Ancien Régime)', in E. Thoen and B. Van Bavel eds., *Land Productivity and Agro-Systems in the North Sea Area (Middel Ages-20th Century): Elements for Comparison. In Comparative Rural History of the North Sea Area; CORN Publication Series 2*, (1999), pp. 30–65.

Devos, G. 'Oostenrijkse Douanestatistiek en de Oostendse Handel in de Tweede Helft van de XVIIIe Eeuw', in, *Colloquium: Economische Geschiedenis van België*, (Brussels, 1972), pp. 335–350.

Dhondt, J. and Bruwier, M. 'The Industrial Revolution in Belgium and Holland, 1700–1914', in C. Cipolla ed., *The Fontana Economic History of Europe*, (London, 1973).

Doursther, H., *Dictionnaire Universel des Poids et des Mesures Anciens et Modernes, Contenant des Tables des Monnaies de tous les Pays* (Amsterdam, 1965).

Douxchamps-Lefèvre, C. 'Le Commerce du Charbon dans les Pays-Bas Autrichiens à la Fin du XVIIIe Siècle', *Belgisch Tijdschrift voor Filologie en Geschiedenis* 46 (1968), pp. 393–421.

——. 'La Statistique Douanière des Pays-Bas Autrichiens', in, *Annales du Congrès de la Fédération CAH de Belgique*, (Brussels, 1969), pp. 123–130.

——. 'La Politique Douanière du Gouvernement des Pays-Bas sous la Règne de Marie-Thérèse', in H. Houtman-De Smedt ed., *Overheid en Economie. Economische Aspecten van de Overheidspolitiek in en met Betrekking tot de Oostenrijkse Nederlanden*, (Antwerp, 1989).

Dries, K. 'Comité voor de Wederzijdse Handel tussen de Duitse Erflanden en de Nederlanden (1768–1777)', in E. Aerts ed., *De Centrale Overheidsinstellingen van de Habsburgse Nederlanden (1482–1795)*, (Brussels, 1994), pp. 793–798.

Duplessis, R.S., *Transitions to Capitalism in Early Modern Europe* (Cambridge, 1997).

Engerman, S.L., *Trade and the Industrial Revolution, 1700–1850*. 2 vols (Cheltenham, 1996).

Engerman, S.L. and O'Brien, P.K. 'The Industrial Revolution in Global Perspective', in R. Floud and P. Johnson eds., *The Cambridge Economic History of Modern Britain*, (Cambridge, 2004).

Epstein, S.R. 'Rodney Hilton, Marxism and the Transition from Feudalism to Capitalism', *Past and Present* 195 (2007).

Everaert, J.G. 'Handel in de Zuidelijke Nederlanden 1650–1795', in, *Algemene Geschiedenis der Nederlanden*, (1977), pp. 185–202.

Findlay, R. and O'Rourke, K.H. 'Commodity Market Integration, 1500–2000', *NBER working paper series* 8579 (2001), pp. 1–69.

Findlay, R. and O'Rourke, K.H., *Power and Plenty* (Princeton, 2007).

Gerschenkron, A., *Economic Backwardness in Historical Perspective* (Cambridge, 1962).

Gillet, M. 'Charbonnages Belges et Charbonnages du Nord de la France aux XVIIIe et XIXe Siècles', in, *Mélanges Offerts À G. Jacquemyns*, (Brussels, 1968), pp. 361–384.

Haagen, W. '"Uitbuiting-door-Handel" als Verklaringsfaktor voor de Vertraagde Industrialisering van de Linnennijverheid in Vlaanderen', *Handelingen der maatschappij voor geschiedenis en oudheidkunde te Gent* XXXVII (1983), pp. 215–243.

Hamilton, A., *Report on Manufactures* (London, 1791).

Harley, C.K. 'Trade: Discovery, Mercantilism and Technology', in R. Floud and P. Johnson eds., *The Cambridge Economic History of Modern Britain*, (Cambridge, 2004), pp. 175–203.

Harley, C.K. and Crafts, N.F.R. 'Cotton Textiles and Industrial Output Growth During the Industrial Revolution', *The Economic History Review, New Series* 48, no. 1 (1995), pp. 134–144.

Hartwell, R.M., *The Causes of the Industrial Revolution in England* (London, 1970).

Hasquin, H., *Une Mutation: Le 'Pays de Charleroi' aux XVIIe et XVIIIe Siècles. Aux Origines de la Révolution Industrielle en Belgique* (Brussels, 1971).

——. 'Nijverheid in de Zuidelijke Nederlanden, 1650–1795', in, *Algemene Geschiedenis der Nederlanden*, (Haarlem, 1979), pp. 124–159.

——, *Oostenrijks België, 1713–1794. De Zuidelijke Nederlanden Onder de Oostenrijkse Habsburgers* (Brussels, 1987).

Heckscher, E. and Magnusson, L., *Mercantilism* (London, 1994).

Heeren, M., *De Kanthandel van de Firma Reyns te Antwerpen in de 18de Eeuw* (1966).

Hobsbawm, E.J., *Industry and Empire: an Economic History of Britain since 1750* (London, 1973).

Horlings, E., *The Economic Development of the Dutch Service Sector 1800–1850* (Amsterdam, 1995).

Houtman-De Smedt H. 'Korte Historische Schets van de Suikerraffinaderij "Cels, Aerts en Compagnie" (1760–1806) en van haar Latere Evolutie (1806–1951)', *Bijdragen tot de Geschiedenis* LXIII (1980), pp. 293–312.

——. 'Charles Proli. Antwerps Zakenman en Bankier, 1723–1786. Een Biografische en Bedrijfshistorische Studie', *Verhandelingen van de Koninklijke Academie voor Wetenschappen, Letteren en Schone Kunsten van België. Klasse der letteren* 45, no. 180 (1983).

——. 'De Zuidelijke Nederlanden en de Oostzee in de 18e Eeuw (Oostenrijkse Periode)', in, *The Interactions of Amsterdam and Antwerp with the Baltic Region, 1400–1800*, (Leiden, 1983), pp. 105–122.

Inikori, J., *Africans and the Industrial Revolution in England: A Study in International Trade and Economic Development* (Cambridge, 2002).

Israel, J., *The Dutch Republic. Its Rise, Greatness and Fall, 1477–1806* (Oxford, 1995).

Janssens, V. 'Het Geldwezen der Oostenrijkse Nederlanden', *Verhandelingen Koninklijke Vlaamse Academie voor Wetenschappen, Letteren en Schone Kunsten van België. Klasse der letteren. Brussel* 29 (1957).

Julin, A., *Les Grandes Fabriques en Belgique Vers le Milieu du XVIIIe Siècle, Académie Royale de Belgique*, (1902).

Komlos, J., *The Habsburg Monarchy as a Customs Union* (Princeton, 1983).

Koninckx, C., *The First and Second Chapters of the Swedish East India Company (1731–1766)* (Kortrijk, 1980).

Kurlansky, M., *Salt, a World History* (London, 2002).

Lafay, G. 'The Measurement of Revealed Comparative Advantages', in M.G. Dagenais and P.-A. Muet eds., *International Trade Modelling*, (London, 1992), pp. 209–234.

Lebrun, P., *L'industrie de la Laine a Verviers pendant le XVIIIe et le Début du XIXe Siècle* (Liège, 1948).

Lebrun, P., Bruwier, M., Dhondt, J. and Hansotte, G., *Essai sur la Révolution Industrielle en Belgique* (Brussels, 1979).

Lefèvre, J. and Lefèvre, P.F., *Etude sur le Commerce de la Belgique avec l'Espagne au XVIIIe Siècle* (Brussels, 1921).

Lemire, B., *Fashion's Favourite. The Cotton Trade and the Consumer in Britain 1660–1800* (Oxford, 1991).

Lenders, P. 'Ontwikkeling van Politiek en Instellingen in de Oostenrijkse Nederlanden. De Invloed van de Europese Oorlogen', *Bijdragen tot de Geschiedenis* 64, no. 1 (1981), pp. 33–76.

Liébin, J., *Bois-du-Luc: Un Charbonnage Hainuyer du 17e au 21e Siècle* (Mons, 2004).

Lis, C. and Soly, H., *Een Groot Bedrijf in een Kleine Stad. De Firma De Heyder en Co. te Lier, 1757–1834* (Lier, 1987).

——. 'Living Apart Together: Overheid en Ondernemers in Brabant en Vlaanderen tijdens de Tweede Helft van de 18e Eeuw', in, *Arbeid in Veelvoud. Een Huldeboek voor Jan Craeybeckx en Etienne Scholliers*, (Brussels, 1988), pp. 131–144.

——. 'Restructuring the Urban Textile Industries in Brabant and Flanders During the Second Half of the Eighteenth Century', in E. Aerts and J.H. Munro eds., *Textiles of the Low Countries in European Economic History*, (Leuven, 1990), pp. 105–113.

——. 'Different Paths of Development. Capitalism in the Northern and Southern Netherlands During the Late Middle Ages and the Early Modern Period', *Review. A Journal of the Fernand Braudel Center for the study of economics, historical systems, and civilizations* 20, no. 2 (1997), pp. 211–242.

List, F., *Das Nationale System der Politischen Oekonomie* (Jena, 1841).

Lyna, D. 'The Cultural Construction of Value: Art Auctions in Antwerp and Brussels (1700–1794)', (UA, 2010).

Maddison, A., *Contours of the World Economy, 1–2030 Ad* (Oxford, 2007).

Magnusson, L., *Nation, State and the Industrial Revolution* (London, 2009).

Materné, J., *De Prijzenadministratie van de Centrale Overheid te Brussel tijdens de 18de Eeuw. Vlaamse, Brabantse, Noordnederlandse, Engelse, Duitse en Baltische Graanprijzen op de Amsterdamse Beurs (1767–1792)* (Brussels, 1994).

McCants, A. 'Poor Consumers as Global Consumers: The Diffusion of Tea and Coffee Drinking in the Eighteenth Century', *Economic History Review* 61, no. supplement (2008), pp. 172–200.

McCloskey, D.N., *The Bourgeois Virtues: Ethics for an Age of Commerce* (Chicago, 2006).

——, *Bourgeois Dignity: Why Economics Can't Explain the Modern World* (Chicago, 2010).

McCusker, J.J. 'The Current Value of English Exports, 1697 to 1800', *The William and Mary Quarterly* 28, no. 4 (1971), pp. 607–628.

Meade, J.E., *An Introduction to Economic Analysis and Policy* (London, 1937).

Mees, J. 'La Statistique Douanière de la Belgique dans la Seconde Moitié du XVIIIe Siècle', *Revue belge d'histoire* 1 (1914), pp. 72–97.

Mendels, F.F., *Industrialization and Population Pressure in Eighteenth-Century Flanders* (New York, 1981).

Michielsen, A. 'Het Volume van de Belgische Handel in de 18e Eeuw', *Tijdschrift voor economie en sociologie* 5 (1939), pp. 206–224.

Michielsen, L. 'Het Kapitalisme te Antwerpen in de XVIIe en XVIIIe Eeuwen', *Nederlandsche Historiebladen* II (1939), pp. 243–262.

Minard, P., *La Fortune du Colbertisme* (Paris, 1998).

Mintz, S.W., *Sweetness and Power: The Place of Sugar in Modern History* (New York, 1985).

Mitchell, B.R. and Deane, P., *Abstract of British Historical Statistics* (Cambridge, 1971).

Mokyr, J., *The Economics of the Industrial Revolution* (London, 1985).

——, *The Lever of Riches: Technological Creativity and Economic Progress* (New York, 1990).

——. 'The Industrial Revolution and the Netherlands: Why Did It Not Happen?' *De Economist* 148 (2000).

——. *The Enlightened Economy. An Economic History of Britain 1700–1850* (New Haven/ London, 2009).

Mollat, M., *Le Rôle du Sel dans l'Histoire* (Paris, 1968).

Morgan, K., *Slavery, Atlantic Trade and the British Economy* (Cambridge, 2000).

Moriceau, J.-M., *Les Fermiers de l'Île-de-France. L'Ascension d'un Patronat Agricole (Xve-XVIIIe Siècle)* (Paris, 1994).

Moureaux, P. 'Le Commerce entre la France et les Pays-Bas Autrichiens dans la Seconde Moitié du XVIIIe Siècle. Une Première Approche des Sources Quantitatives'.

——. 'Un Organe Peu Connu du Gouvernement des Pays-Bas Autrichiens: le Bureau de Régie des Droits d'Entrée et de Sortie', *Belgisch Tijdschrift voor Filologie en Geschiedenis* 44 (1966), pp. 479–499.

——, *Les Comptes d'une Société Charbonnière à la Fin de l'Ancien Régime* (Brussels, 1969).

——, *Les Préoccupations Statistiques du Gouvernement des Pays-Bas Autrichiens et le Dénombrement des Industries Dressé en 1764* (Brussels, 1971).

——, *La Statistique Industrielle dans les Pays-Bas Autrichiens à l'Époque de Marie-Thérèse. Documents et Cartes*. 2 vols (Brussels, 1974–1981).

Multhauf, R.P., *Neptune's Gift: A History of Common Salt*. Vol. 2, *Studies in the History of Technology* (London, 1996).

North, D.C. and Thomas, R.P., *The Rise of the Western World* (Cambridge, 1973).

North, D., Wallis, J. and Weingast, B., Violence and Social Orders. A conceptual Framework for Interpreting Recorded Human History, (Cambridge 2009).

O'Brien, P.K. 'European Economic Development: The Contribution of the Periphery', *Economic History Review* 35, no. 1–18 (1982).

——. 'Imperialism and the Rise and Decline of the British Economy, 1688–1989', *New Left Review* 238 (1999), pp. 48–80.

——. 'Mercantilism and Imperialism in the Rise and Decline of the Dutch and British Economies', *De Economist* 148 (2000), pp. 469–501.

O'Brien, P.K. and Quinault, R., *The Industrial Revolution and British Society* (Newcastle upon Tyne, 1993).

O'Rourke, K.H. and Williamson, J.G. 'After Columbus: Explaining Europe's Overseas Trade Boom, 1500–1800', *Journal of Economic History* 62 (2002), pp. 417–456.

Ogilvie, S.C. and Cerman, M., *European Proto-Industrialization* (Cambridge, 1996).

Ormrod, D., *The Rise of Commercial Empires. England and the Netherlands in the Age of Mercantilism, 1650–1770*. Vol. 10, *Cambridge Studies in Modern Economic History* (Cambridge, 2003).

Paeye, K. 'De Gentse Katoennijverheid op de Internationale Katoenmarkt in de 19e Eeuw', in, *Geschiedenis*, (Gent, 2008).

Parmentier, J., *Oostende & Co: het Verhaal van de Zuid-Nederlandse Oost-Indiëvaart, 1715–1735* (Ghent, 2002).

——, *Het Gezicht van de Oostendse Handelaar* (Ostend, 2004).

Pelizzon, S. 'Grain Flour, 1590–1790', *Review* 23, no. 1 (2000), pp. 87–195.

Pendergrast, M., *Uncommon Grounds: The History of Coffee and How It Transformed Our World* (1999).

Piraux, C. and Dorban, M., *Douane, Commerce et Fraude dans le Sud de l'Espace Belge et Grand-Ducal au XVIIIe Siècle* (Louvain-la-Neuve, 1998).

Pollard, S., *Peaceful Conquest. The Industrialization of Europe 1760–1970* (Oxford, 1982).

Pomeranz, K., *The Great Divergence: China, Europe and the Making of the Modern World Economy* (Princeton, 2000).

Pomeranz, K. and Topik, S., *The World That Trade Created. Society, Culture, and the World Economy, 1400-the Present* (New York, 1999).

Posthumus, N.W., *Nederlandsche Prijsgeschiedenis*. Vol. 1 (Leiden, 1943).

Price, J.M., *Tobacco in Atlantic Trade. The Chesapeake, London and Glasgow, 1675–1775* (Brookfield, 1995).

Pricken, J., *La Douane Belge sous Marie-Thérèse et Joseph II* (Brussels, 1964).

Ricardo, D., *On the Principles of Political Economy and Taxation* (1817).

Riello, G. and McNeil, P., eds., *The Fashion History Reader: Global Perspectives* (London, 2010).

Riello, G. and Parthasarathi, P., *The Spinning World. A Global History of Cotton Textiles, 1200–1850* (Oxford, 2009).

Rifkin, J., *The Hydrogen Economy* (New York, 2002).

Rönnbäck, K. 'Who Stood to Gain from Colonialism? A Case Study of Early Modern European Colonialism in the Caribbean', in, *World Economic History Congress*, (Utrecht, 2009).

Rostow, W.W. 'The Beginnings of Modern Growth in Europe: An Essay in Synthesis', *The Journal of Economic History* 33 (1973), pp. 547–580.

Ruwet, J., *Avant les Révolutions: le XVIIIe Siècle, Etudes d'Histoire Wallonne* (Brussels, 1967).

Ryckbosch, W., *A Consumer Revolution under Strain? Consumption, Wealth and Status in Eighteenth-Century Aalst (Southern Netherlands), Dissertation* (Antwerp, 2012).

Sabbe, E., *De Belgische Vlasnijverheid*. 2 vols (Kortrijk, 1975).

Schneider, E., *Le Charbon. Son Histoire – son Destin* (Paris, 1945).

Schumpeter, E.B., *English Overseas Trade Statistics 1697–1808* (Oxford, 1960).

Schuurman, A., de Vries, J. and Van der Woude, A., *Aards Geluk. De Nederlanders en hun Spullen van 1550 tot 1850* (Amsterdam, 1997).

Serruys, M.W. 'The Austrian Netherlands' Transit Policy and the Port of Ostend: Solving the Crisis of the 'Closure of the Scheldt', in L.U. Scholl and D.M. Williams eds., *Crisis and Transition: Maritime Sectors in the North Sea Region 1790–1940*, (Bremen, 2008), pp. 150–170.

Shaw, J., *Essai sur les Pays-Bas Autrichiens* (London, 1788).

Sheridan, R.B., *Sugar and Slavery: an Economic History of the British West Indies 1623–1775* (Barbados, 1974).

Smekens, F. 'Schets van Aard en Beteekenis der Antwerpsche Nijverheid onder het Oostenrijksch Bewind', in, *Baekelmans Ter Eere*, (1945), pp. 77–108.

Smits, J.-P., Horlings, E. and Van Zanden, J.L., *Dutch GNP and Its Components, 1800–1913, Groningen Growth and Development Centre Monograph Series no. 5* (Groningen, 2000).

Steegen, E., *Kleinhandel en Stedelijke Ontwikkeling: het Kramersambacht te Maastricht in de Vroegmoderne Tijd* (Hilversum, 2006).

Thijs, A.K.L. 'Schets van de Ontwikkeling der Katoendrukkerij te Antwerpen (1753–1813)', *Bijdragen tot de Geschiedenis van het Oud Hertogdom Brabant* (1970), pp. 157–190.

——. 'Aspecten van de Opkomst der Textieldrukkerij als Grootbedrijf te Antwerpen in de Achttiende Eeuw', *Bijdragen en mededelingen betreffende de geschiedenis der Nederlanden* 86, no. 2 (1971), pp. 200–217.

——. 'Hondschootse Saaiwevers te Antwerpen', *Bijdragen tot de Geschiedenis* 54, no. 3–4 (1971), pp. 225–239.

——. 'De Geschiedenis van de Suikernijverheid te Antwerpen (16de–19de Eeuw): een Terreinverkenning', *Bijdragen tot de Geschiedenis* LXII (1979), pp. 23–50.

——. 'De Textielnijverheid', in R. Baetens ed., *Industriële Revoluties in de Provincie Antwerpen*, (Antwerp, 1984), pp. 121–136.

——, *Van "werkwinkel" tot "fabriek." De Textielnijverheid te Antwerpen (Einde 15de-Begin 19de Eeuw)* (Brussels, 1986).

Thoen, E. 'Social Agrosystems' as an Economic Concept to Explain Regional Differences. An Essay Taking the Former County of Flanders as an Example (Middle Ages-19th Century)', in B. van Bavel and P. Hoppenbrouwers eds., *Landholding and Land Transfer in the North Sea Area (Late Midle Ages- 19th Century), CORN Publication Series 5*, (Turnhout, 2004), pp. 47–66.

Tijms, W., *Groninger Graanprijzen. De Prijzen van Agrarische Producten tussen 1546 en 1990*. Vol. 31, *Historia Agriculturae* (Groningen/Wageningen, 2000).

Trenard, L. 'Le Charbon avant l'Ère Industrielle', in L. Trenard ed., *Charbon et Sciences Humaines*, (Den Haag, 1963), pp. 53–102.

Truyens, L., *De Antwerpsche Garentwijndersnatie en haar "Bleyckerye" te Borgerhout* (Brussels, 1943).

Van Aert, L. and Van Den Heuvel, D. 'Sekse als Sleutel tot Succes? Vrouwen en de Verkoop van Textiel in de Noordelijke en Zuidelijke Nederlanden 1650–1800', *Textielhistorische bijdragen* 47 (2007).

Van Bavel, B. and Thoen, E., *Land Productivity and Agro-Systems in the North Sea Area, Middle Ages – 20th Century. CORN Publication Series 2*. Edited by CORN. Vol. 2 (Turnhout, 1999).

Van Buyten, L. 'Bronnen voor de Geschiedenis van de Transitohandel en de Transitowegen in de Oostenrijkse Nederlanden. De Doorvoerhandel op Lorreinen', in, *Histoire Économique de la Belgique. Traitement des Sources et État des Questions. Actes du Colloque de Bruxelles (Ie–IVe Sections)*, (Brussels, 1972).

van Cruyningen, P., *Behoudend maar Buigzaam. Boeren in West-Zeeuws-Vlaanderen, 1650–1850* (Wageningen, 2000).

Van Damme, I. 'Antwerpse Klanten en Kleinhandelaars tussen Continuïteit en Vernieuwing, ca. 1648–ca. 1748', (Universiteit Antwerpen, 2006).

——. 'Pendelen tussen Revoluties en Tradities: Recent Historisch Onderzoek naar de Kleinhandel in de Late Middeleeuwen en de Nieuwe Tijd (ca. 1450–ca. 1850)', *Stadsgeschiedenis* 2 (2007), pp. 54–65.

Van den Eerenbeemt, H.F.J.M., *Op Zoek naar het Zachte Goud: Pogingen tot Innovatie via een Zijdeteelt in Nederland, 17de–20de Eeuw* (Tilburg, 1993).

Van Der Wee, H. 'De Industriële Ontwikkeling in de Nederlanden tijdens de 17de–18de Eeuw. Enkele Kritische Bemerkingen naar Aanleiding van het Debat over de Proto-Industrie en Poging tot Aanvulling van het Synthese-Model', *Academiae Analecta* 46, no. 4 (1984), pp. 57–77.

Van der Wee, H. 'The Western European Woollen Industries, 1500–1750', in D. Jenkins ed., *The Cambridge History of Western Textiles, Part 1*, (Cambridge, 2003), pp. 397–472.

Van Der Wee, H. and Houtman-De Smedt, H., *De Wereldeconomie in Opbouw 1750–1990* (Leuven, 1992).

Van Der Wee, H. and Peeters, T. 'Een Dynamisch Model voor de Seculaire Ontwikkeling van de Wereldhandel en de Welvaart (12e-18e Eeuw)', *Tijdschrift voor Geschiedenis* (1970).

Van der Wee, H. and Van Cauwenberghe, E., *Productivity of Land and Agricultural Innovation in the Low Countries (1250–1800)* (Leuven, 1987).

Van Dievoet, G., *Patrice de Neny (1716–1784) et le Gouvernement des Pays-Bas Autrichiens, Standen en Landen* (Kortrijk, 1987).

Van Houtte, H. 'Contribution à l'Histoire Commerciale des Etats de l'Empereur Joseph II (1780–1790)', *Vierteljahrschrift für Sozial- und Wirtschaftsgeschichte* 8 (1910), pp. 350–393.

——, *Histoire Économique de la Belgique à la Fin de l'Ancien Régime* (Ghent, 1920).

Van Houtte, J., *An Economic History of the Low Countries 800–1800* (London, 1977).

——, *Economische Geschiedenis van de Lage Landen 800–1800* (Haarlem, 1979).

Van Laerhoven, J. 'De Kanthandel te Antwerpen in de 18de Eeuw: de Firma Van Lidth de Jeude', *Bijdragen tot de Geschiedenis* 54, no. 3–4 (1971), pp. 173–190.

Van Meerbeeck, L., *Etude des Relations Économiques des Pays-Bas avec la Grande-Bretagne au XVIIIe Siècle, et plus Spécialement sous les Règnes de Marie-Thérèse et de Joseph II* (Brussels, 1929).

——. 'La Crise Charbonnière et le Problème des Transports en Belgique au XVIIIe Siècle', in, *Premier Congrès International de Géographie Historique*, (Brussels, 1931).

Van Moorhem, T. 'Sociaal Economisch Survey van een Aantal Nieuwe Nijverheden te Gent, 1750–1830 inzonderheid de Suiker-, Tabaks-, Zeep- en Zout-, Papierindustrie, de Speelkaartenfabricatie en de Jeneverstokerijen', (RUG, 1988).

van Tielhof, M., *The 'Mother of All Trades'. The Baltic Grain Trade in Amsterdam from the Late 16th to the Early 19th Century*. Vol. 3, *The Northern World* (Leiden, 2002).

Van Uytven, R., *Geschiedenis van de Dorst. Twintig Eeuwen Drinken in de Lage Landen* (Leuven, 2007).

Van Werveke, H. 'Beschouwing over het Economisch Leven in de Zuidelijke Nederlanden tijdens de XVIIe en XVIIIe Eeuw', *Bijdragen en mededelingen van het historisch genootschap* 61 (1940), pp. LXXXII–CIII.

Van Zanden, J.L. 'Early Modern Economic Growth: A Survey of the European Economy, 1500–1800', in M. Prak ed., *Early Modern Capitalism*, (London, 2001), pp. 69–87.

——, *The Long Road to the Industrial Revolution. The European Economy in a Global Perspective, 1000–1800*. Edited by M. Prak and J.L. Van Zanden. Vol. 1, *Global Economic History Series* (Leiden, 2009).

Vandenbroeke, C. 'De Landbouw en Levensmiddelenpolitiek in de Oostenrijkse Nederlanden', (RUG, 1970–1971).

——. 'De Landbouw en Levensmiddelenpolitiek in de Oostenrijkse Nederlanden', (RUG, 1970–1971).

——. 'Het Prijsonderzoek van de Regering voor de Steden van de Oostenrijkse Nederlanden voor Graangewassen, Vlas en Garen (1765–1794)', in C. Verlinden ed., *Dokumenten voor de Geschiedenis van Prijzen en Lonen in Vlaanderen en Brabant (XIIIe-XIXe Eeuw)*, (Bruges, 1973), pp. 1–166.

——, *Agriculture et Alimentation dans les Pays-Bas Autrichiens*. Vol. 49, *Belgisch Centrum voor Landelijke Geschiedenis* (Ghent, 1975).

——. 'Sociale en Konjuncturele Facetten van de Linnennijverheid in Vlaanderen (late 14e-midden 19e Eeuw)', *Handelingen der maatschappij voor geschiedenis en oudheidkunde te Gent* 33 (1979), pp. 117–174.

——. 'Landbouw in de Zuidelijke Nederlanden 1650–1815', in, *Algemene Geschiedenis der Nederlanden*, (Haarlem, 1980), pp. 73–101.

——. 'The Regional Economy of Flanders and Industrial Modernization in the Eighteenth Century', *Journal of European Economic History* 16, no. 1 (1987), pp. 149–170.

Vanhaute, E. 'Eens Gedronken, Steeds Geschonken'. Over Suikerij en Peekoffie als Surrogaat voor Exotische Drank', in J. Parmentier and S. Spanoghe eds., *Orbis in Orbem. Liber Amicorum John Everaert*, (Ghent, 2001), pp. 539–550.

Veraghtert, K. 'De Havenbeweging te Antwerpen tijdens de Negentiende Eeuw', (Katholieke Universiteit Leuven, 1977).

Vercleyen, J., *Histoire du Charbon* (Brussels, 1965).

Verhulst, A., *Précis d'Histoire Rurale de la Belgique* (Brussels, 1990).

Verhulst, A. and Vandenbroeke, C., *Landbouwproduktiviteit in Vlaanderen en Brabant 14de–18de Eeuw*. Vol. 56, *Belgisch Centrum voor Landelijke Geschiedenis* (Ghent, 1979).

Verlinden, C. and Craeybeckx, J., *Documents pour l'Histoire des Prix et des Salaires en Flandres et en Brabant*. Vol. II (Brussels, 1959–1973).

Verlinden, C. and Scholliers, E., *Dokumenten voor de Geschiedenis van Prijzen en Lonen in Vlaanderen en Brabant* (Bruges, 1959–1973).

Vermaut, J. 'De Textielnijverheid in Brugge en op het Platteland in Westelijk Vlaanderen voor 1800', (RUG, 1974).

Vermoesen, R., *Markttoegang en 'Commerciële' Netwerken van Rurale Huishoudens: de Regio Aalst, 1650–1800, Doctoraatsverhandeling* (Antwerp, 2008).

Viaene, A. 'Proeven van Zijdeteelt in de Vlaanders, 1606–1840', *Biekorf* 58, no. 8 (1957), pp. 225–230.

Vries, P., *Escaping poverty: the origins of modern economic growth* (Vienna University Press, 2013).

Wallerstein, I., *The Modern World-System*. 3 vols. Vol. 2 (New York, 1974).

——, *Mercantilism and the Consolidation of the European World-Economy, 1600–1750*. 3 vols. Vol. II, *The Modern World-System* (New York, 1980).

Walvin, J., *Fruits of Empire: Exotic Produce and British Taste, 1660–1800* (Basingtoke, 1997).

Welling, G.M. 'The Prize of Neutrality. Trade Relations between Amsterdam and North America 1771–1817. A Study in Computational History', (Rijksuniversiteit Groningen, 1998).

Williams, E., *Capitalism and Slavery* (Chapel Hill, 1945).

Wrigley, E.A., *Poverty, Progress, and Population* (Cambridge, 2004).

Wrigley, E.A. and Schofield, R.S., The Population History of England 1541–1871: A Reconstruction (London, 1981).

Index

www.ingramcontent.com/pod-product-compliance
Lightning Source LLC
LaVergne TN
LVHW010640300926
849161LV00005B/998